BEST OF THE JOURNALS IN
RHETORIC AND COMPOSITION

Best of the Journals in Rhetoric and Composition
SERIES EDITORS: STEVE PARKS, JESSICA PAUSZEK, KRISTI GIRDHARRY, AND CHARLES LESH

The Best of the Journals in Rhetoric and Composition series represents an attempt to foster a nationwide conversation—beginning with journal editors, but expanding to teachers, scholars and workers across the discipline of Rhetoric and Composition—to select essays that showcase the innovative and transformative work now being published in the field's independent journals. Representing both print and digital journals in the field, the essays in each addition represent a snapshot of the traditional and emergent conversations occurring in our field - from classroom practice to writing in global and digital contexts, from writing workshops to community activism. Together, the essays provide readers with a rich understanding of the present and future direction of the field.

Essays included in the "Best" series undergo a rigorous review process. First, all essays must have already crossed the threshold to be published in an academic journal in the field. Then, out of all the essays published by a journal, the editor can only select two essays. Next, the "Best" series editors create reading groups across the country. These groups feature full time faculty, adjunct faculty, and graduate students who teach in a range of institutions. In this way, all the nominated essays are assessed and ranked for how they speak to the interests of all those who work in our field – a review process which is unique to the series. The Series editors, plus one guest editor, then make a final selection of essays that have the strongest support from the reading groups for inclusion in a particular volume.

In this way, the Best of Rhetoric and Composition Journals represents the only publication in the field that can truly claim to represent the students, teachers, as well as scholars' collective insight into the pressing issues and important of the current moment. It is for this reason that authors selected for inclusion are celebrated at their home institutions and why journals actively seek to recognition for their work through the series. And it is for its ability of the series to provide the broadest conception of scholarship in our field, that the "Best" publications have found a home in introductory graduate courses and advanced undergraduate courses.

BEST OF THE JOURNALS IN RHETORIC AND COMPOSITION 2017

Edited by Kate Vieira, Vincent Portillo, Jason Luther, David Blakesley, and Steve Parks

Parlor Press
Anderson, South Carolina
www.parlorpress.com

Parlor Press LLC, Anderson, South Carolina, USA

© 2018 by Parlor Press. Individual essays in this book have been reprinted with permission of the respective copyright owners.
All rights reserved.
Printed in the United States of America

SAN: 254-8879

ISSN 2327-4778 (print)
ISSN 2327-4786 (online)

978-1-64317-009-1 (paperback)
978-1-64317-010-7 (Adobe eBook)
978-1-64317-011-4 (ePub)

1 2 3 4 5

Cover design by David Blakesley.
Printed on acid-free paper.

Parlor Press, LLC is an independent publisher of scholarly and trade titles in print and multimedia formats. This book is available in paper and digital formats from Parlor Press on the World Wide Web at http://www.parlorpress.com or through online and brick-and-mortar bookstores. For submission information or to find out about Parlor Press publications, write to Parlor Press, 3015 Brackenberry Drive, Anderson, South Carolina, 29621, or email editor@parlorpress.com.

Contents

Introduction   *vii*
    Kate Vieira, Vincent Portillo, and Jason Luther

ACROSS THE DISCIPLINES
Is WAC/WID Ready for the Transdisciplinary Research
    University?   *3*
    Justin K. Rademaekers

COMMUNITY LITERACY JOURNAL
De aquí y de allá: Changing Perceptions of Literacy through Food
    Pedagogy, Asset-Based Narratives, and Hybrid Spaces   *27*
    Lucía Durá, Consuelo Salas,
    William Medina-Jerez, and Virginia Hill

COMPOSITION FORUM
Mapping the Resourcefulness of Sources: A Worknet
    Pedagogy   *52*
    Derek Mueller

COMPOSITION STUDIES
Teaching for Agency: From Appreciating Linguistic Diversity to
    Empowering Student Writers   *77*
    Shawna Shapiro, Michelle Cox, Gail Shuck, and Emily Simnitt

ENCULTURATION
Weepy Rhetoric, Trigger Warnings, and the Work of Making
    Mental Illness Visible in the Writing Classroom   *104*
    Sarah Orem and Neil Simpkins

HARLOT: A REVEALING LOOK AT THE ARTS OF PERSUASION
Crafting Change: Practicing Activism in Contemporary
    Australia   *126*
    Tal Fitzpatrick and Katve-Kaisa Kontturi

JOURNAL OF BASIC WRITING
Remedial, Basic, Advanced: Evolving Frameworks for First-Year
    Composition at the California State University   *148*
    Dan Melzer

JOURNAL OF SECOND LANGUAGE WRITING
Impact of Source Texts and Prompts on Students' Genre Uptake   *177*
Ryan T. Miller, Thomas D. Mitchell, and Silvia Pessoa

KB JOURNAL
The Syrian Civil War, International Outreach, and a Clash of Worldviews   *210*
Peter C. Bakke and Jim A. Kuypers

LITERACY IN COMPOSITION STUDIES
"The Advantages of Knowing How to Read and Write:" Literacy, Filmic pedagogies, and the Hemispheric Projection of US Influence   *241*
Christa J. Olson and Madison Nancy Reddy

PHILOSOPHY AND RHETORIC
Seeming and Being in the "Cosmetics" of Sophistry: The Infamous Analogy of Plato's *Gorgias*   *271*
Robin Reames

PRESENT TENSE
Implicating the State: Black Lives, A Matter of Speculative Rhetoric   *298*
andré carrington

REFLECTIONS
A Prison Story: Public Rhetoric, Community Writing, and the Politics of Gender   *308*
Michelle Hall Kells

TECHNICAL COMMUNICATION QUARTERLY
Food Fights: Cookbook Rhetorics, Monolithic Constructions of Womanhood, and Field Narratives in Technical Communication   *336*
Marie E. Moeller and Erin A. Frost

WLN: A JOURNAL OF WRITING CENTER SCHOLARSHIP
Service-Learning Tutor Education: A Model of Action   *358*
Lisa Zimmerelli and Victoria Bridges

Introduction

Kate Vieira, Vincent Portillo, and Jason Luther

The year 2017 posed a number of threats to the social organizations that many in the field of composition and rhetoric hold dear: the free press, educational institutions, global peace, humanitarian initiatives, and scientific inquiry, among others. Oceans threatened to swallow islands. Speech was tamped down. Children were taken from families. People were killed, both en masse, and in ways that targeted them on the basis of the color of their skin, their gender, their sexuality.

These, among other events, shaped the social context in which the scholarly work represented in this volume landed, was taken up, and was deemed socially necessary. While these fifteen articles were conceived before 2017, they nonetheless offer a timely message: that the scholarly response to seemingly intractable social problems is to dig deep into a given subject, wring meaning in rigorous ways out of data, and then, crucially, offer ways to help readers put that scholarship to work in our institutions, in our teaching, and in our own writing.

The articles in this volume do just that. Chosen through a competitive process of nomination and review, they reveal anew the vital public role of writing and rhetoric studies in charting productive paths forward. We have organized their contributions into three crucial areas of intervention: how writing organizes knowledge in our institutions, how writing can empower (and disempower) people, and how writing can promote peace.

WRITING IN INSTITUTIONS

First, the articles included among this year's collection provide a number of responses for how composition and rhetoric might attempt to revise its disciplinary approaches to account for a more nuanced, situated, and ultimately responsive and sustainable understanding of its role in the institutions of the world — one that is at once networked and localized; self-aware and transdisciplinary; malleable and necessary. Such revisions are carried out using a variety of lenses — theoretical, historical, and practical — in an attempt to reassess our complicities and responsibilities while offering alternatives and pathways for moving forward.

In "Service-Learning Tutor Education: A Model of Action," Lisa Zimmerelli and Victoria Bridges draw from classroom- and writing center-based service learning models to suggest a sustainable, community-based approach for integrating service learning into tutor education. By forging a longstanding institutional partnership with a public school program in Baltimore called Bridges, Zimmerelli and Bridges describe specific ways that course mechanisms and assessments demonstrate commitment both to tutors and to their communities at large.

Such adaptations via intra- and inter-institutional partnerships are becoming increasingly essential in the 21st century. In "Is WAC/WID Ready for the Transdisciplinary Research University?," for example, Justin K. Rademaekers suggests that traditional WAC-based, write-to-learn pedagogies are ineffective as post-industrial universities use transdisciplinary approaches to solve complex problems, such as cancer and global warming. Problems like these, as Derek Mueller's "Mapping the Resourcefulness of Sources: A Worknet Pedagogy" helps us understand, require an ecological orientation towards knowledge-making in the composition classroom, where sources are not brought *into* texts as much as they are examined "*along* and *across* networked activity systems" so that their constellations are more faithfully rendered through processes of invention and acts of composing.

In "Impact of Source Texts and Prompts on Students' Genre Uptake," Ryan T. Miller, Thomas D. Mitchell, and Silvia Pessoa remind us that while knowledge-making is transdisciplinary and intertextual, acts of composing should be studied with a fine scope, using approaches that account for the cultural values embedded in our assignments, sequences, and those academic genres that condition writing in particular ways. Examining L2 learners at an American university in the Middle East, Miller, Mitchell, and Pessoa show us how variations across different source texts and writing prompts affect the uptake of argumentative writing for particular populations. Those L2 populations, as these authors suggest, are especially affected within institutions that do not carefully consider how specific pedagogical choices about assignments, unit sequences, or suggested readings ripple to affect writers in significantly different capacities.

Highlighting similarly vulnerable writers, in "Remedial, Basic, Advanced: Evolving Frameworks for First-Year Composition at the California State University," Dan Melzer develops a historical case study of California State University's Early Start program, but in this case, at the macro-level of writing program administration. As such, one important outcome of this study is how disciplinary discourses participate in hegemonic transmissions of literacy. Using Critical Discourse Analysis to trace the ways in which a host of CSU actors — including the Chancellor's Office, Board of Trustees, Academic Senate, and English faculty — helped shape the language of remediation and basic writing, Melzer shows readers how the concatenation of texts and events in the public sphere help us to understand the role institutions and expertise play in shaping everyday practices and pedagogies.

Indeed, the languages we circulate help define the very nature of our institutional philosophies. This is the valuable lesson in Robin Reames's "Seeming and Being in the 'Cosmetics' of Sophistry: The Infamous Analogy of Plato's Gorgias," which provides a revisionist reading of *Gorgias*, and specifically Plato's critique of rhetoric — a critique that has traditionally been interpreted as a longstanding argument for rhetoric's association with mere seeming rather than being. By focusing on the use of the term "kommōtikē" within *Gorgias*, as well as the wider imperialistic socio-political context of Greece at the time of its production, Reames suggests that Plato wasn't arguing that rhetoric was "merely" about appearances; rather, his use of kommōtikē signals a more specific material concern for the Athenian polis. In this way, the article suggests that Plato's scorn for rhetoric might be overstated.

Writing for Power

Another key theme is the power of writing in the lives of people in the classroom and in extracurricular spaces. As we see from these essays, writing's power is multifaceted and complex in its ability to both diminish and empower, depending on its users and circumstances. The essays concerned with the power of writing turn their attention to writing's (often detrimental) ability to label and categorize, which in turn can influence future action, as well as development of the self.

Writing has the power to sort, label, and isolate people according to descriptions of gendered and national identity as monolithic categories. In "Food Fights," Marie E. Moeller & Erin A. Frost analyze cookbooks as a genre of technical communication through a feminist lens. Although scholarship has traditionally treated cookbooks as liberatory, they approach the genre through gynotechnic inquiry, which illuminates how the genre works to "discipline and manage women" as it reinforces monolithic understandings of womanhood, woman, and femininity.

In similar ways, writing has the power to label people unfit. In "The Advantages of Knowing," Christa J. Olson and Nancy Reddy describe the Latin American literacy project co-headed by the Walt Disney Company and the U.S. Office of Inter-American Affairs, which, starting in 1941, sought to influence the development of the identity of the Latin American individual through film. The goal of the project was the making of the citizen as part of the modernist project, with an emphasis on literacy, hygiene, and nationalism. Further, they suggest the power of literacy education to create "literacy's others even as it seeks to extend literacy," thereby throttling access to circulation and mobility for some even as it encourages it for others. For example, so-called illiterate individuals in Latin America, who were measured against the value of an American literacy education, were marked with deficiency that could not be reversed, and as such did not have a place in the intra-hemispheric move toward 20th century Americanness.

On the other hand, under certain conditions, categories developed through the power of writing may enable individuals to develop agency over their own lives. In "Weepy Rhetoric," Sarah Orem and Neil Simpkins describe the role of trigger warnings, which might otherwise label the student as disabled, as an access point for people with mental disabilities to take charge of their educations. In this way, they offer examples from courses in which trigger warnings were used to make composition assignments more accessible to people with mental disabilities and provide a sense of agency in the classroom.

Writing can also facilitate the agency of the individual within institutions. In the classroom, students who co-create the curriculum with their instructor become actors enacting an reflective ideology. In "Teaching for Agency," Shawna Shapiro, Michelle Cox, Gail Shuck, and Emily Simnitt are concerned with how instructors might embrace linguistic diversity and also promote multilinguals' linguistic growth. To this end, they describe several approaches to the development of the agency of the student: an assignment in which students articulate the purpose, audience, and form of their projects; an ungraded optional assignment in which students participate in Twitter discussions that are archived; a film project in which multilingual students represent their own identities as writers; and a curricular structure in which students choose, as opposed to being placed in, appropriate writing courses. In short, we recognize the development of the agency of the student-as-actor through the co-development of a composition course as well as its assignments.

WRITING FOR PEACE

A final key theme to arise out of this year's winning articles is the shared desire to use writing and rhetorical analysis to accomplish peace—a message and a mission that is more crucial than ever at the end of a bruising 2017. At a political moment when Latinx families are vilified ("de Aqui de Alla"), when social stratification appears ever more entrenched ("A Prison Story"), when African American lives are consistently threatened by the state and the intransigence of white supremacy ("The State"), when colonialism's legacy continues to reverberate ("Craftivism"), and when armed conflict across the world rages ("The Syrian Civil War"), these articles collectively ask (and answer!): What is the role of writing and rhetoric in promoting peace?

Part of what recommends the articles in this collection is that they do not promise a panacea to the deeply rooted social problem of violence. Instead, they do what the best research does: they detail the context of their studies, and then wade in, with equal parts respect for their subject and rigorous methodology, to illuminate the conditions of oppression, and to propose interventions.

The essays in this collection raise readers' awareness of the complications inherent in projects of rhetorical intervention in violence. In Michelle Hall Kells' cross-genre essay linking the loss (and location) of her son, the deaths of colleagues, and the writing-across-community programs she helped develop, we see how efforts at writing for peace can be stymied by entrenched institutional interests—and yet, the essay provides a hopeful path forward for the development of public writing. Likewise, in "Implicating the State," André Carrington analyzes the Black Lives Matter movement (initiated by black women) as a discursive intervention into white supremacy—a movement that is at once imperative and speculative. "Black lives matter," Carrington shows, is a "promise to uphold." In other words, these essays are clear about what marginalized communities are up against.

Still, in their careful explications of grounded interventions into injustice, readers find hope in writing and in literacy education to promote social change: For example, in Lucía Durá, Consuelo Salas, William Medina-Jerez, and Virginia Hill's "de Aqui de Alla," ethnographers and community educators link Latinx students' home knowledge to an innovative after-school program surrounding food, thus circumventing widely circulated dehumanizing discourses. Similarly, in "Crafting Change," Tal Fitzpatrick and Katve-Kaisa Kontturi show how crafting's emphasis on the materiality of words and symbols can promote what they call a "soft" intervention in patriarchy and racism in Australia, making even radical messages, such as "Fuck your Patriarchy," resonate more widely.

The other side of writing is, of course, reading, or perhaps "listening" for peace. As authors Peter C. Bakke and Jim A. Kuypers of "The Syrian Civil War" show in their analysis of the simultaneously local and global discourses arming both sides, the beginning of peace is understanding the other side's "history, culture, and surrounding discourse."

In their clear-eyed view of violent social structures, and their hope that writing and rhetoric can intervene, these essays join some of the most exciting contemporary work in education, literacy, and rhetorical studies—work that examines the rhetoric of reconciliation, such as Rasha Diab's *Shades of Sulh*, and work that outlines the possibilities of literacy for restorative justice, like Maisha Winn's forthcoming *Justice on Both Sides*. In this way, these articles show writing and rhetoric may have a unique potential to develop peace, that is, to outline a shared commitment to a harmonious social future.

A Note on the Selection Process

The fifteen articles selected for this volume represent discerning, innovative, and eloquent scholarship from numerous journals in rhetoric and composition. Each journal submitted a set of articles, whereby we called upon faculty and graduate students from a range of institutions to read and rank according to the following criteria:

- Article demonstrates a broad sense of the discipline, demonstrating the ability to explain how its specific fo-

cus in a sub-disciplinary area addresses broader concerns in the field.
- Article makes original contributions to the field, expanding or rearticulating central premises.
- Article is written in a style which, while based in the discipline, attempts to engage with a wider audience or concerns a wider audience.

Based on the recommendations of the reviewers, the editors of this collection selected the final list of essays.

We are very grateful, then, to all of the associate editors who have organized and participated in reading groups that helped choose the selected essays. Their generosity, insight, and collaboration made this volume possible, and we are happy to list them here:

Arkansas State
Kristi Costello

Auburn University
Leigh Gruwell and Charlie Lesh

Butte College
Alexandra Matteucci

California State Polytechnic University, Pomona
Kristi Prins

California State University, Chico
Nathan Sandoval

California State University, Fullerton
Martha Webber

Indiana University – Purdue University Indianapolis
Marilee Brooks-Gillies

Johnson and Wales University
Kristi Girdharry

North Carolina State University
Abigail Browning, Chen Chen, Krystin Gollihue, Matt Halm, Hannah Mayfield, Laura Roberts, and Mai Xiong

Texas A&M Corpus Christi
Susan Murphy

Texas Christian University
Rachel Chapman, Lisa Cromwell, Whitney James, Sarah Kelm, Carrie Leverenz, Jessica Menkin, Kayla Sparks, Ashley Sylvester, Wilton Wright

University of California, Merced
Heather Devrickd, Beth Hernandez, Thomas Hothem, Iris Ruiz, and Anne Zanzucchi

University of Central Florida
Justiss Burry, Vanessa Calkins, Brandy Dieterle, Dustin Edwards, Steffen Guenzel, Luann Henken, Dan Martin, Lindee Owens, Laurie Pinkert, Allison Pinkerton, Emily Proulx, Adele Richardson, Stephanie Wheeler, and Thomas Wright

University of Colorado, Colorado Springs
Jarrett Krone

University of Kansas
Frank Farmer

Wichita State University
Danielle Koupf

Works Cited

Diab, Rasha. *Shades of Sulh: The Rhetorics of Arabic-Islamic Reconciliation.* University of Pittsburgh Press, 2016.

Winn, Maisha T. *Justice on Both Sides: Transforming Education through Restorative Justice.* Harvard Education Press, 2018.

Best of the Journals
Rhetoric and Composition

ACROSS THE DISCIPLINES

Across the Disciplines, a refereed journal devoted to language, learning, and academic writing, publishes articles relevant to writing and writing pedagogy in all their intellectual, political, social, and technological complexity. *Across the Disciplines* shares the mission of the WAC Clearinghouse in making information about writing and writing instruction freely available to members of the CAC, WAC, and ECAC communities.

Across the Disciplines is on the Web at http://wac.colostate.edu/atd

Is WAC/WID Ready for the Transdisciplinary Research University?

In "Is WAC/WID Ready for the Transdisciplinary Research University?" (http://wac.colostate.edu/atd/articles/rademaekers2015.cfm) Justin Rademaekers makes a fundamental challenge to current WAC/WID theory and pedagogy. Given our current theoretical (and institutional) focus on interdisciplinary, multidisciplinary, and transdisciplinary work – work that invites and encourages cross-disciplinary collaborations – he asks whether we can sustain a theoretical framework that presupposes discrete sets of disciplinary conventions? The answer to that question, says Rademaekers, is "No." The consequences of that answer include rethinking "writing to learn" pedagogies and reconceiving how we teach complex, rarely stable, often-contended "disciplinary norms" to students. Rather than presenting them as static sets of inflexible conventions, we should help students to see these norms as deeply situated and subject to ongoing negotiation

Is WAC/WID Ready for the Transdisciplinary Research University?

Justin K. Rademaekers

Abstract: Over the past two decades, academic and research institutions increasingly moved toward a transdisciplinary model of knowledge production where collaborations occur among disciplines with seemingly divergent methods and ideologies. More complicated than less- integrated modes of collaboration, transdisciplinary research has been described as an inevitable evolution of knowledge making in advanced and post-industrial societies. The author reviews some of the common communicative barriers that emerge in transdisciplinary and radically interdisciplinary collaborations, and argues that as institutional investments in transdisciplinarity become more tangible, researchers and teachers of disciplinary writing should rethink some approaches to writing to learn pedagogy in WAC/WID. The author posits that writing to learn pedagogy should consider teaching disciplinary conventions as situated and negotiable structures, and outlines some specific curricular approaches that could better prepare students for rhetorical effectiveness in future transdisciplinary collaborations.

Knowledge-making in post-industrial society hinges on transdisciplinary collaboration.[1] Transdisciplinary collaboration, sometimes referred to as *radically interdisciplinary collaboration*, consists of people from very different intellectual and disciplinary backgrounds (such as economics, communications, physics, microbiology, epidemiology, etc.) conducting integrated research to solve some of civilization's most profound problems (such as research on cancer, global climate change, sustainable development, etc.). Professionals in these seemingly divergent disciplines must effectively sit at the same intellectual table and work with one another to address increasingly complex research problems. This means that the future success of transdisciplinary work hinges on preparing writers and communicators who can function, if not thrive, in these transdisciplinary settings; which, not surprisingly, makes transdisciplinary collaboration a central interest for disciplinary writing researchers and teachers.

What differentiates transdisciplinary collaboration from other forms of academic collaboration is that cooperation among participants starts at the very highest levels of integration among disciplines involved. Unlike a multi-disciplinary approach through which collaborators might share and analyze data from their respective disciplines, and unlike an interdisciplinary approach through which collaborators might create overarching concepts among disciplines; transdisciplinary collaborators push the methodological and conceptual bounds of their own respective disciplines, making collaborations both participatory and problem-centered in place of disciplinary allegiance (Newell, 2000; Leavy, 2011). Success in transdisciplinary work depends on participant communicators who are capable of thinking far outside the boundaries of their own disciplinary discourse in order to form situated, problem-centered, and early-integrated methods for problem solving. The readers of this journal, and all those who are an interested in academic discourse and disciplinary writing instruction, should see these transdisciplinary collaborations for what they are: a radical departure from our traditional ways of thinking about disciplinary writing and disciplinary thinking.

The value of diverse disciplines conducting integrated and radically interdisciplinary research is that many of the problems we face in an increasingly-populated and ever-developing world are too complex to be addressed within the confines of a single discipline. This is not to say that highly integrated research is entirely new or untraditional, rather that it is increasingly *essential* in the context of research challenges like global climate change and sustainable development.

The difficulty with making transdisciplinary collaborations successful is that many professionals are trained to function within the parameters of their own discipline. In higher education, teachers and researchers develop expertise in the ways that their profession functions, both discursively and methodologically, and seek to cultivate that knowledge for students participating in their academic programs. Helping students who will become future professionals to acquire this knowledge of their discipline's function through critical investigations of disciplinary language has historically been a foundational goal of WAC/WID curriculums. That latter half of the phrase "learning to write, writing to learn" and the over 40-years of scholarship that has come to be known as writing to learn pedagogy is largely about helping students write to learn disciplinary discourse and understand disciplinary epistemology through language instruction. By cultivating disciplinarity in such ways, WAC/WID curriculums help students learn disciplinary concepts and principles, and perform or enact disciplinary methods and ideologies. Such a view permeates higher education curriculums, including the published principles and best practices of writing in the academic disciplines, writing across the curriculum, and writing in the disciplines.

The primary contention of this article is that a WAC/WID emphasis on disciplinarity is currently, and will be in the near future, insufficient for preparing students for a world that is radically interdisciplinary and transdisciplinary. A review of the common communicative barriers that emerge in transdisciplinary work reveals that the cultivation of disciplinarity creates a plethora of challenges when professionals leave the confines of their discipline and enter into a research collaboration with peers from very different, indeed *divergent*, disciplines. As this article contends, quite often these transdisciplinary collaborations fail to produce meaningful results as a result of entrenched disciplinarity among participants. Many transdisciplinary collaborations divulge into seeming incommensurability among disciplines, most tragically in a time when the success of these collaborations are important for surviving in our rapidly changing world.

An example of such difficulties can be seen in Jakobsen et al.'s 2004 case study of the Interior Columbia River Basin Ecosystem Management Project (ICBEMP), in which transdisciplinary landscape analysis of the Northwestern U.S. was conducted among a team of scientists aiming to address "complex management issues in a planning process for public lands" (p. 18). Jakobsen et al.'s study observes the work of 42 scientists in the ICBEMP with attention to the barriers and facilitators to successful project collaboration. Among the barriers identified, the authors note "the *use* of different scientific methods, such a research design, sampling, data collection, analysis, and interpretation of results between different disciplines" (p. 24) as among the most significant obstacles. The authors further note that while an interdisciplinary writing process was used to help "bridge" this barrier; which saw success among researchers with "overlap in academic backgrounds," among groups where "scientists' backgrounds were very different" publications of findings never happened (p. 24). In examining such important collaborative projects, it becomes clear that rhetoric and writing specialists should invest their energy to find pathways for success in collaborative writing, especially among collaborators from very different backgrounds.

What I suggest in this article is to continue turning our attention to what ought to be an important turn for teaching and research in disciplinary discourse—transdisciplinary knowledge making.

Thinking about WAC/WID principles in light of transdisciplinary work couldn't be more important. Currently, research universities are making growing infrastructural investments in transdisciplinary practices. Arizona State University, for instance, has piloted what they call "The New American University" in which they have "fused disciplines to form new colleges, schools and departments that encourage transdisciplinary collaboration [and]...created new kinds of university structures that promote academic partnerships with the community, industry and government." The University of Vermont launched a 2009 project called the "Transdisciplinary Research Initiative," which takes on projects such as the development of a "national smart grid" in a collaboration that consists of researchers in mathematics, computer science, medicine, economics, engineering, and business disciplines. In 2005, through funding from the National Cancer Institution, the "Transdisciplinary Research on Energetics and Cancer Centers" (TREC) collaborative was formed to address cancers linked to poor diet, exercise and obesity. These ongoing national transdisciplinary research projects through TREC are occurring not just transdisciplinarily, but across different institutions, representing a burgeoning interest and investment in radically inter-disciplinary and transdisciplinary work.

It would be a mistake to think this trend is just about STEM research practices. Transdisciplinary work isn't limited to Research Intensive institutions or graduate student learning—it represents a much broader trend. Those who critique unidisciplinary research and advocate for the surge in transdisciplinary research commonly point to the increasingly complex and transdisciplinary nature of societal problems. Growing concern over enormous scientific and political challenges, such as global climate change, for instance, have resulted in critiques of the limits and boundaries of the traditional disciplinarity of "pure science" disciplines (Gibbons et al., 1994; Heiskanen, 2006; Lenhard et al., 2006). The primary argument in these critiques is that researchers are now faced with problems that cannot be addressed by the "siloed" disciplinary structures that emerged from Enlightenment and Victorian era education. Yet, transitioning toward interdisciplinary structures is quite messy, and riddled with communication challenges.

At their core, I argue that the communication challenges inherent to transdisciplinary collaboration are an important site of inquiry for disciplinary discourse studies and disciplinary writing pedagogy. The aim of this article is to help propel such a conversation forward by providing readers with an entrée into transdisciplinary theory, drawing attention to some of the most common communicative challenges that emerge in transdisciplinary collaborations, and considering some avenues for disciplinary writing research and pedagogy in light of transdisciplinary collaborative work.

An Entrée into Transdisciplinary Theory

The interest in collaborative research practices between seemingly divergent disciplines has been well documented in recent years. Composition and rhetoric scholars have articulated interdisciplinary knowledge making as the deep theoretical structure for English Studies (Kopelson, 2008), as the premiere rhetorical activity of postindustrial society (Payne, 1999), and as the product of a robust feminist rhetorical practice (Royster, Kirsch, & Bizzell, 2012). As interest in interdisciplinary research has grown, so has interest in a more radical form of cross- disciplinary collaboration, which is commonly referred to as transdisciplinary research. What distinguishes transdisciplinary work from other forms of work such as uni-disciplinary, multi- disciplinary, and even inter-disciplinary research, is the degree of integration through which collaboration occurs. Transdisciplinary collaboration occurs at the highest levels of integration among researchers.

In more simple terms, the differences in multidisciplinary, interdisciplinary, and transdisciplinary collaboration can be understood by observing the role of each collaborator in the design of research methods: transdisciplinary work requires participant collaboration earliest in the process, in the design of research methods, and deliberation about conceptual and theoretical orientations. Multidisciplinary work, on the other hand, promotes researchers *returning* to their own respective disciplines for methods design, and in many cases retaining their disciplines conceptual and theoretical perspectives without deliberation among participants. While definitions of these different disciplinary structures vary among researchers and institutions, many cite Patricia L. Rosenfield's 1992 article as a common ground for defining transdisciplinary work. Rosenfield writes:

> Transdisciplinary research can provide a more comprehensive organizing construct. Representatives of different disciplines are encouraged to transcend their separate conceptual, theoretical, and methodological orientations in order to develop a shared approach to the research, building on a common conceptual framework. (p. 1351)

This depiction of transdisciplinary research as "more comprehensive" and *transcendent* to disciplinary "conceptual, theoretical, and methodological orientations" for the purpose of building "a common conceptual framework" differs drastically from a multidisciplinary approach where "each discipline works independently...and the results are usually brought together only at the end; and from an interdisciplinary approach where "different disciplines use their techniques and skills to address a common problem...[but] the results are usually reported in a partial, discipline-by-discipline, sequence" (p.1351).

The most important clarifying characteristic among these different approaches to collaboration is the point at which collaboration begins and participant disciplines are integrated. Lenard et al. (2006) distinguishes transdisciplinary work from other forms of collaborative research through the principles of "early integration" and "late integration." "Early integration," which Lenard et al. (2006) attribute to educational theorist Erich Jantsch, aims to "blur disciplinary boundaries as early as possible," while "late integration," which the authors attribute to educational theorist Hartmut von Hentig, "pleads for the initial preservation of disciplinary boundaries" only to later integrate researchers into a "democratic process within a 'republic of scientists'" (p. 341). The division between the two approaches to integration hinges on whether a disciplined approach and clearly defined disciplinary identities are useful tools once a researcher is entangled in an interdisciplinary environment. Those who believe the integrity of disciplinary identity to be vital to knowledge production may prefer a collaboration with later integration, such as multi- disciplinary collaboration. Those who see disciplinary identity as a situated social construction, and see knowledge production itself as a situated social construction, may prefer collaborations with early integration of participants, such as transdisciplinary or radically interdisciplinary research.

Transdisciplinary projects, in which integration occurs very early in the collaborative process, is a very important site of rhetorical activity that should be of central concern to rhetoric and writing specialists. These moments of blurred boundaries in early integration particularly among traditionally divergent disciplines such as social sciences and natural sciences should be an especially important site of inquiry for disciplinary writing theorists. In these moments of early integration, collaboration is occurring at the methodological and conceptual orders of concern, and because they are sites where the very social assumptions that subtend disciplinarity emerge most definitively, the success and failures of early integration must be examined and better understood.

At the heart of these growing research interests in transdisciplinary work are questions central to studies in disciplinary writing theory and practice: what are good practices for communicating within, among, and beyond disciplines? How do disciplinary genres assist writers in the work of a discipline? How might genres help or limit writers in communicating outside of their discipline? What rhetorical activities promote effective collaboration?

Given the growing urgency of problems that require a transdisciplinary approach, such as global climate change, we might re-imagine some of these disciplinary writing questions in light of transdisciplinary research: what are good practices for communicating about conceptual, theoretical, and methodological orientations with divergent disciplines? What role does genre play in transdisciplinary research, and how might genre theory adapt to transdisciplinary work? What rhetorical activities promote the formation of a common conceptual framework among divergent disciplines in transdisciplinary work? What are some of the common barriers to effective collaboration in transdisciplinary work? Metaphorically, these questions represent an iceberg of inquiry for disciplinary discourse studies for which we have not even begun to investigate the tip.

Some of these questions are hardly new, and have been considered to an extent by scholars in disciplinary writing and communications theory. In the field of technical communication, for instance, there has long been conversation about the transformations which occur when technical writers are involved early in the process, such as on the development team, rather than only after project development has concluded (Bresko, 1991; Fisher, 1999). Yet the infrastructural and intellectual investments that have been made in transdisciplinary collaboration in the past five years alone warrant a renewed urgency for considering the role of disciplinary writing theory in future transdisciplinary universities.

This article will address just one of these questions by outlining some of what I'll call the "common communicative barriers" that emerge in transdisciplinary work with an aim to begin sketching the epistemological character of transdisciplinary work. In reviewing some of these common challenges and characteristics, I hope readers will see new opportunities for critiquing existing writing theory, developing new approaches to writing pedagogy, and consider the changing relevance of WAC/WID theory in a transdisciplinary university and world.

Common Communicative Challenges in Transdisciplinary Work

Identifying communicative barriers and challenges is a useful starting point for understanding the rhetorical activity of transdisciplinary work. Addressing challenges to effective language use is not only a useful premise for research, but helps writing researchers find results that better articulate and justify writing instruction to faculty and administrators throughout the university. A review of existing research on the common challenges in transdisciplinary work is a fruitful starting point for better understanding this trend in transdisciplinary knowledge making.

Of particular use to researchers interested in studies of communicative barriers in transdisciplinary work is Eigenbrode et al.'s "Employing Philosophical Dialogue in Collaborative Science" (2007). This study reviewed seven published studies of inter- and trans- disciplinary collaborations to determine the common barriers that emerged across all studies. The authors aimed to create a system for classifying the common barriers and outline an approach to help cross-disciplinary collaborators identify the "philosophical structure of their research." Eigenbrode et al.'s review of transdisciplinary collaborations are useful for disciplinary writing research because they emphasize specific social and communicative limitations to effective transdisciplinary collaboration, which are echoed in other popular studies of transdisciplinary research (for example Anderson & Scott, 1999; Hargreaves & Burgess, 2009). This makes Eigenbrode et al.'s study a great starting framework for considering opportunities for researchers of disciplinary discourse to reconsider WAC/WID principles and practices in light of transdisciplinary contexts.

Echoing the claims of Lenard et al. (2006), the first barrier described by Eigenbrode et al. is what the authors call disagreements in the "level of integration." The authors describe this barrier as the erroneous tendency to apply the wrong degree of disciplinary integration in cross-disciplinary work. As mentioned previously, the degrees of disciplinarity are frequently classified as "multidisciplinary," "cross-disciplinary," "interdisciplinary" and "transdisciplinary" from order of least epistemologically integrated to most epistemologically integrated. If researchers begin with different intentions for integration, than the discrepancy itself is likely to become a barrier to effective collaboration. The authors confess that a transdisciplinary approach, in which full integration occurs among a variety of divergent disciplines is the ideal, however, a variety of institutional power concerns, such as disciplinary identity, may lead to the wrong level of integration (see also Shove, 2010).

A second major challenge to interdisciplinary collaboration is what Eigenbrode et al. (2007) refer to as "linguistic and conceptual divides." The authors describe these divides as disagreements regarding the specialist terminology used in varying disciplines and the different connotations for the same terms across disciplines. For example, Eigenbrode et al. present the example of "triangulation" as a linguistic and conceptual divide, noting that "triangulation" in the social sciences refers to an entirely different research principle than it does to specialists in navigation and surveying.

The linguistic divides that Eigenbrode et al. (2007) describe are more than semantic divides— they are often at the root of a conceptual divide. For example we can observe a conceptual/epistemological dilemma when we ask: what counts as an observable scientific setting—a strictly controlled lab or a natural (and uncontrollable) ecosystem? Such questions were lively in debates between laboratory Biologists and Environmental Scientists when the environmental science discipline rose to popularity in the mid-20th Century (De Groot, 1992). The word "control" in this example represents more than a linguistic disagreement—it represents a fundamental disagreement on what *counts* as *science*. For some, a natural environment lacks the rigorous *controls* required for information to be repeatable, and is therefore scientifically unreliable. For others, a controlled laboratory setting is merely a fantasy of control, and therefore cannot produce results that are genuinely applicable to the "real" world. So long as biologists and environmental scientists disagree on such a fundamental idea, persistent disagreement is destined to rule the day in collaborative research contexts such as transdisciplinary research.

As discussed earlier in the example of the Interior Columbia River Basin Management Project, these linguistic divides may become serious inhibitors to an interdisciplinary writing process in which collaborators from very different academic backgrounds failed to publish findings. Issues of academic culture such as tenure evaluation, how different disciplines value authorship, and the availability and integrity of journals for publishing interdisciplinary findings, may all accumulate into a disincentive to publish collaborative work. Jakobsen et al. (2004) describe this as a matter of academic culture, which leads to: "questions about authorship, importance of educational level/titles, lack of incentives to work on interdisciplinary projects, and differences in methodological traditions" (p. 28). While these barriers may seem insurmountable, there is hope that as universities invest in transdisciplinary knowledge making structures, the academic culture which reproduces disincentives for collaborative work may begin to change as well.

Disagreements on what counts as *evidence* is perhaps the most epistemologically-systemic barrier to collaboration in transdisciplinary work. Eigenbrode et al. describe this as a "validation of evidence" barrier, which presents a significant challenge when varying or divergent research methods are utilized by the disciplines involved. For example, a social scientist may take citizen input on environmental quality much more seriously as evidence than a chemist might— especially if she can find no "evidence" of the poor environmental quality of which the citizens complain in her chemical analysis of the environment. In my own interviews with social scientists who identify themselves as environmental epidemiologists this disagreement on the value of social input as evidence is commonly down-played by laboratory scientists. To paraphrase one environmental epidemiologist: it means little to a physical scientist that half a town believes there is a medical problem associated with an environmental odor until that physical scientist discovers the chemical root of that odor.

The social context of research is also an important barrier cited by Eigenbrode et al.'s study because it describes the divides that may be political in nature depending upon how a researcher values the input or influence of external stakeholders. Researchers working in physical sciences may be more interested in reducing or attempting to eliminate social (including institutional or governmental) influence on research being conducted; while, researchers from applied social sciences may be more likely to see social context and stakeholder input as a focal point for the research itself—for applied researchers the social context helps define the problem to be addressed (see Karen Barad's (2007) *Meeting the Universe Halfway* for a precise example of recent interest in challenging the notion of pure and un-objective scientific research in laboratories). The social context of research becomes a clear communicative barrier in transdisciplinary research collaborations on environmental topics in which some researchers may be happy to situate their work in light of the urgent need for change in greenhouse gas emissions, while other scientists may feel uncomfortable conducting research in this political framework.

The final two of the seven barriers cited by Eigenbrode et al. (2007) are less common, but essential considerations in transdisciplinary collaborations. The first is what the authors describe as the scientists' "perceived nature of the world." By this Eigenbrode et al. refer to the question of the relation between researcher objectivity and human values, such as morality. The authors argue that divides between researchers on this issue can serve as a serious barrier to collaboration, but most often the address of these divides is "seldom required" (p. 58). Another cited barrier is what the authors refer to as a "reductionist versus holistic science" barrier. Here, researchers who may begin with agreement on integration levels and terminology may differ on how to best approach scientific problems—should the researchers isolate individual components for observation, or look at the problem more broadly without dividing the subject into individual components? Once a decision on this issue has been made, such barriers are less likely to affect the collaboration, however, it is important that decisions on these questions are carefully detailed and agreed upon by researchers very early in the collaboration.

The common communicative barriers that emerge in Eigenbrode et al.'s review of these seven inter- and trans-disciplinary collaborations have value as imports to disciplinary discourse studies. We might summarize some of the common communicative barriers that emerge in transdisciplinary collaborations as follows:

1. Disagreement on issues related to the value of disciplinarity and the point at which input from participants should be integrated.

2. Conceptual and linguistic divides among participants including what counts as science, what methods are appropriate, and what terms mean.

3. Methodological disagreements about what validates knowledge and what counts as evidence.

4. Methods disagreements about how to approach the research problem (i.e. reductionist versus holistic science)

5. Disagreements about the social and political context of research and the role of objective researchers within this context.

These barriers are important to consider because they help researchers of disciplinary discourse understand where language instruction can better prepare students for transdisciplinary collaborative work. These common communicative barriers provide an enormous opportunity for WAC/WID curriculums to consider means for addressing these issues and for improving student ability to function within such collaborations. This is opportunity is especially evidenced by the fact that the communicative barriers that emerge in transdisciplinary collaborations are rooted in participants' failures to identify and discuss the social and rhetorical constitution of their knowledge-making process. That is, participants in the seven transdisciplinary case studies reviewed by Eigenbrode et al. and summarized in this article enter collaborations with their own particular disciplinary conventions for knowledge making, and as such communicative barriers emerge when divergent disciplinary methods, concepts, and terms, such as those between social and physical scientists, become [seemingly] incommensurable. It is the absence of a rhetorical dialogue about disciplinary conventions themselves, including disciplinary concepts, methods, terms, and social/political contexts for the research that leads assuredly to failed transdisciplinary collaboration.

Eigenbrode et al. (2007) agree that the root of these communicative barriers may be the absence of rhetorical dialogue about disciplinary conventions within these transdisciplinary collaborations, concluding their study:

> philosophical assumptions are implicit in this list [of barriers and challenges to transdisciplinary collaboration]. Interdisciplinary or transdisciplinary efforts that involve the synthesis of conceptual schemes may require substantial interactive exploration of these assumptions...under pressure and heat of day-to-day effort, collaborators at any level of integration are exposed to the philosophical assumptions of their partners, but in a piece-meal and uncoordinated way, rarely deliberated. (p. 60)

This emphasis on "philosophical assumptions" that are "rarely deliberated" points precisely to the challenge that WAC/WID scholars might take as a focal point for preparing a university students for future transdisciplinary work. After all, it is the inherently rhetorical and philosophical structure of disciplines and the encouragement of deliberation about such disciplinary structures that WAC and WID researchers have worked for decades to account for in both theory and pedagogy.

IMPLICATIONS OF TRANSDISCIPLINARY WORK FOR DISCIPLINARY WRITING RESEARCH AND PEDAGOGY

Preliminarily, we might begin to see disciplinary writing theory and disciplinary writing pedagogy as well poised for the trend toward transdisciplinary work. Given that transdisciplinary work entails the early integration of social and scientific disciplines, studies of the socially constructed knowledge making practices of disciplines provides valuable insight into how divergent disciplines might functionally collaborate. As such, WAC/WID should have a significant disciplinary investment in transdisciplinary work. Bazerman et al.'s (2005) *Reference Guide to Writing Across the Curriculum* notes, for example, that although there are many manifestations of theories and pedagogies under titles such as "Rhetoric of Science, Rhetoric of Inquiry, Writing in the Disciplines, and English for Specific Purposes" that in fact "…these differently motivated and framed inquiries contribute to a common picture of writing practices in the various disciplines and the relation of those processes to the production and use odisciplinary knowledge…how different disciplines construct knowledge through different textual forms, and the kinds of challenges students must meet when learning to write within their chosen fields" (p. 66). This "common picture" of "how different disciplines construct knowledge through different textual forms" might be understood as a keystone to studying, and perhaps, improving transdisciplinary collaborations.

A collective look at the communicative barriers that emerged in the case studies of transdisciplinary work reviewed by Eigenbrode et al. (2007), reveals that each communicative barrier is partially rooted in the absence of deliberation about disciplinary conventions, and accordingly the tendency for participants in transdisciplinary collaborations to ignore the highly rhetorical nature of the knowledge making practices they bring to such collaborations.

From a post-structural view of language and rhetoric, the communicative barriers (conceptual, methodological, linguistic, and social/political) that emerge in these transdisciplinary collaborations are each constituted by the disciplined effect that language has on a participant's ability to conceptualize, act, and imagine within the epistemological schema of a participant's respective disciplines. For transdisciplinary collaborators to succeed in moving beyond these communicative barriers, they must essentially learn to do the opposite of what WAC/WID pedagogy historically suggests—they must become *un*-disciplined in order to establish a situated and collective disciplinary identity in a radically interdisciplinary/transdisciplinary setting.

Participants must learn about language not as a means for reinforcing disciplinarity and ideology, but as a means for reflexivity, openness, and situated-ness in knowledge making. Participants must learn to deliberate productively about disciplinary conventions, methods, concepts, terms, and social/political contexts if such collaborations are to succeed.

Given this need for open reflection about disciplinary conventions and assumptions, it makes sense that students who may one day be expected to participate in transdisciplinary work should be given a rhetorical education that prepares them to think critically and reflexively about the social structures of their own and peers' disciplinary conventions. Herein lies two major challenges for transdisciplinary universities seeking a rhetorical education that promotes transdisciplinary success: one, many faculty across the disciplines (some would argue a majority) see student comprehension of disciplinarity among the skills acquired in the furthest reaches of a program, such as senior seminars or even graduate-level work; and two, many faculty themselves may not be rooted in disciplines with a tradition of discourse about disciplinary epistemologies.

One way to understand such challenges is to view them as the by-product of a historically disciplinary university structure—the very structure that transdisciplinary knowledge-making aims to contradict by design. As an aside to this article, this means that graduate programs training future university faculty in Ph.D. programs may seek to integrate more discussion of epistemology into their curricula as a means of preparing faculty for holding discussion about disciplinary epistemology with their students. Secondly, and of greater meaning to the focus of this article, universities interested in transdisciplinary work must begin to consider student comprehension of disciplinary epistemology as a threshold concept that should be reflected in student learning objectives, and integrated into course curricula much earlier in four year programs (rather than only in senior seminars, for example).

Aside from these two challenges, there are several clear implications for writing programs at universities interested in transdisciplinary work. Certainly a first step for institutions interested in preparing future students for success in transdisciplinary collaborations is to invest in WAC/WID curriculums that seek to address some of these common communicative barriers. The primary emphasis in such curriculums should be to teach students to think critically and reflexively about the ways in which their disciplines socially construct knowledge-production. This should include reflection on disciplinary epistemology and methodology but also disciplinary terminology and the political/social contexts in which these disciplines might operate. Fortunately, a great deal of this work already exists in WAC/WID practice and theory; but in addition, WAC/WID curriculums should place students in learning environments where they can discuss their disciplines' conventions and deliberate with peers from very different disciplines about their respective disciplinary conventions.

One way that WAC/WID curriculums might seek greater deliberation about disciplinary conventions among students is by re-configuring classroom structures away from epistemologically-related disciplines learning together (i.e. physics, chemistry, and biology students), and toward classrooms that enroll students from highly divergent disciplines in upper- division writing courses together (i.e. physics, economics, history). In a more epistemologically diverse classroom, students can learn to work through the many barriers that emerge during collaborations with peers from divergent disciplinary backgrounds and will be given a chance to practice deliberation about disciplinary discourse which is so badly needed in transdisciplinary settings.

Traditionalists in WAC theory and pedagogy may object to this prospect because there is a great deal of work that takes the rhetorical activity of specific disciplines as a focal point of research, such as "Writing in the Social Sciences" (Steward & Smelstor, 1984); *Professional Academic Writing in the Humanities and Social Sciences* (MacDonald, 1994); or the emergent disciplines of "Business Writing" and "Technical Writing." In suggesting an approach to a WAC/WID curriculum that brings together students from divergent fields with a goal to prepare students for transdisciplinary work, I am not advocating for an abandonment of these traditional, and quite successful approaches. I hope to leave such either/or debates to the pleasure of reactionaries and advocate instead for additional attention to a different kind of classroom structure for institutions interested in the future of transdisciplinary work.

A classroom enrolled with students from highly divergent disciplines could be themed around an applied problem of interest to those students. For example, an applied classroom theme of *Environmental Sustainability*, or *Alleviating Poverty* could draw students from economics disciplines, natural science disciplines, engineering disciplines, business disciplines, and the humanities to work together as collaborative writers addressing an applied problem. There is no doubt that a student trained to think as an economist will have a different approach to addressing environmental sustainability than a student trained in environmental science, or a student trained in English Studies—and that's precisely the point. Struggle will inevitably ensue when students from very different disciplines collaborate on an applied topic like sustainability, but this struggle not only prepares them for rigorous transdisciplinary work, but also forms a valuable pedagogical scene for instructor discussions of disciplinary writing and rhetoric.

The needed adjustments to prepare students for transdisciplinary work largely comes down to a shift away from disciplinarity as the guiding criteria for classroom design and toward applied topics such as environmental sustainability, global climate change, poverty, hunger, or social justice (to name a brief few) as the guiding criteria for classroom design. With applied topics as the guiding criteria for classroom design, WAC/WID leaders can create classrooms where divergent disciplinary frameworks and assumptions that students (and their professors) carry with them in their studies will inevitably emerge. In this difficult collaborative environment, writing emerges not just as a communicative requirement, but also as a means for understanding the perspectives of peers from divergent disciplines, for mediating those differences, and for inventing what can amount to viable solutions to our most pressing social challenges.

In addition to structuring classrooms with students from divergent disciplines around applied problems, writing classrooms interested in promoting transdisciplinary work could also place emphasis on genres whose design helps mediate divergent disciplinary perspectives, such as proposals or visual representations of the applied problem.

In my own interviews with transdisciplinary collaborators, participants commonly reference the grant proposal process as a genre which helped mediate disciplinary differences. Karen Burke LeFevre, in fact, uses the example of "business proposal writing" in her well-known work *Invention as a Social Act* (1987). LeFevre writes of proposal writing: "two or more rhetors collaborate to invent, and in fact, to negotiate, a text. One person may suggest an idea; the other responds; the response becomes a gesture to the first speaker, who then generates another idea...each party must agree, or invention stops" (p. 62-63). There is a great deal of research that needs to be done on the role of proposals as a mediating genre in transdisciplinary collaboration, but there are many indications that such a genre would be useful in an upper-division disciplinary writing course. Transdisciplinary-focused classrooms might also provide an opportunity for studies in visual rhetoric to emerge as an important tool for mediating differences.

Robert Evans and Simon Marvin's "Researching the Sustainable City: Three Modes of Interdisciplinarity" (2006), for example, assesses the function of interdisciplinary collaboration by evaluating three United Kingdom research programs' focus on the design of sustainable cities. In their study of collaboration on the applied problem of sustainability in the U.K., social scientists and engineers struggled to model cities together because of different disciplinary conceptions of traffic patterns. The engineers saw transportation infrastructure as something that had to accommodate the needs of humans; while the social scientists saw transportation infrastructure as relatively fixed, positing instead that human behavior could be accommodated most easily, through policy. The fact that visual modeling in the sustainable cities project brought forth deeply rhetorical disciplinary conventions means that such modeling might be a useful way to draw-out and create an occasion to mediate some of the disciplinary assumptions that threaten a transdisciplinary collaboration's success.

Greater emphasis on the communicative barriers inherent to transdisciplinary work may also suggest new content for WAC faculty workshops. WAC directors and consultants, for example, have had great success helping faculty across the disciplines take ownership over writing instruction within their respective programs. WAC workshops have emphasized the value of writing to learn pedagogy in upper-division courses (Bohr & Rhoades, 2014), have encouraged faculty to discuss the genre systems of their disciplines (Blumner, Eliason, & Fritz, 2001), and have helped faculty across the disciplines consider ways to teach student writing in their disciplines as a process that includes planning, drafting, and revising throughout the semester (Bohr & Rhoades, 2014). WAC faculty workshops for institutions interested in transdisciplinary work might build on these common WAC principles by encouraging faculty across the disciplines to create informal writing assignments which ask students to reflect on the *process* of knowledge making within their disciplines—not informal *writing to learn* about disciplinary content alone. WAC faculty workshops might also encourage faculty across the disciplines to introduce disciplinary genres and methods as dynamic social systems, not as static formulae for disciplinary knowledge making. While this may seem obvious to faculty who are seasoned writers in their fields, WAC directors and consultants directing faculty workshops could discuss the value that teaching disciplinary genres as social systems can have on their students' ability to collaborate with peers from divergent disciplines.

Given the challenge that many faculty themselves may not be confident or trained to discuss and compare disciplinary epistemologies, as mentioned earlier in this essay, WAC workshops may also be a useful tool for training university faculty to hold epistemological conversations about their disciplines with students. Given the nascent development of transdisciplinary university structures many faculty, for example, may have been trained in graduate programs that didn't discuss disciplinary epistemology in explicit ways. Faculty workshops can begin to close this gap in faculty training by providing workshops which help faculty consider the epistemological character of their own disciplines, and by helping to develop the skills for hosting discussions about disciplinary conventions with their students.

Another focal point for WAC faculty workshops at institutions interested in promoting student success in transdisciplinary settings would be to encourage faculty to collaborate on a course writing project among multiple upper division courses across the curriculum. Third and fourth year undergraduate students majoring in Economics might collaborate with third and fourth year undergraduate students majoring in Environmental Studies to write group proposals on a topic such as sustainability. In a setting such as this, upper-division writing projects become an opportunity for students from diverse disciplines to take ownership over their disciplinary knowledge, practice rhetorical deliberation about disciplinary conventions, and produce texts that mediate differences with peers and address authentic applied problems in both disciplines. The classroom discussions about writing, discourse, and knowledge making that might emerge from such a collaboration seem endlessly bountiful. WAC faculty workshops and retreats emphasizing collaboration among divergent disciplines might even become the meeting space through which research collaborations among faculty themselves could sprout early roots.

Conclusion

If we consider the adage "learning to write, writing to learn" that helped define the mission of WAC/WID for some 45 years now, could we not see greater consideration of transdisciplinary collaboration in WAC/WID as an extension of this mission?

The Writing to Learn pedagogy that helps define the work of teachers and researchers of disciplinary discourse hinges on a view of language as a building-block for disciplinary epistemologies. For many, this emphasis on disciplinary writing and rhetoric as epistemic is what WAC/WID is all about. As McLeod and Maimon aptly explain in "Clearing the Air: WAC Myths and Realities" (2000) "Teaching students to write in the disciplines is not an exercise in formalism...it is an exercise in epistemology" (p. 580). Students who are writing to learn, are writing to learn a particular disciplinary epistemology—including the conventions, concepts, methods, terminology and discourses which do the work of disciplines. We ask students to engage in these discourses and the conventions, concepts, methods and terminology that go with them. A central challenge WAC/WID scholars must address is this: the common communicative barriers that emerge in transdisciplinary collaborations suggest that the root cause of communicative barriers in transdisciplinary work are the very epistemological elements that WAC/WID aims to galvanize through writing to learn pedagogy. More specifically, these communicative barriers are rooted in a *static conception of disciplinary epistemology*, and the absence of reflexivity toward disciplinary conventions, concepts, methods, and terms within participating disciplines. This creates a conundrum for WAC/WID programs deeply invested in reinforcing disciplinarity through writing to learn pedagogy, but not an impasse. Generally, we must press on to consider approaches to writing to learn pedagogy which teach disciplinary discourse reflexively, revealing disciplinary conventions, but portraying them as situated, and negotiable in transdisciplinary collaborative settings. Specifically, we should consider ways to integrate writing to learn pedagogy with opportunities for transdisciplinary collaboration, including teaching the skills of negotiating difference among divergent disciplines and teaching written genres that act as tools for mediating such differences. At its best, such an approach would prepare future students for a future that will likely be characterized by transdisciplinary collaboration; but at the very least, engaging students in transdisciplinary discourses can help them see the specific, unique, and situated nature of their own disciplines.

If transdisciplinarity is the future of knowledge-making in a postindustrial society, as institutions and theorists seem to suggest, then we must re-consider the ways in which we cultivate student understanding of disciplinary discourse, and more particularly transdisciplinary discourses. This might require some uncomfortable alteration of WAC/WID pedagogy that aims to reinforce disciplinarity, but there is no better-poised group of scholars for such work than those who study the rhetorical function of academic disciplines.

NOTE

1. The author would like to acknowledge Irwin (Bud) Weisser for expressing early interest in exploring the intersection of transdisciplinary collaboration and WAC/WID pedagogy, as well as Patricia Sullivan and Jennifer Bay for their feedback and guidance on much of the work expressed in this article. Most especially, the author would like to acknowledge Richard Johnson-Sheehan for his assistance in helping the author consider the practical applications of transdisciplinary pedagogy in university curricula. Finally, the author acknowledges his colleagues at West Chester University of Pennsylvania for their spirit and encouragement.

REFERENCES

Anderson, Norman B., & Scott, Paul A. (1999). Making the case for psychophysiology during the era of molecular biology. *Psychophysiology*, *36*(01), 1-13.
Arizona State University. (2013). A new American university. Retrieved from http://newamericanuniversity.asu.edu/.
Barad, Karen. (2007). *Meeting the universe halfway*. Durham: Duke University Press.
Bazerman, Charles, Little, Joseph, Bethel, Lisa, Chavkin, Teri, Fouquette, Danielle, & Garufis, Janet. (2005). *Reference guide to writing across the curriculum*. West Lafayette: Parlor Press and the WAC Clearinghouse.
Blumner, Jacob S., Eliason, John, & Fritz, Francis. (2001). Beyond the reactive: WAC programs and the steps ahead. *The WAC Journal, 12*.
Bohr, Dennis J., & Rhoades, Georgia. (2014, April 27). The WAC glossary project: facilitating conversations between composition and WID faculty in a unified writing curriculum. *Across the Disciplines, 11*(1).
Bresko, Laura L. (1991). The need for technical communicators on the software development team. *Technical Communication, 38*(2), 214-220.
De Groot, Wouter T. (1992). *Environmental science theory: Concepts and methods in a one- world, problem-oriented paradigm*. Amsterdam: Elsevier.
Eigenbrode, Sanford D., O'Rourke, Michael, Wulfhorst, J. D., Althoff, David M., Goldberg, Caren S., Merrill, Kaylani, Morse, Wayde, Nielsen-Pincus, Max, Stephens, Jennifer, Winowiecki, Leigh, & Bosque-Perez,

Nilsa A. (2007). Employing philosophical dialogue in collaborative science. *BioScience*, *57*(1), 55-64.

Evans, Robert, & Marvin, Simon. (2006). Researching the sustainable city: Three modes of interdisciplinarity. *Environment and Planning*, *38*(6), 1009-1028.

Fisher, Julie. (1999). The value of the technical communicator's role in the development of information systems. *IEEE Transactions on Professional Communication*, 42(3), 145-155.

Gibbons, Michael, Limoges, Camille, Nowotny, Helga, Schwartzman, Simon, Scott, Peter, & Trow, Michael. (1994). *The new production of knowledge: The dynamics of science and research in contemporary societies*. Los Angeles: Sage Press.

Hargreaves, Tom, & Burgess, Jacqueline. (2009). Pathways to interdisciplinarity: A technical report exploring collaborative interdisciplinary working in the Transition Pathways Consortium. *Transition Pathways to a Low Carbon Economy*.

Heiskanen, Eva. (2006). Encounters between ordinary people and environmental science—a transdisciplinary perspective on environmental literacy. *The Journal of Transdisciplinary Environmental Studies*, 5(1-2), 1-13.

Jakobsen, Christine H., Hels, Tove, & McLaughlin, William J. (2004). Barriers and facilitators to integration among scientists in transdisciplinary landscape analyses: a cross-country comparison. *Forest Policy and Economics*, *6*(1), 15-31.

Kopelson, Karen. (2008). Sp(l)itting images; or, back to the future of (rhetoric and?) composition. *College Composition and Communication*, *59*(4), 750-780.

Leavy, Patricia. (2011). *Essentials of transdisciplinary research*. Walnut Creek, CA: Left Coast Press.

Lenhard, Johannes, Lücking, Holger, & Schwechheimer, Holger. (2006). Expert knowledge, Mode-2 and scientific disciplines: Two contrasting views. *Science and Public Policy*, *33*(5), 341- 350.

LeFevre, Karen. B. (1987). *Invention as a social act*. Carbondale, IL: Southern Illinois University Press.

MacDonald, Susan. (1994). *Professional academic writing in the humanities and social sciences*. Carbondale, IL: Southern Illinois University Press.

McLeod, Susan, & Maimon, Elaine. (2000). Clearing the air: WAC myths and realities. *College English*, *62*(5), 573-583.

Newell, William H. (2000). Transdisciplinarity reconsidered. Sommerville & Rapport (Eds.) *Transdisciplinarity: Recreating Integrated Knowledge*. EOLSS. 42-48.

Payne, Darin. (1999). Composition, interdisciplinary collaboration, and the postindustrial concern. *Journal of Advanced Composition*, *19*(4), 607-632.

Rosenfield, Patricia L. (1992) The potential of transdisciplinary research for sustaining and extending linkages between the health and social sciences. *Social Science & Medicine.* 35(11), 1343-1357.

Royster, Jacqueline Jones, Kirsch, Gesa, & Bizzell, Patricia. (2012). *Feminist rhetorical practices: New horizons for rhetoric, composition, and literacy studies.* Carbondale, IL: Southern Illinois University Press.

Shove, Elizabeth. (2010). Beyond the ABC: Climate change policy and theories of social change. *Environment and Planning, 42*(6), 1273-1285.

Steward, Joyce S., & Smelstor, Marjorie. (1984). *Writing in the Social Sciences.* Glenville, IL: Scott, Foresman.

Transdisciplinary Research on Energetics and Cancer (2013). Retrieved from http://www.trecscience.org/trec/default.aspx.

University of Vermont. (2013). Transdisciplinary research initiative. Retrieved from http://www.uvm.edu/~tri/?Page=csys.php.

COMMUNITY LITERACY JOURNAL

Community Literacy Journal is on the Web at http://www.communityliteracy.org/

CLJ publishes scholarly work that contributes to the field's emerging methodologies and research agendas and also work by literacy workers, practitioners, and community literacy program staff. Literacy is defined as the realm where attention is paid not just to content or to knowledge but to the symbolic means by which it is represented and used. Thus, literacy makes reference not just to letters and text but to other multimodal and technological representations as well. The complexities of literacy scholarship in the field is undertheorized in a number of important ways. CLJ provides a space for these important voices to be heard and explored.

De aquí y de allá: **Changing Perceptions of Literacy through Food Pedagogy, Asset-Based Narratives, and Hybrid Space**

The authors in this article describe La Escuelita Afterschool Program, an interdisciplinary, inter-institutional, afer-school literacy partnership on the U.S.–Mexico border. The Escuelita Program used food pedagogy to tap into funds of knowledge, bridging home and school literacies. In doing so, the program challenged deficit thinking and enhanced K-6 students' curiosity and engagement around traditional subjects: science, math, reading, and writing. Through a process of experimental curriculum design and a variety of qualitative data collection methods, they discuss how food pedagogy can help to expand the scope of literacy acquisition. The authors remind readers that knowledge not created only in the classroom and to take an asset based view of learning, especially in communities where such assets might be hidden from plain view. They also showcase the possibilities and importance of interdisciplinary, inter-institutional collaborative scholarship.

De aquí y de allá: Changing Perceptions of Literacy through Food Pedagogy, Asset-Based Narratives, and Hybrid Spaces

Lucía Durá, Consuelo Salas, William Medina-Jerez, and Virginia Hill

In this article we describe La Escuelita Afterschool Program, an interdisciplinary, inter-institutional, after-school literacy partnership on the U.S.–Mexico border. The Escuelita Program used food pedagogy to tap into funds of knowledge, bridging home and school literacies. In doing so, the program challenged deficit thinking and enhanced K-6 students' curiosity and engagement around traditional subjects: science, math, reading, and writing. Through a process of experimental curriculum design and a variety of qualitative data collection methods, we discuss how food pedagogy can help to change deficit-based narratives and how it helps expand the scope of literacy acquisition.

Antes de venir a la escuelita sí sabía mucho de maíz pero no se me ocurrió platicarle a mis hijas. Cuando ya vinimos a la Escuelita y que ya era el tema de ese año, y mis hijas me preguntaron "Mami tu sabías de esa planta?" Sí, y por qué no nos habías dicho? Y sabías de esto y esto? Pues sí pero estamos esperando que fuéramos al rancho. Ya ellas empezaron a conocer todo sobre del maíz y que consumimos y que no sabíamos, no sabían que es tan importante sobre el maíz.

> *Before coming to the Escuelita I did know a great deal about corn but I did not think to share that with my daughters. When we began coming to the Escuelita I discovered that was the subject of the year, and my daughters asked me "Mami you knew of this plant?" [I responded] Yes, and [my daughters asked] why didn't you tell us? And [they asked] you knew about this and this? [I responded] Well yes, but I was waiting to go to the ranch. They began learning all about the corn we eat, things we didn't know and why it is so important.*
>
> —"Alicia," La Escuelita Afterschool Program Parent

Our city, situated on the U.S.–Mexico border, ranks consistently low in well-known studies of literacy (Miller). These studies focus on traditional definitions and markers of literacy such as number of bookstores, average educational attainment, and availability of periodical publishing resources. Yet, as we know, literacy is highly complex and involves the intersection of countless internal and external factors. Studies like Miller's decide whose culture has capital, and, in doing so, fuel public perception of literacy deficiencies (Yosso). They exclude more nuanced markers of literacy like bilingualism and biculturalism as proposed in *Generaciones' Narratives* by John Scenters-Zápico. Even when speaking more than one language and being fluent in more than one culture are common, necessary, and valued, as is the case in our location, conversations about literacy focus largely on deficits (Sepúlveda). This is problematic because *global* perceptions of literacy feed into *local* classroom practices, and these classroom practices, in turn, reinforce a learning culture—one that influences what we think we are capable of or destined to accomplish (Engberg and Allen), i.e., the stories we tell ourselves about ourselves (Geertz).

As educator Luis Moll argues, "existing classroom practices underestimate and constrain what Latino and other children are able to display intellectually" (179). Through his concept of Funds of Knowledge, Moll advocates turning to asset-based learning, especially in communities where such assets might be hidden from plain view. "Alicia's" quote at the beginning of this article, originally in Spanish and translated into English, is illustrative of the types of food and literacy connections the Escuelita Program facilitated. In this article we propose food pedagogy as an effective medium to tap into Funds of Knowledge. We describe "La Escuelita Afterschool Program," (Escuelita Program) an interdisciplinary, inter-institutional, after-school literacy partnership in El Paso, Texas.[1] The Escuelita Program used a food pedagogy-based curriculum to challenge deficit thinking and boost K-6 students' curiosity and engagement around traditional subjects: science, math, reading, and writing.

In the sections that follow we explain our theoretical and conceptual perspectives, contextualize our project and study, and answer the following research questions: (1) How does food pedagogy tap into funds of knowledge? (2) How does making connections between "home" and "school" knowledge challenge deficit-based perceptions of literacies? We conclude with a brief discussion of implications and areas for future research.

OUR THEORETICAL AND CONCEPTUAL PERSPECTIVES

Funds of Knowledge

Some areas of academia are beginning to move away from the ideology that knowledge is only created within the classroom space. This transition allows what is generally regarded as untraditional or "home knowledge" to hold as much cultural capital as school knowledge. Moll and other scholars refer to this as Funds of Knowledge (FoK), "knowledge of strategic importance to households" (Moll and Greenberg 323). FoK includes knowledge about farming, medicinal remedies, and home or auto repair, but also institutional access, school programs, and occupational opportunities. FoK "[contrasts] sharply with prevailing and accepted perceptions of working class families as somehow disorganized socially and deficient intellectually" (Moll, Amanti, Neff, and Gonzalez, 134). Re-examining what counts as knowledge opens a space where minority students are seen not as deficient in traditional conceptions of knowledge or literacy, but instead rich in other FoK and literate in other contexts. As argued by Moll et al., "by capitalizing on household and other community resources, we can organize classroom instruction that far exceeds in quality the rote-like instruction these children commonly encounter in schools" (132). Several studies hold FoK at their core for re-examining teacher preparation; they advocate for teachers to recognize, examine, acknowledge, and leverage the FoK with which their students enter the classroom

(See Licona; Calabrese Barton, and Tan; Vélez-Ibáñez and Greenberg; Moll and Greenberg; Moll, Amanti, Neff, Gónzalez).

Asset-Based Community Work and Hybrid Spaces

The concept of FoK dovetails well with asset-based thinking in community work in rhetoric and composition (RC). Asset-based thinking "begins with assets instead of deficits" (Grabill 96). It encourages an ideological stance that gives people agency and credit for their current expertise; positions community members as co-constructors of knowledge, not merely as "clients" in need of a service provided by outsiders (Grabill 96); and encourages active participation instead of passive reception (See Cushman; Grabill; Mathieu; Simmons; Flower; and Long). Although FoK focus on assets and are seen as a desirable pedagogical practice, it is also important to note that enacting such pedagogy in a traditional classroom may be difficult, even more so in an environment of high stakes standardized testing. Science education scholar Miguel Licona argues that a "FoK approach requires teachers to become ethnographers" (869). The extra time educators must take to visit their students' homes and learn their FoK may be asking too much of our teachers.

Several scholars, however, have studied how "hybrid spaces," such as community centers, can be ideal places to reveal and capitalize on students' FoK (See Buxton; Seiler). In their study merging FoK, discourses, and hybrid space in science education, Angela Calabrese Barton and Edna Tan explain the value of hybridity:

> We are interested in notions of hybridity because we have observed how youth take up knowledges, resources, and identities that often go unsanctioned in school. In so doing, they author new identities, drawing from nontraditional funds and Discourses [sic] to renegotiate the boundaries of their participation in class in ways that allow them to build their social identities while establishing epistemic authority. (52, 53)

Hybrid spaces facilitate "meeting halfway" and certain neutrality that allows for non-threatening conversation and shared decision-making. Yet, in addition to finding the right physical space, rhetorical framing is crucial for setting a tone of invitation and co-ownership. Otherwise, how does an "outsider" get an invitation to "help"? In our particular project, we anchored engagement in food.

Food Pedagogy

When we discuss, "food pedagogy" we speak of it from a Food Studies perspective. According to food scholar Warren Belasco,

> [...] "food extends far beyond nutrients, calories, and minerals." A meal is much more than the sum of its parts, for it encompasses what Barthes calls "a system of communication, a body of images, a protocol of usages, situations, and behavior." [...] People use food to "speak" with each other, to establish rules of behavior ("protocols"), and to reveal as Brillat-Savarin said, "what you are." (15)

Food studies is a multidisciplinary, multifaceted discipline that examines the diverse aspects of *food*, from gender, race, class, to psychology, philosophy, consumption, production and distribution (See Counihan and van Esterik). In our use of "food pedagogy," food is an "object, site, target and 'technology' of education and learning" and is a "*vehicle for learning*" (emphasis in the original, Flowers and Swan 419, 423). "Food pedagogy" is "a congeries of education, teaching and learning about how to grow shop for, prepare, cook display, taste, eat and dispose of food by a range of agencies, actors and media; and aimed [at] a spectrum of 'learners' ... " (426). All of these activities are packed with tacit knowledge, and by making such everyday knowledge explicit, we have the opportunity to make explicit both traditional literacies, typically learned in books or school, and FoK. We propose that food pedagogy has great rhetorical weight as an entry point to engaging community literacies. Scholars and practitioners in the field of education have found creative ways to elicit FoK, and we believe that by putting the work that is being done in education, RC, food studies and food pedagogy in conversation will allow more fruitful harvests of information about the groups we work with.

OUR PARTNERSHIP

How We Came to Be

Our Escuelita Program team is part of an interdisciplinary research group formed in 2011 at The University of Texas at El Paso (UTEP). The mission of this group has been to develop, implement, and document integrated intervention programs that contribute to health and educational equity among Hispanic populations, particularly through translational research. The Escuelita Program is a spin-off of this group. During initial meetings, which took place at the UTEP library, notions of literacy, STEM, culture, and cooking surfaced, and curiosity solidified around the following questions:

- How is it that in bilingual communities like ours conversations focus so much on deficits?
- What would happen if we re-wrote the script of our literacy story? How might we see traditional literacies (science, math, reading, and writing) through a cultural lens?
- Might we see changes in the ways our students perceive themselves? Might we see changes in the ways students are perceived by others? Might we see changes in students' educational outcomes?

The team grew to include faculty and graduate students in science education, RC, literature, food studies and art; resident relations specialists from the Housing Authority of the City of El Paso (HACEP); teachers and aides from a local school district; and students in grades K-6 and their parents. Our common interdisciplinary and inter-institutional denominator? Food. We decided to use food pedagogy to anchor lessons, hands-on cooking, and conversations about ourselves and our heritage.

Our ultimate goal was to write and test a curriculum specifically for after-school programs that used food as a "hook" for students to engage traditionally challenging concepts or subjects. The pilot project (which we also to refer to as Year 1) was titled "The HACEP-UTEP After-school Pilot Project: Promoting Scientific and Literacy Skills through Culture-based Activities." It came to be known informally as the Escuelita Program (*escuelita* is a diminutive, and endearing, term for school in Spanish). The project in Year 2 was titled "Using Corn to Bridge Home and School Literacies: A Culture-based, After-school Curriculum Merging Science, Math, Geography, History, Reading, and Writing."

HACEP and The Escuelitas. HACEP manages 6,500 public residential units comprising multi-family, scattered sites, and elderly communities, which represent 40,000 residents whose average annual income is below $10,000. According to Holly Mata et al., single females with children comprise over fifty percent of HACEP households. Almost half of HACEP residents are under the age of 14. HACEP residents are predominately of Hispanic heritage (98%) and mostly Mexican immigrants and Mexican-Americans.

HACEP hosts four Escuelita sites. Escuelitas are both programs and physical spaces (usually one room with access to the larger community center) contained in the different HACEP community centers throughout the city. A teacher and several tutors or aides from one of the local school districts work with students from that community after school. Among the school district and HACEP communities, Escuelitas are generally perceived as places where students receive tutoring and enrichment activities or do homework.

Educational Partners and Curriculum Overview. The two institutional educational partners for this project were UTEP and a local school district.[2] Collaborating partners from these institutions included

> **William Medina-Jerez**—PI of the Escuelita Program. He is originally from Colombia and is an Associate Professor in Science Education. He worked with three cohorts of pre-service elementary teachers in science education as part of the project.
>
> **Lucía Durá**—Co-PI for the project. She is an Assistant Professor in RC with a background in participatory action research, language, food writing, and food pedagogy.
>
> **Consuelo Salas**—Ph.D. student in RC with a background in Food Studies. She designed and implemented sessions with Dr. FS on food and culture. She conducted ethnographic research using Activity Theory during the project and provided observational feedback for the collaborating team.
>
> **Francisco Valente Saénz**—M.A. art student who worked on a separate collaborative, public art project with HA residents. He introduced Drs. Medina-Jerez and Durá.
>
> **Meredith Abarca**—Associate Professor of English Literature and a Food Studies scholar. She implemented one session in Year 1 and helped to co-design and implement the curriculum in Year 2. She brought a Food Studies and culture lens to the project.

Virginia Hill and Sonia Legarreta—two resident relations specialists from HACEP, who link residents with services that can improve quality of life.

Ms. GB—Escuelita teacher for Year 1. She worked diligently with the students in between formal Escuelita sessions on vocabulary-building and reading and writing.

Ms. IH—an art teacher from Ms. GB's school who documented our work using photography and video and facilitated use of the school's computer lab when needed for art projects.

Ms. ML—Escuelita teacher for Year 2. She was instrumental in helping us design age-appropriate activities. Her daughter was also an Escuelita participant.

Ms. JS—school district Specialist and official partnership liaison.

School district tutors—two to three tutors from the school district supported the work of the Escuelita students and teachers. They did not participate in planning sessions but were present at feedback/research sessions.

Methodology

Curriculum Development as a Design Experiment

Inspired by Calabrese Barton and Tan's science education study on "Funds of Knowledge and Discourses and Hybrid Space," we approached our work of curriculum development as a design experiment. A design experiment in educational research, as explained by Cobb, Confrey, diSessa, Lehrer, Schauble, is meant "to develop a class of theories about both the process of learning and the means that are designed to support that learning" (10). Design experiments are necessarily (1) praxis-based, (2) interventionist, (3) prospective—based on a hypothesis, (4) iterative, and (5) immediately relevant to practitioners, i.e., resulting theories are pragmatic (Cobb et al. 9-11). In a way similar to Calabrese and Tan, we used our design experiment to address simultaneously problems of practice and develop/test principles of teaching and learning that might be applicable beyond the original research site.

Data Collection and Analysis

Given the speculative and iterative nature of conducting a design experiment, we drew from a variety of data collection methods to reflect on the process and products and feed insights back into project design over the course of each school year. In Year 1, we collected data anchored in food-based lessons. This included artifacts (e.g., drawings, writing, and photographs/video), narratives (oral and written), and observations (several of us kept research journals). We also conducted focus groups with family members and interviewed children participants. In addition to these methods, in Year 2 we added an Activity Theory ethnography, which Consuelo conducted for a methods course in her doctoral program, and asset-based, participatory methods: Appreciative Interviews (AIs) (Lipmanowicz & McCandless), Cultural Memory Banking (CMB) (Handa & Tippins), Participatory Interviews, and Participatory Drawing and Narrations. We analyzed all data continuously as a team using Glaser & Strauss' constant comparative method to extract key themes. We also employed visual discourse analysis to interpret the composition, context, and reception of images (See Christmann and Durá et al.).

Curriculum Design and Implementation

Our first research question asks, how does food pedagogy tap into funds of knowledge? To answer this question, in this section we describe key insights from the recursive curriculum design and implementation process. In the mode of Jessica Seinfeld who writes healthy recipes under the auspices of "yummy" foods, in Year 1 we set out to write a curriculum for the Escuelita Program that used food to "grab" students' attention so that they may explore science, math, reading, and writing along the way. We also aimed to re-write the script of our literacy story by viewing traditional school literacies through a cultural lens.

We used food to anchor all lessons, invited parents to participate often, incorporated art as much as possible, and coordinated lessons with the seasons or holidays, e.g., planting time, harvest time, Thanksgiving, etc. (Gónzalez and Moll). Each session contained one or more 90-minute lesson. The curriculum sequence we followed in Years 1 and 2 is in table 1.

Table 1. Curriculum Sequence for Year 1 and Year 2 Design Experiment

YEAR 1	YEAR 2
	Preliminary Session with Families: "Appreciative Interviews" (AIs) and "Cultural Memory Bank" (CMB). Escuelita Program team brings home cooked meal to share with parents.
Session 1: "The Favorite Plate" Ms. CG, guides students in the design of a colorful plate representing their favorite meal using the 5 Ws as a heuristic.	Session 1: "Where does corn come from?" Incorporates history and geography in tracing the historical migration of corn from different areas of the world to the students' plates. Writing activity: map and corn diagram with various species (i.e., yellow, blue, hominy, Peruvian) and their descriptions.
Session 2: "Practicing with Cooking Techniques" Prior to this session Ms. CG prepares a glossary of the terms students practice using. Students perform different cooking techniques, e.g., measuring, mixing, and folding. They prepare calabacitas (Mexican squash side dish), merengues (meringues), and melcochas (Colombian caramels) with guidance and are introduced to food science.	Session 2: "What food is made with corn?" Incorporates cultural history and nutrition in making direct connections with familiar recipes. Recipe reading and writing activities using visual-to-written templates (See fig. 1).

Year 1	Year 2
Session 3: "Cooking with Families." Students read bilingual books: Adelita and the Veggie Cousins/Adelita y las primas verduritas and A Day without Sugar/Un día sin azúcar. Each family brings a vegetable and/or a fruit to be used in preparation of a soup and fruit skewers. Students and their parents practice the cooking techniques and write a family recipe (using a template) that uses at least one fruit and/or vegetable.	**Session 3**: "Who makes foods made with corn?" Incorporates cultural history in greater depth, including family history. Uses a cultural artifact exhibit as teachers provided a metate (stone grinder), hand molino (mill), tortilla press, and comal (hot plate) to demonstrate culturally significant traditional ways of processing corn in the home. Students interview a family member or neighbor using a template to record responses. They also bring a corn "artifact" and write a short story about it. **Interim Session with Families:** Videotaped family member interviews and potluck.
Session 4: "Revising Recipes." Students go through a peer review process of their family recipes and revise with help of tutors. Students write a recipe for cold sandwich wraps using a visual-to-writing template (See fig. 1).	**Session 4**: "What other things are made with corn?" Teachers demonstrate the multiple uses of corn. Demonstration of physical objects that are also made with corn; for example, batteries, etc. Students not only have the opportunity to write, but physically see how science uses food for purposes outside of nutrition.
Session 5: "The Ideal/Colorful Plate." Introduction of the USDA/Harvard/Michelle Obama plate for comparison with the students' initial plate. Students color the "Obama" plate and work on a third plate: their "improved" favorite plate, which they explain.	**Session 5**: "Why is corn important?" Students reflect on the information they have learned throughout the unit, and considered the various cultural, historical, and scientific implications of corn. In a group writing exercise or through picture books students compose a story of why they believe corn is important.

Year 1	Year 2
Sessions 6 and 7: "The Faces of Food." In Part I, students use bagels and vegetables to represent a family member's face. They tell an oral story about the person. In Part II, students use ingredients for Mexican tostadas to create a face that expresses how they feel that day. They describe their face and that particular emotion(s).	
Culminating Event with Families: Students and their families received a compilation of the Escuelita recipes, including Escuelita and family recipes.	**Culminating Event with Families**: Stories are compiled, formatted into an illustrated book/booklet, and presented to the wider housing, school district, and university community.

Year 1 Insights

At the end of Year 1 our team learned four key lessons. First, constant with the process of design experiments as a methodology, the curriculum was under constant revision. For example, we added Sessions 6 as a result of Meredith and Consuelo joining the team. Meredith had done the bagel face activity in a different setting and introduced us to it. We then added the tostada face—Session 7—for cultural relevance as we learned that some students were unfamiliar with bagels. Second, we found that some of the most successful moments involved family members cooking with students and family members sharing recipes. Recipes are a conversation starter, even within family units. For example, students had questions for their parents about the techniques and the origins of the recipes. Third, we learned that positioning students as makers and doers brings out other ways of knowing. This ontological dimension is a valuable aspect of food pedagogy. Making or cooking allows students to work with their hands and learn something about themselves. It also enables them to "know" what they are describing in oral or written form. Students felt that if they lacked the vocabulary for something, "showing" was a valid technique. Art as "doing" worked in a similar way. Using a visual to written template, students draw the steps in a recipe first and then describe the steps in words (See fig. 1 below). This meets students where they are and allows all of them to be active participants, regardless of skill level.

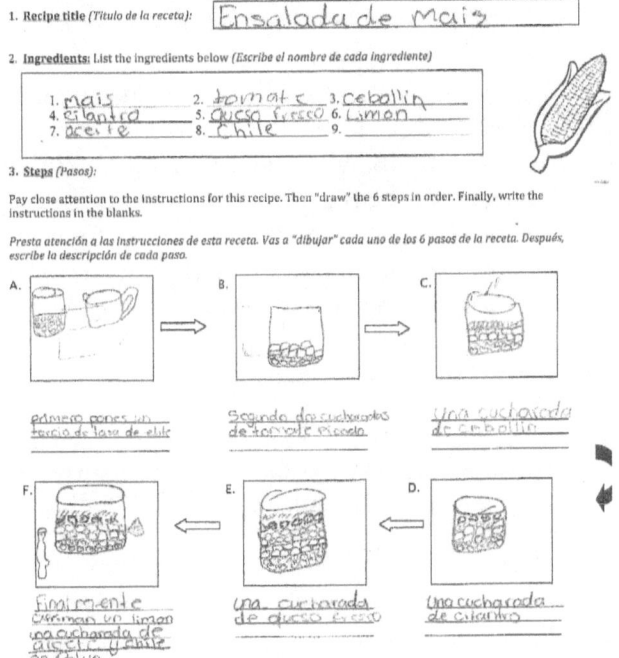

Figure. 1. Visual to Written Recipe Template

A fourth lesson is leveraging the richness of our linguistic backgrounds, e.g., hybridity. When students had the ability to choose a language for a particular activity, they didn't feel "stuck." And yet, the curricular structure gave them plenty of opportunities to also practice their more challenging language.

Year 2 Insights

Based on what we learned in Year 1, in Year 2 we began the program with a greater emphasis on participatory and asset-based techniques. We decided to focus on an agricultural theme that would be relevant for everyone involved—something that everyone had access to, that was in our daily diets, and that grows in the area. We chose corn. And seeing the value of family narratives in Year 1, we decided to incorporate appreciative interviews and cultural memory banking from the first session. AIs are meant to discover and build on the root causes of success—as opposed to failure or barriers (Lipmanowicz & McCandless). Using AIs, questions are structured for positive discovery and storytelling, e.g., think back to when you were growing up, what was your favorite food? Who would make it? What do you remember about the tastes, ingredients? When would you eat it? Where? We used this question sequence in our first session with families to begin to populate our CMB. We used a CMB to "store" all of our findings from interviews, focus groups, observations, field trips, and lessons. This CMB was displayed on the walls of the Escuelita site and was available for all participants to populate with words, sentences, and images. Field trips during Year 2 included visits to local food factories, grocery stores, and a local corn maze; they were planned to help reinforce lessons within the class time.

At the end of Year 2, in the summer, our team met to compile lessons into a written curriculum for replication. We analyzed the findings from both years, and we structured the curriculum document as a recipe in which we explained these findings as "Essential Ingredients." Our instructions for the users read:

> We have framed this thematic unit as a recipe—not one to be followed to the letter, but one to be adapted to your needs. Some ingredients, we have found, are essential. They are what helps create bridges between home and school. Others are more flexible. Their quantities can be tweaked a bit more. In this section we describe the key ingredients for the unit. *¡Buen provecho!* Enjoy! (Medina-Jerez, Durá, & López)

The essential ingredients we describe in the curriculum are

- Food pedagogy not only helps to "break the ice" in any group, it also helps to tap into students' "Funds of Knowledge" and empowers students in the "doing." Students are able to learn *about* food as the topic engages a wide variety of people, but they are also able to learn *through* food: "food can be a useful teaching tool to develop an understanding of science and math concepts" (Phillips, Duffrin & Geist 24).
- A hybrid space (after-school) provided opportunities for creativity without the pressure of state assessments (tests and standards). It also provided opportunities for family members to attend and to talk to each other.

- A locally important food theme that lends itself to conversations about heritage and that is infinitely "explorable" serves as a good point of departure for inquiry. We found an agricultural theme to be relevant. Other locations might choose a theme that is relevant for other reasons, i.e., geography, industry, history.
- Family involvement grounds the FoK discovery process in heritage and home practices. It also maximizes the likelihood that ideas children bring home will be adopted/sustained.
- Inquiry structure—framing this as an exploration helps us all learn together instead of the educators as teachers and the participants as learners.
- Art, hands-on activities, field-trips and guest teachers, in ways similar to food, position students as makers and doers, creating a space for physical meaning-making, increased-self awareness, and different perspectives/new narratives.
- Explicit "transfer" language helps participants make connections about knowledge and ways of knowing from one sphere to the other.

Aligning the Classroom and Kitchen Spaces: Threads from Participants

In order to answer our second question—how does making connections between "home" and "school" knowledge challenge deficit-based perceptions of literacies?—we first describe the three part process of using "*charlas culinarias*" to make connections. We then present insights, which we have grouped thematically using a constant comparative method (Glaser & Strauss), from data collected from students, parents, and teachers over the course of Years 1 and 2 of the Escuelita Program.

Making Connections through *Charlas Culinarias*

If indeed our realities are shaped by language—by the stories we tell ourselves—then changing those stories becomes crucial in order to challenge deficit-based perceptions. Abarca explains that *charlas culinarias* "[...] represent spoken personal narratives, testimonial autobiography, and a form of culinary memoir [...] (166). In the Escuelita Program, we worked to create an environment that asked parents of student participants to speak to their culinary FoK within the hybrid space of a classroom and community center. Eliciting these stories through *charlas* was a first step towards making connections between home and school. We did this in a couple of ways: (1) recipe sharing and cooking together in Year 1, and (2) integrating AIs, Participatory Interviews, and the CMB in Year 2. Through our *charlas* we attempted to move through three steps:

> Step 1: Inviting the parents to share their stories about food, production, and consumption both with their children and with other families and creating a space where those stories are cherished and valued;
>
> Step 2: Fostering an environment that allowed families to recognize their food production, consumption, and distribution knowledge as a literacy, i.e., knowledge that perhaps they had never before considered to be a literacy but simply a means of providing for their families;
>
> Step 3: In going through steps 1 and 2 with the parents, we used food to tap into students' funds of knowledge and (1) create a sense that what occurs in the kitchen is a valuable literacy; 2) make explicit connections to multiple subjects, science, geography, reading, writing, history, and using food to expand students' notions of those subjects.

Cooking as a Scientific Process

At the onset of Year 2, we conducted AIs with parents. This *charla* took place with families around a simple question: "What foods do you eat or make that have corn?" We asked parents to speak in pairs, then in fours, and then shared with the whole group stories about their cultural cooking practices as well as who they were, where they were from, and a bit about their family history. The parents explained that never before had they considered that their caloric funds of knowledge or food preparation, could be scientific; however, in the AIs parents described, for example, that they had knowledge of how to start a fire without the use of the stove—using firewood outside. Once the fire was lit, they then had the know how to keep the flame at the right temperature to prepare the foods. Parents, especially mothers, also had knowledge of various recipes involving the *nixtamalización* process (soaking corn in lime and boiling it to facilitate grinding and enhance the *masa's* (corn dough) nutritional value), different types of corn for different uses, and different tools that were used to process the corn such as the *metate* (stone grinder) for grinding and the *comal* (hot plate) for cooking. We "stored" this knowledge in the CMB.

Valuing Food Literacies

Midway through Year 2, we held a potluck to which parents brought their favorite recipes made with corn. The students conducted Participatory Interviews. They followed an interview format and were videotaped asking their parents questions about their favorite dishes and recipes made with corn. It is worth noting that, in large part, parents were not shy in front of the camera. Rather, they were enthusiastic to share more stories, and they asserted that they were very happy to share food with us as we had done with them. Thus the tone for the session was generous and festive.

Through the *charlas*, parents were able to take on an authoritative role in their FoK as preparers of food. One working parent talked about the importance of *sazón*. In her interview she explained why one should make food taste good: "Es importante tener buena sazón. Si a la gente le gusta la comida le van a preguntar a uno como la hizo y le van a pedir más." For this parent, good tasting food was a commodity. She said that if food tasted good people would want to know how it was made, and in a financial pinch, one could sell it. She further explained that she felt equipped to sell food if she ever lost her job. Other parents talked about the importance of passing down their heritage through food—mostly to their daughters; although one parent said she would also pass it to her son. At the end of Year 2, we conducted participatory drawing activities with parents, asking them to depict signs of change "before" and "after" engaging in the Escuelita Program. "I had never given importance to where food comes from," said one parent. "Now when we're eating, we have these conversations." Another parent talked about valuing her roots and explained that when they go to the ranch in the future her children want to help warm the tortillas and learn about more things you can do with corn: "El rancho es un vil rancho, de adobe. [Ellos] no quieren salir de la cocina, donde se hacen las tortillas. Pero cuantas cosas se hacían con el maíz? [Y]o, conocía muy poquito." A parent added that her daughter now wants to discuss similarities and differences with other Latin cultures.

Students as Makers and Doers

Cooking activities in the Escuelita Program were designed to support the translation of everyday practices into authentic learning opportunities to practice scientific habits of mind that include predicting, calculating, observing, and inferring, among others. While engaged in the cooking activities, students were able to practice reading and writing skills included in the planning, preparation, and presentation of each recipe and activity (e.g., follow directions, summarization, compare and contrast) both in Spanish and in English. A prevalent theme for both years of the Escuelita Program was that student participants stayed active and engaged with the projects both within the Escuelita setting and at home in the kitchen space. In the end-of-year focus groups, students spoke about which activities they remembered most or found to be their favorites. Students from Year 1 (even at the end of Year 2 when we conducted follow-up interviews) remembered the activities that involved cooking: making soup, fruit skewers, and *merengues* and *melcochas*. Students from Year 2 remembered tortillas to make *quesadillas*, visiting the grocery store and reading food labels, making a colorful corn salad, and doing a silk-screen painting of their favorite take-aways from the year with a narration. Similarly, when we asked students about the differences they saw between the work they do at the Escuelita and the work they do in their regular classrooms, students from both years pointed to the "doing." "Here we are working together," one student said. "Here we do activities. At school we do more worksheets," another student said.

In their before/after drawings and narrations parents from Year 1 noted that their children do tasks such as help wash vegetables, chop vegetables, and read the ingredient labels. They also say things like, "I am a chef" or "this ingredient tastes good with this other one." In explaining before/after changes at the end of Year 1, Ms. GB said that while most of the Escuelita participants were not in her class at school, they would very proudly say hello to her in the hallway. To her this was significant as she explained that students from lower grades (she teaches 6th grade) do not customarily speak to or reach out to teachers from higher grades, much less publicly.

In the case of students from Year 2, they read food labels and tell their parents when corn is an unexpected ingredient, such as with hamburger buns or ketchup. Students from Year 2 also replicate easy recipes such as the corn salad with their parents. Ms. ML noted the significance of this theme: "Before, students were just observers. They would watch their parents. Now they do things. They can do things that they watched others do, and that's empowering!" She also added that this curriculum is similar to what students in "Gifted and Talented" classes get, and this population is not typically exposed to such programming. Virginia and Sonia also observed that students stayed excited and were more engaged throughout the year with our involvement; they noted that students transferred some ideas from the cooking sessions to the garden project in their residential community.

Conclusion: *De aquí y de allá*

The saying, "Ni de aquí, ni de allá" in Spanish means "from neither here nor there." It refers to the immigrant's conundrum of physical and metaphorical liminality. Our title, *De aquí y de allá*, is a both/and proposition. The work presented in this article challenges deficit-based perceptions by bridging home and school literacies. It encourages a both/and perspective instead of either/or. Through the Escuelita Program we have described how food pedagogy taps into family FoK. Honoring and bearing witness to FoK laid the groundwork for a learning environment that encouraged students to engage in what they were are already familiar with, value it, see it as a literacy, and use it to learn other subjects. Food pedagogy, in tapping into funds of knowledge, helps to expand the scope of literacy acquisition by changing the narrative about what people can expect from themselves. And learning by doing builds the confidence and know-how to transfer literacies (broadly speaking) or skills from one space to another. It is through this framework that communities traditionally seen as illiterate can begin to expand and question traditional notions of literacy.

There is great potential in food-literacy partnerships, and this is just the beginning. As food continues to trend, so can explorations and experiments with food pedagogy. Many aspects of this project can be investigated further, e.g., reading and writing artifacts, learning STEM subjects through food, the epistemological and ontological dimensions of food pedagogy, and the relationship between food pedagogy and learning outcomes. We encourage other scholars and practitioners to apply the Escuelita model of community engagement with their local communities in a way that makes sense to their context.

And we welcome conversations that further inquiry as we continue to explore the Escuelita Program's curriculum replication.

Notes

1. The Escuelita project was funded by The University of Texas at El Paso's College of Education Research Grants for Associate Professors program. We are thankful for this financial support. We also thank Meredith Abarca for her influence in the design, facilitation, and documentation of this work; for guiding us into the field of Food Studies; and for reviewing this manuscript. We are indebted to all Escuelita students and families and to our collaborating partners Sonia Legarreta, Francisco Valente Saenz, Ms. IH, Ms. GB, Ms. ML, and Ms. JS. This work would not be possible without their participation and feedback.

2. In accordance with our confidentiality agreements, we are using pseudonyms for school district partner names.

Works Cited

Abarca, Meredith E. *Voices in the Kitchen: Views of Food and the World from Working Class Mexican and Mexican American Women*. College Station: Texas A&M Press, 2006. Print.

Belasco, Warren. *Food: The Key Concepts*. New York: Berg, 2008. Print.

Buxton, Cory. "Creating contextually authentic science in a low performing urban elementary school. *Journal of Research in Science Teaching* 43.7 (2006) : 695–721.

Calabrese Barton, Angela and Edna Tan. "Funds of Knowledge and Discourses in Hybrid Space." *Journal of Research in Science Teaching* 46.1 (2009) : 50-73. Print.

Calabrese Barton, Angela, Toby J. Hindin, Isobel R. Contento, Michelle Trudeau, Kimberley Yang, Sumi Hagiwara, and Pamela Koch. "Underprivileged Urban Mothers' Perspective on Science." *Journal of Research in Science Teaching* 38.6 (2001) : 688-711. Print.

Carlton Parsons, Eileen and Heidi B. Carlone. "Culture and science Education in the 21st century: Extending and making the cultural box more inclusive." *Journal of Research in Science Teaching* 50.1 (2012) : 1-11. Web. 28 May 2015 doi: 10.1002tea.21068

Christmann, Gabriela B. "The Power of Photographs of Buildings in the Dresden Urban Discourse. Towards a Visual Discourse Analysis." *Forum: Qualitative Social Research Sozialforschung* 9.3 (2008) : np. Web. 28 May 2015.

Cobb, Paul, Jere Confrey, Andrea diSessa, Richard Lehrer, and Leona Schauble. "Design Experiments in Educational Research." *Educational Researcher* 32.1 (2003) : 9-13. Print.

Counihan, Carole and Penny Van Esterik. "Why Food? Why Culture? Why Now? Introduction to the Third Edition." *Food and Culture: A Reader*. 3d ed. Eds. Carole Counihan and Penny Van Esterik. Routledge: New York, 2013. Print.

Cushman, Ellen. *The struggle and the tools: Oral and literate strategies in an inner city community*. Albany: SUNY Press, 1998. Print.

Durá, Lucía, Laurel J. Felt, and Arvind Singhal. "What Counts? For Whom? Cultural Beacons and Unexpected Areas of Programmatic Impact." *Journal of Evaluation and Program Planning*, 44 (2014) : 98-109. Print.

Edbauer Rice, Jenny and Jeff Rice. *Pre/Text: A Journal of Rhetorical Theory Food Theory*. 21.1-4 (2013). Print.

Engberg, Mark E. and Daniel J. Allen. "Uncontrolled destinies: Improving opportunity for low income students in American higher education." *Research in Higher Education* 52.8 (2011) : 786-807. Web. 18 May 2015

Flower, Linda. *Community Literacy and the Rhetoric of Public Engagement*. Carbondale: Southern Illinois UP, 2008. Print.

Flowers, Rick and Elaine Swan. "Introduction: Why food? Why pedagogy? Why adult education?" *Australian Journal of Adult Learning*. 52.3 (2012) : 419-430. Print.

Frye, Joshua and Michael Bruner. *Rhetoric of Food*. New York: Routledge, 2012. Print.

Geertz, Clifford. *The Interpretation of Culture: Selected Essays*. New York: Basic Books, 1973. Print.

Grabill, Jeffrey T. *Community Literacy Program and the Politics of Change*. New York: SUNY Press, 2001. Print.

Glaser, Barney and Anselm Strauss. *The Discovery of Grounded Theory: Strategies for Qualitative Research* New Brunswick: Aldine Transaction, 1967; 2012. Print.

González, Norma E, & Moll, Luis. "Cruzando el puente: Building bridges to funds of knowledge." *Journal of Educational Policy*, 16.4 (2002) : 623-641. Print.

Hagiwara, Sumi, Angela Calabrese-Barton, and Isobel R. Contento. "Culture, food, and language: Perspectives from immigrant mothers in school science." *Cultural Studies of Science Education*, 2 (2007) : 475-499. Print.

Handa, Vicente C. and Deborah J. Tippins. "Cultural Memory Banking in Preservice Science Teacher Education." *Research Science Education*. 42.6(2012): 1201-1217. Print. doi:10.1007/s11165-011-9241-6

Licona, Miguel M. "Mexican and Mexican-American children's funds of knowledge as interventions into deficit thinking: opportunities for praxis in science education." *Culture Studies of Science Education* 8 (2013) : 859-872. Doi 10.1007/s11422- 0139515-6. Print.

Lipmanowicz, Henri and Keith McCandless. "Appreciative Interviews." *Liberating Structures: Innovating by Including and Unleashing Everyone. E&Y Performance* 2.4 (2010) : 6-9. Web 30 May 2015.

Long, Eleanore. *Community Literacy and the Rhetoric of Local Publics* West Lafayette: Parlor Press, 2008. Electronic.

Mata, Holly, Maria Flores, Ernesto Castañeda, William Medina-Jerez, Josue Lachica, Curtis Smith, and Hector Olvera. "Health, hope, and human development: Building capacity in public housing communities on the U.S.–Mexico border." *Journal of Health Care for the Poor and Underserved* 24.4(2013) : 1432-1439.

Matheiu, P. *Tactics of hope: The public turn in English composition*. Portsmouth, NH: Boynton/Cook, 2005. Print.

Medina-Jerez William, Lucía Durá and Marisela Lopez. "Bridging Home and School literacies at The *Escuelita*: A Recipe for Engaged Asset-Based Learning." 2014. Unpublished Microsoft Word File.

Moll, Luis C. "Literacy research in community and classrooms: A sociocultural approach." *Theoretical Models and Processes of Reading*. 4th edition. Robert B. Ruddell and Norma Unrau Eds. Robert B. Ruddell and Harry Singer Newark: International Reading Association, 1994. Print.

Moll, Luis C., Cathy Amanti, Deborah Neff and Norma Gonzalez. "Funds of Knowledge for Teaching: Using a Qualitative Approach to Connect Homes and Classrooms." *Theory into Practice. Qualitative Issues in Educational Research* 31.2 (1992) : 132-141. Print.

Moll, Luis C. and James B. Greenberg. "Creating zones of possibilities: Combining Social contexts for instruction." *Vygotsky and Education: Instructional Implication and Applications of Sociohistorical Psychology*. Ed. Luis C. Moll London: Cambridge UP, 1992. 319 - 348. Print.

Miller, John W. "Overall Rankings," Central Connecticut State University, 2013.Web. 30 May 2015.

Philips, Sharon K, Melani W. Duffrin and Eugene A. Geist. "Be a Food Scientist." *Science and Children* 41.4 (2004) : 224-29. Web. 31 May 2015.

Scenters-Zapico, John. Generaciones' Narratives. Logan: Utah State UP, 2010. Electronic.

Schilb, John. "Special Focus: Food." *College English* 70.4 (2008) : 345- 436.

Seiler, Gale. "Reversing the "standard" direction: Science emerging from the lives of African American students." *Journal of Research in Science Teaching*, 38.9 (2001) : 1000–1014.

Sepulveda, Enrique. "Overcoming Deficit Thinking." *CT News Junkie*, 17 Sep 2012. Web. 30 May 2015.

Simmons, W.M. *Participation and power: Civic discourse in environmental policy decisions*. New York: SUNY, 2007. Print.

U.S. Census Bureau. "State and County QuickFacts: El Paso County, Texas." The United States Census Bureau, 22 Apr. 2015. Web. 28 May 2015.
Vélez-Ibáñez, Carlos G. and James B. Greenberg. "Formation and Transformation of Funds of Knowledge among U.S. Mexican Households." *Anthropology and Education Quarterly* 23.4 (1992) : 313-335. Print.
Yosso, Tara J. "Whose culture has capital? A critical race theory discussion of community cultural wealth." *Race Ethnicity and Education* 8.1 (2005) : 69-91. Web. 18 May 2015.

Author Bios

Dr. Lucía Durá is Assistant Professor of Rhetoric and Composition in the Department of English at The University of Texas at El Paso (UTEP). Her research focuses on innovative approaches to organizational and social change, intercultural communication, risk communication, and the discourses of health and medicine. Her recent work on positive deviance and intercultural communication has yielded numerous peer-reviewed presentations and publications. She is currently working on several positive deviance projects that combine education and race critical theory.

Consuelo Carr Salas is a fourth year doctoral candidate at the University of Texas at El Paso. She is the inaugural recipient of the Centennial Outstanding Doctoral Student Strauss Research Fellowship from the Department of English. Her research interests include visual rhetoric and the intersection of food studies and rhetoric.

Dr. Medina-Jerez is an Associate Professor of Science Education in the Department of Teacher Education at the University of Texas-El Paso (UTEP); he teaches undergraduate science methods courses, as well as graduate level courses on science teaching in bilingual classrooms. Before moving to UTEP, he was an Assistant Professor of Science Education at the University of Wyoming for five years, and before that he completed his post-doctoral appointment at Arizona State University (ASU) in both the College of Education and the Schools of Life Sciences. While at ASU, Dr. Medina-Jerez collaborated in research projects related to the use of technology in elementary school classrooms with English Language Learners (ELLs) (College of Education), and in aggression behavior studies of house finches

(School of Life Sciences). Dr. Medina-Jerez earned his Ph.D. (2005) and M.S. (2002) in Science Education from the University of Iowa.

Ms. Hill has been with the Housing Authority of the City of El Paso for the past six years working as a Resident Relations Specialist. Prior to working with HACEP she worked for the Workforce Centers for 18 years. Ms. Hill has spent almost 25 years working with low and very low income persons assisting and encouraging them to leave public assistance and become self-sufficient. She believes children are the future of this nation, and that our current education system needs to change to allow them to lead the world.

COMPOSITION FORUM

Composition Forum is a peer-reviewed journal for scholars and teachers interested in the investigation of composition theory and its relation to the teaching of writing at the post-secondary level. The journal features articles that explore the intersections of composition theory and pedagogy, including essays that examine specific pedagogical theories or that examine how theory could or should inform classroom practices, methodology, and research into multiple literacies. *Composition Forum* also publishes articles that describe specific and innovative writing program practices and writing courses, reviews of relevant books in composition studies, and interviews with notable scholars and teachers who can address issues germane to our theoretical approach.

Composition Forum is on the Web at http://compositionforum.com/

Mapping the Resourcefulness of Sources: A Worknet Pedagogy

Mapping the Resourcefulness of Sources: A Worknet Pedagogy

Derek Mueller

"Writing is one of the activities by which we locate ourselves in the enmeshed systems that make up the social world" (Cooper 373).

Opening: Locating Sources *Along* Systems

In her 1986 essay, "The Ecology of Writing," Marilyn Cooper expressed a preference for "an ecological model of writing, whose fundamental tenet is that writing is an activity through which a person is continually engaged with a variety of socially constituted systems" (367). Cooper's articulation of an ecological view was—for Rhetoric and Composition—one of the earliest to appear in what today has become too teeming an arena for any one Burkean parlor to host, much less contain. Numerous scholars and practitioners[1] have adopted, expressed, and extended in sophisticated ways ecological understandings of writing activity systems. While the array of perspectives on writing ecologies over nearly three decades grows ever more vast, much of this work builds upon or in other ways accords with Cooper's ideas that ecological systems are "inherently dynamic" (368), that they spill fortuitously beyond bounded contexts, and that a simple web provides a conceptual metaphor and a visual model sufficient for grasping (and eventually venturing along) the topographies of such systems.

I begin with Cooper's prescient article both because her ideas underpin the logic of the pedagogy and project that I develop in this paper and because I present the project using "The Ecology of Writing" as a model source. The project responds to a concern for approaches to source-based academic writing that frame sources too reductively as materials to be slotted *into* writing. In a contemporary frame, the project I introduce resonates with Douglas Brent's arguments for rethinking the value of the research paper, where he notes its connective facility for students (i.e., source-based research operating as a way to aid students in realizing linkages across disciplines). Brent writes, "with the writing task in the foreground and the content more in the background, we can spend a great deal of time working students through various phases of getting to know source texts that they will need in order to answer their particular research questions" (48). In addition to helping students get to know source texts, worknets function heuristically from the earliest stages of inquiry, emphasizing how work with sources can operate as rhetorical invention. Research questions are oftentimes instigated by encounters with what others have written. As such, the approach reinforces for writers a generative relationship between coming up with viable research questions and reading exploratorily for dimensions of sources they had not considered before, dimensions that are germane to rethinking researchable questions as the questions morph and take on better defined shapes. Worknets extend this premise into practice, locating students' work with sources not only in middle and late stages of a project's development, such as happens when writers seek and enlist sources only as evidence to support claims (i.e., a supportive approach), but at an earlier juncture, while a project is still somewhat messy, still taking shape (i.e., an inventive approach). The approach offered here is flexible insofar as it remains open to what constitutes a researchable question. As presented, it is also informed by alternative approaches to research processes, such as the collection and annotation practices Geoffrey Sirc emphasized in "box-logic" and the nomadic, Barthes-influenced "anything whatever" Jeff Rice introduced as an aspect of his 1963 hip-hop machine. Both of these approaches value the juxtaposition of uncanny, striking artifacts—an inventive mélange of song lyrics, photographs, snippets of text. Together these produce uncanny instigations that spark more intense interest in research than do topic-based alternatives.

I call the project *worknets*. Worknets offer researching writers a means of locating and tracing sources *along* and *across* networked activity systems (Spinuzzi). Worknets treat sources as *complexly enmeshed resources* for rhetorical invention and, in effect, as *constellations of activity* whose tracing may prove generative throughout a researching writer's many stages of active inquiry. Sources are suspended among many disparate forces while writers compose; they are rather like tiny knots held in part among a skein of ties that coalesces motives, arguments, references, generalist and disciplinarily-situated vocabularies, sites of production, and space-time coordinates. As such, source-based writing stands to be enriched by adopting an explicitly networked logic when engaging sources.

The word worknets comes from Bruno Latour's *Reassembling the Social,* a book in which he introduces Actor-Network Theory, a methodology developed to trace and account for associations among divergent, oftentimes non-obvious, actors. Latour mentions worknets fleetingly and as a playful inversion of *networks* because worknets place an explicit emphasis on action, whereas networks can appear inert, like static snapshots. Latour writes, "Really, we should say 'worknet' instead of 'network'. It's the work, and the movement, and the flow, and the changes that should be stressed. But now we are stuck with 'network' and everyone thinks we mean the World Wide Web or something like that" (143). By naming the project "worknets," I hope for its network logic to be evident as it foregrounds some of the ways relations among articles, people, things, places, moments, and activities manifest *as* a particular research source, whatever the source may be. With this in mind, the word "worknets" refers to *the specific project* in a teaching context as well as *the networked, associational aspects of a research source* that are traceable and that by tracing can lead researching writers to rhetorical invention and further inquiry. The approach seeks to render a source's associations traceable in such a way that powerfully augments inquiry and related research-based writing processes for students. In effect, the guiding, sustained question in a worknets-based pedagogy is, how is a particular source entangled in an associative web, constituted by both obvious and non-obvious traces? Recognizing a source's associative web enlarges its footprint and makes it knowable as the culmination of constellated activity. Insights stemming from this support inquiry and invention because they demystify the orienting contexts from which the source emerged, rendering more explicitly hints of the behind-the-scenes mess and divergent forces borne out through the source as it takes shape, eventually as a tidy manuscript that circulates and ages.

In the project this paper introduces, I attend to four *worknet phases*, or aspects of sources that, once surfaced, may illuminate promising possibilities for further inquiry: *semantic, bibliographic, affinity-based*, and *choric*. These four phases are by no means exhaustive, but I have presented them as a scaffolded set, meaning that they build from one to the next, offering a practical schema for attending to highly salient dimensions of a research source. The *semantic* phase examines high frequency and load bearing words and phrases (i.e., vocabulary). The *bibliographic* phase attends to source reference (i.e., citations), noticing both how the sources operate in the article and following-up on selected references list for further discovery work. The *affinity-based* phase dwells on authorship (i.e., professional and intellectual kinship). It looks into who wrote the article, what else they have written, the author's intellectual genealogy (i.e., collaborators and mentors), and the occasion for the source's composition. The *choric* phase inquires into serendipitous and coincidental events occurring at or near (in place and time) the source's development (i.e., generative surrounds). Tracing each of the four phases for one research source involves illustrating the phases and writing an account for each of them that explores how selected associations have materialized and how those ties could be generative for an emerging research project. Each phase is exemplified more fully in the second half of the paper.

For instructors who teach research-based academic writing, worknets stand to strengthen the relationship between reading, invention, and formal, explicit citation. They enlarge and render more vividly apparent the source's contexts, which in turn helps writers realize the differences between casual (or requirement-obliging) citation and source use that is likely to be more rhetorically astute due to greater engagement with the source. Worknets bring sources more fully into view, so writers can make decisions about source use mindful of other possibilities. In this sense, worknets hinge between a specific *project* that applies the tracing of associations for a specific research source and a *pedagogy* or rationale guiding priorities for writing instruction that frames research as cognizance of and participation in networked activity systems.

Worknets respond directly to concerns raised in The Citation Project, an ongoing study of the ways college writers use sources, and echoed in Alison Head's study of student views of search processes. According to these studies, many students engage only shallowly with sources, and they also tend to be uncertain about techniques for gauging quality of sources and eventually retrieving full sources beyond second-hand references and abstracts more likely to be free-circulating online. Head's study of research writing practices by students in the humanities and social sciences, for instance, reports findings indicating much uncertainty related to search and retrieval (para. 18). She also notes that many students look to professors for guidance, which adds urgency to the matter of how to teach research well. If search, retrieval, and responsible use are not self-evident, they warrant explicit instruction. A similar charge of ownership of and responsibility for this pattern is reiterated at The Citation Project web site: "If instructors know how shallowly students are engaging with their research source—and that is what the Citation Project research reveals—then they know what responsible pedagogy needs to address" (para. 3). In addition to addressing the Citation Project's conclusions about shallow engagement with sources, a worknets-based approach also reinforces the interconnections among sources by making such connections explicit. Mapping connections is likely to influence the ways writers recognize themselves as entering into conversations that pre-exist them, and careful, slow work with sources prepares writers to decide more effectively about how to use sources later as support, whether by direct quotation, paraphrase, or summary. In light of the Citation Project's findings, instructors oftentimes know *what* "responsible pedagogy needs to address," indeed. A worknet pedagogy supplies a *how*.

Worknets as a "Constructive Phase" Pedagogy: Prepositioning and Wandering Resourcefulness

Cooper's ecological approach responded to timely debates in the 1980s about the most ethical frames through which to think about and teach writing. Her argument acknowledged tensions between her social view and its counterpart, which preferred to understand writers as solitary, as isolated. Instead of seeing particular moments in a writing process as *more* enmeshed ecologically than others, such as an emphasis on delivery or audience might privilege, Cooper suggested that "language and texts are not simply the means by which individuals discover and communicate information, but are essentially social activities, dependent on social structures and processes not only in their interpretive but *also in their constructive phases*" (my emphasis, 366). A worknets-based pedagogy regards Cooper's attention to constructive phases to be a critical distinction worth drawing upon. Accepting and acting upon source use as a constructive phase sees exploratory collection and annotation as vital from the earliest stages of inquiry and invention. Worknets, then, assume writers and sources ought to function as a symbiotic hybrid would, with each dependent upon and acting with the other all along. This adjustment, which finds its theoretical footing in Latour's consideration of hybrids in *We Have Never Been Modern*, calls on us to suspend the convenience of conceptual dichotomies (e.g., writer and source as discrete, separate actors) and to consider them instead as integral and mutually entangled (10). Search and retrieval of sources, therefore, are not only acts of composing but they also are *social* acts: acts that find writers and sources as associatively entangled and implicated in one another (i.e., "writer" is virtually the same as "writer with sources"; "sources" are virtually the same as "sources with writer"). The temporary fusion of identifications must not be mistaken for "social" in the commonplace sense of interpersonal engagement, affability, or conversational palling around. Rather, the idea of hybridity in this context, as a way to reconsider source-based writing as social, requires us to recognize as more thickly interconnected than we are accustomed to noticing a constellation of people, things, and forces of which the writer and source, through writing, are indelibly becoming a part. Immersing into this web, which is akin to noticing it and viewing it as a heuristic fund for invention during constructive phases, helps the writer compose inventively, if exploratorily, and in time to "connect with [whatever may surface as] the relevant idea system" (369).

To tease out this hybridity just a bit further, it will help to provide context related to commonplace prepositions for research-based academic writing and also to address more fully how an ecological conception of the "writer+sources" hybrid presents a social, resourceful alternative pedagogy for composition practitioners. The purposes in elaborating these principles are two-fold: 1) to suggest that commonplace prepositions for naming what students do with sources warrant mindful attention, and 2) to suggest how a worknet-based approach to teaching research writing foregrounds source use as a social, or ecology-building act. That is, writing with sources fashions a web of associations of which one's writing is inseparable as a continuation and an outgrowth.

Prepositioning

Richard Lanham's discussion of the generative oscillation between looking *at* and looking *through* interfaces, whether pages or lit screens or other presentational surfaces, is well-known among his many contributions to rhetorical education. Lanham theorizes this bi-stable condition in *The Electronic Word*, and the artifacts he analyzes in this case are hypertext and digital interfaces as well as our perspectival relationships to them. Lanham claims a value in differential orientations capable of shifting attention to "frontstage/backstage" in keeping with the logic indicated by each respective preposition in the tandem (72). As an update to Lanham's consideration of at/through and keeping with the context of interfaces, Collin Brooke recently factored in a third preposition, *from*, which adds a more explicit emphasis on networked participation and identification: "With interfaces, it is no longer sufficient to speak simply of an at/through distinction that leaves the position of the viewer, user, or reader unexamined. Just as we look *at* and *through* interfaces, we also look *from* a particular position, and that position is both macro- and microperceptual" (140). With Brooke's contribution, Lanham's bi-stability was revised, updated, and improved upon; in its place, a more network-based account of pluralized conceptions of our interactions as well as a sensible and well-theorized recognition of the ways prepositions produce easy-to-overlook frames for thinking and acting.

In Brooke's update to Lanham's at/through distinction and its more explicit emphasis on networks, I find the exigency for re-evaluating commonplace prepositions applied to source use. Consider the prepositions typically associated with source use and citation in researched academic prose. What are writers commonly urged to do with sources?[2] Which prepositions—think of them as *god prepositions*—have become so freely and frequently invoked in research writing instructional discourse as to appear ubiquitous and universal?

Take an example from Andrea Lunsford's *The Everyday Writer*: "Here are some general guidelines for integrating source materials *into* your writing" (emphasis added, 186). Later in the same section on "Research," under the subheading, "Integrating sources and avoiding plagiarism," Lunsford writes, "Carefully integrate quotations *into* your text so that they flow smoothly and clearly *into* the surrounding sentences" (emphasis added, 187). For the sake of comparison, David Blakesley and Jeffrey Hoogeveen's *The Brief Thomson Handbook* puts it this way: "Signal phrases...introduce and integrate source material *into* writing" (emphasis added, 164). I must be careful to acknowledge that my purpose here is only to provide a couple of illustrative examples by way of sampling, not to introduce a comprehensive study of contemporary handbooks in circulation. That the preposition *into* is easy to locate in a few of the handbooks I happened to have on my office shelf does corroborate a tacit sense many teachers of writing have, that "into" is frequently used to pre-position source materials relative to their landing place in the new document. In fact, when it comes to source use and the orienting terms for what we ask students to do with sources, *into* seems to be the commonest preposition.

Into is predisposed to a centripetal or in-bound pathway. The English language, however, lacks a preposition antithetical to this one; there is no *out-to*, only *from*. And we are all familiar with a framing discourse for research writing that talks about taking materials *from* sources and integrating materials *into* the new composition. Yet, much in the same way Brooke regarded Lanham's at/through pairing as inadequate for expressing the contingent agencies of "viewers, users, and readers" who encounter interfaces, I argue that the preponderance of *from* and *into* prepositions provide a linear but not yet network-based conceptual frame for source use, particularly when we seek to emphasize a source-using-writer hybrid acting throughout all phases, including a constructive phase. A worknets-based pedagogy deliberately complicates the *into-* ward gesture (suggested by this preposition) with an outward-venturing alternative: *along*.

In *Lines: A Brief History*, cultural anthropologist Tim Ingold draws a distinction between the logics of *along* and *across* as these prepositions relate to modes of travel. Although both prepositions (and the dispositions implied by each) convene outward-bound conceptions of movement, acts of traveling *across*, which Ingold equates with transport, imply an itinerate route, or, that is, a route whose ultimate destination is pre-determined: "[T]ransport is destination oriented. It is not so much a development along a way of life as a carrying across, from location to location, of people and goods in such a way as to leave their basic natures unaffected" (77). To provide a counterpoint, Ingold explains how particular cultures, such as the Inuit living in Arctic regions, are exemplars of an along-oriented mode of path-making, for "*as soon as a person moves he becomes a line*" (emphasis in original, 75). Relatedly, the writer+source hybrid becomes a mesh of lines, threaded along and building toward aggregate pathways or channels of inquiry. This is a slightly different way of thinking about source use than the from/into prepositions usually make available to writers, but the preference I've explained here for an along/across alternative does not need to eclipse more conventional approaches to source use. Rather, the prepositions along and across provide different ways to think about how writers can way-find with sources at all phases of composition, including the constructive phase.

Making Sources Resourceful, or Writing Along "Wiggly Paths"

Sources become more fully visible as ecologically enmeshed *resources* when we begin to think in terms of the prepositional alternatives sketched above. An *along* manner or attitude, drawing upon Ingold's study of lines, foregrounds the participatory sociability of source use—the webs writers actively build and ask readers to traverse with them—more than the from/into pairing does. From/into connotes slotting; along/across, on the other hand, suggest radial continuity, a kind of carrying-on. I want writers to realize how this along/across framework opens sources to rhetorical invention because it yields multiple possibilities for connection and exploration. The along/across spectrum offers centrifugal, or outward-moving, alternatives to its dead-endist, lift-and-load counterpart, from/into.

As such, the notion of resourcefulness—or using everything available, as much as possible—relates to I.A. Richards' discussion of the wandering resourcefulness of words in "Speculative Instruments." Countering structuralist reductions of the relation between words and meanings, Richards seeks a systematic approach to the problem of meaning that allows for shifting connotations:

> All these [central intellectual] words wander in many directions in this figurative space of meaning. But they wander systematically, as do other wanderers, the Planets. By fixing a limited number of positions, meanings, for them, we may help ourselves to plot their courses. But we should not persuade ourselves that they must be at one or other of these marked points. The laws of their motions are what we need to know: their dependence upon the positions of the other words that should be taken into account with them. (38)

The constellatory metaphor brings systematic wandering to bear on "what we need to know" about words when using them. For words and their multiple valences, Richards introduces a conceptual frame—the paths of planets—to explain shifting between fixed and emerging relations. Because sources depend upon small semantic networks,

Richards' distinction is useful for qualifying a definition for resourcefulness that locates it in this tension between anchor and drift. Analysis of a source must hold mutual regard for established contexts while also allowing for semiotic drift, or wandering, implicated with new and emerging contexts.

To explain what this means for source use, I am drawn to Richards's suggestion in the passage above that readers need to know "the laws of their motions." When using sources, writers are often concerned with strategically positioning summary, paraphrase, and direct quotation based on rhetorical and discursive considerations, some explicit and some tacit. The laws of motions for sources often fall inexactly between the constraints imposed by context and whatever gesture might extend from or altogether break with those constraints. Resourcefulness is in this case about finding potential and foraging for pathways similar to the prepositional adjustment that favors along/across as opposed to from/into. In fact, for source use, Richards' discussion of resourcefulness bears strong resemblance to the respective along/across frames introduced by Ingold, and both of these aspects are amplified in the visual representations of each worknet phase because the hub and spoke model represents the source at an up-close scale, as dwelling among these paths and as one small intersection in a much larger networked constellation. Source use settles into an orbit or loop that alternates between constraints and drift, or between itinerate and exploratory movements. For researching writers, neither purely itinerate nor purely exploratory manners of source use will suffice; writers skillful in source use must alternate between these movements because source-based writing requires frequent, decision-making oscillation between source and new text.

Mapping the resourcefulness of sources may proceed after adjusting the default prepositions associated with source use and while aspiring to maintain a balance between the itinerate (across) and exploratory (along). Because this second gesture—making sources resourceful—is closely related to method, perhaps one further illustration of the logic this worknets-based pedagogy builds upon will serve before turning to the project itself.

In his book, *Placeways*, Eugene Walter juxtaposes method and *tao* as two distinctive approaches to wayfaring:

> [T]he *tao* remains close to the contours of natural landscape and avoids rationalization, preferring wiggly paths or irregu-

lar courses of water. In contrast, the Greek sense of *hodos* or "route" expects rationalization. Our term, "method," which means a way of proceeding but implies rational conduct, comes from the Greek words *meta* plus *hodos*. (Walter 185)

Methodical approaches to source use can be helpful, but I find them especially promising when we foreground our thinking about *met-hod* in relation to the term's Greek ancillaries *meta-* (beyond) and *-hodos* (paths) (Walter 185). With this in mind, *method*ical approaches to source use are not so much lockstep processes of search, retrieval, selection, and integration, but rather as routes across and beyond particular problems. Simply, methodical approaches to source use can become restrictive too early in an inquiry process if we understand source consultation and use as following too narrow or monolithic a set of procedures. When approaches to research writing tolerate stagnant or unquestioning operations, source integration risks turning to unchecked ritual—a flat but requisite gesture involving finding and slotting excerpts. In general, this is what I wish to avoid in my teaching of research-based writing. My intention is neither to abandon methodical approaches to source use nor to put too deeply in doubt rationalist sensibilities about the functions of sources in researched writing. Rather, worknets as an alternative framework may provide a complementary approach that supports writing conceived and carried out along "wiggly paths or irregular courses." In relation to the distinction Walter draws between method and *tao*, a worknets- based pedagogy makes the most of the resourcefulness of sources. Furthermore, it does so with mutual regard for the value in rationalist aims and purposeful source use, on the one hand, and exploration along "wiggly paths," or a *tao* sensibility, on the other.

What, then, is available for us *to do* with sources that is at once in service of these traditional goals and yet simultaneously encouraging writers to move above and beyond typical pathways of retrieval, reading, and citation? The following section showcases the worknets project that, extending from the pedagogical framework I have elaborated up to this point, provides an alternative to conventional and methodical approaches to source use—that is, it formulates a response to the *What else can we do?* question—a response as concerned as The Citation Project is with "what students are actually doing with their sources" (para. 1) as with what else they could be doing to develop facility with textual research.

Worknets: Course Context

I first developed this project for a section of WRTG326: Research Writing I taught at Eastern Michigan University in the Fall 2010 semester. The course typically enrolls second-, third-, and fourth-year students from a wide variety of majors, a slight majority of whom identify with programs in English Studies, such as Written Communication, English Education, and Journalism. The course promises "to explore the strategies, format and styles of writing appropriate for academic research with emphasis on the student's own field of study" (Eastern Michigan University Academics n. pag.).

Due to the many fields of study represented in the course, I sought to create a project flexible enough that students in different fields would gain similar insights into the resourcefulness of sources in spite of distinctive disciplinary frames from which they researched. A second priority was to dwell at length on a specific source and to be diligent about surfacing many different aspects of its entanglements, which I suspected was atypical compared with other approaches to source use students were already experienced with. Finally, I wanted to craft the project so it would build through intervals—small pieces students could share with each other and with me. Furthermore, working in intervals means each worknet phase could be temporarily held apart from the others, but the series of phases would build in succession toward a more thickly enmeshed representation of traceable associations woven, branching, and threaded across one another. At each interval, students wrote an account of the specific worknet phase surfaced through each of four approaches: *semantic, bibliographic, affinity-based,* and *choric.* Each phase also included an illustration—a simple diagram consisting of links and nodes—produced using Google Drive Drawing.[3]

The worknets project demonstrated in the next section took shape over six weeks, running from Week Four through Week Ten in a fifteen-week semester. Students developed it while attending to other course readings and an array of research-based activities—an inquiry memo, ongoing course readings, self-selected readings with annotations, and a semester-long inquiry-based research project informed by *The Craft of Research* by Joseph Williams, Wayne Booth, and Gregory Colomb. Together, the four phases constituted 20% of the overall grade for the course.

Four Worknets Phases

To begin, each student selected a germinal article published since 1980. I emphasized that the article choice must be made with care because we would be making multiple passes along the source to illustrate the four respective worknet phases. Choosing sources also involved reading the full text of the article, of course; however, I did not want to place too much value on perfect alignments between the article and the emerging focus of their sustained research projects because I was seeking to sponsor a more exploratory relationship to research-based inquiry, even as students began with provisional areas of inquiry, or topics, related to their fields of study. That is, at the same time students were searching for and selecting an article appropriate for their four worknet phases, they were also drafting inquiry memos that articulated *possible* researchable questions related to their majors. For some, the two were tightly integrated, but for others, they bore a looser correspondence. Articles with at least a handful of citations were better, for the purposes of the worknets, than articles that cited three or fewer outside sources. Once everyone selected a source to map according to its networked associations, the project called for creating the first of four phases.

Semantic

The semantic phase concerns *vocabulary*—words and phrases that appear in the article itself and whose in-context reference and meaning can be more deeply examined as well as traced to peripheral ideas suited to further exploration. In a manner similar to what Richards calls for, honing in on specific references recognizes the function of words and phrases as speculative instruments that can augment inquiry, refine research questions, and bolster related search processes. In practical terms, taking the words and phrases themselves as resources, the writer could use these terms to query various search engines, to set up a Google Search Alert,[4] or to consult the *Oxford English Dictionary* attentive to the each word's root elements and etymology.

Techniques for surfacing a semantic worknet in an article include reading and annotating with attention to high-occurring words and phrases, reading and annotating for unusual turns of phrase or highly specialized language, or using freely available, web-based platforms to identify frequently appearing terms, such as Tagcrowd.com or Wordle.

net. The first two approaches privilege close work with the source *while* reading it; thus, these may complement conversations we want to have with students about note-taking and indexing sources for a specific project. The web-based approach, on the other hand, operates by a different logic that finds a value in getting some distance on the original source. Tagcrowd.com and Wordle.net will translate the full text version of the source, provided it is a digital version whose text can be copied and pasted, into a weighted list.

With a selection of words and phrases identified, the writer may revisit the locations on the page to look for variations in usage. To return again to Marilyn Cooper's "The Ecology of Writing," for example, the development of a semantic worknet phase indicated the following two-word phrases, or bi-grams, in the article (with number of occurrences in parentheses): cognitive process (13), ecological model (8), textual forms (8), process model (8), and solitary author (7) (See Figure 1.) The written account based on this semantic worknet might dig more deeply into "process model." What exactly is a "process model" in the context of the article? In what other ways has "process model" figured into scholarship about writing contemporaneous to Cooper's article or in the nearly three decades since?

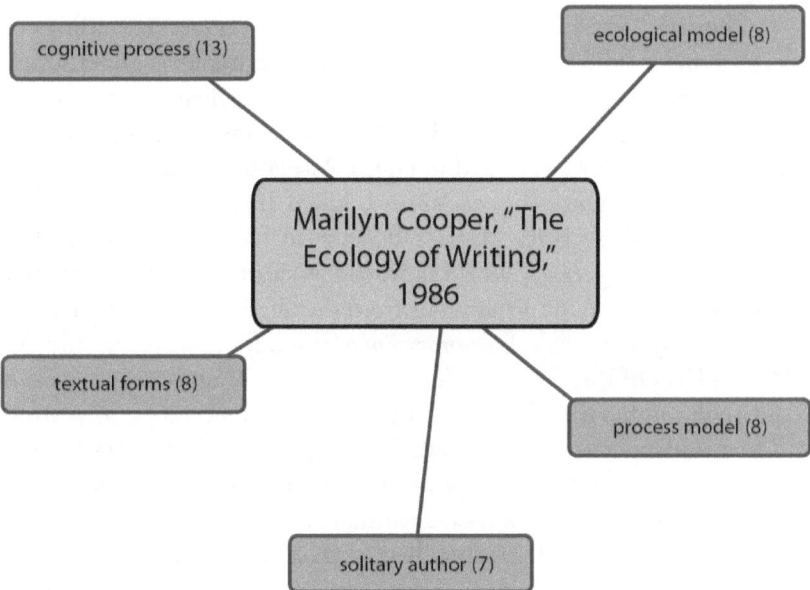

Figure 1: Semantic worknet phase.

Bibliographic

Whereas the semantic worknet phase is concerned principally with the text of the source and the recurrent words and phrases therein, the bibliographic phase accounts for the sources it cites. This turn to references perhaps passes without much critical consideration among those with experience in research writing. This is because references lists or works cited supply researching writers with a ready list of sources in the neighborhood of the initial source. The bibliographic worknet only asks that we notice references more deeply, that we read them on the lookout for citations likely to prove somehow useful to the project.

Techniques for establishing a bibliographic worknet amount to noticing sources and selecting a few of them to retrieve and read from those listed. The motives for selection need not be too narrowly defined, although they could be based on different ways of identifying source types (e.g., scholarly sources; chapters, articles, and monographs; primary, secondary, and tertiary sources) or dates (e.g., divide all references into three equally divided units based on the overall period covered, then choose one from each timeframe). The bibliographic phase can also challenge students to trace the selected references back into the article itself to look at how they are set up, framed, and how frequently they are mentioned.

Cooper's "The Ecology of Writing" cites 32 sources. Certainly collecting and reading all of them would be a formidable undertaking, but settling on three to five of them would nevertheless prove worthwhile to enlarge the scope of the inquiry drawing on Cooper's work. The worknet phase illustrated in Figure 2 isolates four references: Kenneth Burke's *A Grammar of Motives*, Lloyd Bitzer's "The Rhetorical Situation," Shirley Brice Heath's *Ways With Words*, and George Dillon's *Constructing Texts*. Working from this short list, the writer would attempt to retrieve these materials from the library, and having tracked down a copy of Burke's *A Grammar of Motives*, for example, would ask, What pieces of Burke's work does Cooper use? What other sections of the book might, at a glance, extend the idea of an ecology of writing? When students select and retrieve full monographs, I don't ask them to read the entire book but rather recommend they look selectively into a chapter or section used in their germinal article. Chapters and articles, however, warrant a full reading. Again, the key to a bibliographic worknet is that it turns to references as a method for enriching inquiry.

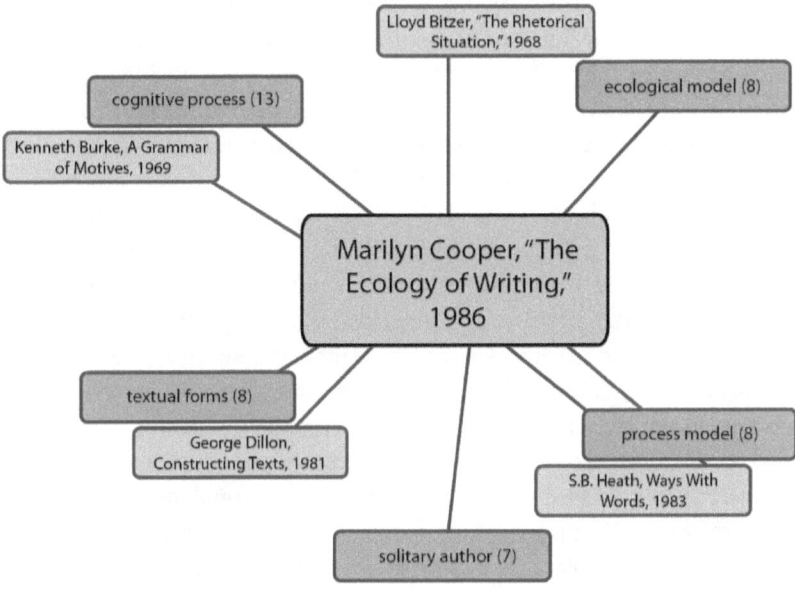

Figure 2: Bibliographic worknet phase.

Affinitybased

The affinity phase (See Figure 3.) focuses on an author's working relationships: collaborations, professional appointments and associations, graduate program of study, and identifiable intellectual influences. Whereas the semantic and bibliographic worknets take root in the text itself, affinity worknets turn to questions of authorship. Affinities may be loose or strong, short-lived or enduring, professional or personal, but whatever constitutes them, taking stock of them, which is to say rigorously noticing them, may prove a resource that can substantially shape a particular line of inquiry related to the focal source. Affinity-based worknets pursue as traceable associations those aspects of sociability and worldview that may be more difficult to identify in any one article.

Affinity-based worknets and the forms of evidence they are built upon are not as obvious. To begin surfacing an affinity-based worknet, a researching writer might search for other work by the primary author of the source. Are there co-authors listed? A second technique for monographs would be to look at the acknowledgements section or the dedication. Affinity-based worknets also consider the programs in which someone has studied, the faculty they worked with there, and the cohort they belonged to. Are there any patterns identifiable in other work done by these scholars and teachers? Relatedly, what was the focus of the author's dissertation or thesis research? Who was on the author's dissertation committee? What areas of focus are evident in their work? The tracing of affinities works with gradually larger spheres to consider a broader variety of forces likely to have influenced the author. This is time-consuming work, and it yields irregular, often unverifiable results. Nevertheless, the deliberate consideration of influences and affinities may be germane to an emerging research question for a writer who has identified the source as foundational. For example, noticing collaborations expands a genealogy of people and ideas. Consider a source on multimodal composition. Affinities in other work related to design and computational methods would suggest those as opportunities for further exploration; alternatively, affinities with scholars in composition theory and assessment would suggest slightly different connections. Mapping these affinities proves conductive insofar as it illuminates relationships that, because they span people and ideas, suggest interdisciplinary pathways for further exploration and examination.

Again, setting out from Cooper's 1986 essay, one would ask, what affinities can I find? Remember that the worknet does not need to exhaust all possibilities but rather only locate, select, and include a few choice affinities related to Cooper's career. For example, Cooper collaborated with Cynthia Selfe on an article in 1990. In 1980, Cooper's dissertation research at the University of Minnesota, *Implicatures in Dramatic Conversation*, focused on H. Paul Grice. She worked with Dennis Lynch and Diana George on an award-winning article in 1997. Without delving too far into Cooper's biography, we have picked up a couple of points that may prove fortuitous. Because the worknets initiate this tracing as invention, the process does not lend itself to determining preemptively the utility of any lead. Instead, the point is to generate a confluence of associations that fan out from the source and that, by tracing these associations, writers begin to realize as available a greater range of possibilities for connecting Cooper's work to their emerging research interests.

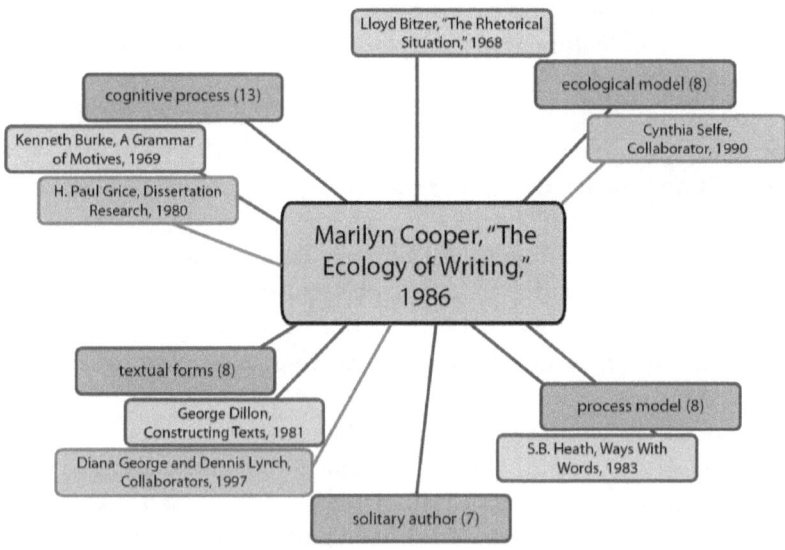

Figure 3: Affinity-based worknet phase.

Choric

Choric worknets draw on the idea of *chora*, an alternative to topical or *topoi*-based invention. Thomas Rickert elaborates on the concept and examines its theoretical genealogy in "Toward the Chora":

> [Jacques] Derrida and [Gregory] Ulmer in particular utilize inventional methods that could be called choric, as opposed, for instance, to topic invention, because of the way they attribute inventional agency to non-human actors such as language, networks, environments, and databases. They demonstrate that the *chora* is of rhetorical interest because it transforms our sense of what is available as means for persuasion, or, more precisely, of what is available as means for r hetorical generation, in line with an expanded notion of spatiality that complexifies traditional divisions among discourses, minds, bodies, and circumambient environs. (253)

The pedagogy and project I am introducing could be broadly described as choric, but earlier phases of it, such as the semantic phase, could be more conventionally understood as topical relative to the way Rickert describes choric invention. Thus, although the other worknets could be considered choric, this phase of the project is more playfully far-afield in its willingness to explore time-place coincidences—the ambient surrounds—for rhetorical generation, or invention.

Like the affinity worknet phase (Figure 3) a choric phase is not concretely grounded in the text of the article. Rather than attend to scholarly and intellectual ties as the affinity worknet does, it explores coincident objects and events from popular culture in the interest of enlarging context—something like what Rickert calls "circumambient environs." Establishing a choric phase involves exploring the time and place the article was occasioned from and listing corresponding moments, even though they may at first seem an odd assortment (See Figure 4.)

Cooper's article was published in 1986, the same year *Ferris Bueller's Day Off* played in theaters, Chinese economist Deng Xiaoping was celebrated as *Time*'s Man of the Year, Al Capone's vault was opened, Bill Buckner missed the ground ball, and Da Yoopers released their first album, "Yoopanese." The choric worknet instigates surprising, uncanny insights through juxtaposition. These disparate elements may or may not turn out, ultimately, to be inspiring or influential. They come with no guarantees. Identifying this particular phase (3-5 pop cultural coincidences), however, *can* stir new researchable questions, as follows: How do ideas of process and ecology generalize to the economic theories embraced by Deng Xiapong? Or how does an ecological approach to writing change the ways we might think about school movies from 1986, such as *Ferris Bueller's Day Off* or *Back to School*? Even further, at yet another degree removed, how do ecological models underscore or shed light on developments in the middle of Ronald Reagan's presidency, relating to the war in Nicaragua, the environmental movement in the mid-1980s, or the Iran-Contra affair?

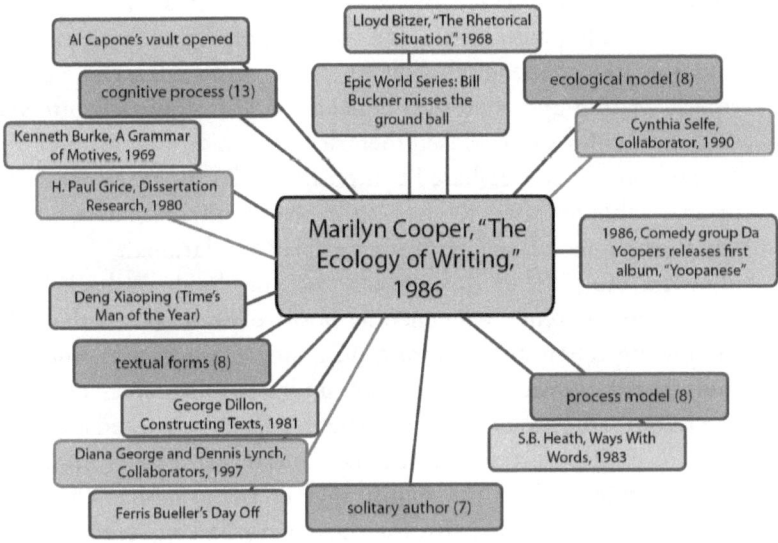

Figure 4: Choric worknet phase.

To Conclude, Further Enmeshed

Depending on previous experiences with textual research, commonplace thinking about source use may change sharply as a consequence of the worknets-based pedagogy and project introduced in this paper. The pedagogy requires a deliberate, mindful adjustment in pre-positions typically associated with source use, as well as slow and patient movements concerned with the coinciding spheres the germinal article could be said to be enmeshed within: semantic, bibliographic, affinity-based, and choric.

The four phases produces a constellated abundance—copious options, among which writers can pick and choose. For instance, the project involving an ecological model, comedic movies about schooling, and Cooper, Lynch, and George's "Moments of Argument" article, would by this method yield a promising research focus—on agonism in contemporary rhetorical education, perhaps—that became available only through the mapping of associations premised on a balance between itinerate (across) and exploratory (along) processes. Tracing each worknet phase, drawing it, and writing an account that explains the ties that have materialized and how those ties are generative for an emerging research project—these practices encourage researching writers to pause, dwell, and reflect upon sources and in such a manner that can challenge shallow reference while still serving goals of research writing and rhetorical education. This approach offers a flexible structure for source-based rhetorical invention that generalizes to most attempts at source-based composition; that is, its method offers a transferable heuristic for writing in many other situations, particularly those in which academic sources are foundational.

Following the pilot of this project, the anecdotal feedback I received was and has remained generally positive. Some noted that the idea of slowing down and hovering on a single source was uncommon but that it proved invaluable for understanding and engaging with the resourcefulness of sources. Other feedback suggested creating worknets for multiple articles during the semester. Still other informal comments inquired about the significance of the graphical element, which was more labor intensive for those who had no previous experience using concept mapping or drawing applications. From very early on in the development of this project, I considered the visual representation to be important as a way to map into a simplified, two-dimensional frame the spatio-conceptual relations emanating through the germinal source. I continue to find a value in this aspect of the worknets, but I also acknowledge that the worknets project could be successful using other approaches, such as hand-illustrated sketches or written accounts only.

There remain many possibilities for worknets-based projects, including applying it to several articles, as I have already mentioned. By sharing in-progress documents across groups or an entire class, students could also develop worknets collaboratively and later consult them as an inventional commons. This would work well in a research-based writing class using a common domain of inquiry. The worknets project also scales vertically and horizontally, reaching deep into the university curriculum: it could be taken up in a first-year writing course, an upper-division writing intensive course in a variety of disciplines, and in a graduate seminar. Yet another possibility would be to explore other aspects of the germinal article, such as the ages of the sources it draws upon, or the density of the sources in-context (i.e., noticing when sources are involved thickly or thinly). Each of these speculative openings maintains an interest that persists throughout this paper—an interest in enriching and prolonging encounters with sources.

Acknowledgments

Several generous, incisive colleagues influenced the shape of this article through conversation and responses to drafts, including Jen Clary-Lemon, Kate Pantelides, Rebecca Moore Howard, and participants in the Eastern Michigan University Advanced WAC Institutes over the last two years.

Notes

1. Early turns to ecologies to theorize or understand composition can be found in Richard Coe's 1975 *CCC* article, "Eco-logic for the Composition Classroom," as well as in Louise Wetherbee Phelps's *Composition as a Human Science* (1988), which has as its first section, "Constructing an Ecology of Composition." Contemporary examples of ecological thinking about writing are in ever-growing supply, available in *Ecology, Writing Theory, and New Media* (2011), edited by Sidney Dobrin, as well as in Nathaniel Rivers and Ryan Weber's 2011 *CCC* article, "Ecological, Pedagogical, Public Rhetoric."

2. This question could also evaluate the verbs commonly used in contexts urging students to write with sources.

3. The visual representations of worknets displayed in the article were created in Google Drive Drawing, a free-to-use online application suited to creating labeled elements, drawing lines among them, and storing the in-progress illustration for future additions. One-color off-prints of these sketches may not reflect that each worknet is differently color-coded. Google Drive Drawing makes the project of colors, spacing among nodes, and typeface changes relatively intuitive to apply, though proficiency with these settings will likely require practice and explicit instruction. Google Drive Drawing also provides an export command that allows writers to save the image as a .jpg file, which can then be inserted into a document.

> Use of Google's free online platforms for creating drawings or word-processed documents must acknowledge two important points. First, teaching with these platforms is rather like standing on shifting sands because they may change at any time, including while you are in the midst of a project or project making use of them. Second, using Google Docs or any other Google service requiring a user account will necessitate signing up, and while this is a relatively innocuous-seeming step, it includes accepting Google's Terms of Service. I recommend faculty who ask students to use Google platforms for required coursework explicitly acknowledge the Terms of Service and reserve time for anyone with reservations to discuss the alternatives available.

4. Google Search Alerts are standing searches configured to send email or RSS notifications each time Google encounters a new occurrence of the term. In effect, it establishes an algorithm suited to searching the freshest of what's available--relative to a particular query--on the web. For more, visit http://www.google.com/alerts

Works Cited

Brent, Douglas. "The Research Paper and Why We Should Still Care." *WPA* 37.1 (Fall 2013): 33-53. Print. Brooke, Collin Gifford. *Lingua Fracta: Toward a Rhetoric of New Media*. New York: Hampton, 2009. Print. Citation Project. "What is the Citation Project?" Web. February 8, 2012.

Coe, Richard M. "Eco-Logic for the Composition Classroom." *College Composition and Communication* 26.3 (Oct. 1975): 232-237. Print. Cooper, Marilyn. "The Ecology of Writing." *College English* 48.4 (1986): 364-375. Print.

Dobrin, Sidney, ed. *Ecology, Writing Theory, and New Media: Writing Ecology*. Routledge Studies in Rhetoric and Communication Ser. New York: Routledge, 2011. Print. Eastern Michigan University Academics. "2011-2012 Undergraduate Catalog." Web. January 22, 2012.

Head, Alison J. "Beyond Google: How Do Students Conduct Academic Research?" *First Monday* 12.8 (2007): n. pag. Web. February 8, 2012.

Howard, Rebecca Moore, Tricia Serviss, and Tanya Rodrigue. "Writing from Sources, Writing from Sentences." *Writing & Pedagogy* 2.2 (2010): 177-192. Print. Ingold, Tim. *Lines: A Brief History*. New York: Routledge, 2007. Print.

Lanham, Richard. *The Electronic Word*. Chicago: U Chicago P, 1993. Print.

Latour, Bruno. *Reassembling the Social*. Clarendon Lectures in Management Studies Ser. New York: Oxford UP, 2005. Print.

---. *We Have Never Been Modern*. Trans. Catherine Porter. Cambridge, Mass.: Harvard UP, 1993. Print. Phelps, Louise Wetherbee. *Composition as a Human Science*. New York: Oxford UP, 1991. Print.

Richards, I.A. "Speculative Instruments." *Professing the New Rhetorics: A Sourcebook*. Theresa Enos and Stuart Brown, eds. Prentice Hall: Englewood Cliffs, NJ. 8-39. Print.

Rice, Jeff. "The 1963 Hip-Hop Machine: Hip-Hop Pedagogy As Composition." *College Composition and Communication* 54.3 (2003): 453-471. Print. Rickert, Thomas. "Toward the *Chora*: Kristeva, Derrida, and Ulmer on Emplaced Invention." *Philosophy and Rhetoric* 40.3 (2007): 251-273. Print.

Rivers, Nathaniel, and Ryan Weber. "Ecological, Pedagogical, Public Rhetoric." *College Composition and Communication* 63.2 (Dec. 2011): 187-218. Print.

Sirc, Geoffrey. "box-logic." *Writing New Media: Theory and Applications for Expanding the Teaching of Composition*. Ed. Anne F. Wysocki, et al. Logan: Utah State UP, 2004. 113-148. Print.

Spinnuzi, Clay. *Network: Theorizing Knowledge Work in Telecommunications*. New York: Cambridge UP, 2008. Print. Walter, Eugene V. *Placeways: A Theory of the Human Environment*. Chapel Hill: U North Carolina P, 1988. Print.

© Copyright 2015 Derek Mueller.

Licensed under a Creative Commons Attribution-Share Alike License.

COMPOSITION STUDIES

Composition Studies is on the Web at http://www.uc.edu/journals/composition-studies.html

The oldest independent periodical in the field, *Composition Studies* is an academic journal dedicated to the range of professional practices associated with rhetoric and composition: teaching college writing; theorizing rhetoric and composing; administering writing related programs; preparing the field's future teacher-scholars. We welcome work that doesn't fit neatly elsewhere.

Teaching for Agency: From Appreciating Linguistic Diversity to Empowering Student Writers

Martinez's article models and argues for the value of employing counterstory as a powerful method for representing marginalized peoples' experiences and perspectives in rhetoric and composition. Counterstory, as Martinez eloquently and persuasively describes, lays bare the workings of racism on people's lives and thus offers a framework for validating researchers' embodied experiences. This method also prioritizes narrative as an effective means by which to foreground racism and its effects on people of color. This article was selected because the author represents voices and experiences that continue to figure too minimally in composition journals.

Teaching for Agency: From Appreciating Linguistic Diversity to Empowering Student Writers

Shawna Shapiro, Michelle Cox, Gail Shuck, and Emily Simnitt

In this article, we build on conversations about linguistic diversity in writing studies, proposing a framework by which instructors and administrators can promote the empowerment of multilingual writers. Our framework, which we call "teaching for agency," recognizes the resources that linguistically diverse students bring to our writing classrooms, but also takes into account these students' needs and goals regarding English language development. We articulate a process in which students gain greater awareness and control of the opportunities for action available to them, and learn to evaluate the effects of their decisions as writers and scholars. Practitioners can help to facilitate this process, we argue, by creating optimal conditions within which students can make informed decisions. After presenting the teaching for agency framework, we describe how we have employed it at our own institutions, through assignments that provide an authentic and relevant rhetorical context for student writing, as well as programmatic policies that offer multiple pathways for student success. By foregrounding agency as a central construct in the teaching of writing, we hope to demonstrate our respect for what students already know and can do with language, and our commitment to expanding every student's linguistic and rhetorical repertoire.

In recent years, discussions within writing studies about language difference have burgeoned. As Paul Kei Matsuda argues, this growth is due partly to the recent attention given to translingualism as an approach to linguistic diversity and partly to the increase of multilingual writers at many institutions of higher education. Many of these conversations have focused on the importance of promoting a positive, inclusive view of language—a stance we also endorse. There is widespread agreement that multilingualism[1] should be seen as an asset or resource, rather than a deficit or obstacle, and that our classroom instruction should reflect the valuing of multiple linguistic codes.

Linguistic diversity is a useful place to begin conversations about multilingual writers, as it may compel instructors and administrators to enact more equitable classroom practices and institutional policies. But often overlooked in these discussions is multilingual students' own goal to continue developing as English language users. In other words, a focus on appreciation alone may leave behind classroom practices that are explicitly aimed at promoting English language development. And yet pedagogies focused primarily on language development run the risk of perpetuating a deficit orientation toward multilingual writers, causing those students to be seen only in terms of the gaps in their English knowledge. The questions that we continue to wrestle with, then, are as follows: How can we treat students as developing writers/language users without promoting a deficit view of second language (L2) writers and writing, and without reproducing stigmatizing pedagogies and policies? How do we honor the knowledge and linguistic resources all students bring to our courses and programs, while also promoting their growth as writers and language users?

We suggest that foregrounding the concept of student agency can enhance conversations about language difference, recognizing the resources multilingual students bring to writing, while also promoting linguistic growth. While the term "agency" has been employed within writing studies and other disciplines in various ways (see Canagarajah, "Agency"; Duranti; Lu and Horner; Miller), it has not been widely used within composition to inform how we address multilingual writers across a full spectrum of language backgrounds. Our aim in this article is to flesh out what we mean by agency, including the conditions, pedagogies, and institutional practices that make agency possible for multilingual writers.

In the remainder of our article, we articulate the central elements of teaching for agency and describe how we each have enacted this approach in our own writing pedagogies and programs. We conclude by discussing how this theoretical framework may be applied in other contexts in which multilingual students write. Our aim is to complement the recent—and welcome—moves in writing studies toward adopting linguistically inclusive practices, by presenting a pedagogical framework that is informed not only by an appreciation for linguistic diversity, but also by a commitment to empowering multilingual writers.

Understanding Agency

The practices we propose here are rooted in the idea that each linguistic, rhetorical, political, and institutional act is a choice that in turn shapes the language, writing, thoughts, beliefs, and actions of other people. Within a broad understanding of social action, its impacts, and the available choices human actors have, we will discuss the relationship of agency to writing pedagogy and institutional practice, particularly in relation to undergraduate multilingual writers in U.S. institutions of higher education.

The framework we develop here articulates relationships between action, awareness, and optimal conditions—critical components of agency—as they apply to the work of writers, writing instructors, and writing programs:

1. Students as agents have a degree of control over their own acts related to writing and writing development.
2. In order to have greater control over these acts, students need to notice that an action needs to be taken, understand the range of possible actions, be aware of the context of the action, and be able to evaluate the possible effects of a given action.
3. In order to help student writers develop greater awareness, writing instructors and program administrators need to create optimal conditions—from classroom activities and assignments that help students to notice and utilize particular rhetorical and linguistic practices, to program structures that help writers make informed choices about their academic lives.

We will take each component of agency in turn. At the core of our conceptualization of agency is action. Agency has been defined broadly to include all actions, intentional and not, and encompasses the idea that all actions have impacts on others (Cooper; Duranti). As teachers and program administrators, we are interested in raising writers' awareness of those impacts and increasing students' sense of control over their acts as writers. Acts can be as specific as choosing a particular word or as broad as choosing a particular writing course. In order for an act to be agentive, from our perspective, there must be options for action. Those options are opened and constrained by particular micro- or macro-contextual factors. Multilingual writers have access to multiple linguistic codes, language and literacy practices, and rhetorics, thereby acting as linguistically agile agents of their own communicative messages (Cook; Jordan). However, students still developing their knowledge of the dominant language or language variety may experience constraints because they have fewer linguistic resources to choose from in that language. These students also face the same constraints experienced by all students, such as an instructor's evaluation criteria, the bounds of an assignment, their own educational histories, or time pressures.

Central to the ability to take action is the idea of "noticing" that an action needs to be taken and awareness of the available actions one might take. Indeed, as explained by psychologist John Godolphin Bennett, "Unless we notice, we cannot be in a position to choose or act for ourselves" (i). Linguists have taken up this concept of "noticing" to explain how language development occurs, including students' development as writers (Schmidt; Swain). Noticing includes identifying problems in a text which might compel a writer to revise their work, or rejecting certain rhetorical conventions (Qi and Lapkin; Swain). Here, we broaden noticing to encompass any moment when a student feels called upon to take action as a writer, including selecting a particular path through a writing program.

Once a writer is aware that action needs to be taken, she then must be aware of the range of available actions and the existing constraints on those actions. She must also have the necessary knowledge for informed decision-making. Key areas of knowledge for multilingual writers include linguistic, generic, rhetorical, and cultural knowledge, as well as an understanding of U.S. educational culture. Awareness not only guides writing acts, such as specific linguistic choices while drafting and revising, but also aids writers in evaluating their own writing. Greater awareness of the effects of actions includes a better understanding of how readers might perceive their writing (including recognizing what would be "marked" for a native English speaker), a sense of the perspectives the writer has to offer on a topic, and information about the possible consequences of a course placement decision. As illustrated in fig. 1, greater awareness leads to greater control. Thus, the framework for writer agency may be summarized as such (see fig. 1).

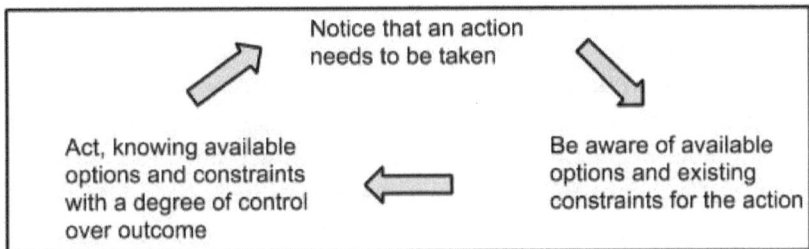

Fig. 1. Writer Agency.

To facilitate this awareness, writing instructors and program administrators need to create opportunities for students to exercise agency. Tanita Saenkhum, in her study of multilingual writing placement, lists as acts of agency "negotiating, choosing to accept or deny [their placements], self-assessing, planning, questioning, and making decisions" (126) and argues that "these acts of agency will be possible when conditions for agency are optimal" (126). Our goal as instructors and administrators, then, is to create optimal conditions for success, no matter a student's English proficiency level on being admitted. Instructors and administrators must recognize the constraints that students must inevitably work under, while also expanding opportunities for students to shape the contexts in which they write and act. Teaching for agency, then, might look like this:

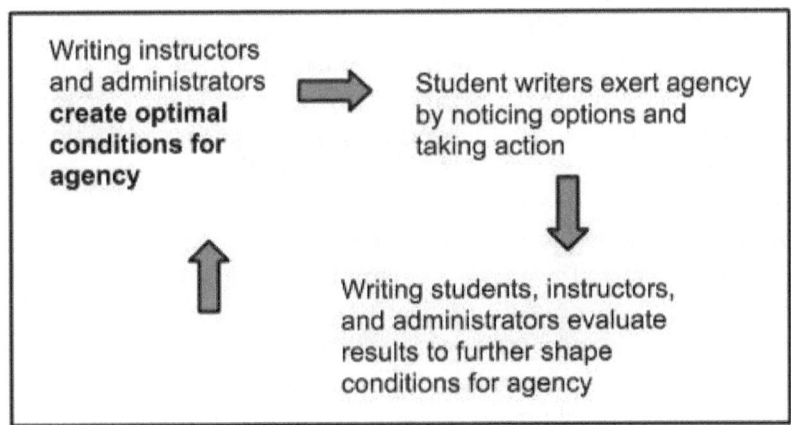

Fig. 2. Creating Optimal Conditions for Agency.

In the remainder of this article, we introduce assignments, pedagogical strategies, and curricular options that we have developed at our respective institutions. We also explore the necessary conditions for students to become aware of the choices available to them and the possibilities for negotiation, so they can not only act, but also understand how those actions affect their own and others' lives.

Pedagogical and Programmatic Practices for Agency

Writing Beyond the Classroom (Shawna Shapiro)

This assignment is part of a writing course entitled "The English Language in a Global Context," which students select through guided self-placement at Middlebury College, a small liberal arts college in Vermont. The course supplements the instruction students receive in writing-intensive seminars taught by faculty across the curriculum. I designed this course in response to a request from colleagues for an offering that would appeal to both L1 and L2 writers with a range of abilities and would provide language support in a non-remedial environment. "Writing beyond the Classroom" is the final course assignment and requires that students write about a lingering issue from the course for an outside audience.

Students exercise agency at various points throughout this project. They first write a proposal, articulating an audience and purpose for their work. After receiving feedback, they revise the proposal and develop an annotated bibliography of sources that have informed their thinking on the topic. As they develop their projects, students are asked to pay close attention to genre and register—to "break out" from the academic norms that shaped their other papers. To heighten students' rhetorical awareness, we examine sample texts, noting choices the writers made to fit audience expectations. When submitting the final draft, students submit a Writer's Memo, reflecting on their rhetorical choices. I have received a wide range of projects, including persuasive letters, editorials, narrative essays, informational brochures, and a variety of creative works (see "snapshots" below). In my feedback and evaluation, I focus on rhetorical awareness, informed decision-making, and self-evaluation, guided by the following questions:

1. Is the project relevant to the course? Does it reflect the learning and thinking we have done throughout the semester?
2. Is the writer able to articulate linguistic and/or rhetorical choices they made, and to explain the rationale behind those choices? Are they aware of how their work meets and/or diverges from genre conventions?
3. Can the student explain how this project reflects their growth as a writer?

To illustrate the range of student work, as well as the negotiation and reflection that occurs throughout the writing process, I offer brief snapshots of three students' projects.

Fernando, an international student from Mexico, wrote a letter addressed to our college's Center for Social Entrepreneurship—an entity with which he had become heavily involved. Fernando had noticed that the center had very few resources on social entrepreneurship in non-English languages. He found this problematic, as many of the initiatives undertaken by the center were in countries where English is not a dominant language. His letter opens as follows:

> Dear everyone at CSE,
>
> In our meeting last Friday I told you that you would help me with one of my final assignments. . . . I was fortunate enough to have the freedom to create my own final project for my [writing] class, and . . . I chose to write a letter—to you. In it I will tell you the story of the journey that led me to Social Entrepreneurship, and I will also talk about a problem that hinders its reach and development.

Fernando goes on to argue for shared "transcreation" of materials, which he says involves making key concepts relevant to "the context of [readers'] own culture and daily experience." Fernando wanted his letter to have a confident, professional tone while also referencing his personal experiences. Reflecting on his final draft, he said,

> The tone is right for the intended audience—it is personal to keep the connection I have with them . . . but it is also slightly academic to convey the importance that the issue has for me. I am very satisfied with the way I connected my own story with

the issue that I present, and I believe this makes the writing stronger.

In a personal email to me near the end of the semester, Fernando wrote, "[W]hat a great feeling it is when one can integrate classes and what one loves most."

Emily, a second generation Chinese American, wrote an essay for other Middlebury students, entitled "Loss of a Mother Tongue." In her Writer's Memo, Emily said, "My goal for this project is to capture that feeling of uncertainty, of not knowing where one stands in the scheme of things, of feeling alone and angry at being different, yet feeling proud to be so." In the first half of the essay, Emily shares stories from her childhood that highlight the complexity of her linguistic and cultural identity. Later, these stories culminate in a social critique: "In the eyes of the American education system, language is the least important of standards. . . . But not if it's English. . . . Any other language, and the educations system force it out of children."

Emily's tone in the essay was fairly colloquial—an intentional choice she justified as follows: "I wanted this piece . . . to capture the feeling of in-betweenness, and above all [to be] relatable." To help illustrate her "in-betweenness," Emily recounted typical conversations she had with older relatives, which included dialogue in Cantonese. To make these conversations more accessible, she represented the Cantonese in Pinyin, which uses the Roman alphabet, rather than in Chinese characters. Emily also used her narration to convey the gist of the conversation, rather than offering a direct translation:

> My mother . . . asked me: "Nei num-ji nei hai zhong-goc yen ah-hai mei-goc yen?" Are you Chinese or American? There was no preface to this question. It came out of nowhere—that's the thing with my mother, she just comes out and hits you with things like that.

Emily exercised agency as well when presenting her work to the class, by performing her reading dramatically, using a variety of voices and gestures. She received a warm round of applause from her classmates afterward.

Eirene, an international student from Malaysia, wrote an editorial article, "The Non-National National Language," which targeted a Malaysian audience. Eirene's goal was to highlight and challenge negative attitudes toward "Manglish"—a colloquial mix of Malay and Malaysian English. Keeping her audience in mind, Eirene made frequent references to cultural and political dynamics in Malaysia. She also employed frequent code-switching among English, Malay, and Manglish, which she felt was an important way to underscore her claim that Manglish should be a source of pride, rather than embarrassment. When reading Eirene's early drafts, I realized I lacked the cultural and linguistic knowledge to grasp the nuances in her argument. To make the writing more accessible, Eirene chose to include footnotes explaining cultural or historical references and translating the sections written in Manglish and Malay. One example of this is in this passage: "But in all honesty, though I grew up learning the language, I feel no affinity to *Bahasa Melayu* (BM) as my national language. I say *Bahasa Melayu* and not, *Bahasa Malaysia* because well . . . who am I kidding?" In a footnote here, Eirene explained that "Bahasa Melayu" meant "Malay Language," while "Bahasa Malaysia" meant "Malaysian Language." She continued, "The government changed the name of the language from the Malay language to the Malaysian language in order to reinforce the idea that this was our national language and not an ethniccentric language." Without this information, I would not have grasped the relevance of this subtle difference to her broader argument. While the inclusion of footnotes may be incongruent with the genre of a newspaper article, those footnotes were crucial not just for me, but for the first-year writing awards committee: I submitted Eirene's piece, and she was named one of five finalists.[2]

These snapshots illustrate the process by which students exert agency as writers: They create a project about which they are knowledgeable and passionate; they make informed rhetorical choices throughout the writing and presentation process; and they reflect deeply on those choices, as well as on their growth as writers.[3]

Writing in the Twittersphere (Emily Simnitt)

In a section of first-year writing designed to support multilingual writers at Boise State University, I use a Writing about Writing (WAW) approach, which requires students to engage in primary research into their own and others' literacy practices (Downs and Wardle). The content of the course provides students the academic language and methods through which to honor, discuss, and explore their experiences with language acquisition, multilingual negotiation, and English-language literacy. The formal writing assignments provide scaffolding and support for students to gain experience in genres of academic writing. This curriculum sets the stage for additional ways in which students can choose to share their developing knowledge about writing in an academic environment.

To encourage further exploration of multiple literacies, I invite students to join an optional, ongoing Twitter chat about writing, language, and identity. The choice to participate via Twitter offers a low-stakes opportunity for agency, as students explore the content of the course (academic writing) in a flexible, often more familiar, format. Students may feel little rhetorical control over academic writing in English, but many of these same students are comfortable micro-composing on mobile devices, whether on Twitter, other social media, or simply texting.

This Twitter chat originated during a campus-wide conference at Boise State University presented by multilingual students taking English 123, a course designed to support multilingual writers, as Gail will further describe below (see also Shuck). At the spring 2012 conference, my students, who had been researching technology and writing, invited attendees to live-tweet about what they saw, learned, and experienced during the conference and to label each tweet with the hashtag #123chat or #197chat. The hashtag acts as a searchable marker, allowing those interested to follow and join in the conversation from semester to semester.

Before each conference, I bring archived tweets into class as an object of analysis, showing how the tweets become meaningful as a compilation. Together, we notice patterns of language use and content, categorizing types of tweets and considering what tweets indicate about the expressed identity of the Twitter user (teacher? student? presenter? multilingual?). This analysis in turn facilitates student awareness of the available choices for constructing tweets.

In reading through the chat from spring 2015, students might notice how Twitter can strengthen community (see also Lomicka and Lord). For example, tweets express encouragement and congratulations to presenters from friends and strangers alike: "You are the best group dude" (Almutari), "It was a great opportunity to learn about all these cultures" (Abochnb), or, "So confident" (aldihani). They might also notice how tweets highlight resonating ideas from presentations, offering ideas for students' own projects. A presentation on homesickness elicited this batch of tweets: "This conference remained me of my first semester at boise state" (Abochnb); "I can relate to missing where you from! I miss California" (Herrera); "Who doesn't miss his home?" (AbulGreen); and "Missing home is normal feelings to many students" (Alrashidi). Students might also notice meta-commentary on what is happening during the conference and how the audience for student work goes beyond the classroom and the conference itself. For example, this tweet calls attention to a chat participant outside of the state: "This guy from Tennessee [emoji of a hand pointing down to the username at the end of the tweet] And he is watching the conference from hashtag #197chat @hsulmutairi_" (Almutari).

While they are reading the #197chat feed, I draw students' attention to presenters' rhetorical choices and how they are received by the tweeting audience. One presentation that elicited many responses argued that use of social media in one's personal life influences how one writes in academic genres. The presenters argued that the most important factor influencing writing is the tool used, most often a computing device where writers send emails, check social media, and write academic papers. To visually represent how use of the same device results in the blending of genres, this group drew on one member's skill with Video Scribe, a program that animates whiteboard drawing, to make a video. In the video, a picture of a cell phone appeared and then disappeared. Next came a picture of a blender. Written to one side of the blender was "Formal Writing," with "essay, resume, research paper" listed below. On the other side, under the label "Informal Writing," students listed "e-mail, social media, journals." As the video continued, each of the terms flew into the blender, and the blender whirred.

As students presented, the audience of their peers, instructors, and faculty from across the university tweeted. Two pictures of the blender appeared in the Twitter feed, with one respondent asking, "How did you do this animation?" (Nogle). The presenters responded using subsequent tweets. Several more conference participants tweeted praise of the video, including, "Wow, great video. I'm going to have to try video scribe" (Donahue). Another attendee tweeted, "Do you think that writing style will be changed with the social media?" (abullah_q45), and other tweets appeared to restate the argument that technology use leads to genre blending. These tweets extended the WAW-based class discussion about technology and writing and showed the students how their choice and use of technology communicated their main point.

This exchange and traces of the presentation remain on Twitter for future students to find and analyze, creating a space to reimagine students' academic work for other audiences. The conference and the Twitter chat do not replace the study and practice of academic writing in English. Rather, they give students opportunities to share ideas, gain confidence, and support each other. Using the Twitter chat as an object of analysis prior to their participation shows students ways to exercise control and agency beyond more standard academic genres. When students analyze the language of tweets from previous conferences, they reach the conclusion that tweets do not need to be in Standard Written English to be rhetorically successful. Drawing students' attention to the informality and register of the tweets highlights the difference between the rhetorical situation on Twitter and that of academic genres in the university. While students develop academic language in formal essay assignments, Twitter increases opportunities for written language interaction in a different genre with an immediate, familiar audience.

I do not grade or evaluate the chat. Instead, my evaluation of whether Twitter provides useful rhetorical opportunities for students involves my own noticing of how the chat makes its way into class discussions, final portfolios, and student reflective writing. I point this out to my students. In this way, I help students see how the linguistic and rhetorical choices in the chat affect conversations in other contexts. I encourage them to seek opportunities to actively participate in a larger scholarly conversation.

Agency through a Film Project (Michelle Cox)

This film assignment served as a capstone for an international section of First Year Writing (FYW) at Dartmouth College that is enrolled through directed self-placement and stretches across two quarters. In designing the section, I considered the many challenges facing international multilingual students at Dartmouth, a small Ivy League college set in a rural area in the third "whitest" state in the country (U.S. Census Bureau). Dartmouth's student culture is dominated by fraternities, and the college prides itself on its long-held traditions and competitive atmosphere. The quarter system compresses courses to 9.5 weeks, ramping up the pace, and with it, the reading and writing load. Students without previous experience in English-medium academic environments need to quickly turn their textbook knowledge of English into their primary means for communicating and learning. And students without previous experience in U.S. education systems need to quickly acquire the knowledge of genres, writing processes, and research strategies assumed by faculty across the curriculum. Further, the first year of college is a time when international and U.S.-born students alike negotiate their identities. Therefore, I wanted my course to lead to greater awareness of issues related to multilingualism and second language writing development, allowing students to have greater control when making decisions about self-representation in their writing.

My goals during the first quarter, then, were for students to better understand their own English language and literacy development, position themselves as English users within the global arena (rather than only as Dartmouth students), and explore cultural differences in writing. During this term, students read about second language writing development, World Englishes, and textual ownership, while writing a language and literacy narrative, a research report on a variety of English, and a researched argumentative essay on plagiarism (see the Appendix for a list of course readings). My goal for the second quarter was for students to apply this knowledge while producing original research, writing a proposal for an undergraduate research grant, and engaging in a term-long film project.

For the film project, groups produced short films that targeted a Dartmouth audience (such as faculty or peers) and chose topics related to material covered during the first term. Scaffolding allowed students first to analyze samples (student films, as well as *Writing across Borders*, a film for faculty on multilingual writing) and then to complete separate stages of the project: a pitch (which identified the primary audience and message), a treatment plan (a more developed plan), a storyboard and script (which laid out the visual and sound elements), the rough cut (a draft of the film), and then the final cut. Each stage was presented for review by peers, a consultant from the college's media center, the course writing fellow, and me.

While creating the films, students were challenged to think carefully about audience and identity. One group, who wanted their film to target international peers and promote pride in international identity, struggled with how to handle the voiceover (Kudakwashe, Orzisk, and Sung). Concerned that their audience would have difficulty understanding their accents, the group considered asking a native-English speaking student to serve as narrator. During a class workshop, however, their peers asked if this decision would conflict with their message. They ultimately decided to do their own narration. The final cut of their film, "Speak Up! (a movie by internationals for internationals)," opens with the narrator telling us, "About ten percent of Dartmouth students are international. These students—*we*—create an environment that contributes to a valuable and unique Dartmouth experience." The narrator appears on camera a minute into the film, when he shares results from a survey conducted by the group and states that they also interviewed international students on their challenges. He then says, "Please, hear *our* voices," and walks off camera. These uses of first person show how the decision to serve as narrator led to stronger performance of identification with international students in the film. The remainder of the film shares clips of international students discussing challenges in adapting to U.S. culture, strategies they used to overcome these challenges, and final words for international peers: "Be proud of your heritages," "Be proud of your culture," and "Be proud of your accent."

A second group, who wanted to persuade domestic peers to value international students more, struggled to find an effective rhetorical approach (Bekele, Golanda, and Janjua). During a workshop, peers pointed out that the tone of their film could be considered negative and perhaps accusatory toward domestic students, as they seemed to be blaming domestic students for not knowing more about international students. To soften the tone, the group chose to frame the film with a series of questions. Their film, "Unity in Diversity: Internationalism at Dartmouth," opens with the question, "Did you know that in the Class of 1925, there was only one international student at Dartmouth?" followed by a clip of a hand flipping through a 1925 class yearbook and stopping at a photo of a Chinese international student. The words, "And now?" come on the screen, after which we see a series of short clips, showing international students answering the questions, "Where are you from?" and "What is your first language?" The film then moves to short clips of domestic students guessing answers to questions about Dartmouth international student demographics, followed by the correct answers and data on how many Dartmouth students answered the question correctly on a survey distributed by the group. The final question of the film, "So what? Why is internationalism important to Dartmouth anyway?" is followed by interview excerpts featuring the Director of International Student Programs and writing program faculty, who the group felt would add credibility to the film. The positive feeling that runs throughout the film is created by the humor with which the domestic students' responses are presented, the statements made by Dartmouth staff highlighting the benefits of working with international students, the upbeat music that runs in the background ("Best Days of My Life" by American Authors), and the message in the final frame, "Let's appreciate internationalism."

A third group, who wanted to empower international peers as writers, struggled to find approaches that would convince students to make use of available writing support (Bing and Pejanovic). Their classmates told them that raising awareness of available resources would not be enough, as information about the resources already existed. Their film, "Second Language Adaptation: Writing at Dartmouth for International Students," opens with information meant to persuade international students that they need writing support, sharing data from a survey they conducted (e.g., "41% of international students did not feel ready for college-level writing before coming to Dartmouth") interspersed with clips of international students discussing their writing struggles. Then, a frame announces, "Don't panic! We will introduce you to people who will make writing at Dartmouth easier." Headshots of the film's producers are shown traveling along a campus map, followed by clips of representatives from the programs they visit, including the library, writing program, and writing center. The most powerful moment in the film comes at the end, when one of the international students who had described her struggles with writing in English earlier is revealed to be a writing center tutor. Smiling broadly, she tells us, "Here I am. I am an international student, but I am teaching American students how to write."

With this curriculum, I was pushing back against the tendency in academic communities for others to craft the representations of multilingual students' identities (Costino and Hyon; Ruecker; Saenkhum). I sought to create optimal conditions for agency by inviting students into the academic conversation on second language writing, equipping students with the same literature and tools that academics have access to, and providing a venue for self-positioning as international students at Dartmouth. Overall, I would say the project successfully met these goals. Students also successfully advocated for multilingual students through their films, promoting inclusion, pride in diversity, and community, and produced films they felt proud of, as indicated by three groups' choice to publish their films on YouTube.

Curricular Structures and Informed Student Choice (Gail Shuck)

In addition to creating optimal conditions for agency in assignments and classroom practices, those of us with administrative roles can create optimal conditions for students to decide among multiple curricular options. In this section, I describe a pilot FYW course at Boise State University that addresses students' language development needs without relying on deficit-oriented practices and provides options that honor students' ability to make informed choices.

This pilot option is a six-credit, one-semester course called Accelerated English 101 for Multilingual Students (hereafter, "Accelerated English"), which fulfills the first-semester FYW requirement. More similar to the Accelerated Learning Program (ALP), with its support studio linked to a mainstream course (Adams, Gearhart, Miller, and Roberts) than to a stretch program (Glau), Accelerated English bypasses the second of two pass/fail ESL[4] courses and moves students to the required FYW courses (English 101 and 102) more quickly. Placement into the Level I or Level II ESL course or into FYW is determined by an in-house timed essay test. International students take this test during their orientation, and U.S.-resident multilingual students are guided toward this test by certain responses on our online self-placement website or through advising.[5] Accelerated English offers three hours of extra class time per week and a class size of fifteen. In letting students bypass one ESL course, Accelerated English helps to alleviate the pressures that some multilingual students are under, from scholarship restrictions to financial concerns to the stigma of "remedial" courses.

The course is a direct response to recent increases in two populations at Boise State: Saudi and Kuwaiti students on government scholarships, on one hand, and students who came to the U.S. as refugees, on the other. This latter group is often not identified for English proficiency evaluation. They may have very low SAT or ACT scores, or they may be exempt from needing a standardized test at all for admission because the admissions policy exempts applicants over twenty-one years old. These increases have posed some population-specific challenges. Government-sponsored students, warned that they must "compete with native speakers," are likely to try to avoid ESL courses, sometimes waiting a semester or more to take the placement test again, hoping their English will have improved enough to bypass ESL courses, or seeking FYW courses at other institutions with fewer barriers to enrollment. While avoidance of ESL courses is certainly a form of agency, the lack of curricular alternatives, coupled with insufficient information about the implications of avoiding, makes for less than optimal conditions.

For refugee or immigrant students, a central problem is a lack of awareness about multilingual-specific classes or support programs, which stems from the lack of a solid infrastructure of support and information for U.S.-resident English learners. Once informed of their options, however, these students often take the pass/fail ESL courses to ease into the university, receive credit toward graduation, and protect their GPAs. Without a system that adequately identifies students most in need of such information, U.S.-resident multilingual writers often find themselves in English 101 or its four-credit ALP version, English 101-Plus ("English 101P"), often without the English proficiency to be successful in those courses.

These contextual constraints highlight an additional challenge: international as well as resident students' being admitted without the English proficiency or reading and writing experience—even in their native languages—required to be academically successful. Providing a faster path through the FYW program was appealing, but only if we increased the support for English language and writing development, which would benefit multilingual students from a wide variety of backgrounds.

Without the new course, the entire sequence would look like this for a student who placed into ESL Level I (English 122):

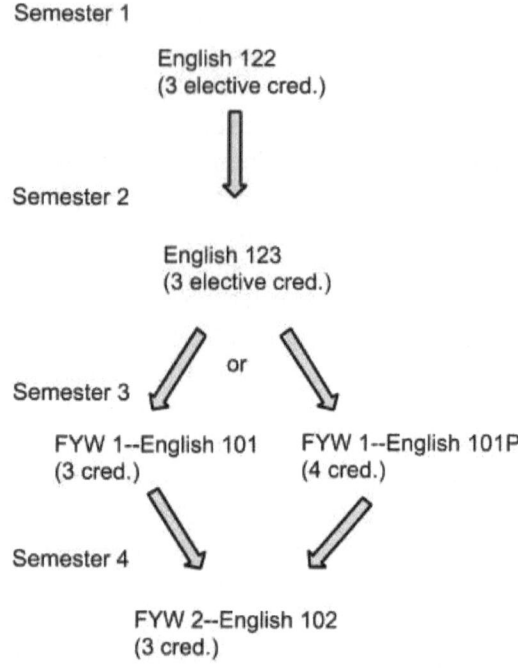

Fig. 3. Limited Choice and a Longer Path without Accelerated English.

The one institutionally sanctioned course choice a student can make comes after passing English 123, at which point the student may choose English 101 (3 credits) or a 4-credit, class-plus-studio option called English 101P. Some English 101P instructors have reported that one weekly studio hour is not sufficient for these two newer populations to be successful. Although these stories are anecdotal, these instructors, despite their preparation to teach L2 writers, have seen students with lower English proficiency levels struggle in FYW.

Since we began offering Accelerated English two semesters ago, many students have preferred it to the two-course ESL sequence and to the avoidance strategies many previous students chose. Demand has been very high. The following illustration can help to explain why.

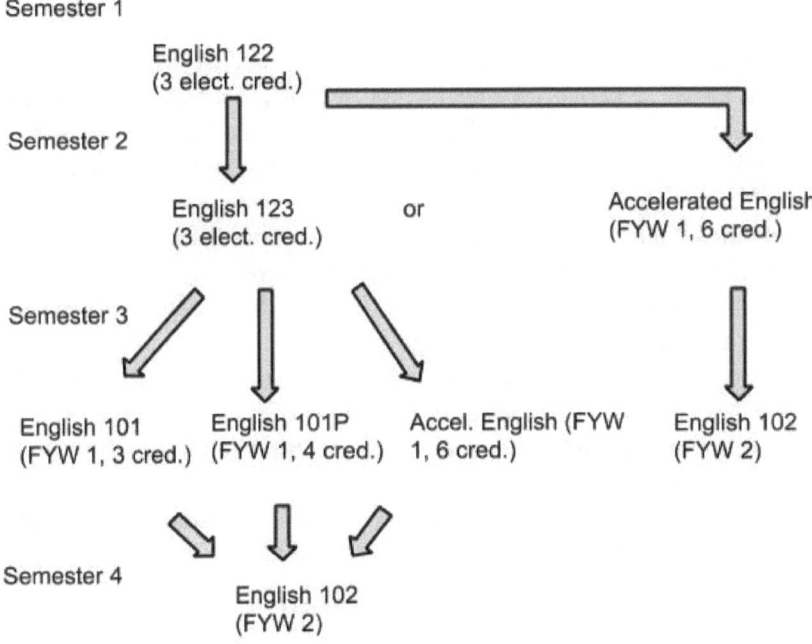

Fig. 4. More Choice and a Shorter FYW Path with Accelerated English.

As illustrated in Figure 4, students who pass English 122 may choose to move more slowly through the course sequence and take English 123 next before attempting English 101, or they may jump to Accelerated English, after which they would take English 102. A student who takes the English 123 path can then choose among three options for fulfilling the first-semester FYW requirement. With both a shorter path and a greater number of options, students have more opportunities to make agentive decisions. We will be collecting data on students' performance in English 102 over the next few semesters, which we hope will demonstrate comparable success in English 102 regardless of the students' choice at each juncture.

Despite the delays entailed by a two-course preparatory sequence, I have continued to offer English 122 and 123. Even when there are alternatives, some students have chosen these courses. They want the time, the support, and the opportunity to take low-risk but credit-bearing courses, as well as the comfort of being in a class with other second-language writers (Costino and Hyon). Having options as well as information empowers multilingual students to decide how they want to complete their FYW requirement.

Students who choose Accelerated English over the slower ESL sequence have experienced one unexpected advantage of Accelerated English: the greater impact that the six graded credits have on GPAs. The higher stakes seem to be leading these students to be more engaged than they typically are in the pass/fail ESL courses. It is too early in the pilot to document these claims, but in informal conversations, all four of the Accelerated English instructors have reiterated this point. If true, this outcome would suggest that students are investing in their own success—agents at work.

A survey of all of the students enrolled in the spring 2015 and fall 2015 Accelerated English and English 123 classes was revealing. Asked the most important reason for their choosing the course they were in, the students in Accelerated English were split between "finishing faster" and "wanting time and support." The most commonly chosen answers were as follows:

Table 1. Top Reasons for Choosing the 6-credit Option

Reason for Choosing Accelerated English	Percentage of Students (Number)
I wanted to finish composition requirements faster.	25% (21)
I wanted the extra time and support of the 6-credit option.	24% (20)
A friend or advisor told me to take it.	11% (9)
English 101 seats were full.	8% (7)

The finding that seven students enrolled in Accelerated English even though they were eligible for English 101 is striking, as they chose a 6-credit course over a 3-credit course a semester later. This could be explained by a desire for a more supportive experience or a desire to finish faster. In either case, they made their own agentive decisions.

The students in English 123 were asked the same question. Their primary reason for choosing English 123 was that they did not know or understand that Accelerated English was a way of bypassing English 123. Two of the 14 English 123 respondents had hoped to enroll in Accelerated English, but it was full. Ten (71%) answered simply that English 123 was the next course in the sequence or that the test placed them into English 123, revealing a lack of awareness among some students that Accelerated English was an option.

As my coauthors have illustrated, offering options is one way to create conditions for agency. Having an institutionally recognized choice, where there were only back-door choices in the past, is crucial. So is accurate information. Some students, for example, have expressed a concern that a six-credit course would be too difficult. The reality is that Accelerated English offers more support—not more work—than English 101. I have addressed these concerns where possible in impromptu information sessions, announcements by instructors of English 122, and more formal presentations to students, advisors, and international services staff, but more awareness-raising needs to be done. Once they recognize that the additional credits are for in-class support, students can better evaluate the effects of enrolling in Accelerated English. I am also deepening my partnerships with the FYW Program and other units to increase students' awareness of options and of the implications of their choices. That awareness is a critical component of empowering multilingual writers to make informed decisions and be academically successful.

Concluding Thoughts

As the above examples show, agency is a useful framework for both micro-level and macro-level analysis, from a single assignment to an institutional structure. The examples illustrate how we, as writing instructors and program administrators, seek to create optimal conditions for multilingual student agency, by building options for students and by working to increase awareness so those students can make informed decisions about those options. This awareness includes increased knowledge of second language writing itself, of the politics of English, and of the effects of different linguistic and rhetorical choices. That knowledge, in turn, increases students' control over how they navigate an assignment or writing program, how they position themselves in a text and in the wider community, and how they continue developing as English users.

Although our examples reference undergraduate writing courses and programs, this agency framework would also be useful for increasing multilingual student agency in other contexts, such as writing-in-the-disciplines courses, graduate writing programs, writing centers, and K-12 settings. Within these contexts, what options for linguistic, rhetorical, generic, and programmatic action exist? What, in the assignment, curriculum, or wider rhetorical, cultural, and political contexts, constrains writers' options? What constitutes "sufficient information"—what do students need to notice—for students to make informed decisions about these options? How can we, as instructors and program administrators, use this information to create optimal conditions for multilingual student agency? And how do we respect student choices, even when their choices (such as avoiding an ESL section) do not seem advantageous, from our perspective as instructors or administrators? Promoting student agency does require a degree of trust in the student, providing spaces for students to both thrive and stumble. We are convinced, however, that stumbling leads to learning and resilience, and that the rewards of teaching for agency far exceed the risks.

Notes

1. We have chosen not to use the term "translingual" to refer to our overall project or to students. As Suresh Canagarajah (*Translingual Practice*) has argued, "translingualism" has become an umbrella term that includes the use of multiple languages, discourses, and registers (in other words, the term refers to a set of language practices employed by all language users). In this article, we limit our discussion to students who use English as an additional language. Thus, we alternate between "multilingual" and "second language (L2)," terms widely used to describe this population. We acknowledge that neither term is wholly accurate to describe learners of English in the U.S. However, "multilingual" values the many linguistic resources students bring, and "L2" connects our work to the field of second-language writing studies, which has made important contributions to theory and pedagogy for working with learners of English as an additional language.

2. The article was eventually published in an online Malaysian newspaper—without the footnotes.

3. Another published piece from this project is at http://translingual.org/2013/05/06/reflexiones-en-bilingue/.

4. We use the term *ESL* here, in part to highlight these courses' "pre-101," non-requirement-fulfilling status. "ESL" does not appear in the catalog title of those courses.

5. The online self-placement process has some junctures at which students can identify themselves as multilingual and answer questions about their experiences with reading and writing in English and other languages. However,

the online placement questionnaires have very text-heavy questions that some multilingual students do not understand. Some admitted that they clicked answers at random and ended up with a 101 placement, despite their lack of comprehension of the language of the questionnaire. The FYW Placement Coordinator and I (Gail) are working toward a more nuanced way to identify students who would be best served in a course designed to facilitate their English language development without overwhelming them.

Works Cited

Adams, Peter, Sarah Gearhart, Robert Miller, and Anne Roberts. "The Accelerated Learning Program: Throwing Open the Gates." *Journal of Basic Writing* 28.2 (2009): 50-69. Print.
(abdullah_q45). "Do you think that writing style will be changed with the social media?" 15 April 2015. 9:47 a.m. Tweet.
(Abochnb). "It was a great opportunity to learn about all these cultures." 15 April 2015. 10:03 a.m. Tweet.
(AbulGreen). "Who doesn't miss his home?" 15 April 2015. 10:01 a.m. Tweet.
---. "This conference remained me of my first semester at boise state." 15 April 2015. 9:59 a.m. Tweet.
Aldihani, Abdulatif (abdullateefq8). "So confident." 15 April 2015, 10:05 a.m. Tweet.
Almutari, Omar. (OmarAlmutari). "You are the best group dude." 15 April 2015. 9:59 a.m. Tweet.
Alrashidi, Anwur. (anwur123). "Missing home is normal feelings to many students." 15 April 2015. 10:03 a.m. Tweet.
Bekele, Ekshesh, Donie Golanda, and Maieda Janjua. "Unity in Diversity: Internationalism at Dartmouth." Online video. *YouTube.* YouTube, 8 Mar. 2014. Web. June 2015. <https://www.youtube.com/watch?v=-bYB5snc1ec>.
Bennett, John Godolphin. *Noticing.* Sherborne: Coombe Springs P, 1976. Print. The Sherborne Theme Talks Ser. 2.
Bing, Jun, and Luka Pejanovic. "Second Language Adaptation: Writing at Dartmouth for International Students." Online video. *YouTube.* YouTube, 6 Mar. 2014. Web. June 2015. <https://www.youtube.com/watch?v=eUNP23Dac6Q&feature=youtu.be>.
Canagarajah, A. Suresh. "Agency and Power in Intercultural Communication: Negotiating English in Translocal Spaces." *Language and Intercultural Communication* 13.2 (2013): 202-24. Print.
---. *Translingual Practice: Global Englishes and Cosmopolitan Relations.* New York: Routledge, 2013. Print.
Cook, Vivian. "Evidence for Multi-Competence." *Language Learning* 42 (1992): 557-91. Print.

Cooper, Marilyn. "Rhetorical Agency as Emergent and Enacted." *CCC* 62.3 (2011): 420-49. Print.
Costino, Kimberly A., and Sunny Hyon. "'A Class for Students Like Me': Reconsidering Relationships among Identity Labels, Residency Status, and Students' Preferences for Mainstream or Multilingual Composition." *Journal of Second Language Writing* 16.2 (2007): 63-81. Print.
Donahoe, Jillian. (littlestDonahoe). "Wow, great video. I'm going to have to try video scribe." 15 April 2015. 9:50 a.m. Tweet.
Downs, Douglas, and Elizabeth Wardle. "Teaching about Writing, Righting Misconceptions: (Re)Envisioning 'First-Year Composition' as 'Introduction to Writing Studies.'" *CCC* 58.4 (2007): 552-84. Print.
Duranti, Alessandro. "Agency in Language." *A Companion to Linguistic Anthropology*. Ed. Alessandro Duranti. Malden: Blackwell, 2004. 451-73. Print.
Glau, Gregory J. "The 'Stretch Program': Arizona State University's New Model of University-level Basic Writing Instruction." *WPA: Writing Program Administration* 20.1/2 (1996): 79-91. Print.
Herrera, Robert. (RobertH88771204). "I can relate to missing where you from! I miss California." 15 April 2015. 10:00 a.m. Tweet.
Jordan, Jay. *Redesigning Composition for Multilingual Realities*. Urbana: NCTE, 2012. Print.
Kudakwashe, Clement, Odon Orzisk, and Taeho Sung. "Speak Up! (a movie by internationals for internationals)." Online video. *YouTube*. YouTube, 6 Mar. 2014. Web. June 2015. <http://www.youtube.com/watch?v=j3_keBWOTvM>.
Lomicka, Lara, and Gillian Lord. "A Tale of Tweets: Analyzing Microblogging Among Language Learners." *System* 40.1 (2012): 48-63. Science Direct. Web. 10 July 2014.
Lu, Min-Zhan, and Bruce Horner. "Translingual Literacy, Language Difference, and Matters of Agency." *College English* 75.6 (2013): 582-607. Print.
Matsuda, Paul Kei. "The Lure of Translingual Writing." *PMLA* 129.3 (2014): 478-83. Print.
Miller, Carolyn R. "What Can Automation Tell Us about Agency?" *Rhetoric Society Quarterly* 37 (2007): 137-57. Print.
Nogle, Christi. (ChristiNogle). "How did you do this animation?" 15 April 2015. 9:47 a.m.
Qi, Donald S., and Sharon Lapkin. "Exploring the Role of Noticing in a Three-Stage Second Language Writing Task." *Journal of Second Language Writing* 10 (2001): 277-303. Print.
Ruecker, Todd. "Improving the Placement of L2 Writers: The Students' Perspective." *WPA: Writing Program Administration* 35.1 (2011): 92-118. Print.

Saenkhum, Tanita. "Investigating Agency in Multilingual Writers' Placement Decisions: A Case Study of The Writing Programs at Arizona State University." Diss. Arizona State University 2012. Web. 1 Aug. 2015.

Schmidt, Richard. "Attention, Awareness, and Individual Differences in Language Learning." *Proceedings of CLaSIC 2010*. Ed. Wai Meng Chan, Seo Won Chi, Kwee Nyet Chin, Johanna W. Istanto, Masanori Nagami, Jyh Wee Sew, Titima Suthiwan, and Izumi Walker. Singapore: National U of Singapore, Centre for Language Studies, 2010. 721-37. Web. May 2015. <http://nflrc.hawaii.edu/PDFs/SCHMIDT%20Attention,%20awareness,%20and%20individual%20differences.pdf>.

Shuck, Gail. "Ownership of Texts, Ownership of Language: Two Students' Participation in a Student-Run Conference." *The Reading Matrix* 4.3 (2004): 24-39. Print.

Swain, Merrill. "Languaging, Agency and Collaboration in Advanced Language Proficiency." *Advanced Language Learning: The Contribution of Halliday and Vygotsky*. Ed. Heidi Byrnes. London: Continuum, 2006. 95-108. Print.

U.S. Census Bureau. *State Rankings: The 2012 Statistical Abstract*. Washington: GPO, 2012. Web. Oct. 2015. <www2.census.gov/library/publications/2011/compendia/statab/131ed/2012-statab.pdf>.

Writing across Borders. Dir. Wayne Robertson. Oregon State U, 2005. Film.

Appendix: Reading List from Dartmouth FYW Course

Bloch, Joel. "Plagiarism: Is There a Difference across Cultures?" *Indonesian Journal of English Language Teaching* 3.2 (2007): 139-51. Print.

Carson, Joan. "Becoming Biliterate." *Journal of Second Language Writing* 1.1 (1992): 37-60. Print.

Harushumana, Immaculee. "Blinding Audacity: The Narrative of a French-Speaking African Teaching English in the United States." *Reinventing Identities in Second Language Writing*. Ed. Michelle Cox, Jay Jordan, Christina Ortmeier-Hooper, and Gwen Gray Schwartz. Urbana: NCTE, 2010. 232-9. Print.

---. "Colonial Language Writing Identities in Postcolonial Africa." *Reinventing Identities in Second Language Writing*. Ed. Michelle Cox, Jay Jordan, Christina Ortmeier-Hooper, and Gwen Gray Schwartz. Urbana: NCTE, 2010. 207-31. Print.

Howard, Rebecca Moore. "A Plagiarism Pentimento." *Journal of Teaching Writing* 11.2 (1993): 233-46. Print.

---. "Understanding 'Internet Plagiarism.'" *Computers and Composition* 24.1 (2007): 3-15. Print.

Krachu, Braj. "World Englishes: Agony and Ecstasy." *Journal of Aesthetic Education* 30.2 (1996): 135-55. Print.

Kubota, Ryuko. "My Experience of Learning to Read and Write in Japanese and English as L2." *Reflections on Multiliterate Lives*. Ed. Ulla Connor and Diane Belcher. Clevedon: Multilingual Matters, 2001. 96-109. Print.

Leki, Ilona. "History of Writing Instruction in English as a Second Language." *Understanding ESL Writers: A Guide for Teachers*. Portsmouth: Heinemann, 1992. 3-9. Print.

---. "Models of Second Language Acquisition." *Understanding ESL Writers: A Guide for Teachers*. Portsmouth: Heinemann, 1992. 10-24. Print.

Sasaki, Miyuki. "An Introspective Account of L2 Writing Acquisition." *Reflections on Multiliterate Lives*. Ed. Ulla Connor and Diane Belcher. Clevedon: Multilingual Matters, 2001. 110-9. Print.

Tsai, Ming-Daw. "Learning is a Life-Long Process." *Reflections on Multiliterate Lives*. Ed. Ulla Connor and Diane Belcher. Clevedon: Multilingual Matters, 2001. 135-40. Print.

You, Xiaoye. "The Choice Made from No Choice: English Writing Instruction in a Chinese University." *Journal of Second Language Writing* 13.2 (2004): 97–110. Print.

ENCULTURATION

enculturation
a journal of rhetoric, writing, and culture

Enculturation was launched in 1996 by two graduate students. In twenty years it has never been affiliated with a press or organization and has only had minimal institutional support by one university. Currently it is hosted on an individual's server and supported with one RA through the University of South Carolina. Almost all of the managerial, editorial, and production work continues to be done by young faculty and graduate students in the field of rhetoric and composition. The mission of the journal has generally been to publish broader ranging interdisciplinary work related to rhetoric and composition that is more theoretical or media-oriented.

Enculturation is on the Web at http://enculturation.net/

Weepy Rhetoric, Trigger Warnings, and the Work of Making Mental Illness Visible in the Writing Classroom

"Weepy Rhetoric," by Sarah Orem (Smith College) and Neil Simpkins (University of Wisconsin-Madison) speaks to an exigency of broad cultural concern as well as being of particular concern to educators and rhetorical scholars. Trigger warnings, while starting with a concern for genuine disabilities grounded in trauma, jumped ship at the popular level and generated a backlash against overly sensitive and overprotected students, on the one hand, and political correctness gone wild on the other. The authors, however, show how trigger warnings work to make mental illness visible in the classroom by revealing the interrelation of physical and psychological injury. *Weepy rhetoric*, they argue, gives difficult, messy emotion a place in the classroom and they chart strategies for employing trigger warnings, mental illness, and real emotions in composition pedagogy. The editors at Enculturation chose "Weepy Rhetoric" because it is an excellent example of the way scholarship can speak to broad concerns without falling prey to reductive perspectives, polemical response, or rendering the public overly academic. Instead, they turn these concerns into productive occasions for thinking and learning.

Weepy Rhetoric, Trigger Warnings, and the Work of Making Mental Illness Visible in the Writing Classroom

Sarah Orem and Neil Simpkins

"In a sense, the predicament is to understand what kind of community is composed of those who are beside themselves."

—Judith Butler, *Undoing Gender*

WARNING FOR: #ABLEISM #SUICIDE #TRANS VIOLENCE #RACISM #MENTAL ILLNESS #VIOLENCE #DEATH

Within the span of a few months, from late 2013 to mid-April 2014, a cascade of op-eds began appearing in web magazines and newspapers decrying the threat of a new public enemy: trigger warnings, textual tags attached to a variety of media that alert readers and viewers that the ensuing material could spur a mental health crisis. In response to emerging student requests for professors to use trigger warnings in classrooms, journalists suggested trigger warnings "structur[e] public life around the most fragile personal sensitivities" (Jarvie) and "bubble-wrap students against everything that might be frightening or offensive to them" (Times Editorial Board). While rhetoric and writing scholar Kathleen Livingston favors trigger warnings, deeming them "one part of a larger practice of consent," English professor Karen Swallow Prior worries they constitute a form of "empathic correctness" arising from the "sensitivity cultivated within an entire generation of overprotected kids." Likewise, Northwestern University professor Laura Kipnis complains that trigger warnings belie undergraduates' desire to remain "cocooned from uncomfortable feelings."

Trigger warnings have long been used in feminist-, queer-, and disability-activist settings online, but the public discussion of trigger-warned syllabi came specifically on the heels of the ratification of

Oberlin College's 2013 Campus Sexual Violence Elimination Act. In response to the act's publication, Oberlin's Office of Equity Concerns issued a list of "Support Resources For Faculty," delineating strategies for meeting the needs of student survivors of sexual violence ("Support Resources"). The document—nonbinding due to its status as a list of recommended resources—encourages faculty to implement trigger warnings in order to make classrooms more accessible to students with PTSD. Subsequently, students on other campuses called for trigger warnings in their own university syllabi. On February 18, 2014, undergraduate Philip Wythe wrote in Rutgers University's *Daily Targum* that trigger warnings offer a "compromise" between the desire to support trauma survivors and the need to protect civil liberty. A few days later, on February 25th, 2014, the University of California-Santa Barbara's student senate issued resolution #805 calling for faculty to "list trigger warnings" on syllabi to aid students with psychiatric disabilities (A.S. Senate).

In the crossfire of student advocacy for and faculty critiques of trigger warnings, the writers of this article were left feeling disoriented. We are both rhetoric and writing scholars who live with chronic mental illness. We both write about our disabilities in academic as well as informal and online contexts. Years ago, we met in a corner of the Internet where trigger warnings are *de rigueur*, and our friendship formed as we discussed how best to balance therapy, medication, doctors visits, and mental illness with the demands of academic life. We believed that navigating academic careers while mentally ill demonstrated our resilience, but as journalistic and scholarly op-eds on trigger warnings populated our computer screens, we learned that the opposite conclusion was being drawn by some: only recently, we participated in a highly public online conversation about trigger warnings in which a fellow academic declared that "PTSD is the new 'my dog ate my homework.'"

At that moment, we felt compelled to question: How does online writing about trigger warnings rhetorically construct mentally ill students and scholars? How do mentally ill persons intervene in such discourses? And what work could trigger warnings perform in the writing courses we teach?

Because they call attention to the emotional pain of students, trigger warnings tap into longstanding assumptions about mental illness—namely, that mentally ill persons are merely malingering, dwelling unnecessarily with emotional pain, and in need of toughening up. A mental illness like depression is, according to psychotherapist Julia A. Boyd, regularly interpreted as a personal fault—a propensity to be "lazy" or "unmotivated" (15). Meri Nana-Ama Danquah concurs in her memoir *Willow Weep for Me*, a narrative exploration of her psychiatric illness, that mental illness is not typically "looked upon" as "legitimate" (144).

In a curious rhetorical maneuver, rather than contesting assumptions about the sensitivity of mentally ill persons, Oberlin's trigger warning recommendations ask faculty to pay *more* attention to students' feelings. "Be sensitive and supportive," it advises. Offer "emotional support and validation." Understand the "range of emotion[s]" present "during and after a trigger" ("Support Resources"). Perhaps trigger warnings lean into pathologizing discourses about mental illness in order to find productivity in them? Such is our proposal: we argue that trigger warnings function as what we term *weepy rhetoric*, a mode of crying through text. Pouring out difficult, messy emotions in academic spaces, trigger warnings function as reverse discourse, reclaiming damaging assumptions about the mentally ill. In what follows, we will show how trigger warnings work to make mental illness[1] visible by revealing the interrelation of physical and psychological injury. Then, after reflecting on our own experiences with trigger warnings, we will chart some strategies for employing them in composition pedagogy.

TW: Textual Weeping

Trigger warnings operate through written, printed, or digital text and, as such, are an inherently "graphic" and visual mode of communication (Bernhardt 168). Mental illness, however, is typically understood as an *in*visible phenomenon—a disability that is not easily legible on a body's surface. Therefore, individuals who "experience emotional distress" are sometimes accused of not being truly "sick," writes Anna Mollow, and are assumed to be "merely malingering" (285). Within higher education, the claim to mental illness can meet special resistance from what José Muñoz sees as a scholarly imperative to "insis[t] on the need for a rigorous deployment of evidentiary procedure" (8). Because trigger warnings work to reveal a cluster of bodily symptoms that are characteristically invisible, their proponents ask others to accept as legitimate something that can lack visible evidence.

Often, when we mentally ill disclose our disability, we do so knowing that others may believe we are exaggerating our emotional pain. This critique is evident in Jack Halberstam's widely circulated blog post "You Are Triggering me! The Neo-Liberal Rhetoric of Harm, Danger and Trauma." In it, Halberstam encourages young generations of activists to focus more on "systemic" oppressions rather than "individuals and their woes." Comparing trigger warning advocates to cultural feminisms of the 1970s and '80s, Halberstam goes so far as to describe both groups as a "messy, unappealing morass of weepy, hypo-allergic, psychosomatic, anti-sex, anti-fun, anti-porn, pro-drama, pro-processing post-political subjects." Halberstam's essay is a sincere attempt to think through the difficulties of moving from personal experiences of pain and discrimination to coalitional politics. Yet at the heart of his essay is a claim that mentally ill persons are "weepy"—wallowing in pain.

Are students who ask their professors to use trigger warnings weepy? In its colloquial sense, "weeping" refers to sadness. According to the *Oxford English Dictionary*, the adjectival term "weepy" describes a particularly negative emotional experience in which one feels "mournful" or "maudlin" ("Weepy, adj."). Oberlin College's "Support Resources" begins with such an expression of sadness:

The statistical evidence about the impact of sexualized violence on college students is sobering. According to the CDC's 2010 National Intimate Partner and Sexual Violence Survey (NISVS), almost 1 in 5 women (18.3%) and 1 in 71 men (1.4%) have experienced rape. [...] In an Oberlin class that contains 20 students, we estimate that there may be about 2 to 3 students in the class who have experienced some form of sexualized violence.

Explicitly underscoring student suffering by describing the "sobering" pervasiveness of rape, Oberlin's "Support Resources" situates trigger warnings within a "mournful" rhetorical context.

In its verb form, "weeping" constitutes "a visible and audible display of emotion" ("Weep, v."). The performance of sadness articulated via weeping includes both corporeal and emotional sensations. Weeping "manifest[s] the combination of bodily symptoms (instinctive cries or moans, sobs, and shedding of tears) which is the natural, audible, and visible expression of painful [...] emotion." As a noun, a "weep" refers to the excretions of the human body: "an exudation, percolation, or sweating of moisture" ("Weep, n."). The adjective "weepy" also refers to the ickier aspects of the flesh: "exuding moisture, damp, oozy" ("Weepy, adj."). The concept of "weeping" therefore illustrates how physical and psychological symptoms of pain emerge coterminously.

While physical pain and injury are often seen as visible phenomena, mental or emotional distress is often understood as invisible, as we have just remarked. Weeping, therefore, is a dramatic performance of making visible the complex interrelation of emotional and physical, visible and invisible pain. It is a concept rooted in the embodiment of emotional pain.

Trigger warnings evoke Joshua Gunn's notion of "the cry"—communication that draws "the auditor's attention to the role of the physical body [...] as well as the fact that the body is easily fucked with" (24). By requesting a trigger warning, a student necessarily testifies to a history of experiencing pain, whether arising from sexual assault, physical violence, mental illness, or some combination of the three, and indicates that these impact her continued daily life, both mentally and in the material space of the classroom.

A trigger warning, we suggest, *weeps*. It is *weepy rhetoric*—a method of calling attention to pain through language, while foregrounding the interrelation between emotional pain (such as mental illness) and physical pain (including assault or sexualized violence). Visibly displaying through text a history of surviving physical and psychological injury, a trigger warning (TW) is itself a Textual Weeping.

Reclaiming pathologizing notions about the over-sensitivity of the mentally ill, a trigger warning is a form of reverse discourse - a political strategy whereby a marginalized group speaks back to power in the same terms that have historically been used to oppress them (Foucault 101). Thinking about trigger warnings as a form of weepy rhetoric maps the complexities of how mentally disabled persons are simultaneously denied rhetorical agency and afforded particularly rich rhetorical tools by virtue of being dis/abled (by psychiatric difference as well as by pervasive discrimination). Weepiness has a double edge: it is a characteristic pejoratively applied to trigger warning users as well as a powerful rhetorical tool that opens new ways to move through the discourses that surround us.

Because the boundaries between "acceptable" pain and disabling pain are not always easy to draw, using weepy rhetoric can be dangerous. According to Catherine Prendergast, mental illness "supplants one's position as a rhetor," denying "rhetoricability"—the rhetorical force a particular rhetor's communication holds—to the mentally disabled ("On the Rhetorics" 47, 56). For Jenell Johnson, mental illness stigmatizes rhetors, marking them as having "*kakoethos*, or bad character" (461). The more apparent a mental disability becomes to others, the more the mentally disabled rhetor loses rhetorical force and credibility.

In op-eds by humanities faculty, mental illness is frequently construed as simple discomfort instead of a true disability. For example, the *Inside Higher Ed* article "Trigger Warnings are Flawed," written by seven women and gender studies professors, conjectures that students ask for trigger warnings because they want a "guarantee" that they "will not experience unexpected discomfort" in classroom settings (Freeman et al.). Likewise, poet and author CAConrad's contribution to *Entropy* magazine's roundtable "On Trigger Warnings" questions the degree to which PTSD constitutes a disability at all. "In the end," Conrad writes, "whether we consider PTSD a disability or not I'm not seeing how trigger warnings is [sic] the answer" (Milks et al.). Linking mental illness with discomfort lends those with mental illness bad character; in these cases, students with mental illness are seen as a malingering force lessening the quality of classroom instruction.

Some faculty evince frustration with the chronic nature of mental illness and trauma, which cannot always be immediately resolved or addressed. The authors of "Trigger Warnings are Flawed" suppose that faculty members are "not trained to handle traumatic reactions" and recommend that professors direct students concerned about being triggered in the classroom to "independent campus offices that handle documentation, certification, and accommodation plans" (Freeman et al.).[2] Rhetorically relegating mental disability to the purview of separate campus mental health centers, this article constructs mentally ill students as unmanageable by the average professor.

After a large amount of popular and scholarly pushback, Oberlin retracted its trigger warning recommendations in April of 2014. But, following Catherine Prendergast's call for composition instructors to take seriously the writing practices that our students bring us ("Fighting Style"), we view the public and scholarly debate over trigger warnings as an opportunity to look more closely at what these tools might be able to do (or are already doing) for the disabled students that we teach and for ourselves as well. The process of weeping is painful, but it is also healing. Wounds weep when they heal. Just like a mending sore leaks pus and fluid, a trigger warning brings into the world (via text) the nasty, painful histories that someone who might use a trigger warning has lived through while allowing mentally ill students to find a way to navigate the world around them. Trigger warnings ask us to consider how reading and writing make the body and mind vulnerable together.

What if we, as composition scholars, embrace the messy emotions that trigger warnings highlight through written, print, or digital text? To explore this possibility, we will reflect on our own experiences with trigger warnings (or the lack thereof) in classrooms and digital spaces through two narratives. In doing so, we follow Shayda Kafai's recommendation that those who "theorize madness" are well-served by writing "in the first person" and by "claiming self-knowledge." In the first narrative that follows, "Performing Vulnerability," Sarah Orem reflects on what it's like to be inside a rhetoric classroom that does *not* employ trigger warnings. The second narrative, "Writing on the Edge," documents Neil Simpkins's experiences using trigger warnings in a digital community whose users are frequently at risk for suicide.

I. Performing Vulnerability

The year I passed my comprehensive exams and began writing my doctoral dissertation, my OCD symptoms worsened to the point that I was completely housebound. I would, eventually, recover. I would, eventually, finish writing and defend my dissertation. I distinctly remember, during my recovery process, having a conversation with a colleague who complained that they dreaded students with disabilities enrolling in their courses. My colleague worried aloud that students asking for disability accommodations "don't look disabled, a lot of the time."

Asking for accommodations when you don't look disabled (or disabled enough) is hard. So when I was a student I didn't ask for them.

I remember one particular instance when I wish I *had* asked for a trigger warning as a student. I'm thinking of a semester in which I signed up for a graduate seminar titled "Performative Rhetorics," which was led by a big-name professor who I desperately wanted to impress. The course explored theories of performativity by John Searle, J.

L. Austin, Judith Butler, and Jacques Derrida, and each week, one student was required to present a short paper applying the course readings to a text of their own choosing. Roughly halfway through the semester, a student delivered a paper on "the rhetoric of the suicide letter." I hazily recollect that the presentation used theories of rhetorical performativity to unpack David Foster Wallace's fiction, but I couldn't say for sure. I simply don't remember. I do remember that the paper incorporated graphic descriptions of how someone might commit suicide.

Having OCD means regularly experiencing "intrusive thoughts"— unwanted, unexpected, and distressing thoughts that fill my mind without my control. My intrusive thoughts revolve around the fear that I might hurt myself if I lose control of my mental faculties. Clinicians call this variant of OCD "Harm OCD." People who have Harm OCD are not violent, but instead have "frequent powerful doubts on the theme that something they have done or will do will lead to harm" for themselves or others (Penzel 302). My disorder has led me to perform elaborate daily rituals to assure myself that I am not on the verge of going "crazy" and hurting myself, even though I have no history of suicidal ideation.

As I sat in that graduate seminar, listening to another student detail the ways someone might kill themselves, my mind overtook me. I wasn't "out" as a person with a mental illness, so my classmates and the professor would have been bewildered if I had bolted for the door or run crying into the bathroom, which is what I wanted to do. I panicked, caught in a loop of irrational thoughts: *What if I hurt myself? What if I kill myself? Is this discussion a sign that I'm going to hurt myself?* I spent the class, mentally, somewhere else, struggling to hold on against an onslaught of electrifying fears. It took me days to come down from the panic attack and begin eating again (I lose my appetite when I am very triggered).

Though I missed out on the discussion of Wallace's literature, I did get a practical lesson in Judith Butler's theory of vulnerability: how the shared nature of social life makes all individuals vulnerable to one another. According to Butler, being embodied implies experiencing "mortality, vulnerability, agency: the skin and the flesh expose us to the gaze of others but also to touch and to violence" (21). Butler concedes that vulnerability is often difficult and painful to experience. I certainly didn't like it. My initial reaction to being triggered in class was to soldier on through the pain. In the intensely competitive atmosphere of a PhD program at a Research I institution, I believed I had to toughen up. I eschewed any display of weakness (or, weepiness).

But Butler also defines vulnerability as a powerful state to inhabit. To acknowledge the vulnerability that permeates life is not to be "resigned to a simple passivity or powerlessness" (23). Rather, such acknowledgement can uniquely enable acts of empowerment and agency. Though I saw myself as weak, I was also power*ful* in other ways. I'd survived clinically "extreme" OCD and gone on to graduate study. If I had asked the professor for a trigger warning, I would have simultaneously disclosed the vulnerability I experience when in the middle of a trigger and testified to a history of surviving with a mental health disorder. I would have also taken the risk of making my illness more visible to my peers. What would it mean to view a student's request for the use of a trigger warning not as a desire to "avoid discomfort," but instead as a testament to having survived abuse, psychiatric illness, or violence?

Butler insists that contemporary politics should seek to "sustain" various "precarious lives across the globe," and I view trigger warnings as one such device that can "sustain" students who live with psychiatric illness (23). If the professor or the student presenting their paper had offered a trigger warning by saying "trigger warning for suicide" verbally or offering a heads-up via email ahead of class, I could have skipped class that day, or even just that specific paper presentation. Potentially, I would not have had to cope with the panic attacks that derailed my studies for days after the class was over. Granted, by missing class I would have missed out on the day's lesson, but I missed the lesson anyway. I don't remember it—I was far too deep in the throes of OCD ruminating and panic.

Trigger warnings can help mentally disabled students navigate the kairotic space of the classroom—especially a writing or rhetoric classroom such as the one I occupied. As Margaret Price describes, kairotic spaces are "characterized by all or most of these criteria":

1. Real-time unfolding of events
2. Impromptu communication that is required or encouraged
3. In-person contact
4. A strong social element
5. High stakes. (61)

The predominance of kairotic spaces in academic life particularly affects how well both students and faculty access higher education. Kairos in Price's construction can be disabling, or at least marshaled by non-disabled individuals to create inaccessible spaces. Many classrooms incorporate all of these kairotic criteria, particularly in the writing- or reading-focused classroom. Students are expected to attend real-time discussion of works regularly, where they have in-person contact with both their peers and the person assigning them a grade. Students' ability to perform socially in the space is usually tied to a participation grade that can directly impact their final grade. Writing, literature, and cultural studies classes often fulfill a general-education requirement, and failing the class would mean needing to retake the same or a similar course. As such, the stakes for these classrooms are high.

Trigger warnings can help mitigate some of the issues that students with mental illnesses, such as myself, might have in maneuvering through a classroom's kairotic space. With trigger warnings, a student who might experience a flashback or panic attack from a graphic depiction of rape or suicide can allow that event to unfold in a place of his or her choosing. In class, the student would be prepared for conversations to potentially center on this triggering element. The student's ability to navigate in-person contact and the social element of the classroom may be increased if he or she is aware of where the conversation might lead. And because students are typically discouraged from leaving the classroom mid-lecture, trigger warnings signal a professor's awareness that a student might need to briefly excuse themselves from the room to experience a trigger in private.

II. Writing on the Edge

To be transgender is to live a life knowing many of your Internet and in-real-life trans friends will die. It means being seen as at risk for suicide—or, on the other end, as expendable. The first time I attached a trigger warning to my personal writing occurred when, at an awards banquet, the mother of a young trans person who had committed suicide at my college commended me for staying alive. She noted that she pitied me for the struggle I would face being trans. That evening, I wrote on my blog:

APRIL 13, 2011

on being pitied (tw for suicide)

"How can one turn out/ the pockets of his love/ and not fear the inventory."
paul guest, "such as myself," notes from my body double

At the time, I was also struggling with the most severe period of incapacitating depression and suicidality thus far in my life, and others around me—including fellow transgender friends in my corner of t2 about their mental state—even suicidality. In some cases, these warnings work in personal narratives to focus the power of pain; trigger warnings in the most personal of writing spaces sometimes replace the titles of posts where writers narrate their everyday experiences with mental disability. For example, in a post I wrote in 2013 describing how graduate school was both driving me mad and giving me life, the title of my blog entry is simply a trigger warning.

OCTOBER 22, 2013

tw: suicide

i am writing this 45 minutes before i have to tutor for three hours and then ride the bus for an hour

Though I wasn't thinking about why I titled this post with a trigger warnings at the time, titling it as such signaled the content of the post (depression/suicidal ideation) and allowed me to write more frankly about my experiences. It allowed me to weep, openly.

The inventive power of trigger warnings has been harnessed in some writing classrooms, particularly creative writing classrooms. For example, Andrea Lawlor has found that trigger warnings can catalyze invention and creation when used collaboratively. In a roundtable facilitated by *Entropy Magazine*, she explains:

The last time I worked with students who wanted to use trigger warnings, in the Trans*/Queer Writing Group [...] one of my clever students created an anonymous collaborative document on the web (http://collabedit.com), so people could anonymously list things for which they wanted warning. We compiled our list, which was fairly short and comprised of pretty common categories (sexual violence, suicide, cutting, etc.), and people mostly did offer warnings when they included representations of these subjects in their pieces—which they did! including self-identified survivors, who sometimes wrote pieces which very graphically depicted some of the things on the trigger list[....] Trigger warnings in a workshop might allow student writers to write in MORE compelling, more honest, more powerful ways about our world, which includes trauma. (Milks et al.)

In Lawlor's classroom, students and the professor decided together if they were to use trigger warnings and what they would warn for. This collaborative approach helped open up conversations about how we write about trauma and how others experience what we write.

Trigger warnings are a tool that writers could use to navigate the "embodied writing" that personal narratives so frequently constitute. As William Banks describes, personal writing can replay violent experiences, which, "once inscribed on the body," are "difficult to erase and, as such, may control the readings we do of ourselves, our experiences, and others" (25). In many composition classrooms, we ask instructors to teach narrative writing and expect students to write personal narratives that explore their lives; Tara Wood has noted that requirements to write personal narrative that do not take into account experiences of disability may force students to write essays that reproduce the trope of "overcoming" disability or to "[re-enforce] the 'normal' body" (38). Trigger warnings can help instructors frame conversations about disability and traumatic experiences, de-emphasizing the "colonizing" effect that assigned personal narratives can have (Wood 38).

Trigger warnings are a way, particularly with narrative writing, to help make our writing more accessible to people with mental disabilities, whose bodies and minds continue, like a palimpsestic document, to be inscribed with layers of violence. Elizabeth Brewer, Cynthia Selfe, and Melanie Yergeau have argued that we must work to create "cultures of access" around writing, both in how composition and rhetoric scholars write to each other in academic contexts and in how we teach students to write (Yergeau et al.). They note that we should teach students how to make their writing "easily readable: by ensuring that they are in a digital form accessible by screen readers (and not simply a PDF with a single image unrecognizable to optical character scanners), by offering aural forms of such texts, or by providing large-print versions of such texts" (153). By using a trigger warning, a writer acknowledges that their narratives can cause bodily and mental pain. Beyond our responsibilities to our readers, trigger warnings may allow broader access to writers as they open a wider range of experiences to draw from in narrative.

Deterritorializations

If weeping, according to the *Oxford English Dictionary*, entails the "exudation or dripping of moisture generally," then weeping represents a practice that produces tangible matter which touches, rubs up against, or leaves marks on the surrounding landscape ("Weeping, n."). Weeping on a friend's shoulder in a moment of sadness leaves a wet splotch of residue on their shirtsleeves. When we weep we leak onto the persons, things, and environments around us. Likewise, trigger warnings allow student writers to impact the classrooms they move through by calling attention to difficult emotions. To reveal how trigger warnings grant students more authorial, creative power, the rest of this essay will outline concrete strategies for employing trigger warnings in rhetoric and writing classrooms.

Some professors, such as the AAUP Committee on Academic Freedom, have voiced fears that student trigger warning advocates are attempting to exert control in the classroom. To the extent that trigger warnings in higher education might, in the committee's words, "interfere" with "the choice of course materials and teaching methods," these concerns are not unfounded (Committee A). But is it strictly undesirable for students to shape their own learning practices? For theorists of feminist pedagogy, who have long been suspicious of hierarchical models of education, the goal of college instruction should be precisely to "recognize and encourage" students' "capacity" to "theorize and to recognize their own power" (Weiler 34). Trigger warnings work to equalize the traditionally hierarchical relationship between professors and students in the classroom.

With her permission, we offer a trigger warning statement authored by Tekla Hawkins, an assistant professor at the University of Texas Rio Grande Valley, as an example of the way trigger warnings can situate students and professors as equal participants in a writing classroom. Hawkins's policy statement was used in an undergraduate course taught at The University of Texas at Austin titled "Visual Rhetoric." On the course website, under the heading "Course Policies," Hawkins writes:

> This course uses trigger warnings as a matter of standard practice.
>
> Triggers are words or phrases that can cause extreme reactions. These reactions may range from anger or embarrassment to full panic attacks. Giving trigger warnings is required in many online communities, and is becoming more common in public spaces. Common triggers include but are not limited to: addiction (of any kind), self-harm (of any kind), child harm, sexual assault, and racism.
>
> Behind the link below[4] are some comments that might be triggering. As you can see, these are comments that might occur in casual conversation (as they are examples from on campus), and yet can still be harmful to others. Phrases and subjects you might be more familiar with as upsetting are descriptions of alcoholic behavior in a novel, victim blaming in a news story, or of course active threats of any kind. When addressing these kinds of topics in writing, put warnings near the top of your page or in the subject line. When addressing these kinds of topics in conversation, you can warn by saying "warning for racism" or something similar before you go on. This may seem odd at first, but becomes normalized very quickly.
>
> As in any humanities class we will be discussing texts that contain material about the hard questions faced by any culture; this is what makes them worth discussing. In general, triggers are the result of personal experiences. It is easy to be kind, and reactions to personal experiences are nothing to be ashamed of. [...] It is impossible to plan or warn for every exigency, but as a group, we can be sensitive about potentially sensitive discussions.

In this trigger warning statement, Hawkins acknowledges her responsibility as an instructor to accommodate students. She asks students, "as a group," to actively participate in creating a classroom that is inclusive to mentally disabled students. She and her students might make errors in this mutual project ("it is," she remarks, "impossible to plan or warn for every exigency"), but what's important in this trigger warning statement is not that mistakes are made but that the class engages in a good-faith effort to consider psychiatrically disabled students' needs. This statement also notes the power of casual and formalized language to shape attitudes towards mental disability. As Elizabeth Brewer notes, if "attitudes toward disability" represent "an integral part of what disability studies scholars are writing about when it comes to accessibility" (Yergeau et al.), then Hawkins's statement helps students develop reactions to disability that are thoughtful and nondiscriminatory.

Hawkins's course policy statement also underscores that trigger warnings constitute a writing practice which originated in online spaces. Trigger warnings are always in some way informed by their digital origins, and as such, debates surrounding the use of trigger warnings in university classrooms are tied to concerns of technological innovation and digital media production. Alex Reid speculates that social media's ability to "enable a wider audience" of readers for scholarly discourse might help "deterritorialize" academic thought and allow for a more "heterogeneous" group of individuals to consume it. Reid suggests that digital media holds the capacity to make scholarship more "accessible." Though he does not explicitly mention disability, we argue here that Reid's insight can be read as a disability insight. Trigger warnings' position as both an accessibility tool and a textual practice that emerged from the Internet offers an imperative for scholars to study disability and digital media together.

Reid concedes that, despite his vision that digital scholarship could allow for a more accessible public of readers of scholarly work, many academics are cautious with the "crowded space[s] of social media" for "fear" of being "exposed" or challenged. Student groups who argue for the inclusion of trigger warnings on university syllabi are harnessing a digital practice in order to critique academic norms and make academic spaces more accessible. To some extent, the blog posts we examine in this essay that speak against student-led accessibility efforts seem to desire a return to the traditional "scholarly identity and authority" that Reid sees digital scholarship potentially challenging. Trigger warnings *do* allow students to challenge professors' traditional authority. They represent a site where students are rejecting a passive role in the classroom.

Another concern persistently voiced by faculty is the fear that trigger warnings will censor course content relating to topics of race, gender, or sexuality. The seven authors of "Trigger Warnings are Flawed," for example, believe that if trigger warnings become "mandat[ory]" on college campuses, "faculty of color, queer faculty, and faculty teaching in gender/sexuality studies, [and] critical race theory" will be the likely targets of attempts to censor course material, putting such faculty at risk for administrative censure and attack (Freeman et al.). Such concerns have merit, especially in climates where faculty have drawn criticism for speaking openly against racism, homophobia, or class stratification.[5] Efforts will have to be made, therefore, to distinguish between moral or personal objections to reading specific course content and the fact of a text being difficult to access because of a disability issue.

Because trigger warnings point, unflinchingly, to pain and hurt, they position users as performing the wrong affect for the classroom, collective, or digital space; they defy the drive to be pleasant or decorous. Sara Ahmed explains that minority subjects—women, queer people, disabled people, and people of color—are often expected to appear happy, embodying "lightness, humor, and [shared] energy" (43) in order to cover over histories of oppression (87). Since trigger warnings frequently mark pain that is explicitly gendered or racialized, like rape or police violence, they perform the kind of work that Ahmed suggests is forbidden by dominant systems of oppression. Undoing interlocking oppressions, according to Ahmed, involves the work of "speak[ing] out about … unhappiness" (60) and "expos[ing] the bad feelings that get hidden, displaced, or neglected under public signs of joy" (65). Trigger warnings might, therefore, be more oriented to the intersectional than they are given credit for.

We believe that trigger warnings or assignments that take being triggered into account can balance the needs of disabled students with the teaching of race, sex, and gender. Typically, trigger warnings are an additive and not a subtractive phenomenon: professors *add* a "TW" to their syllabus or give a vocal trigger warning in class rather than excise material from a syllabus. Moreover, the institutional origin of most calls for trigger warnings undercuts fears that they will become "mand[atory]" on "college campuses." For example, while UCSB student resolution #805 encourages a university-wide "mandate" to include trigger warnings on syllabi, the lack of policy-making authority held by this particular student organization attests to the fact that resolution #805 would not be mandatory at all (A.S. Senate). At the end of the document, the authors of the resolution concede that they are "urg[ing]" for a policy change and intend to broach their demands with the university's Academic Senate—a group of professors who do hold policy-making power. The push for trigger warnings in this instance represents bottom-up student activism, not top-down institutional authority.

As an example of the ways in which professors can take triggering material into account while still teaching topics including race, sex, and gender, we turn to an assignment authored by Patricia Roberts-Miller, Professor of Rhetoric and Writing at UT-Austin. In her course "Principles of Rhetoric," Roberts-Miller requires three major papers. For each paper, she gives several possible topics that students can write on. Each topic includes material relating to race or gender. For example, the first assignment asks students to: "Use a concept from Jasinski [...] in order to write a rhetorical analysis of one of the following texts. Focus on one or two specific strategies in order to argue for your interpretation of the relationship between rhetorical strategies and authorial intention, historical context, intended audience, or impact." Roberts-Miller offers the following topics that students can explore:

David Walker's *Appeal To the Colored Citizens of the World*. Walker was a black abolitionist who wrote a text condemning slavery and arguing for self-defense. People in the South were terrified of this text, and called out the militia simply because copies of it were found.

Pickup artists. We looked in class at Steelball's website, and discussed the audience and interpellation—that, whatever Steele's actual audience, his intended audience is mildly misogynist, stuck in the 80s-90s, entitled, and determinist in human relations; he interpellates that audience to see themselves as simply needing more confidence, more misogyny, more entitlement, and more faith in determinism. How rhetorically different are more recent pickup artist sites such as http://www.puatraining.com/?

Ruth Benedict, "Races of Mankind." Benedict wrote this initially as a pamphlet for soldiers explaining what was wrong with Nazism (it's common for troops to be given such material). It was outrageously controversial, and pulled from circulation by southern Senators and members of Congress who objected to its criticism of racism. Yet, by modern standards, it feels fairly racist. What rhetorical concept explains Benedict's strategies and the outcome?

In our conversations with her, Roberts-Miller described designing the architecture of this assignment so as to avoid triggering students. The assignment given above *requires* students to grapple with anti-black racism, misogyny, sexualized violence, or anti-Semitism. However, as Roberts-Miller explains, if a student finds a particular topic especially difficult to write 1250 words on, they can choose a different one. Roberts-Miller's assignment therefore broaches racism, violence, and sexism while giving students multiple options for how they approach these topics. The assignment does not censor but, instead, puts each student in charge of her own education.

Conclusion

In our experience, many professors and faculty members are already doing the kind of work performed by trigger warnings—briefly notifying students that what they're about to read or watch might be graphically violent. The language of the "trigger warning," as we see it, explicitly frames this kind of notification within a disability context. If we, as educators of English, writing, and composition, truly hope to include psychiatrically disabled students in our classrooms, we must listen closely to these students. We must take seriously their stated needs, especially given the fraught nature of claiming disability and accessing accommodations.

Notes

1.In this article, we will use terms like "mentally ill," "psychiatrically or mentally disabled," and "Mad" to refer to persons who live with mental illness. We use "mentally disabled," in the manner of Margaret Price, to indicate people with a wide variety of mental illnesses and cognitive disabilities who are rarely brought together in medical contexts but who often find solidarity together in everyday life (2). "Mentally ill" denotes a kind of impairment that produces "suffering" as well as societal discrimination (Mollow 288, 287). The term "Mad," capitalized, refers Mad Pride, a "psychiatric disability activist" movement (Lewis 115).

2.If a professor does feel uncomfortable supporting a student in the middle of a trigger, using trigger warnings seems to be one way to ensure that the student doesn't have a traumatic reaction during their class.

3.We want to briefly note the importance we see in asking for consent to use personal blogs as a source for academic writing. As such, we have decided to reflect on our own online writing rather than selecting examples from our Internet networks.

4.At the bottom of her trigger warning statement, Hawkins includes a link to a separate page that contains phrases common to student parlance that might be triggering.

5.For example, English professor William S. Penn was suspended from his post at Michigan State University after critiquing racism in the U.S. Republican party in 2013; in 2012 theologian Tina Beattie was dis-invited from appearing for a lecture at the University of San Diego because of her advocacy for gay marriage; and in 2013 College of the Mainland in Texas fired tenured political science professor David Michael Smith because, many speculate, of his vocal support of employee's rights.

Works Cited

Ahmed, Sara. *The Promise of Happiness*. Durham: Duke UP, 2010. Print.

A.S. Senate. "A Resolution to Mandate Warnings For Triggering Content in Academic Settings (02262014:61)." *A.S. Senate*. UCSB, 25 Feb. 2014. Web. 22 Aug. 2014

Banks, William P. "Written through the Body: Disruptions and 'Personal' Writing." *College English* 66.1 (2003): 21-40. Print.

Bernhardt, Stephen A. "The Shape of Texts to Come: The Texture of Print on Screens." *College Composition and Communication* 44.2 (1993): 151-175. Print.

Boyd, Julia A. *Can I Get a Witness?: For Sisters when the Blues is More Than a Song*. New York: Dutton, 1998. Print.

Butler, Judith. *Undoing Gender*. New York: Routledge, 2004. Print.

Committee A on Academic Freedom and Tenure. "On Trigger Warnings." *American Association of University Professors*. AAUP, Aug. 2014. Web. 29 Jun. 2015.

Danquah, Meri Nana-Ama. *Willow Weep for Me: A Black Woman's Journey Through Depression*. New York: Ballantine, 1998. Print.

Freeman, Elizabeth, Brian Herrera, Nat Hurley, Homay King, Dana Luciano, Dana Seitler, and Patricia White. "Trigger Warnings Are Flawed." *Inside Higher Ed*. Inside Higher Ed., 29 May 2014. Web. 4 Jul. 2014.

Foucault, Michel. *The History of Sexuality, Volume 1: An Introduction*. New York: Vintage Books, 1990. Print.

Gunn, Joshua. "On Recording Performance or Speech, the Cry, and the Anxiety of the Fix." *Liminalities: A Journal of Performance Studies* 7.3 (2011): 1-30. Print.

Halberstam, Jack. "You Are Triggering me! The Neo-Liberal Rhetoric of Harm, Danger and Trauma." *Bully Bloggers*. Bully Bloggers, 5 Jul. 2014. Web. 22 Aug. 2014.

Hawkins, Tekla. "Course Policies." *rhe 315: visual rhetoric spring 2015*. Tekla Hawkins, 2015. Web. 22 Oct. 2015.

Jarvie, Jenny. "Trigger Happy." *New Republic*. The New Republic, 3 Mar. 2014. Web. 24 Jun. 2015.

Johnson, Jenell. "The Skeleton on the Couch: The Eagleton Affair, Rhetorical Disability, and the Stigma of Mental Illness." *Rhetoric Society Quarterly* 40.5 (2010): 459-478. Print.

Kafai, Shayda. "The Mad Border Body: A Political In-Betweeness." *Disability Studies Quarterly* 33.1 (2013): n. pag. Web. 26 Aug. 2014.
Kipnis, Laura. "Sexual Paranoia Strikes Academe." *The Chronicle of Higher Education*. The Chronicle of Higher Education, 27 Feb. 2015. Web. 24 Jun. 2015.
Lewis, Bradley. "A Mad Fight: Psychiatry and Disability Activism." *The Disability Studies Reader*. 4th ed. Ed. Lennard J. Davis. New York: Routledge, 2013. 115-131. Print.
Livingston, Kathleen Ann. "On Rage, Same, 'Realness,' and Accountability to Survivors." *Harlot* 12 (2014): n. pag. Web. 24 Jun. 2015.
Milks, Megan, CAConrad, Jos A. Charles, Andrea Lawlor, Sarah Schulman, Aishah Shahidah Simmons, and Anna Joy Springer. "On Trigger Warnings, Part I: In the Creative Writing Classroom." *Entropy*. Entropy, 14 Apr. 2014. Web. 22 Aug. 2014.\
Mollow, Anna. "'When *Black* Women Start Going on Prozac…': The Politics of Race, Gender, and Emotional Distress in Meri Nana-Ama Danquah's *Willow Weep for Me*." *The Disability Studies Reader*. 2nd ed. Ed. Lennard J. Davis. New York: Routledge, 2006.283-299. Print.
Muñoz, José Esteban. "Ephemera as Evidence: Introductory Notes to Queer Acts." *Women and Performance: A Journal of Feminist Theory* 8.2 (1996): 5-16. Print.
"On Trigger Warnings." *AAUP.org*. American Association of University Professors, Aug. 2014. Web. 25 Jun. 2015.
Penzel, Fred. *Obsessive-Compulsive Disorders: A Complete Guide to Getting Well and Staying Well*. Oxford: Oxford UP, 2000. Print.
Prendergast, Catherine. "The Fighting Style: Reading the Unabomber's Strunk and White." *College English* 72.1 (2009): 10-28. Print.
---. "On the Rhetorics of Mental Disability." *Embodied Rhetorics: Disability in Language and Culture*. Ed. James C. Wilson and Cynthia Lewiecki-Wilson. Carbondale, IL: Southern Illinois UP, 2001. 45-60. Print.
Price, Margaret. *Mad at School: Rhetorics of Mental Disability and Academic Life*. Ann Arbor: U of Michigan P, 2011. Print.
Prior, Karen Swallow. "'Empathetically Correct' is the New Politically Correct." *The Atlantic*. The Atlantic Monthly Group, 23 May 2014. Web. 24 Jun. 2015.
Reid, Alex. "Exposing Assemblages: Unlikely Communities of Digital Scholarship, Video, and Social Networks." *Enculturation* 8 (2010): n. pag. Web. 26 Aug. 2014.
Siebers, Tobin. *Disability Theory*. Ann Arbor: U of Michigan P, 2008. Print.
"Support Resources for Faculty." *Office of Equity Concerns*. Oberlin College, n.d. Web. 2 May 2014.

The Times Editorial Board. "Warning: College Students, This Editorial May Upset You." *Los Angeles Times*. Los Angeles Times Media Group, 31 Mar. 2014. Web. 24 Jun. 2015.

"Weep, n." *OED Online*. Oxford: Oxford UP, 2015. Web. 24 Jun. 2015.

"Weep, v." *OED Online*. Oxford: Oxford UP, 2015. Web. 24 Jun. 2015.

"Weeping, n." *OED Online*. Oxford: Oxford UP, 2015. Web. 24 Jun. 2015.

"Weepy, adj." *OED Online*. Oxford: Oxford UP, 2015. Web. 24 Jun. 2015.

Weiler, Kathleen. "Friere and a Feminist Pedagogy of Difference." *Debates and Issues in Feminist Research and Pedagogy: A Reader*. Ed. Janet Holland, Maud Blair, and Sue Sheldon. Philadelphia: Multilingual Matters, 1995. 23-44. Print.

Wood, Tara. "Overcoming Rhetoric: Forced Disclosure and the Colonizing Ethic of Evaluating Personal Essays."*Open Words: Access and English Studies* 5 (2011): 38-52. Web. 2 Nov. 2015.

Wythe, Philip. "Trigger Warnings Needed in Classroom." *The Daily Targum*. Rutgers University, 18 Feb. 2014. Web. 22 Aug. 2014.

Yergeau, Melanie. "Disable All the Things: On Affect, Metadata, & Audience." Computers and Writing Annual Conference. Washington State University, Pullman, WA. 6 Jun. 2014. Keynote Address.

Yergeau, Melanie, Elizabeth Brewer, Stephanie Kerschbaum, Sushil K. Oswal, Margaret Price, Cynthia L. Selfe, Michael J. Salvo, and Franny Howes. "Multimodality In Motion: Disability and Kairotic Spaces." *Kairos: A Journal of Rhetoric, Technology, and Pedagogy* 18.1 (2013): n. pag. Web. 25 Jun. 2015.

HARLOT: A REVEALING LOOK AT THE ARTS OF PERSUASION

Harlot: A Revealing Look at the Arts of Persuasion is a peer-reviewed digital journal dedicated to exploring

Harlot is on the Web at http://harlotofthearts.org/

rhetoric in everyday life. The journal's title gestures toward historical references to rhetoric as "the harlot of the arts," a pejorative perspective that Harlot seeks to challenge. The mission of the journal is to bridge rhetorical scholarship and popular discourse by creating a space for critical—but inclusive and informal—conversations about rhetoric amongst diverse publics. To that end, its peer review process includes reviewers from within and outside academic contexts who prioritize collaboration and revision; accepted submissions are typically succinct, savvy, and richly mediated.

Crafting Change: Practicing Activism in Contemporary Australia

In "Crafting Change," Fitzpatrick and Kontturi explore the rhetorical potential of the craftivism movement, in which makers work together to create positive change. The authors' layered positions as scholars, artists, and activists enrich the discussions of their own practices. Tal explains her strategic use of textiles, a personal legacy from her grandmother, to trigger political moments; Katve-Kaisa reflects on two very different communal crafting projects as embodied, relational activism. Together, their work blurs conventional lines among theory, practice, art, and scholarship. Though firmly rooted in context, it transcends disciplines and connects makers through shared hope "that small and soft actions can lead to political change." In this way, "Crafting Change" expands the audience's understanding of rhetorical craft and criticism.

Crafting Change: Practicing Activism in Contemporary Australia

Tal Fitzpatrick and Katve-Kaisa Kontturi

This article brings together thoughts and practices of two Melbourne-based women working across the fields of craftivism, practice-led research and contemporary art history. While introducing and analysing Australian craft(ivist) projects, this article also suggests new concepts useful in tackling the contemporary phenomenon of craft activism.

When understood conventionally, activism is regularly associated with loud and ardent messages, outspoken charismatic leaders, and forms of protest such as mass demonstrations, processions, rallies, strikes, and sit-ins. These actions are often seen as too confrontational and antagonistic, as well as futile, as they are understood rarely to result in the outcomes hoped for (Corbett, 2013). Simultaneously, online activism has exploded, with great numbers of people turning towards digital strategies such as e-petitions, social media awareness-raising campaigns, crowd-sourcing, and online fundraising for acting on their values. However, while these forms of digital engagement attract a significant number of people, some question how well online activism translates into real-world action. The growing skepticism around the possibility of driving real-world change using online strategies alone has given rise to terms such as "clicktivism" and "slacktivism" (Parks, 2013). These terms further emphasize the need to activate activism anew, to find novel ways to engage people with issues of social, political, and environmental justice.

Driven by the notion that sustainable change comes about as a result of the compound effect of many small actions and ideas that over time become a groundswell of opinion, craftivism looks to engage with anyone and everyone in conversation and reflection around critical issues and wicked problems.

In the context of this shift away from both antagonistic and entirely digital forms of activism, we have witnessed the emergence of a new form. This peculiar form of activism looks to affect real-world change through a movement that combines the principles of social, political, and environmental justice with individual creativity, the act of making by hand, the power of connecting with other like-minded people, and a spirit of kindness, generosity, and joy.

The movement we speak of is **craftivism!**

Over the past ten years craftivism has gained global traction: individual creations, craft collectives and large-scale projects have received a lot of attention both within and outside the world of activism. The movement encompasses different entanglements of craft and activism, from knitting scarves for the homeless (SWAP; Knitting for Brisbane's Needy; KOGO), making quilts for children in hospital (Inspiration Quilts, 2014; Quilts for Kids, 2015; Victorian Quilters Inc. Australia; Blanket Lovez, 2015), claiming the streets for women (Just, 2014), and yarn-bombing tanks (Moore & Prain, 2009), creatively reusing marine waste in order to drive a thriving social enterprise in Kenya (Sole, 2015), or making fluffy toy vaginas and flinging them over power lines as a strategy for challenging the censorship of female genitalia (Corbett, 2014). Driven by the notion that sustainable change comes about as a result of the compound effect of many small actions and ideas that over time become a groundswell of opinion, craftivism looks to engage with anyone and everyone in conversation and reflection around critical issues and wicked problems.

Margaret Mayhew with her rugs at the Refugees Are Welcome rally, October 2014. Photo: Katve-Kaisa Kontturi

Our essay situates itself in contemporary Australia, where questions of postcolonialism and multiculturalism—especially the treatment of Indigenous people, asylum seekers, and immigrants—are burning. Other popular craftivist issues encompass gender and climate change. These are the issues around which the craft projects we introduce in this essay have been created. Our contribution is both practical and theoretical. It draws on personal experience with and participation in a selected set of craft projects, and, using these as case studies, rethinks and widens the concept and practice of craftivism. This approach means that any theoretical or conceptual suggestions we offer grow from the practices of making.

Also, our positions within the field of craftivism are multiple and thus offer us a rich starting point for evaluation. Tal Fitzpatrick is a textile artist, craftivist, and community development worker currently undertaking a practice-based PhD on Craftivism and the Political Moment. Katve-Kaisa Kontturi, for her part, is a research fellow and curator interested in how fabrics—including knitted, crocheted, and stitched ones—can facilitate cultural relations.

To locate our work in the political landscape of Australia and to illustrate contemporary craftivism, let's start with a practical example.

Knit Your Revolt is a voluntary, Australia-based network of crafters that aims to raise awareness around issues relating to gender and the treatment of asylum seekers by the current right-wing, neoliberal government headed, until very recently, by Tony Abbott (Australia's Prime Minister at the time of writing. He was deposed this month in a leadership spill). *Knit Your Revolt* operates as a loose network of "rad crafters" who are not aligned with any political or other organization, but instead get organized via social media. Over the past two years their knitted protest banners, public performances, and crafty interventions have been causing a stir in several major cities across Australia, including Canberra, the nation's capital.

Two craftivists from Knit Your Revolt hold up knitted banners in front of Parliament House in Canberra, February 2015. Photo: Knit Your Revolt, https://www.facebook.com/KnitYourRevolt

In March 2015, on International Women's Day, *Knit Your Revolt* infamously crashed an official Women's Day even—hosted by then-Prime Minister Tony Abbott, who was also the Minister for Women—bafflingly held at a men's-only club in Brisbane (SBS, 2015, Mar 6). The activists organized a creative parade to turn up at the venue. Women and men adorned in colorful knitted balaclavas, beards, and chains held up signs that read: "Minister for Women: Not in my name!" and "Knit Your Revolt: Chain Gang of Broken Hearts and Dreams" (SBS, 2015, Mar 6). The protest achieved national media coverage and resulted in a broader debate around misogynist politics.

The craftivist projects introduced and analyzed in our essay are concerned with this softening, engaging power of materials and processes of making.

Through their integration of craft and adversarial political activism, *Knit Your Revolt* has been able to create a space where dissenting voices are not so easily closed down or dismissed by the media. Indeed, the group has been repeatedly successful in gaining positive media coverage and support for their campaigns. The ability to use craft to soften the blow of dissent is a unique strength of the craftivist movement. As UK artist, activist, and craftswoman Inga Hamilton (2010) explains, "All over the world, activists take a stand against moral injustice and social inadequacies. The very nature of fighting for justice can lead to aggression and tense situations, and artwork can bring powerful, positive messages to the community, but when craft gets involved, it seems to soften the blow so the message is both more heartfelt and quick-witted" (p. 27).

The craftivist projects introduced and analyzed in our essay are concerned with this softening, engaging power of materials and processes of making. Some are more outspokenly political than others. However, all rely on the idea that small and soft actions can lead to political change.

Tal will begin by introducing some of her symbol-filled soft wall hangings and continue by drawing a connection between her grandmother's textile art and her own current craftivist practice, as well as discussing their specific means of political action. Then Katve-Kaisa will reflect on her experiences of participating in two different craft-based workshops that perhaps exceed the boundaries of traditional activism. In this way, our essay widens the understanding of craftivism, both in terms of its history and as a mode of activist practice.

Tal Fitzpatrick at the Black Friday rally, Melbourne, March 2015. Photos: anonymous via Black Friday Rally Facebook page.

Making Space for Opinion | by Tal Fitzpatrick

My craftivist practice is strongly grounded in the feminist history of using textile art as a strategy for political action. Like countless women before me (Perry, 1999), I use textile-based craft practices such as appliqué quilting and embroidery to create objects and artworks with a message. For me, the power of these craft objects lies both in their aesthetic, tactile qualities and in the fact that they are, in many ways, everyday functional objects. This power is amplified by the subversive use of crafts, and their association with feminine domesticity and private life, to comment publicly upon politics, power, and public life—all of which are traditionally associated with masculinity (Parker, 2010).

Recently, I made two quilted wall hangings: one with the words "No Justice No Peace" appliquéd onto it as a response to the #BlackLivesMatter campaign, and the other with the words "Fuck your Patriarchy." I was compelled to make these works because of an overwhelming sense of outrage and despair in the face of current world events. As a maker, creating these works provided me with an avenue for addressing my own feelings of helplessness. Through the process of making, I find that I'm able to channel my rage into something constructive that can be shared with others who may (or may not) feel the same way. Since making these hangings, I've used them as protest banners that I take to public rallies in Melbourne, Australia, where I live. For example, in March 2015 I used them in a Black Friday rally against the forced closure of rural Aboriginal communities in Western Australia.

An important strategy for inciting people to start asking questions through my practice is sewing together different layers of meaning, associations, and cultural references.

While walking in public with these works, I notice that they attract special attention because of their materiality and the obvious amount of time that has gone into making them. People regularly stop me to ask: Did you make these? What do they mean? While some people come up to tell me why they like them, even more share a personal story about their own connections with the practice of craft. On the other hand, when these works were hanging in a community gallery, I observed people being very offended by the use of bad language. Others politely asked around as to what the word "patriarchy" meant. Whatever the response was, these moments where strangers feel compelled to interact and reflect can be understood as points of rupture where a kind of political space is opened up, if only briefly.

For Betsy Greer, writer, maker, and editor of *Craftivism: The Art of Craft and Activism* (2014), the very essence of craftivism lies in "creating something that gets people to ask questions; we invite others to join a conversation about the social and political intensions of our creations. Unlike more traditional forms of activism, which can be polarizing, there is a back-and-forth in craftivism ... It turns us, as well as our work, into vessels of change" (p. 8).

An important strategy for inciting people to start asking questions through my practice is sewing together different layers of meaning, associations, and cultural references. I do this using not just written language, but also visual cues, metaphors, and symbolism, combining different textures and materials to form an enticing tactile surface. This way, rather than glancing over the written words and responding only to the text, people are enticed to engage with other senses and ways of knowing: they are compelled to touch and feel with their hands, to dwell with their eyes. In this manner, the crafted works trigger memories, emotions, and associations that provide multiple entry points to the work.

This strategy of layering meaning in order to make a political work more intriguing is something I learned from my grandmother, textile artist Dawn Fitzpatrick. Over a period of thirty years, starting in the mid-1970s, Dawn made large-scale figurative textile wall hangings, a practice she referred to as "cloth art." Her work, which was often political and almost always incorporated symbolism relating to her own faith, combined quilting, patchwork, machine embroidery, appliqué, and drawing and painting techniques.

Dawn Fitzpatrick, *The Slide, Ein Karem* (1992) Photo: Tal Fitzpatrick

One of Dawn's many politically intriguing works is known as *The Slide, Ein Karem*. This hanging depicts the unique sculptural slides at a playground in Jerusalem, where two Jewish mothers were stabbed to death by an Arab while waiting for their children. This piece was her "soft" response to a situation in which authorities refused to erect a memorial plaque for the murdered women, as "innocence must prevail, not bitter memories" (Fitzpatrick, 2010). Dawn depicts the children on the slides as butterflies, writing: "The butterfly can be a symbol of rebirth, an emblem of the soul fluttering free." By way of cloth art, she was able to create a different kind of memorial to the memory of this tragedy. This hanging acts as a touchstone, a memory device for sharing a story that was too traumatic and too politically fraught to enshrine into words on a plaque. Yet at the same time, depending on how many of the symbols and clues you can read in the work, the full story it tells is likely to entirely escape you.

Tal Fitzpatrick, *Fuck Your Patriarchy* (2014), 90cm x 100 cm, machine-quilted wall hanging made using new and recycled materials and fabric marker. Photo: Tal Fitzpatrick

Like Dawn, I look to create hangings that patch together different symbols, textures and significance in order to allow audiences to weave their own meaning into the work. In my "Fuck Your Patriarchy" hanging, there are, among other things, biblical symbols—such the apple (core), the snake, and the "unclean" raven, which Noah sent out from the ark, but which never returned—and butterflies. It is here, in this space of ambiguity, confusion, and conflict, that the potency for discussion inspired by the work is found: What does this mean? What is the story behind this work? Why did someone take the time to make it? These are questions that can only be resolved through conversation.

Philosopher and political theorist Jacques Rancière's (2009) thinking can help us to articulate how such an approach to activism might be effective. According to Rancière, the goal of the activist is to open a space for inquiry where anyone can speak as long as they are aware that whatever they say can and will be questioned and challenged by others. These open spaces for conversation are those where we feel empowered to share our opinion. Rancière describes these temporal spaces as *political moments*: "A political moment occurs when the temporality of consensus is disrupted. It occurs when a force is capable of exposing the imagination of the relevant community and of contrasting it with a different configuration of the relationship of each individual to everyone else" (p. ix).

However, these political moments, where political debate and what Rancière calls "dissensus" are tolerated, are becoming increasingly hard to come by in societies fixated on consensus. Furthermore, political moments are further delegitimized because they are centered around opinion, and since Plato, "opinion" has largely been understood as the opposite of thought. To reclaim the importance of opinion, Rancière argues:

Opinion is actually the space in which the possibilities of thought and the mode of community these possibilities define are determined. Opinion is not a homogenous space for the lowest form of thought, but rather a space in which to debate what can be thought under particular circumstances and what the consequences of this thought might be. (p. ix)

For craftivists, the implications of this celebration of creativity and individual opinion are that there is great power in creating engaging spaces where a diverse cross-section of people can express their opinions and contribute to a broader debate. As Greer explains, "The creation of things by hand leads to a better understanding of democracy, because it reminds us that we have power" (p. 8). So while some might criticize craftivism for being too "nice" or too gentle, for me, craftivism is effective precisely because it avoids antagonism in its preference for physical and material-based processes for exchanging opinions.

As a craftivist, I'm not so much interested in trying to convince people to think or behave in a specific way. Rather, I'm more concerned with how my material practice can trigger *political moments*—or spaces where opinions can be expressed, stories told, and dissensus explored. For me, at its core, craftivism is about reclaiming and restoring our own political agency through a process of making opinionated works that encourage people to ask questions and engage with different ideas and with each other. It is an imaginative and creative force capable of bringing about real-world change, however small it may be.

Katve-Kaisa Kontturi knitting with Tjanpi Desert Weavers and working on the Big Knitted Welcome Mat community project. Photos: Katve-Kaisa Kontturi (left) and Kate Just (right)

Crafting Relational Activism |
by Katve-Kaisa Kontturi

In this section, I continue to widen the conventional understanding of contemporary craftivism by reflecting on two projects that, in their own ways, made me rethink what can be thought of as activist practice. In July 2015 I took part in a basket-weaving master class run by Tjanpi Desert Weavers at the Victorian College of the Arts, University of Melbourne. The Tjanpi Desert Weavers are a group of Indigenous Australian women from the Central Desert, the so-called Red Center. Like people who are invited to give master classes usually are, these women are masters of a certain technique: basket-weaving. They excel in fiber art.[1] They held the class just before the opening of the Tarrawarra Biennial, a contemporary art exhibition organized in co-operation with the prestigious Melbourne Art Fair, in which they were likewise invited to participate alongside major Australian artists. This year, their work was also presented at the Australian Pavilion during the Venice Biennale.

Tjanpi Desert Weavers with their work at the completion of the Tarra Warra Camp. Front left to right: Niningka Lewis, Yangi Yangi Fox, Roma butler, Molly Miller, Rene Kulitja. Back left to right: Fiona Hall, Mary Pan, Nyanu Watson, Angaliya Nelson. Photo by Jo Foster. 2014. Copyright Tjanpi Desert Weavers, NPY Women's Council.

When we as art students and teacher-researchers entered the class, we didn't quite know what to expect. The briefing was very brief indeed: we learned that our teachers were in Melbourne for the first time and that for our teachers, Melbourne felt as outback as their desert was to us. They had travelled thousands of kilometers, and they didn't speak much English. Also, they had brought all the materials we needed with them: the grass we would use had grown in the red desert ground.

There were no verbal instructions or concrete illustrations of how to proceed and no technologies involved, other than the needles passed to us, and grass and fiber ubiquitously piled around us. I sat next to a teacher called Molly, and without many words, she grabbed some fiber and started a basket by making the first knot. Then she began to integrate the grass by weaving the fiber around it: there was a basket silently in the making.

Fiber art in the making. Photo: Katve-Kaisa Kontturi

To learn how to weave, we couldn't but follow our teacher's skillful hands—her body moving with the basket in becoming. Observing Molly and other students around me, I learned a lot. We worked in almost complete silence; we didn't chat, we didn't make friends as one often does when crafting together. In fact, I don't even remember the faces of my fellow crafters very well. Individuals were not really the issue: all we did was to focus on learning to work with the fiber, to feel the fiber, and to add the grass filling to make the basket beautifully round. We learned by making and following each other and our teacher weaving fiber. By doing that, we learned more than just how to make baskets. Working side by side, elbow to elbow, rhythmically repeating the phases of basket-making, we wove not only certain fiber objects, but each other, closer together.

Of course, inequalities dividing Indigenous and non-Indigenous Australians could not possibly be overcome during one or two master classes. But still, something happened: the sensation of possibility through collaboration was felt as our bodies worked closely together, learning from each other. This is what I would call a subtle sort of relational activism, one based not on grand gestures or loud demands, but on bodily relatedness (Manning, 2009; Massumi, 2011) and hence on the increasing feeling of communality.

Some weeks after participating in the Tjanpi Desert Weavers' master class, I participated in another community-based craft project led by Kate Just, a US-born contemporary artist living in Melbourne, who specializes in knitted sculptures. The project took place in and was funded by the City of Greater Dandenong, which, since 2002, has been one of Australia's official "refugee welcome zones." The aim of this public project was to bring together local people of multiple ethnic backgrounds by collaboratively producing a Big Knitted Welcome Mat (the title of the project).

Knitting the big welcome mat. Photo: Kate Just

I joined the project when it had already begun, so I benefitted from being surrounded by people who already knew what they were doing. I hadn't knitted for years, and my sole language of knitting was Finnish. Therefore, I struggled a bit to get going and became all the more confused when I realized that knitting terms also differed according to American and Australian/British conventions. But soon the confusion transformed into an invigorating discussion of how "knit" and "purl" were expressed in different languages, and when and how it was that we had learned to knit—whether the process took place in Australia, Chile, Finland, Malta, Italy, Singapore, Russia, or China. Side by side and each in their particular way, we knitted together, and also learned from each other. But this time, we were not silent. As we sat and knitted, we chatted about our everyday practices and differences in our lives. The giant doormat, with its more than 100 squares of multiple textures and different stitches, bore witness to this process of discovering our differences.

A close-up of the welcome mat. Photo: Kate Just

When I thought about how the mat had come to embody diversity, difference, and close connection, I remembered how we had received clear instructions of what to do. Indeed, in comparison to the Tjanpi Desert Weavers' master class, we were provided with a detailed how-to: the red squares were supposed to be 20 x 20 cm in size, and 104 of them were needed to construct the mat. Although there were clear rules, I didn't feel restricted. Later, I understood that knitting instructions worked as "enabling constraints." In Erin Manning (2013) and Brian Massumi's (2010) relational philosophy, "enabling constraint" means something that triggers action and does not restrict creativity, but rather, encourages it within certain limits.

It was through these enabling constraints that our knitting project brought together bodies of women of different ages and of multiple ethnic and social backgrounds in a way that wouldn't have been otherwise possible. It was when we were putting the mat together and attaching the letters to form the word "welcome" that we worked closest together. We had to climb to the table, stretch our arms, and twist our necks. Without the project, and its material restrictions, we would never have worked in such close bodily proximity. That is, we wouldn't have learned to relate our bodies to each other in such an intimate manner while remaining relative strangers to each other. This comes close to Joanne Turney's (2009) claim in *The Culture of Knitting* that "knitting is a great leveler: the one activity or practice that can bring people together and overcome difference, creating harmonious environments in which sociability is at the forefront" (p. 144).

Working in close proximity. Photo: Kate Just

Although I share Turney's genuinely affirmative understanding of what communal crafting *can do*, there are significant differences in our thinking. I would not claim that crafting can overcome differences or create harmony. Rather, if a greater extent of communality is achieved, it is because people have learned to open their individual bodies and to feel how their relation to other bodies is both constitutive and indispensable. This does not erase differences, but rather, teaches us how we can cope with them, *relate* to them, live with them towards the future. This is how craftivism as relational activism works.

Brief Moments, Slow Processes, Subtle Relations: Craftivism as Micropolitics

In this essay, we have provided a glimpse into some of the diverse forms of craft-based activism currently being practiced in Australia. As practitioners and participants, we have taken part in rallies, created visually complex wall hangings, and attended a basket-weaving master class and a community knitting project. While the adversarial style of criticism typical of many "rad crafters" is not present in the projects we have introduced, we nevertheless understand them as craftivist practices. The reason for this is that they all create space and possibilities for change, and therefore for the imagining and making of a better world, by means of crafting.

What we want to suggest is that craftivism as micropolitics is as political as any macro political action such as large-scale demonstrations or the implementation of a new law.

From *Knit Your Revolt*'s media-attracting activism that bursts with witty slogans highlighted by bright colours to the quiet process of being taught to weave baskets by the Tjanpi Desert Weavers, what brings the projects together is their ability to open up political moments. Whereas for Rancière, political moments are first and foremost *temporal* spaces for opinions to be expressed and debates provoked, we want to emphasize that the material-physical practice and tactile materials of craft-making are indispensable for these moments to occur. However, as we have described, in crafting and thinking with craft objects, we are dealing with a very specific kind of materiality: a materiality that is felt as it triggers memories and opinions as bodies open up for collaboration, and as sensations of possibility for mutual futures arise between bodies closely relating to one other.

In our understanding, the repetitive, rhythmic, and time-consuming movement indispensable for crafting—whether communal or individual, or involving machine-sewing, embroidery, basket-making, crocheting, or knitting—is not only thoroughly material, but relational. This sort of conception of materiality as *(micro)movement* is characteristic of new materialist thinking. Instead of grand-scale and calculable transformations in society, new materialism looks for tiny or almost imperceptible actions, and believes in their potential to produce change (van Dolphijn & van der Tuin, 2013; Kontturi, 2014). This focus and belief in the transformative power of brief political moments, slow repetitive processes, and subtle yet sensible relations is called *micropolitics*.

What we want to suggest is that craftivism as micropolitics is as political as any macro political action such as large-scale demonstrations or the implementation of a new law. Its political efficacy lies in its ability to engage with diverse groups of people and provide them with a sustainable way of interacting, communicating, and taking action with one another.

Notes

1. In addition to painting, fiber art is one of major sources of income for Indigenous Australian communities, which is, understandably, a controversial issue in itself; they have no choice but to produce art that sells well, that looks Aboriginal enough and is of economic value on the art market. However, Tjanpi Desert Weavers art is said to be truly innovative, therefore exceeding any presumptions of what their art should look like. See Tiriki Onus and Eugenia Flynn and Diane Moon.

References

Blanket Lovez. (2015). Blanket Lovez. Retrieved from www.blanktlovez.com.
Corbett, Sarah. (2014). Interview with Sarah Corbett of the Craftivist Collective. In Greer, Betty (Ed.) *Craftivism: The Art of Craft and Activism* (pp. 203-212). Vancouver: Arsenal Pulp Press.
Fitzpatrick, Dawn & McGorman, Lee. (1975). *Cloth Art* [24 slides] Sydney: Crafts Council of Australia.
Fitzpatrick, Dawn. (2010). *Inside the gates of Jerusalem*. Unpublished Manuscript. Tal Fitzpatrick's personal archives.
Greer, Betty. (2014). Knitting craftivism: From my sofa to yours. In Greer, Betty (Ed). *Craftivism: The Art of Craft and Activism* (pp. 24-36). Vancouver: Arsenal Pulp Press.
Hamilton, Inga. (2014). Daily narratives and enduring images: The love encased by craft. In Greer, Betty (Ed.) *Craftivism: The Art of Craft and Activism* (pp. 24-36). Vancouver: Arsenal Pulp Press.
Inspiration Quilts. (2014). *Inspiration quilts*. Retrieved from www.inspirationalquilts.com.au/donations.html
Just, Kate. (2014). *Just's Hope and Safe project*. Retrieved from http://www.katejust.com/hope-safe
Knit One Give One. (n.d.). *Knit one give one*. Retrieved from www.knitonegiveone.org
Knitting for Brisbane's Needy. (n.d.). *Knitting for Brisbane's needy*. Retrieved from www.knittingforbrisbanesneedy.com.au
Kontturi, Katve-Kaisa. (2014). Moving matters of contemporary art: Three new materialist propositions. *AM: Journal of Art and Media Studies*. 5.
Manning, Erin. (2009). *Relationscapes: Movement, art, philosophy*. Minneapolis: Minnesota University Press.
Manning, Erin. (2013). *Always more than one*. Durham and London: Duke University Press.
Manning, Erin & Massumi, Brian. (2014). *Thought in the act: Passages in the ecology of experience*. Minneapolis: Minnesota University Press.

Massumi, Brian. (2010). On critique. Inflexions 4 Retrieved from www.inflexions.org/n4_t_massumihtml.html.
Massumi, Brian. (2011). *Semblance and event: Activist philosophy and the occurrent arts.* Minneapolis: University of Minnesota Press.
Moon, Diane. (2009). *Floating life: Contemporary Aboriginal fibre art.* South Brisbane: Queensland Art Gallery.
Moore, Mandy & Prain, Leanne. (2009). *Yarn bombing: The art of crochet and knit graffiti.* Vancouver: Arsenal Pulp Press.
Onus, Tiriki & Flynn, Eugenia. (2014, Aug 13). The Tjanpi desert weavers show us that traditional craft is art. *The Conversation.* Retrieved from http://theconversation.com/the-tjanpi-desert-weavers-show-us-that-traditional-craft-is-art-30243
Park, Andy. (2013 Nov 18). Clicktivism: Why social media is not good for charity. *The Feed, SBS online.*
Parker, Rozsika. (2010). *Subversive stitch: Embroidery and the making of the feminine.* London: I. B. Tauris.
Perry, Gillian. (1999). *Gender and art: Art and its histories series.* New Haven: Yale University Press.
Quilts for Kids. (2015). Quilts for kids. Retrieved from http:www.quiltsforkids.org/volunteer/
Rancière, Jacques. (2009). *Moments Politiques: Interventions 1977–2009.* New York: Seven Stories Press.
SBS (2015, March 6). Female protesters dressed as men try to crash LNP event. *SBS Online.* Retrieved from www.sbs.com.au/news/article/2015/03/06/female-protesters-dressed-men-try-crash-lnp-event.
Scarves with a Purpose. (n.d.). Scarves with a purpose. Retrieved from www.scarveswithapurpose.com
Sole, Ocean. (2015). Cleaning beaches, creating masterpieces. *Ocean Sole.* Retrieved from www.ocean-sole.com.
Tarrawarra Biennial 2014: Whisper in My Mask. Tarrawarra Museum of Art. Retrieved from ww.twma.com.au/exhibition/tarrawarra-biennial-2014-whisper-in-my-mask/
Turney, Joanne. (2009). *The culture of knitting.* New York: Berg Publishers.
van Dolphijn, Rick & van der Tuin, Iris. (2009). *New materialism: Interviews & cartographies.* Open Humanities Press.
Victorian Quilters Inc. Australia. (n.d.) Victorian Quilters, Inc. Australia. Retrieved from www.victorianquilters.org.

Tal Fitzpatrick is a Melbourne-based textile artist, craftivist, and community development worker who is currently completing a PhD with the Centre for Cultural Partnerships at the Victorian College of the Arts, University of Melbourne. Having taken up her paternal grandmothers' figurative approach to appliqué quilting Tal's practice-led research explores the intersections between socially engaged art, activism and feminist and new materialist approaches to craft. For more information on Tal's latest projects, please visit: www.praxial-practice.wordpress.com

Katve-Kaisa Kontturi works as a postdoctoral fellow in the Victorian College of the Arts at the University of Melbourne. She is a founding member of the European New Materialist Network, and has devoted her academic career to the study of relational materialities of art and the body. Kaisa enjoys curating affective exhibitions, the bodily rhythm of crafting, and dressing in beautifully patterned vintage frocks.

JOURNAL OF BASIC WRITING

> *Journl of Basic Writing* is on the Web at https://wac.colostate.edu/jbw/

Journal of Basic Writing is a refereed print journal founded in 1975 by Mina Shaughnessy, who served as the journal's first editor. *JBW* is published twice a year with support from the Office of Academic Affairs of the City University of New York. Its editors are full-time CUNY faculty. Basic writing, a contested term since its initial use by Shaughnessy in the 1970s, refers to the field concerned with teaching writing to students not yet deemed ready for first-year composition. Originally, these students were part of the wave of open admissions students who poured into universities as a result of the social unrest of the 1960s and the resulting reforms. Though social and political realities have changed dramatically since then, the presence of "basic writers" in colleges and universities—and the debates over how best to serve them—persist. *JBW* publishes articles related to basic and second-language writing using a variety of approaches: speculative discussions that venture fresh interpretations; essays that draw heavily on student writing as supportive evidence for new observations; research reports written in non-technical language that offer observations previously unknown or unsubstantiated; and collaborative writings that provocatively debate more than one side of a critical controversy. The articles we are submitting this year take on the social, political, and pedagogical questions related to educational access and equity that are at the core of *JBW's* history and mission.

Remedial, Basic, Advanced: Evolving Frameworks for First-Year Composition at the California State University

The language of remediation has had a critical, often limiting, impact on how we think about basic writing. As our understandings of student literacies and language politics have grown, we see the need for new frameworks to re-term, and so refigure, our work on political-structural levels. In this article, Dan Melzer takes on the evolution of frameworks around pre-freshman and freshman writers in the California State University, reminding us of basic writing's mission of access, at the same time citing embedded remediation discourse for its limiting effects. Progressing from "remedial" to "basic" to "advanced," he supports CSU's recent refiguring of writing instruction to move beyond the "discoursal limits" of previous frameworks and their effects.

147

Remedial, Basic, Advanced: Evolving Frameworks for First-Year Composition at the California State University

Dan Melzer

ABSTRACT: *In this essay I conduct a Critical Discourse Analysis of the language surrounding the California State University (CSU) Chancellor's Office latest plan to curb remediation, the Early Start program. I consider Early Start in the context of what I argue is the evolution of three major frameworks for Basic Writing in the CSU: the CSU Chancellor's Office Remedial Writing Framework that focuses on deficiency and gatekeeping; the Basic Writing Framework that developed in the 1970s as a way for CSU's writing teachers to defend access for underserved students; and the emerging Advanced Writing Framework, which eliminates Basic Writing and redefines one semester of composition as advanced and a two semester stretch course as mainstream. I trace three themes in the "discourse event" of Early Start: Early Start's relation to historical discourse on remediation, replication of discourse norms by the media, and faculty complicity in the discourse of the Remedial Writing Framework. Based on my analysis of the ways that it disrupts the dominant discourse of remediation and basic skills, I argue the Advanced Writing Framework provides hope of changing the nature of the discourse.*

California has played a central role in the national discourse about remediation and Basic Writing. From Mike Rose's analysis of "the language of exclusion" in the institutional discourse surrounding remediation at the University of California (UC), to Ed White and the California State University (CSU) English Council's politicking to prevent the CSU Chancellor's Office from implementing a multiple-choice test for college writing equivalency, to Tom Fox's defense of access for the diverse CSU student population, to Jane Stanley's analysis of the rhetoric of remediation at UC Berkeley, Basic Writing teachers in California have fought against manufactured literacy crises and the discourse of students as "deficient" and in need of "remediation" of "basic skills."

Despite this continued resistance to the language of exclusion and despite the growth in the 1970s of extensive Basic Writing programs to support underserved students, writing teachers at the CSU have not been able to change an enduring remedial framework of deficiency and basic skills that to this day shapes the discourse of the CSU Chancellor's Office, the Board of Trustees, the media, and even many CSU teachers. As Mary Kay Crouch and Gerry McNenny conclude in their overview of remediation in California, "Looking Back, Looking Forward," "Looking historically at the CSU's attempts to grapple with what it views as the 'problem' of remediation, we see that the solutions proposed during each cycle of concern have rarely varied" (64). Crouch and McNenny share my concern regarding the CSU's history of top-down mandates that label students as deficient based on timed tests, but they stop short of arguing that much of this history has been shaped by a discursive framework that has endured despite the rise of Basic Writing programs. The latest effort of the Chancellor's Office to curb remediation, the Early Start program, exemplifies the endurance of a remedial framework of deficiency and basic skills, the recycling of the same misguided solutions to the "problem" of remediation, the inability of CSU Basic Writing programs to change the discourse, and the unintentional complicity of CSU teachers in the language of exclusion.

The idea for Early Start began with the CSU Board of Trustees, and in 2010 Early Start came down as a date from the Chancellor's Office and was implemented in 2012. Early Start forces students who score below the cut score of 147 on a timed writing test—the English Placement Test (EPT)—to engage in a "remediation" activity before their first semester of college. As Crouch and McNenny reference, at most CSUs nearly half of incoming students are placed into non-credit bearing "remedial" or Basic Writing courses, and now these students are being asked to take even more coursework at their own expense before the start of the regular semester. The Early Start activity that is required of students who score below 147 on the EPT can be a summer course at a CSU campus, a community college basic writing course, or a brief online course—all paid for by the student.

Through a Critical Discourse Analysis, I contrast the remediation and basic skills discourse of Early Start—what I refer to as the Remedial Writing Framework—with the discourse of an approach to first-year composition emerging in the CSU that involves replacing testing and tracking with Directed Self-Placement (DSP); shifting from a series of non-credit bearing Basic Writing courses to a mainstream, two-semester cohorted stretch course; and relabeling the one-semester composition course as "advanced." I refer to this emerging mainstreaming approach as the Advanced Writing Framework. The Advanced Writing Framework acknowledges that *most* CSU students will need more than one semester of composition to succeed, and it disrupts the discourse of remediation while retaining support for underserved students. I argue that the Advanced Writing Framework presents the best hope for CSU writing teachers of disrupting the discourse of the Remedial Writing Framework that has endured despite the rise of Basic Writing programs. Although my focus is the CSU, the endurance of the Remedial Writing Framework, the complicity of Basic Writing teachers and other allies in this framework, and the emergence of the Advanced Writing Framework connects to national narratives on remediation, Basic Writing, and mainstreaming, as well as current scholarly discussions in the field of Basic Writing.

These scholarly discussions about the state of Basic Writing and basic writers often focus on the endurance of the language of remediation and basic skills—what Bruce Horner refers to as "a debilitating sense of having to keep fighting the same fights, making the same arguments, over and over again" ("Relocating" 6). Like Horner and Rose, I am interested in tracing the replication of the institutional discourse of remediation and the ways that discourse reduces students' complex and fluid literacies to a static set of deficiencies in basic skills. I argue that Early Start is evidence that the language of remediation and basic skills will continue to endure and replicate despite the resistance of Basic Writing teachers and despite the support provided to underserved students by Basic Writing programs. I am especially interested in turning a spotlight on Basic Writing teachers' unintentional complicity in the language of exclusion, since this complicity speaks to the pressing need for imagining alternatives to Basic Writing programs and the discourse that inevitably attaches to the Basic Writing enterprise, despite our best intentions.

In their article "In the Here and Now: Public Policy and Basic Writing," Linda Adler-Kassner and Susanmarie Harrington argue that "we need to develop rhetoric and action that will change the nature of the debate" (37) and work against the naturalized frames of students as deficient and remediation as a temporary problem to be solved. One way to change the naturalized frames of students as deficient is to consider models of mainstreaming alternatives to Basic Writing, as scholars such as David Bartholomae, Ira Shor, Mary Soliday, and Kelly Ritter have encouraged us to do. The Advanced Writing Framework is a unique model in that it has helped CSU writing teachers disrupt the language of exclusion not by mainstreaming "basic" students but by reframing the "mainstream" composition course as "advanced" and what is now labeled "basic" as mainstream—a move that I argue has the potential to change the nature of the discourse.

HISTORICAL FRAMEWORKS FOR FIRST-YEAR WRITING AND REMEDIATION IN THE CSU

Before I contrast the discourses of the Early Start and Advanced Writing Frameworks, I want to offer a brief history of the evolution of Basic Writing in the CSU. The tone for the gatekeeping approach of the Remedial Writing Framework was set in the 1960 Master Plan for Higher Education in California. The Master Plan mandated that students' writing abilities be tested before entering a UC or CSU and argued that standards should be high at the UC and the CSU since "the junior colleges relieve them of the burden of doing remedial work" (66). To help further relieve this "burden" of remediation, in the early 1970s the Chancellor's Office and Board of Trustees began working on a plan to use a multiple-choice test designed by the Educational Testing Service (ETS) as a college writing equivalency that would have resulted in a large percentage of incoming students testing out of composition entirely. Ultimately, the Chancellor's Office goal was to replace the teaching of composition with a test. This targeting of composition was met with outrage by the CSU English Council, a group of English Teachers across CSU campuses who rallied against the test and worked to persuade the Chancellor's Office that the test was reductive and invalid. However, even when the Board of Trustees relented on the multiple-choice equivalency test after the public outcry of the English Council and granted permission for a placement test into Basic Writing courses, they retained the discourse of the Remedial Writing Framework, proclaiming in 1975 that the new test and curriculum will involve "basic skills and remedial improvement" (CSU Task Force on Remediation 2).

Ed White was a faculty member at CSU San Bernardino at the time the Chancellor's Office was planning to implement the ETS multiple-choice test, and he played a central role in persuading the CSU to instead adopt what was to evolve into the EPT, a placement test created by CSU writing teachers. The EPT, which combines indirect and direct assessment of student writing, was originally scored by CSU writing teachers and used to place students into either Basic Writing or mainstream courses based on cut scores. The rise of Basic Writing programs throughout the CSU system in the 1970s connects to the implementation of the EPT as a placement tool. As White points out, "until the placement program began, the CSU was not authorized to offer writing courses below the regular freshman level" (79). The implementation of the EPT and the growth of Basic Writing programs in the late 1970s mark the emergence of what I am referring to as the Basic Writing Framework, a framework that works in opposition to the Chancellor's Office Remedial Writing Framework and which is still the norm at most CSUs. Under this framework, Basic Writing teachers have been able to defend access to the CSU of underserved students by using the EPT as a tool to place students into one of a series of "basic" or "developmental" courses. Although White and other CSU writing teachers argued that Basic Writing courses should be credit-bearing, the Chancellor's Office felt that this would lower CSU standards, and Basic Writing courses at the CSU remain non-credit bearing to this day—as they do at many institutions across the U.S.

Despite the victory of Basic Writing teachers in protecting access for underserved students, the Chancellor's Office and Board of Trustees have continued their attempts to eliminate remediation. A report published in 1983 by the California Postsecondary Education Commission, *Promises to Keep*, bemoans the "decline in basic skills" (10) and recommends reducing remediation within the next five years. The 1987 review of the Master Plan creates a taxonomy of college writing where "pre-college" remediation is equated with "skill deficiencies," and the plan recommends phasing out remediation at the CSU and UC. A 1995 report by the Committee on Education set as a goal that by Fall 2001 all entering CSU students would possess "basic skills." Another report by the Chancellor's Office and Board of Trustees aimed to reduce remediation to 10% by 2007 (LAO 2). These attempts reflect what Mike Rose refers to as the "myth of transience": "if we can just do *x* or *y*, the problem will be solved—in five years, ten years, or a generation—and higher education will be able to return to its real work" (355).

A group of CSU WPA's began to grow frustrated with both the misguided assumptions of the Chancellor's Office ideology and the inability of Basic Writing programs to change this ideology, and in conversations at English Council meetings and their local campuses, they began to search for an alternative that would eliminate the stigma of remediation without denying support for underserved students. This alternative to the Remedial and Basic Writing Frameworks, which I refer to as the Advanced Writing Framework, has been implemented at a handful of CSU campuses that have replaced the EPT with Directed Self-Placement (DSP) and have eliminated Basic Writing by turning what was once considered the mainstream course—a one-semester option—into an "advanced" writing course, and turning what was once labeled "basic" or "remedial"—a series of non-credit bearing courses—into a two-semester cohorted stretch course that is considered mainstream. The stretch course has the same outcomes and assignments as the advanced course, but a smaller class size and a slower pace. The Advanced Writing Framework changes the discourse associated with both the Remedial Writing Framework and the Basic Writing Framework by replacing the term "mainstream" with "advanced" and replacing the terms "basic" and "remedial" and "developmental" with "mainstream." Because the Advanced Writing Framework relies on DSP, it also presents students and the general public with a more sophisticated definition of college writing than the multiple-choice "basic skills" assessment and formulaic timed writing of the EPT.

When considered in the context of the evolution of Basic Writing in the CSU, Early Start is of special interest because of the way it brings all three of the frameworks I outline into conflict: the recycling of the Chancellor's Office Remedial Writing Framework; the response to this recycling from the teachers who developed the Basic Writing Framework; and the beginnings of a disruption of the discourse of Early Start and the Remedial Writing Framework by the emerging Advanced Writing Framework. A critical analysis of the discourse of Early Start reveals that despite the rise of Basic Writing in the CSU and the good intentions of Basic Writing teachers—and sometimes *because* of those good intentions—the discourse of remediation and basic skills remains dominant.

DISCOURSE ANALYSIS AND BASIC WRITING

Critical analysis of public discourse has been a focus of a number of scholarly critiques of remediation. In addition to the work of Rose, Fox, and Stanley in California, Basic Writing scholars have focused on the ways that terms like "basic" and "remedial" have caused negative perceptions of underserved students and the programs developed to support them. Bruce Horner analyzes the ideology that informs the discourse surrounding Basic Writing, and especially its history at CUNY, in "Discoursing Basic Writing." Horner warns against naturalizing basic writing and basic writers, and instead argues for a view of basic writing as a set of social practices, occurring in historical and political contexts, and not merely skills acquisition. Steve Lamos also looks at CUNY and the early discourse surrounding open admissions and uses a critical race lens in his analysis. Lamos encourages us to pay attention to the ways basic writing students are racialized in the open admissions debate and how that racialized discourse maintains white power structures. Linda Adler-Kassner and Susanmarie Harrington analyze the dominant narratives surrounding basic writing in *The New York Times* and *Minneapolis Star Tribune* in *Basic Writing as a Political Act.* They argue that these narratives, which include the portrayal of literacy as an autonomous set of skills, are frames controlled by administrators and the media rather than teachers.

Another important critical analysis of remediation, and the one that most clearly paves the way for the Advanced Writing Framework, is Kelly Ritter's analysis of the discourse of Basic Writing at Yale and Harvard in *Before Shaughnessy*. Ritter questions definitions of Basic Writers and argues that basic writing is an institutional construct. Ritter argues for the "erasure of the label *basic* altogether" (129), and she proposes instead sequences of credit-bearing courses that are labeled only by numbers such as 1, 2, and 3. Each course in a sequence is considered "introductory" in the sense that all the courses are helping prepare students for complex academic literacies, and are not labeled "basic" or "developmental." Ritter's goal is to encourage a "model that eliminates the stigma, as much as possible, from different levels of preparedness in first-year writing" (141).

None of these authors who critically analyze public discourse on Basic Writing explicitly use a Critical Discourse Analysis (CDA) approach, but all of them conduct a close analysis of the language we use to describe remediation and Basic Writing programs and students in order to focus on the problems with public perceptions and beliefs regarding these terms and concepts. CDA, with its central aim to "explicate abuses of power promoted by [texts] by analyzing the linguistic/semiotic details in light of the larger social and political contexts in which those texts circulate" (Huckin, Andrus, and Clary-Lemon 107), is an ideal approach for thinking about Basic Writing and remediation. Ruth Wodak describes the focus of CDA as analyzing "structural relationships of dominance, discrimination, power and control when these are manifested in language" ("Critical Linguistics" 53). Along with Norman Fairclough, Wodak outlines a number of principles of CDA, including the assumption that discourse constitutes society and culture and always does ideological work, that discourse is historical, and that discourse is a form of social action ("What CDA is About" 271-80). With its focus on power and ideology, a CDA lens forces us to look at the language of remediation with a critical eye and consider the social and cultural consequences of the labels we use to describe college writing courses and college writers. Teun A. van Dijk asserts that the ultimate goal of CDA is to resist social inequality and push towards alternative paradigms for social problems (352-53). From Rose to Horner to Adler-Kassner to Ritter, Basic Writing as a profession has been taking a critical perspective on the discourse of remediation in order to resist social inequality. Rarely, however, have scholars taken an *explicit* CDA approach to remediation and Basic Writing. It is also rare that scholars have included the language of Basic Writing teachers themselves in this critical analysis of the discourse of remediation.

I turn a CDA lens on Early Start with the ultimate goal of resisting the social inequality of the Remedial Writing Framework and showing the limits of the Basic Writing Framework's success in challenging the discourse of remediation of basic skills. An analysis of the discourse of Early Start reveals that only a change in the nature of the discourse will move us beyond the enduring Remedial Writing Framework.

CDA ANALYSIS OF EARLY START: HISTORICAL DISCOURSE AND THE REPLICATION OF DISCOURSE NORMS

The documents from the Chancellor's Office promoting Early Start, the reaction to Early Start in campus and city newspapers, and the response to Early Start from faculty represent what discourse theorists such as Fairclough and Wodak refer to as a "discourse event." In the case of Early Start, the discourse event involves a series of intertextual executive orders, policies, press releases, newspaper articles, and resolutions that shape how students from socioeconomically marginalized groups are portrayed and that replicate norms from prior discourse surrounding remediation in California as well as the national discourse on remediation. A discourse analysis of Early Start reveals three primary themes: 1) Early Start as historical discourse, 2) the replication of discourse norms in the media reporting on Early Start, and 3) teacher complicity in the Remedial Writing Framework.

CDA often focuses on a corpus of interrelated texts (Huckin, Andrus, and Clary-Lemon). To illustrate the ways that Early Start reinforces the Remedial Writing Framework, I collected public documents associated with Early Start that I located through searches of the Chancellor's office website, CSU campus websites, and city and school newspapers. This corpus of texts includes the Chancellor's Office Executive Order implementing Early Start, press releases regarding Early Start from the Chancellor's Office, resolutions against Early Start from CSU academic senates, and twenty-three articles from campus and city newspapers across California published from 2010-2013.

I focus my analysis of these documents on the language of exclusion of the Remedial Writing Framework, and especially the familiar and enduring language that points to the "semantic macrostructures" that dominate the discourse event: *remedial*, *deficient*, and *skills*. In discourse analysis, semantic macrostructures are the global meanings of discourse—the key words and concepts that point to broader themes (A. van Djik "Multidisciplinary CDA" 99). As I traced the semantic macrostructures of *remedial*, *deficient*, and *skills* throughout the texts in my corpus, three themes emerged. Discourses are "always connected to other discourses which were produced earlier" (Fairclough, Mulderrig, and Wodak 372), and one CDA theme that emerged in my research is the connection of the language of Early Start to prior

Chancellor's Office executive orders and reports, as well as national reports on alleged literacy crises. Wodak emphasizes "the mediating and constructing role of the media" (7) in discourse events, and another theme in the discourse event of Early Start is the way the language of the Chancellor's Office press releases was uncritically replicated in campus and city newspapers.

The language of exclusion of the Chancellor's Office was also replicated by CSU teachers. Allan Luke argues thatcommunities bothresistandbecome "complicit in their own moral regulation" (9). Luke says about this complicity, "When and where these discourses are internalized by the subject as her or his own constitute the moment of noncoercive discipline par excellence" (9). CSU teachers and activists were often unintentionally complicit in the replication of the Remedial Writing framework, and this complicity—this "noncoercive discipline"—is the final theme I trace in my discussion of Early Start. Teacher complicity is also the most troubling theme, since a change in the discourse is unlikely to occur if even Basic Writing teachers reinforce the Remedial Writing Framework.

Early Start as Historical Discourse

The language of Early Start, Executive Order 1048, is what CDA theorists refer to as "historical discourse" in that it echoes the discourse of earlier executive orders. The semantic macrostructures of the language of exclusion of the Remedial Writing Framework is prominent throughout EO 1048. EO 1048 states that "incoming freshmen who have not demonstrated proficiency in English and/or mathematics will be required to begin remediation prior to the term for which they have been admitted." In the discourse of Early Start, as in the language of exclusion in the UC system that Rose critiqued, remediation is a "scholastic quarantine" for entering first-year students "until their disease can be diagnosed and remedied" (Rose 352). That diagnosis is the EPT, and it is assumed by EO 1048 that a timed impromptu test is a valid measurement of "proficiency in English." EO 1048 highlights the fact that "Deficiencies in mathematics and/or English are to be determined by test scores." Students who are not considered proficient are to be segregated into a remedial activity so that they can begin "addressing deficiencies in mathematics and/or English."

This discourse of EO 1048 echoes the ideology of deficiency and basic skills of earlier executive orders, such as EO514, passed in 1989, which states that "students who do not demonstrate the requisite competence are required to enroll in a CSU Writing Skills program to correct deficiencies before undertaking baccalaureate English courses." EO665, which was passed in 1997, requires students to complete remediation in one year in order to "ensure that deficiencies in student writing skills are corrected as efficiently and expeditiously as possible." This discourse of deficiency also echoes prior reports involving the Chancellor's Office, such as the "CSU Plan to Reduce Remedial Activity, 1985-1990," which recommends diagnostic testing in high school to "alert students to their deficiencies," and the 1987 California *Master Plan Renewed*, which describes remedial students as, "Students who are nearly college ready, but exhibit serious multiple skills deficiencies that require instruction at two levels below the Freshman level in English" (52). The discourse of Early Start is not only a replication of the historical discourse of Chancellor's Office executive orders and reports, but also a replication of national metanarratives about remediation. In recent national reports that manufacture literacy crises such as the National Commission on Excellence in Education's *A Nation at Risk*, the Spelling's report *A Test of Leadership*, and the Education Commission of the States' *Blueprint for College Readiness*, declining scores on standardized tests are cited as evidence of the failure of students to learn basic skills in K-12, and remediation is portrayed as a waste of taxpayer dollars. *A Nation at Risk* cites the need for "remedial" courses in "basic skills" in English as one indicator of risk for American education, while at the same time calling for more standardized testing to track students into "remedial interventions." *A Test of Leadership* bemoans the decline in literacy and the number of college students wasting taxpayer dollars in "remediation" mastering English "skills" that "should have been learned in high school" (viii). *Blueprint for College Readiness* cites the "alarmingly high" number of students with "academic deficits" who are in "remedial" courses (31). The historical discourse of the CSU Chancellor's office is shaped by the semantic macrostructures of the national discourse on remediation that has remained virtually unchanged since the first college writing "remedial intervention," English A at Harvard, in the late 1800s.

Replication of Discourse Norms in the Media

Following the establishment of EO 1048, the Chancellor's Office released a series of press releases that contain the semantic macrostructures of the language of exclusion: *remedial, deficient,* and *skills*. The goal of Early Start, according to the Chancellor's Office press releases, is to "begin the skills-building process before students arrive on campus for their freshman year" (par. 1). The press releases say that Early Start is designed for students "who need to improve their skills in English" with the goal of "addressing deficiencies earlier." In the discourse of the Chancellor's Office, echoing the national narratives of *A Nation at Risk* and the Spelling's report, the writing "deficiencies" are located within the student, not within the socioeconomic circumstances of the CSU's primarily working-class population. These deficiencies can be addressed by improving "skills," which can somehow be accomplished once and for all in a shortened summer course.

The discourse of EO 1048 and the Early Start press releases was replicated throughout articles in campus and city newspapers, either through direct quotations or paraphrase by journalists who adopted the language of the Remedial Writing Framework as the "common sense" (Luke 12) discourse on the subject. For example, the word "remediation," and the attendant concept that students labeled remedial are deficient, was replicated in many of the titles of the articles:

- CSU Launches Program To Alleviate Remedial Student Issues (Addison)
- Cal State Campuses Overwhelmed by Remedial Needs (Krupnick)
- California State University Wants Struggling Students to Take Remedial Courses Prior to Freshman Year (Krieger)
- University to Force Remediation (Bailey)

These titles reinforce the idea that the problem resides within the students— they are "struggling" and "remedial." The CSU system is portrayed as "overwhelmed" by these remedial students, without any acknowledgment that underserved students are the norm at an institution whose alleged mission is to serve working-class Californians. As Horner argues, basic writing students' "location on the periphery is ideological, obtaining even in institutions where basic writers constitute the statistical norm" ("Relocating" 9). At some CSU campuses, the EPT places nearly 70% of students in remediation, making them peripheral in name only.

Replication of the Remedial Writing Framework's discourse norms occurred in many newspaper articles, reinforcing the notion of Early Start as a discourse event with limited and limiting semantic macrostructures. The italics I added in the following excerpts from campus and local newspaper articles indicate language lifted directly from or paraphrased from the Chancellor's Office press releases:

> Approximately half of CSU's regularly admitted freshmen are *not proficient* in math and/or English and are required to take *developmental courses* during their initial year of college.

> Wracked with frustration over the state's legions of *unprepared* high school graduates, the California State University system next summer will force freshmen with *remedial* needs to brush up on math or English before arriving on campus.

> The Cal State system's *remedial* pressures have, for the past few years, led many students to take *basic* classes at community colleges.

> Instead of combining *remedial* courses with normal courses during the student's first year, the goal is to have the student take those courses beforehand during the summer.

In addition to replicating the semantic macrostructures of the language of exclusion, the media replicates the Remedial Writing Framework's contrast between "remedial" and "developmental" and "basic" courses with "normal" courses. This basic/normal distinction is both informed by and reinforces the portrayal of "the legions of unprepared high school graduates" as inherently deficient and in need of quarantine until they can learn basic skills to "brush up" on their "remedial needs."

Bartholomae argues that this basic/normal distinction is what we have "learned to think through and by" in the field of Basic Writing (8), and although most CSUS Basic Writing teachers resist this way of thinking, in California the media has certainly learned to think of college students in terms of this dichotomy. When CSU composition teachers created "basic" and "developmental" writing programs in the 70s, they intended, like Mina Shaughnessy at CUNY, to replace the language of "remedial" and "deficient" with less oppressive terms. However, the discourse event of Early Start reveals that basic and developmental writing have been coopted by the Remedial Writing Framework. The names of CSU's "basic writing" and "developmental writing" programs reinforce a basic/normal dichotomy—an issue that leads us to consider teacher complicity in the language of exclusion.

Complicity of CSU Teachers in the Remedial Writing Framework

Luke argues that complicity in oppressive discourse is not "simple topdown ideological manipulation" (9). Communities participate in discourse in ways that involve both working against the discourse and becoming complicit in their own oppression. Luke explains that when discourses are internalized, then noncoercive discipline has been achieved by those in power (9). The problem of complicity in dominant discourse and internalization by teachers of the language of exclusion is illustrated in the voices of faculty quoted in articles about Early Start. A few faculty members quoted in the articles, for example, simply reiterate the Chancellor's Office view that students are deficient. In this section of the essay I once again italicize the language of the Remedial Writing Framework to highlight the ways CSU teachers are caught in this historical discourse.

One composition instructor was quoted in an article as saying, "Obviously, there are an awful lot of entering students who do need *remediation*" (qtd. in Carmona). A remediation director at another college was quoted as saying, "We're all trying to figure out how to handle these students who are woefully *unprepared*" (qtd. in Krupnick). The use of the term "remediation" and the idea that there are an overwhelming number of students that need remediation was not just stated by faculty who spoke in favor of Early Start. Other faculty quoted in newspaper articles offer strong critiques of Early Start, but do so using terms from the language of exclusion of the Remedial Writing Framework. One educator and activist who has been a staunch defender of the CSU's mission to serve diverse, first-generation college students was quoted as saying, "*Remedial* students did not fail to prepare for CSU. *Remedial* students are the majority. *Remediation* can be seen as a social justice remedy because if *remedial* education was not available in the CSU then many fewer students would have access to a college education in California" (qtd. in Bordas). Another teacher known for her leadership role in composition throughout the CSU was quoted as saying, "I do not believe this program will be effective. I definitely don't think it will be more effective than what we already do....If we don't have it our students would be fine. They aren't going to improve in any way that's measurable and that's going to reduce their time in *remediation*" (qtd. in Kernes).

The language of exclusion was also replicated by faculty in resolutions against Early Start. Consider this excerpt from the CSU Academic Senate's resolution against Early Start:

> The Academic Senate of the California State University (ASCSU) recognizes the value of diverse campus approaches to moving fully qualified first-time freshmen (FTF) who require additional *skill acquisition (remediation)* in English or mathematics to achieve *proficiency* either prior to, or during, their first year of enrollment.

In this resolution, composition is conceived of as "skill acquisition" and students are expected to become proficient in these basic skills by the end of their first year, as if writing is a finite set of skills that can be completed in a few semesters. The sentence above was repeatedverbatimina number of CSU campus Faculty Senate resolutions against Early Start. The resolution against Early Start passed by the Faculty Senate at San Jose State University contains sentences that reproduce the language of the Remedial Writing Framework:

> In particular, there is a disproportionate percentage of underrepresented students requiring *remediation* and the Early Start requirement further reinforces the message that they don't belong at the University; and San José State already has effective *remediation* programs directed and taught by experts in the field.
>
> Many in the *remedial* education community feel that there is an eternal existence of *remedial* students despite manifold attempts to "fix" them. *Remediation* has always had more to do with how these students are labeled and perceived than who they actually are. (2)

The discourse of these resolutions reinforce the concept of the internal remedial student, and it speaks to Victor Villanueva's argument that it is time "to move away from the concept that basic writers are in need of remedies" (97). Part of moving away from this concept of students perpetually in need of a remedy is getting beyond the language of remediation that teachers as well as administrators and the media continue to replicate. Even as they work against Early Start, faculty are trapped in the semantic macrostructures of the language of exclusion of the Remedial Writing Framework: *basic*, *remedial*, and *skills*. The language used by CSU faculty to critique Early Start supports Rose's point that "we end up arguing with words that sabotage our argument" (342). What the CSU needs to truly disentangle itself from the Remedial Writing Framework is new words, and a new discourse framework.

THE ADVANCED WRITING FRAMEWORK: DISRUPTING THE DISCOURSE

The required first-year composition course has its roots in remediation, and the language of exclusion is not unique to courses labeled "basic" or "developmental." As Mathew Pavesich argues, "Built into the very fiber of composition, and its *raison d'être*, is the notion of remedial normalization as crisis response" (91). Sharon Crowley's abolitionist argument—that first-year writing will not lose its remedial status until the requirement itself is eliminated—presents one alternative to the Basic Writing Framework. A possible abolitionist solution for the CSU would be to eliminate both Basic Writing and first-year composition and encourage campuses to see writing as a shared responsibility through writing across the curriculum or writing in the disciplines programs. Another way of framing the issue, however, is to make the argument that most students need more than a single semester of focused, integratedreading andwriting instructionby a compositionspecialist to help prepare for the complexities of academic literacies. A handful of CSUs have persuaded their campuses that a single semester of composition should not be considered mainstream but advanced.

There are five campuses that have made this shift away from the EPT and the basic/normal dichotomy. These five campuses—San Francisco State University, Fresno State University, CSU Channel Islands, CSU San Bernardino, and CSU Sacramento—ask students to complete a Directed SelfPlacement (DSP) survey rather than using their EPT cut score for placement. Students may choose to take either a one-semester course that is considered an advanced writing experience or a two-semester cohorted stretch course which is considered the mainstream option, with additional adjunct tutoring options for students in either path. Fairclough argues than an important part of critical discourse analysis is finding "resistant texts" and "alternative representations" (134), and I argue that the Advanced Writing Framework presents alternative semantic macrostructures that disrupt Early Start and the Remedial Writing Framework and help CSU teachers break from historical discourse norms of deficiency, skills, and testing.

The curriculum structure of the Advanced Writing Framework combines a variety of the models that William Lalicker outlines in "A Basic Introduction to Basic Writing Program Structures," and the inspiration for the approach at these five CSU campuses certainly comes from Basic Writing theory and practice. It is critical to note, however, that none of these campuses perceives of or labels the stretch course as Basic Writing. Lalicker is not alone in associating stretch courses with Basic Writing. Adler Kassner and Harrington in *Basic Writing as a Political Act*, George Otte and Rebecca Williams Mlynarczyk in "The Future of Basic Writing," and Greg Glau in his articles about the stretch program at Arizona State University, all associate stretch with basic writing. This is not a criticism of these authors: most stretch programs are associated with Basic Writing and "basic" writers. Pavesich argues that DSP and remediation alternatives like stretch and studio are problematic when they lead students to place themselves in courses that are not considered "normal," and this is where the reframing of the one-semester course is key.

By introducing discourse that defines the one-semester course as "advanced" or "accelerated" and the stretch course as mainstream, these five CSU campuses have accomplished what Ritter calls "a shift in program design that does not eliminate necessary assistance for these writers but also does not rhetorically separate them from other writers in the university" (13). To discuss the effects of the shift from the Basic Writing Framework to the Advanced Writing Framework, I cite the language used on the DSP and first-year writing program websites and brochures of these five campuses.

The Discourse of the Advanced Writing Framework

At both CSU Channel Islands and CSU Sacramento, the dominant discourse that the EPT is a valid way to measure writing ability and place students into composition courses is explicitly disrupted. The welcoming letter that the CSU Channel Islands writing program includes on their DSP website lets students know that "at CSUCI, we don't believe single timed essays can reliably predict how students will perform in writing classes. We believe students and writing are far more complex than any single score can suggest." The letter goes on to assure students, "You'll certainly do a better job of placing yourself than a single timed test would." The CSU Sacramento DSP website explains that "Sac State students used to enroll in first-year composition courses based on their scores on the English Placement Test (EPT). We do not, however, believe that a multiple-choice, timed exam is the best way to determine a student's skills and placement."

In addition to challenging the validity of the timed impromptu test, the discourse of mainstreaming at these CSU campuses challenges the "normal/ basic" dichotomy and instead introduces the terms "strong" and "average" to define the differences between the one-semester course and the two-semester stretch course. This is evident in the DSP placement survey instruments of Fresno State, Channel Islands, and San Francisco State. All three institutions use the phrase "I think of myself as a strong reader and writer" as the first criterion for self-placement into the one-semester course, and "I think of myself as an average reader and writer" for self-placement into the twosemester course. The literacy self-survey that is a part of the CSU Sacramento DSP instrument asks students if they have "more than average" experience reading and "more than average" experience writing. The one-semester composition courses at these CSU campuses are for "strong" students, and the two-semester option is the average. Otte and Williams Mlynarczyk say of DSP: "With this model, entering students are advised of the availability of basic writing courses and left to make their own decision as to whether to take BW or regular composition" (17). In the Advanced Writing Framework, there is no basic/regular dichotomy for DSP. As the DSP brochure of CSU Channel Islands states: "There are no remedial writing courses at CSUCI, so whichever choice you make, you'll be in a course that counts toward graduation and in which you will be expected to produce college-level writing." This distinction of "strong" versus "average," as opposed to "normal" versus "basic," is reinforced in the titles of the first-year writing courses. At Fresno State, the course title of the one-semester composition option is "Accelerated Academic Literacy." In their DSP brochure, Fresno State says of their stretch course: "Unless you really excel in English, we suggest this option." The brochure warns students that the one-semester course "is an advanced class, and to choose this option you need to be a very competent reader and writer, ready toread complex essays, develop research supported analyses and complete assignments at a faster pace." The course title of the one-semester composition option at San Bernardino is "Advanced Composition." On the DSP website, it is labeled as the "most aggressively paced first-year writing option." The one-semester course is described as "intended for students who are confident, flexible readers and writers, have familiarity with academic conventions and habits of mind, and are self-directed and self-motivated." It is important to note that despite the similar language used, this kind of reframing is quite different from Peter Adams' Accelerated Writing Program, which involves accelerating Basic Writing through a specific kind of mainstreaming but does not focus on redefining the one-semester course as accelerated or advanced for all students and does not necessarily use DSP.

The DSP survey instruments and websites from all four institutions do recognize that mainstream first-year writers at an institution such as the CSU, which has an explicit mission of access to college for first-generation students, will not always have the same literacy backgrounds as the students entering the University of California system or private institutions like Stanford. The stretch courses are for students who are "unsure what to do when confronted with difficult texts," "have trouble coming up with good topics and ideas," "need to learn how to use outside sources," and "could use some brushing up on grammar and punctuation." These are not the qualities of "remedial" or "basic" students but of typical CSU students. CSU San Bernardino describes the stretch course option that lasts three academic quarters as:

> Intended for the typical entering college students who may feel somewhat nervous about reading and writing at the college level and/or whose previous writing experiences have focused primarily on forms of writing, like the 5 paragraph format, Schaffer paragraphs, and other systematic approaches to writing development.

Despite this acknowledgment that the expectations of college-level writing will be a challenge for *most* entering students at the CSU (and not just those labeled remedial by a timed test), DSP recognizes the assets students bring with them to college writing. The DSP website at CSU San Bernardino states that "students who are admitted to CSUSB have successfully met expectations for high school writing; they are college-ready students." CSU Sacramento emphasizes that "students enter the university already having a variety of writing skills and strategies. It is our mission to build upon these to prepare students for the complex reading, thinking, and writing tasks that will await them in their university classes and beyond." The CSU Sacramento DSP website also makes an effort to discuss multilingual students' assets. It states that the multilingual versions of each course "focus on the experiences and languages that multilingual students bring to the classroom—using them as a resource for learning and refining students' academic reading and writing." Unlike the basic skills language of the discourse of Early Start, the language of DSP and stretch composition presents a more nuanced view of college reading and writing, in large part because the terms are in the control of composition specialists rather than ETS or the Chancellor's Office. With the discourse in the control of writing teachers, students who were once labeled "remedial" or "basic" can now be more accurately labeled as "typical," and what was once wrongly labeled mainstream—a mere one semester of composition instruction—can be more properly labeled as "advanced" or "accelerated."

Table 1 outlines the ways in which the discourse of the Advanced Writing Framework disrupts both the Remedial and Basic Writing Frameworks. It summarizes the evolution in the teaching of composition in the CSU from indirect assessment to direct assessment to self-assessment; from testing and tracking to choosing; from composition as a remedial basic skills course to composition as an advanced course in complex academic literacies; and from a separate writing curriculum for remedial and mainstream to an integrated writing curriculum.

Table 1: Comparison of Writing Frameworks in the CSU

Remedial Writing Framework	Basic Writing Framework	Advanced Writing Framework
Indirect assessment of writing ability through a multiple-choice test designed and scored by ETS	Direct assessment of writing ability through a timed writing test designed and scored by CSU writing teachers	Self-assessment of writing processes and habits through DSP activities designed by CSU writing teachers
Testing to exclude	Testing to sort	Self-assessment to choose
Targeted population of students labeled "remedial" writers	Targeted population of students labeled "basic" or "developmental" writers	All students labeled "college writers"
One-semester first-year composition course as "normal," preparatory courses as "remedial"	One-semester first-year composition course as "mainstream," preparatory courses as "basic" or "developmental"	One-semester first-year composition course as "advanced," stretch course as "mainstream"
Different curriculum in "normal" and "remedial" courses	Different curriculum in "mainstream" and "basic" courses	Different pacing in one-semester and stretch courses but the same curriculum

Table 1 reveals how the Advanced Writing framework disrupts the discourse of the Remedial Writing framework in ways that the Basic Writing Framework was not able to: by eliminating the semantic macrostructures "remedial" and "basic" and "skills"; by eliminating high stakes timed testing as a tool to track and label students; by erasing the basic/normal dichotomy; and by making two semesters of composition the mainstream and one semester advanced. Composition teachers who are concerned about being complicit in the discourse of remediation and basic skills can reflect on Table 1 to consider which column their own programs align with and what steps they can take to move their programs away from testing, tracking, and the normal/basic distinction.

LOOKING BACK, LOOKING FORWARD AGAIN: CONCLUSIONS AND RECOMMENDATIONS

My argument for the Advanced Writing Framework is not a criticism of the work of the first generation of CSU Basic Writing teachers; nor is it a dismissal of what has been the strategic benefit of the term and the concept of "Basic Writing" in protecting resources for underserved students in the CSU. Shaughnessy's relabeling of remediation as "Basic Writing" was a savvy rhetorical move away from exclusionary language that CSU writing teachers were wise to adapt at the time. Shaughnessy's intention was toavoid both the term "remedial" (with its emphasis on personal defects) and "developmental" (with its implications that students are cognitively stunted). Deborah Mutnick argues that "basic writing, for all its internal contradictions, has played a vital role in increasing access to higher education" (72), and the creation of Basic Writing programs in the CSU system in the 1960s and 70s was a savvy move to protect access for socioeconomically disadvantaged students and provide them the support they needed to succeed in college writing. The recent creation of alternatives to non-credit bearing remedial coursework under the Advanced Writing Framework has been a savvy move as well, and one that has helped save the resources garnered by Basic Writing programs from right-wing attacks on access and entitlement and from budget cuts that have decimated state support for remediation in the past decade. I believe Basic Writing programs across the country can take away a number of lessons from the current evolution in first-year composition in the CSU, and I believe the Advanced Writing Framework represents more than just a rhetorically savvy move; it represents the possibility of escape from the "political-semantic web" (Rose 342) of the language of exclusion.

Changing the Nature of the Discourse

Based on my analysis of the emerging Advanced Writing Framework in the CSU, I feel there are strategies WPAs and writing teachers can use to help change the nature of the debate and disrupt the discourse of the Remedial Writing Framework that endures not just in California but across the United States. The most important of these strategies is toavoid labeling college writing courses or programs "remedial," "developmental," or "basic." There are times that it may be strategically necessary to use these terms and concepts to ensure the survival of a program, but it is up to composition teachers to remove these semantic macrostructures from the discourse norms. The discourse event of Early Start reinforces that if we continue using these terms, the Remedial Writing Framework will endure and replicate in the language of administrators and the public.

I believe it is also important for WPAs and writing teachers not to be complicit in labeling students "remedial," "developmental," or "basic" when discussing college writers and college writing courses with faculty, administration, and the media or when designing writing assessment and placement. As the CSU faculty quoted in campus and city newspapers reporting on Early Start and the faculty senate resolutions against Early Start reveal, as long as teachers use the language of exclusion, we unintentionally replicate the dominant discourse of the Remedial Writing Framework even as we argue against it. In an Advanced Writing Framework, the current writing assessment best practice that works against labels that stigmatize college writers in the minds of the public is Directed Self Placement. The history of Basic Writing in the CSU reveals that regardless of who designs the content of a timed writing test, who scores the test, or what the placement nuances are, administrators, faculty, students, and the public will associate a timed test with passing or failing, and with sorting the "normal" students from the "deficient" students. As my analysis of the emerging Advanced Writing Framework in the CSU emphasizes, DSP helps ensure that writing teachers control the discourse of assessment and placement. It can be a challenge to argue for DSP in the context of national and local discourses that assume that timed writing tests are valid indicators of college readiness and that "remedial" students won't be capable of making decisions about which writing course is best for them. At the CSU it took decades of politicking through English Council and at local campuses to persuade the Chancellor's Office to allow DSP to replace the EPT. WPAs who are working to change a remedial framework that dominates both nationally and locally at most institutions cannot expect change to happen overnight.

At most institutions of higher education, a one semester composition course is considered mainstream, and typically more than one semester of preparation in first-year composition is labeled "basic" or "developmental" or "remedial." The Advanced Writing Framework makes the case that one way to disrupt the normalized discourse of alleged literacy crises and legions of underprepared students draining taxpayer money is to rethink how much coursework in composition *most* entering college students will need to prepare for complex academic literacies. Rather than defining one semester of first-year composition as "mainstream" or the "norm," we should define it as "advanced" or "accelerated." We need to disabuse administrators and the public of the normalized discourse that fifteen weeks of reading and writing instruction from a composition expert is enough for most students to make the transition from high school to college literacies. Connected to this recommendation is the strategy of labeling anything beyond one semester of composition—whether it is stretch or studio or some other configuration—as "mainstream" rather than "basic" or "developmental" or "remedial." By defining the stretch course as the mainstream option, the CSU campuses in my study have worked toward eliminating the discourse of the Remedial Writing Framework without eliminating the amount of instruction and support most students will need to succeed in college reading and writing. The experience of the CSU system shows that we can change the discourse of our curriculum, our professional identities, and our disciplinary and public conversations. We can stop using terms like "remedial" or "basic" or "developmental." We can frame our research on the assets diverse students bring to college writing and less on the challenges and problems the students we label "basic writers" present. We can resist the urge to track and separate the "basic" from the mainstream—in our curriculum, in our research, at our conferences, and in our journals.

The shift from the Remedial Writing Framework to the Basic Writing Framework in the 1970s was important and necessary, and this shift protected access for underserved students, but the discourse event of Early Start further emphasizes that what this shift failed to do was change the nature of the discourse of remediation and basic skills. To truly disrupt the discourse of the Remedial Writing Framework, we need to recognize our own complicity in this discourse and work to move beyond the discoursal limits of the Basic Writing Framework. Replacing the language of exclusion and the discourse of the Remedial Writing Framework will not be easy or fast. But if administrators, politicians, the media, and our fellow faculty can so quickly and easily adopt and replicate the language of exclusion that we ourselves have at times been complicit in supporting, there is reason to believe that they will adopt new assumptions and a new discourse if we lead the way.

Works Cited

Adams, Peter, Sarah Gearhart, Robert Miller, and Ann Roberts. "The Accelerated Learning Program: Throwing Open the Gates." *Journal of Basic Writing* 28.2 (2009): 50-69. Print.

Addison, Brian. "CSU Launches Program to Alleviate Remedial Student Issues." *Long Beach Post* 8 Feb. 2013. Web. 1 Sep. 2015.

Adler-Kassner, Linda, and Susanmarie Harrington. *Basic Writing as a Political Act: Public Conversations about Writing and Literacies.* New York: Hampton Press, 2002. Print.

---. "In the Here and Now: Public Policy and Basic Writing." *Journal of Basic Writing.* 25.2 (2006): 27-48. Print.

Bailey, Joe. "University to Force Remediation." *The Collegian* 9 Apr. 2010. Web. 1 Sep. 2015.

Bartholomae, David. "The Tidy House: Basic Writing in the American Curriculum." *Journal of Basic Writing* 12.1 (1993): 4-21. Print.

Bordas, Ally. "Early Start Program." *Fullerton Sentinel* 8 Feb. 2011. Web. 1 Sep. 2015.

California State Postsecondary Education Commission. *Promises to Keep: Remedial Education in California's Public Colleges and Universities.* Jan. 1983. Web. 30 May 2015.

California State University Academic Senate. "Opposition to Impending Implementation of Mandatory Early Start Programs." 8 May 2009. Web. 1 September 2015.

California State University English Council. "Position Statement: Mandatory Early Start." Apr. 2010. Web. 5 June 2015.

California State University Office of the Chancellor. "Executive Order 1048." June 2010. Web. 16 April 2015.

California State University Public Affairs Office. "CSU Freshmen to Get an Early Start on Critical Skills." 7 Feb. 2012. Web. 10 Dec. 2014.

California State University Task Force on Remediation. "CSU Plan to Reduce Remedial Activity 1984-1990: A Report Submitted at the Request of the California Postsecondary Education Commission." Mar. 1984. Web. 23 May 2015.

Carmona, Ariel. "Cal State's Early Start Program Sparks Opposition." *CalWatchdog.com* 30 July 2012. Web. 1 Sep. 2015.

Commission for the Review of the Master Plan of Higher Education. *The Master Plan Renewed: Unity, Equity, Quality, and Efficiency in California Postsecondary Education*. July 1987. Web. 2 June 2015.

Crouch, Mary Kay, and Gerri McNenny. "Looking Back, Looking Forward: California Grapples with 'Remediation.'" *Journal of Basic Writing* 19.2 (2000): 44-71. Print.

Crowley, Sharon. *Composition in the University: Historical and Polemical Essays*. Pittsburgh: University of Pittsburgh Press, 1998. Print.

Education Commission of the States. *Blueprint for College Readiness: A 50 State Policy Analysis*. 2014. Web. 9 June 2015.

Fairclough, Norman. "Critical Discourse Analysis as a Method in Social Scientific Research." *Methods of Critical Discourse Analysis*. Eds. Ruth Wodack and Michael Meyer. Thousand Oaks, CA: Sage, 2001. 121-38. Print.

Fairclough, Norman, Jane Mulderrig, and Ruth Wodak. "Critical Discourse Analysis" *Discourse Studies: A Multidisciplinary Introduction*. Ed. Teun A. van Dijk. Thousand Oaks, CA: Sage, 2011. 357-78. Print.

Foucault, Michel. *The Archaeology of Knowledge and the Discourse on Language*. New York: Pantheon. 1972. Print.

Fox, Tom. *Defending Access: A Critique of Standards in Higher Education*. Portsmouth, NH: Boynton/Cook, 1999. Print.

Glau, Gregory. "*Stretch* at 10: A Progress Report on Arizona State University's Stretch Program." *Journal of Basic Writing* 26.2 (2007): 30-48. Print.

---. "The Stretch Program: Arizona State University's New Model of University-Level Basic Writing Instruction." *Writing Program Administration* 20.1-2 (1996): 79-91. Print.

Horner, Bruce. "Discoursing Basic Writing." *College Composition and Communication* 47.2 (1996): 199-222. Print.

---. "Relocating Basic Writing." *Journal of Basic Writing* 30.2 (2011): 5-23. Print. Huckin, Thomas, Jennifer Andrus, and Jennifer Clary-Lemon. "Critical Discourse Analysis and Rhetoric and Composition." *College Composition nd Communication* 64.1 (2012): 107-29. Print.

Kernes, Justin. "Early Start Program to Begin Next Summer." *The Pioneer* 10 Nov. 2011. Web. 1 Sep. 2015.

Krieger, Lisa. "California State University Wants Struggling Students to Take Remedial Courses Prior to Freshman Year." *San Jose Mercury News* 18 Mar. 2010. Web. 1 Sep. 2015.

Krupnick, Matt. "Cal State Campuses Overwhelmed by Remedial Needs." *Contra Costa Times* 11 December 2011. Web. 1 Sep. 2015.

Lalicker, William. "A Basic Introduction to Basic Writing Program Structures: A Baseline and Five Alternatives." *Basic Writing e-Journal* 1.2 (Winter 1999). Web. 10 Dec. 2013.

Lamos, Steve. "Basic Writing, CUNY, and 'Mainstreaming': (De)Racialization Reconsidered." *Journal of Basic Writing* 19.2 (2000): 22-43. Print.

Legislative Analyst's Office. "Initial Review of CSU's Early Start Program." Jan. 2014. Web. 3 June 2015.

Liaison Committee of the State Board of Education. *A Master Plan for Higher Education in California, 1960-1975*. Sacramento: California State Department of Education, 1960. Web. 30 May 2015.

Luke, Allan. "Text and Discourse in Education: An Introduction to Critical Discourse Analysis." *Review of Research in Education* 21 (1995-1996): 3-48. Print.

Mutnick, Deborah. "The Strategic Value of Basic Writing: An Analysis of the Current Moment." *Journal of Basic Writing* 19.1 (2000): 69-83. Print.

National Commission on Excellence in Education. *A Nation at Risk: The Imperative for Educational Reform*. 1983. Web. 8 June 2015.

Otte, George, and Rebecca Williams Mlynarczyk. "The Future of Basic Writing." *Reference Guides to Rhetoric and Composition: Basic Writing*. Parlor Press and The WAC Clearinghouse, 2010. Web. 7 June 2015.

Pavesich, Matthew. "Reflecting on the Liberal Reflex: Rhetoric and the Politics of Acknowledgment in Basic Writing." *Journal of Basic Writing* 30.2 (2011): 84-109. Print.

Ritter, Kelly. *Before Shaughnessy: Basic Writing at Yale and Harvard, 1920-1960*. Carbondale, Southern Illinois UP, 2009. Print.

Rose, Mike. "The Language of Exclusion: Writing Instruction at the University." *College English* 47.4 (1985) 341-59. Print.

San Jose State University Academic Senate. "Opposition to the Implementation of Mandatory Early Start Programs." 14 Feb. 2011. Web. 1 Sep. 2015. Shaughnessy, Mina. *Errors and Expectations: A Guide for the Teacher of Basic Writing*. New York: Oxford UP, 1977. Print.

Shor, Ira. "Our Apartheid: Writing Instruction and Inequality." *Journal of Basic Writing* 16.1 (1997): 91-104. Print.

Soliday, Mary. *The Politics of Remediation: Institutional and Student Needs in Higher Education*. Pittsburgh: University of Pittsburgh Press, 2002. Print. Spelling's Commission. *A Test of Leadership: Charting the Future of U.S. Higher Education*. U.S. Department of Education, 2006. Web. 8 June 2015.

Stanley, Jane. *The Rhetoric of Remediation: Negotiating Entitlement and Access to Higher Education*. Pittsburgh, PA: University of Pittsburgh Press, 2010. Print.

van Dijk, Teun A. "Critical Discourse Analysis." *The Handbook of Discourse Analysis*. Eds. Deborah Schiffrin, Deborah Tannen, and Heidi Hamilton. Malden, Mass: Blackwell, 2001. 352-71. Print.

---. "Multidisciplinary CDA: A Plea for Diversity." *Methods of Critical Discourse Analysis*. Eds. Ruth Wodack and Michael Meyer. Thousand Oaks, CA: Sage, 2001. 95-120. Print.

Villanueva, Victor. "Subversive Complicity and Basic Writing Across the Curriculum." *Journal of Basic Writing* 32.1 (2013): 97-110. Print.

White, Edward. "The Importance of Placement and Basic Studies: Helping Students Succeed Under the New Elitism." *Journal of Basic Writing* 14.2 (1995): 75-84. Print.

Wodak, Ruth. "Critical Linguistics and Critical Discourse Analysis." *Handbook of Pragmatics*. Ed. Jan Östman and Jef Verschueren. Amsterdam: John Benjamins, 2006. 50-70. Print.

---. "What CDA is About." *Methods of Critical Discourse Analysis*. Eds. Ruth Wodack and Michael Meyer. Thousand Oaks, CA: Sage, 2001. 1-13. Print.

Dan Melzer is Director of First-Year Composition at the University of California, Davis. His research interests include writing across the curriculum, multiliteracies, and writing program administration. He is the former Writing Across the Curriculum Coordinator at California State University, Sacramento

JOURNAL OF SECOND LANGUAGE WRITING

The *Journal of Second Language Writing* is on the Web at https://www.journals.elsevier.com/journal-of-second-language-writing

The *Journal of Second Language Writing* is devoted to publishing theoretically grounded reports of research and discussions that represent a contribution to current understandings of central issues in second and foreign language writing and writing instruction. Some areas of interest are personal characteristics and attitudes of L2 writers, L2 writers' composing processes, features of L2 writers' texts, readers' responses to L2 writing, assessment/evaluation of L2 writing, contexts (cultural, social, political, institutional) for L2 writing, and any other topic clearly relevant to L2 writing theory, research, or instruction.

Impact of Source Texts and Prompts on Students' Genre Uptake

Miller, Mitchell, and Pessoa uniquely combine two perspectives on genre—Rhetorical Genre Studies and Systemic Functional Linguistics—to investigate intertextuality and argumentative writing in the context of a first-year undergraduate world history course at an American university in the Middle East. Their analysis demonstrates how professors' choice of source texts and writing prompts influence the extent to which students produce the argument genre expected of them in their discipline. The study contributes to research on intertextuality by shedding light on the relationships between course materials and student writing and advances genre studies by showing how two genre traditions can be profitably integrated. It also has important pedagogical implications for the teaching of argumentative writing in the disciplines.

* Reprinted from the *Journal of Second Language Writing* 31 (2016): 11–24. © 2016, with permission from Elsevier.

Impact of Source Texts and Prompts on Students' Genre Uptake

Ryan T. Miller, Thomas D. Mitchell, and Silvia Pessoa

Abstract: Argumentative writing is a vital but challenging genre for university students, particularly second language writers. While much is known about different factors that make it challenging, in this paper, we focus on an underexplored factor: the intertextual relationship between source texts, prompts, and student writing. We analyze student writing in a first-year history class at a branch campus of an American university in the Middle East, and more specifically, how source texts and writing prompts condition whether students produce the expected argument genre. We draw from two perspectives on genre: Rhetorical Genre Studies, with its focus on the highly contextualized nature of writing, provides a useful lens through which to view intertextuality; Systemic Functional Linguistics, with its explicit focus on language, provides tools for studying writing development in school genres. Results suggest that source texts that do not contain an explicit argument and prompts that ask for students' opinion may facilitate students' uptake of argument. The study has pedagogical implications for improving alignment between an instructor's goals and expectations, assignment design, and the writing students produce.

1. INTRODUCTION

Learning to write arguments is a crucial part of students' induction into university-level work (Wu & Allison, 2005) and writing argumentatively is "one of the greatest challenges many English language learners (ELLs) are likely to face" (Hirvela, 2013, p. 67). This is in part because L2 university writers may still be in the process of "learning the valued genres of academic communication" (Tardy, 2009, p. 4). Thus, even when these students are expected to produce arguments, they do not always meet this expectation. This gap between the instructor's expectation and the writing that students produce may stem from varied and overlapping factors, including lack of academic preparation (Allison, 2009, Harklau, 1994, Harklau, 2001, Hirvela, 2013), organization of ideas (Coffin & Hewings, 2004), balancing authoritative voice with inclusion of multiple perspectives (Coffin and Hewings, 2004, Miller et al., 2014), and justifying claims with appropriate evidence (Silva, 1993). In this paper, we focus on an underexplored factor: the intertextual relationship between source texts, prompts, and student writing. We analyze student writing in response to source texts and prompts in a first-year history class at a branch campus of an American university in the Middle East. Our analysis demonstrates how source texts and writing prompts condition whether students produce the expected argument genre.

In higher education, students often write from source texts and in response to prompts (Hirvela and Du, 2013, Horowitz, 1989). The relationships among a source text, prompt, and student writing can be thought of as a type of intertextuality, or the relationship between two or more texts. Because university-level writing involves not only putting forth one's own ideas, but representing those ideas in relation to prior discourse in discipline-specific ways, intertextuality is an important aspect of academic writing (Tardy, 2009). Research on intertextuality between source texts and L2 writing has mostly focused on textual borrowing, plagiarism, and summary writing (e.g., Pecorari, 2003), with limited focus on how features of source texts influence student writing, particularly argumentative writing. Research on intertextuality between writing prompts and L2 writing has mostly focused on the context of standardized assessment (e.g., Horowitz, 1986, Horowitz, 1989), with limited focus on classroom contexts. Very little attention has been paid to the interplay between source texts, writing prompts, and student writing.

To study how source texts and prompts condition student writing, we draw from two perspectives on genre that have seldom been combined: Rhetorical Genre Studies (RGS; Freadman & Medway, 1994) and Systemic Functional Linguistics (SFL; Halliday & Mathiessen, 2004). RGS, with its focus on the highly contextualized nature of writing, provides a useful lens through which to view intertextuality. Specifically, we use Freadman, 1994, Freadman, 2002 notion of *uptake*—how one genre invokes another genre in response—to consider how source texts may influence the genre students produce (i.e., their uptake). We also draw on Bawarshi's (2003) application of uptake to the conditions that writing prompts create for student texts. We extend this work on uptake into an L2 setting, while also adding detailed linguistic analysis of the genres students produce.

For this analysis, we draw on SFL because of its explicit focus on language and the tools it provides for studying writing development in school genres. From an SFL perspective, genre is a "staged, goal-oriented, social process" (Martin, 1992, p. 505). We use Coffin's (2006)typology and linguistic descriptions of history genres to closely analyze student writing. Although SFL approaches to genre have been widely applied in the study of history writing, this has primarily been at the elementary and secondary school levels (e.g., Christie and Derewianka, 2008, Llinares and Pascual Peña, 2015, Martin, 1992, Schleppegrell et al., 2004), not in university settings.

In the next section, we discuss prior research on intertextuality between source texts and student writing, and between prompts and student writing. Then we describe in more detail how we draw on the RGS and SFL perspectives on genre. Finally, we introduce school history genres, with a focus on the Argument genre.

2. Literature Review

2.1. Intertextuality, source texts, and prompts

University students in many disciplines are frequently expected to write arguments from source texts (Davis, 2013, Hirvela and Du, 2013, Horowitz, 1989, Keck, 2006, Keck, 2014, Shaw and Pecorari, 2013). Writing from source texts can be challenging as it requires students to engage in "complex reading and writing activities and make contextualized decisions as they interact with the reading materials and the assigned writing tasks" (Hirvela & Du, 2013, p. 87). Much of the literature on intertextuality between source texts and student writing has focused on textual borrowing and plagiarism (see, e.g., Abasi et al., 2006, Keck, 2010, Pecorari, 2003, Plakans and Gebril, 2013, Shi, 2012, Weigle and Parker, 2012, Wette, 2010). However, fewer studies have looked at how specific aspects of the source text affect student writing. Keck (2014) showed that expository texts, more than narrative texts, tend to generate greater textual borrowing among both L1 and L2 students, resulting in more texts that mirror the sequence of ideas in the source text. Yu (2009) found that a number of aspects of source texts—including macro-organization, frequency of unfamiliar words, topic familiarity, and length of source texts—affected students' ability to summarize the source text.

Another form of intertextuality common in higher education is writing in response to prompts. Much of the research on prompts has considered their role in language tests (e.g., Hamp-Lyons and Mathias, 1994, Hinkel, 2002, Horowitz, 1986, Horowitz, 1989, Kobrin et al., 2011, Kroll and Reid, 1994), with less attention to the use of prompts in classroom writing assignments or how they affect student writing (Oliver, 1995, Reid and Kroll, 1995). Oliver (1995) found that the quality of student writing is affected by the types and amount of rhetorical specification of topic, purpose, and audience in the prompts. Studies focusing on task complexity have suggested that more complex prompts may encourage students to write more effectively by, for example, producing more accurate writing (e.g., Kobrin et al., 2011, Kuiken and Vedder, 2008, Ong and Zhang, 2010).

Specifically addressing the use of prompts in history classes is the work of Coffin (2006) and Llinares and Pascual Peña (2015). According to Coffin (2006), "Unless a writing task/exam question is formulated in clear, unambiguous terms and/or supported with supplementary guidance and support, students may produce a genre that is not the 'target' genre expected by a teacher" (p. 169). Consequently, it is important that teachers deconstruct the goals of the task with the students, are consistent in the wording of the prompt, and make it explicit "that different genres are given greater weight and value in different contexts" (p. 169). Llinares and Pascual Peña (2015) investigated use of oral prompts in history classes and found that the types of questions teachers ask can affect the genres students produce in classroom discussions.

2.2. RGS and SFL approaches to genre

To study how source texts and writing prompts condition student writing, we draw from two perspectives on genre: RGS and SFL. The RGS approach views genre as social action (Miller, 1994) and focuses on socio-rhetorical aspects of genre such as discourse community, audience expectation, rhetorical situation, and intertextuality. Within this approach, writing is viewed as highly complex and contextualized, with a wide range of factors that influence the final product, many of which are invisible to students and instructors alike. Among these are intertextual factors, or influences from other texts (Johns, 2011).

Following an RGS perspective, the intertextuality between source texts, prompts, and student writing could be considered using Freadman, 1994, Freadman, 2002 concept of uptake, or the ways that genres elicit other genres in response. Freadman (2002) argues that genres create socio-rhetorical conditions for other genres to take up in response, such as a jury's finding creating the conditions that a judge's sentencing takes up. The relationships between genres are not always one-to-one, however, and there could be a range of possible uptakes in response to a text, which Bawarshi (2008, p. 81) describes as a text's "uptake profile." According to Freadman (2002), some texts are designed to elicit certain kinds of uptakes, and some uptakes may be more valued or expected than others. In university-level writing, source texts may create conditions for certain ranges of uptakes and different source texts may have wider or narrower uptake profiles. Part of the task for student writers, then, is to become aware of how to select an appropriate genre in response to another genre. However, the need for this awareness is often invisible to both students and instructors and may result in a lack of explicit instruction, leading to uptake profiles that are wider than instructors expect.

The concept of uptake has also been applied to the relationship between prompts and student writing. Building on Freadman (2002), Bawarshi and Reiff (2010) argue that "the assignment prompt creates the conditions for the student essay" (p. 86), inviting students to take up specific positions in their writing. Although prompts may provide room for alternative positions, student uptakes of prompts that differ from the desired uptake are often seen as failures (Pelkowski, 1998, cited in Bawarshi, 2003).

While still emphasizing the social dimension of genre, SFL investigates how language is used to make meaning to achieve the goals of a genre. Although variation between contexts is acknowledged, the SFL perspective contends that "within that variation, [there are] relatively stable underlying patterns of 'shapes' that organize texts so that they are culturally and socially functional" (Feez, 2002, p. 53), and thus genre instruction focuses on making language and language choices explicit and scaffolding students' production of increasingly complex genres (Martin & Rose, 2008). SFL's explicit focus on language provides tools for the detailed analysis of school genres. Researchers who use SFL have taken these tools into classrooms, enabling teachers to make the language of academic writing explicit for students, and resulting in writing improvement, particularly for L2 writers (e.g., Brisk, 2014, Dreyfus et al., 2015).

2.3. School history genres

Genres of school history writing have been studied extensively from an SFL perspective. These studies have identified a number of distinct history genres and their linguistic features. Coffin (2006) describes these genres along a sequence of development (Table 1). Students initially learn to write chronologically organized, story-like Recording genres, such as Autobiographical and Biographical Recounts (which retell a person's life), Historical Recounts (which retell events in chronological order), and Historical Accounts (which explain the reason for a specific chronology). Students then move toward Explaining genres, which are organized by cause-and-effect relationships. Later, students progress toward writing more abstract Arguing genres, which incorporate complex interrelationships among ideas, evaluations of information and perspectives, and attention to the possibility of multiple interpretations of a historical event.

Table 1. School history genres.

Genre family	Genres
Recording genres	1. Autobiographical Recount
	2. Biographical Recount
	3. Historical Recount
	4. Historical Account
Explaining genres	5. Factorial Explanation
	6. Consequential Explanation
Arguing genres	7. Exposition
	8. Challenge
	9. Discussion

Note: Based on Coffin (2006).

The transition to writing Arguing genres is difficult for many students (Martin, Maton, & Matruglio, 2010). Students must select and evaluate facts, and interpret, generalize, and transform these facts to create meaning (Eggins, Wignell, & Martin, 1993). Although expert writers of historical arguments skillfully perform this knowledge transformation (i.e., "integrating content as interpreted evidence for an argument"), novice writers tend to engage more in knowledge telling (i.e., "listing… document content as discrete information bits") without abstraction and evaluation (McCarthy Young & Leinhardt, 1998, p. 25). Given the difficulty of transitioning to Arguing genres for all students, but particularly L2 writers, studying the factors that may influence argumentative writing is important.

2.4. The present study

In our study, we draw on Freadman, 1994, Freadman, 2002 and Bawarshi, 2003, Bawarshi, 2008, Bawarshi and Reiff, 2010) descriptions of uptake for understanding intertextual relationships of source texts and prompts with student writing. We combine this theoretical framework with the linguistic descriptions of history genres from the SFL perspective (e.g., Coffin, 2006, Schleppegrell, 2004). Although RGS and SFL are usually thought of as distinct and separate perspectives (however, see Aull, 2015, for another example of combining RGS and a linguistic perspective on genre), combining these perspectives was useful in our study. The explicit attention to intertextuality in RGS offers important insights in the study of genre, while the explicit linguistic descriptions of history genres in SFL are especially useful for the study of L2 writing (and for L2 writers and writing teachers) and offer systematic tools for analysis and classification of genres.

Our study also extends the previous work on the use of source texts and prompts by investigating how source texts and prompts, both individually and in combination, influence students' genre uptake in a classroom setting. Our research questions were:

1. How does variation across source texts affect students' uptake of the intended Argument genre?
2. How does variation across prompt wordings affect students' uptake of the intended Argument genre?
3. How does the combination of source text and prompt affect students' uptake of the intended Argument genre?

3. Methods

3.1. Data source and context

In the present study,[1] we draw on data from a required first-year undergraduate world history course at a branch campus of an English-medium university in the Middle East that largely follows the curriculum of the main campus in the United States. The course, titled Introduction to World History, was a one-semester overview of major historical milestones from ancient Babylon to modern-day globalization. The data were collected as part of a larger study of academic writing at the university.

The 70 students enrolled in the course came from linguistically and culturally diverse backgrounds, with the majority from the greater Middle East. The average TOEFL iBT score was 97 (equivalent to above C1 level in the Common European Framework of Reference; Educational Testing Service, 2015), indicating that students were generally proficient users of English.

Assignments in the course, all designed by the history professor,[2] included reading and discussing academic and historical texts, and writing six short (1–3 page) argumentative essays about the texts. Eleven readings were assigned, ranging from five to 25 pages in length, and students could choose any six to write about. In each essay, students selected a prompt, choosing from among three to five options, typically based on a single source text.

To supplement our analysis of student writing, we draw on assignment descriptions, grading rubrics, and ongoing conversations with the professor.[3] A substantial proportion (30%) of the grading rubric was dedicated to "Argument," specifying that essays should have a clear thesis statement supported by relevant evidence from the source text, and that there should be "clear relevance of the argument to the question asked." The rubric also emphasized that students should be sensitive to biases and limitations in the sources, suggesting that the professor valued interpretative work beyond reporting the content of the source text. Although he expected argumentative writing, argument was not taught as a genre in this course.

3.2. Text analysis

The motivation for this analysis emerged during a separate project (see Miller et al., 2014), in which we noticed that although the history professor expected students to produce arguments, many students did not. Because of this perceived gap between the professor's expectations and students' genre uptake, we conducted a systematic analysis of the genres that students produced, following Coffin's (2006) typology of history genres and the conditions created by two source texts and the corresponding prompts.

3.2.1. Coding for genre

The 83 essays analyzed include writing from 70 students (13 wrote about both source texts). All three authors independently coded the genre of each essay, and discussed differences until reaching agreement. Based on our data, we modified Coffin's (2006) typology of history genres by incorporating the Report genre[4] (Veel, 1997). To code for genre, we focused on the essays' global structure (genre stages), purpose, and key language features (Coffin, 2006, Schleppegrell, 2004). These features are described in Table 2.

Table 2. Descriptions of genre categories found in the student writing.

Genre	Social purpose	Stages	Key language features
Historical Account	To account for why events happened in a particular sequence	1. Background 2. Account sequence 3. (Deduction)	Temporal organization; language of cause-and-effect; presents events as agentive in bringing about subsequent events
Explanation	To explain the reasons/factors that contribute to a particular outcome To explain the effects/consequences of a situation	1. Outcome/Input (multi-part macro-Theme) 2. Factors/Consequences 3. (Restatement of factors/consequences)	"Text time" rather than temporal organization; orders causes and consequences with numeratives and connectives; construes significance of events through evaluative lexis and clause structures; presents causes and consequences as facts via non-modalized verbs
Descriptive Report	To organize and describe the attributes, properties, behaviors, etc. of a single class of object	1. Topic (multi-part macro-Theme) 2. Attributes, properties, behaviors, etc. 3. (Restatement of attributes, properties, behavior, etc.)	Taxonomical organization; presents descriptions and generalizations as facts via non-modalized verbs

Genre	Social purpose	Stages	Key language features
Argument (Exposition)	To put forward a point of view or argument	1. (Background) 2. Thesis 3. Arguments 4. (Counter-arguments) 5. (Concession) 6. Reinforcement of thesis	Logical organization; evaluates and comments on historical information, supported by evidence; holds interpretations of history as tentative (not factual) that have to be argued for; aligns reader to the position advanced in the thesis via interpersonal resources

Note: Adapted from Coffin (2006), Schleppegrell (2004), and Veel (1997). Genre stages in parentheses are optional.

Historical Accounts are essays that "explain why events occurred while maintaining the 'what' of history in the form of a timeline" (Coffin, 2006, p. 58). In our data, Accounts typically began by summarizing previous historical events (Background), and then presenting an account of events as they unfolded over time (Account sequence). Thus, their global organization was chronological, often manifested through time encoded in marked Themes (i.e., the beginning of a clause: Before the…, During the…, After the…).

Explanations use cause-and-effect relations, not time, as the organizing principle. Students' Explanations were typically organized by a macro-Theme—the opening generalization in a text that serves to predict the text's overall development (Martin, 1992)—that had multiple parts, such as, "Disease affected culture in India, China, and Egypt." Students followed the macro-Theme with body paragraphs that elaborated multiple, simultaneous causes (in the case of Factorial Explanations) or effects (Consequential Explanations), each of which corresponded to a part of the macro-Theme. As Coffin explains, these causes and effects are "presented as categorical, objective 'facts' rather than a set of propositions that have to be argued for" (p. 71) (e.g., *one important effect is…* vs. *this effect is important because…*).

Following Veel (1997), Descriptive Reports were essays that were structured by a taxonomy reflecting the social purpose of "describ[ing] the attributes [or] properties… of a single class of object" (p. 172). These essays had paragraphs united under individual common subclasses of the taxonomy that did not support an overarching argument in the macro-Theme. As with Explanations, the macro-Theme often had multiple parts, with body paragraphs corresponding to each part. For example, one Descriptive Report had a macro-Theme of "By looking at the Hammurabi Code we can conclude many important points and facts which tell us about Babylon's political system, social structure, and economy," followed by three body paragraphs describing each of these, without an over-arching argument that they supported.

Essays were coded as Arguments if they had a central thesis that made a claim in the macro-Theme and a majority of body paragraphs were consistent with and supported this claim. A key distinction between non-argumentative and argumentative history genres has to do with whether the writer acknowledges multiple perspectives on the topic through the use of interpersonal language. To analyze these linguistic resources, we used Martin and White's (2005) Appraisal framework, particularly the resources of ENGAGEMENT. In non-argumentative genres, the focus is on providing "relatively categorical explanations of historical phenomena" (Coffin, 2006, p. 77) with linguistic resources that present information as factual. When writers present information as factual, relying on bare assertions or presuppositions, they are expressing no room for alternative points of view and projecting complete agreement onto the reader. These are termed *monoglossic* (single-voiced) propositions and are typically realized via non-modalized verbs (e.g., the simple present tense). In argumentative genres, on the other hand, writers "hold interpretations of history as tentative" (Coffin, 2006, p. 76), using *heteroglossic* (multi-voiced) propositions to acknowledge multiple perspectives, evaluate information, and guide the reader toward accepting their perspective. They do so using resources such as modality, concede and countering moves, explicit reference to other voices, and moves that comment on discourse to help align the reader to the writer›s perspective (Martin and White, 2005, Miller et al., 2014).

3.2.2. Prompts

We analyzed the prompts' wording to determine the genre each seemed to create conditions for. We based our analysis on Llinares and Pascual Peña's (2015) application of Dalton-Puffer's (2007) classification of academic questions to history classrooms. Llinares and Pascual Peña (2015) analyzed the history genres (also using Coffin, 2006) that students produced in oral responses to teachers' questions for facts (objective happenings), explanation (how something happened or elaboration of facts), reasons (reasons or causes why something happened), and opinions (personal opinion about a fact). They found that questions for facts (e.g., *What happened...?*) and reasons (*Why...?*) were the most common to trigger Historical Accounts and Explanations, whereas questions for opinions (*Do you think...?*) were the most common to trigger Argument.

3.2.3. Source texts

We focused on student responses to two source texts. The first consisted of excerpts from Hammurabi's Code, laws devised by the Babylonian king Hammurabi circa 1754 B.C. Hammurabi's Code is a numbered list of laws and associated punishments for breaking the laws (e.g., "205. If the slave of a freed man strike the body of a freed man, his ear shall be cut off"; codes ranged in length from 10 to 90 words each). As such, there is no overarching claim that is made and supported throughout the text. Furthermore, there is no sequence of events; instead, each particular law presents isolated cause-and-effect relationships.

The second source text was a slightly abridged excerpt from the third chapter of historian William H. McNeill's (1976) book, *Plagues and Peoples*. The chapter is a macro genre[5] describing relationships between humankind and disease. McNeill argues for his interpretation of events by drawing on multiple primary and secondary sources and evaluating their validity. For example, in the following passage, McNeill justifies his interpretation that the existence of parasites prevented Chinese expansion:

All these assertions remain uncomfortably abstract and *a priori*. As in the case of the Middle East, there is little hope of discovering from ancient texts exactly what the humanly dangerous parasites may have been. Still, ancient writers often betray keen awareness of the disease risks in the South. Thus, Ssu-ma Ch'ien, the founder of Chinese historiography, who lived from about 145 to 87 B.C., tells us [...] This is authoritative testimony, for Ssu-ma Ch'ien made a personal tour.... (1976, pp. 104–105)

Here McNeill evaluates historical sources, conceding that they are not completely indisputable ("All these assertions remain uncomfortably abstract and *a priori*"), but then countering with claims about their reliability ("Still, ancient writers often betray keen awareness of the disease risks in the South"). McNeill makes use of interpersonal resources to persuade the reader to adopt his historical assessment based on his explicit reasoning, including his evaluation of available information. Thus, this brief excerpt is indicative of the substantial differences between this text and Hammurabi's Code, which contained no such explicit argumentative features.

In our preliminary analysis, we noticed that the differences between these two texts may have affected students' uptake. In addition to these differences, the selection of Hammurabi's Code was useful as the first reading of the semester—providing insight into what students could produce with limited university instruction—in contrast to the McNeill text, the fourth reading in the semester.

4. Results

While the professor's expected uptake for each essay was Argument, we found that the prompts and source texts had wider uptake profiles, with students producing several non-Argument genres. We found that not all of the prompts created conditions to be taken up as Arguments, and that one of the source texts facilitated Argument uptake while the other did not.

Following Dalton-Puffer (2007) and Llinares and Pascual Peña (2015), we analyzed the language of each of the prompts and found that three were questions for opinion, while four were questions for facts or explanations. Out of 43 essays written in response to questions for opinions, most (35, or 81.4%) were Arguments, so we termed these Argument Conditioning Prompts. Of the 40 essays written in response to questions for facts or explanations, only 14 (35.0%) were Arguments, so we termed these Non-Argument Conditioning Prompts.

We found that Hammurabi's Code resulted in a much higher proportion of Arguments (43 out of 59, or 72.9%) than the McNeill text (six out of 24, or 25%). Thus, we termed Hammurabi's Code an Argument Facilitative Source Text and McNeill a Non-Argument Facilitative Source Text.

Our analysis revealed four combinations of prompt and source text that conditioned students' uptakes (Fig. 1): (1) Argument Conditioning Prompt + Argument Facilitative Source Text; (2) Non-Argument Conditioning Prompt + Argument Facilitative Source Text; (3) Argument Conditioning Prompt + Non-Argument Facilitative Source Text; and (4) Non-Argument Conditioning Prompt + Non-Argument Facilitative Source Text. An Argument Conditioning Prompt combined with the Argument Facilitative Source Text resulted in 30 out of 31 essays (96.8%) being Arguments. The Non-Argument Conditioning

Prompts, when combined with the Argument Facilitative Source Text, resulted in 13 out of 28 essays (46.4%) being Arguments. On the other hand, the Argument Conditioning Prompts, when combined with the Non-Argument Facilitative Source Text, resulted in five out of 12 essays (41.7%) being Arguments. The Non-Argument Conditioning Prompts, when combined with the Non-Argument Facilitative Source Text, resulted in only 1 out of 12 essays (8.3%) being an Argument.

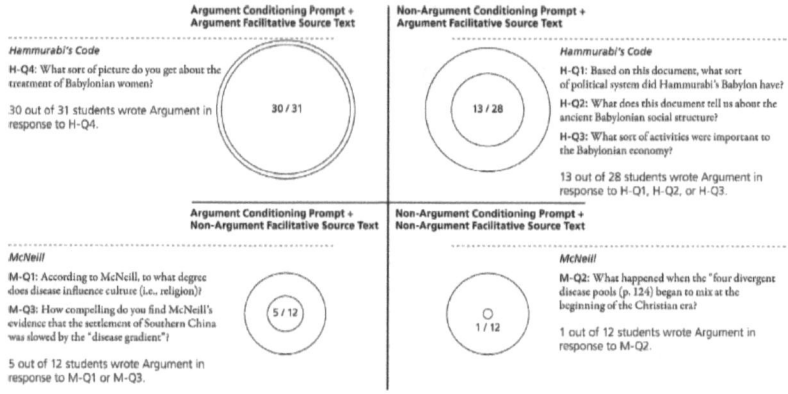

Fig. 1. Overview of findings.

In the following sections, we illustrate these findings with analysis of representative examples of student uptakes for each combination.

4.1. Argument Conditioning Prompt + Argument Facilitative Source Text

H-Q4, because it directly addresses the student ("do *you* get"), is a question for opinion (Dalton-Puffer, 2007), the type Llinares and Pascual Peña (2015) found most likely to result in Argument. Similarly, in our study, 30 of the 31 students who responded to this prompt produced Arguments, and we categorized H-Q4 as an Argument Conditioning Prompt (Table 3).

Table 3. Genres Produced in response to Hammurabi's Code, Question 4 (H-Q4).

Prompt	Argument	Report	Total
H-Q4: What sort of picture do you get about the treatment of Babylonian women?	30	1	31

This result suggests that the conditions created by this prompt and the Hammurabi source text were extremely favorable to Argument. Not only were the students responding to an Argument Conditioning Prompt, they were doing so in response to Hammurabi's Code, which is a list of laws. While the Code includes laws that outline provisions, expectations, and punishments that are particular to women, it never makes any overt evaluative statement about the treatment of women. Thus, to effectively answer the prompt, students needed to interpret the meaning of the laws and make claims about what they indicated about the status of women. The lack of an explicit argument in the source text appears to have facilitated interpretation and analysis, given that the majority of the students used the laws to support their own claims.

The 30 students who wrote Argument followed the stages of Argument, including a thesis in the macro-Theme position, support, and reiteration. The thesis was a central claim based on a subjective interpretation of Hammurabi's laws. Students supported their claims with evidence of laws indicative of that interpretation, and they tied this evidence back to the overarching claim. Most essays supported a claim that Hammurabi's laws were "harsh," "rigid," or "unfair," while a few claimed that they were "fair" (or "rigid, but fair"). For example, one student argued that, "women were considered to be much less important than the men." In a paragraph focused on women receiving different punishment than men for the same crime, the student cited a relevant law as evidence, followed by the assertion that "this demonstrates that the laws were very biased against Babylonian women." Thus, this student made use of ENGAGEMENT (Martin & White, 2005) moves by bringing Hammurabi's voice into the text and guiding the reader toward accepting her perspective with the use of "this demonstrates."

Only one student took up H-Q4 with a Report, which had a multipart macro-Theme but without an overarching claim. This essay was similar to Reports written in response to other prompts, which we discuss in detail below.

4.2. Non-Argument Conditioning Prompt + Argument Facilitative Source Text

H-Q1, H-Q2, and H-Q3 can be categorized as questions for facts (Dalton-Puffer, 2007), a type Llinares and Pascual Peña (2015) found not well suited to Argument. While the phrasing of H-Q1 ("What sort of") is similar to H-Q4 (discussed above), H-Q1 does not solicit the students' opinion through direct address. In H-Q2, there seems to be a tension between asking for fact ("what does this document tell") and asking for opinion ("tell us"). Although the phrase "tell us" does make the prompt more personal, we find it does not really solicit students' opinions, especially when compared to more direct wordings, such as "What sort of picture do you get about the ancient Babylonian social structure?" Finally, H-Q3 appears to invite the students to produce a list of activities without arguing why they were important. Therefore, we categorized H-Q1, H-Q2, and H-Q3 as Non-Argument Conditioning Prompts (Table 4).

Table 4. Genres produced in response to Hammurabi's Code, Questions 1–3 (H-Q1, H-Q2, H-Q3).

Prompt	Argument	Report	Total
H-Q1: Based on this document, what sort of political system did Hammurabi's Babylon have?	4	5	9
H-Q2: What does this document tell us about the ancient Babylonian social structure?	8	9	17
H-Q3: What sort of activities were important to the Babylonian economy?	1	1	2
Total	13	15	28

Although they are Non-Argument Conditioning Prompts, they generated a significant number of Argument uptakes. Again we suggest that the features of the source text had some bearing on these results. Hammurabi's Code never makes an explicit argument about the type of political system it represents (H-Q1), the social structure of ancient Babylon (H-Q2), or the activities that were important for the society (H-Q3). The Hammurabi text appears to have conditioned some students to make inferences based on their interpretation of the laws' content, in spite of the prompt, further indicating that Hammurabi's Code is an Argument Facilitative Source Text.

The 13 students who wrote Arguments took up these prompts by making a claim in the macro-Theme and supporting their perspective with evidence from the text, following the stages of Argument. For example, in response to H-Q1, one student proposed that Hammurabi's Code "represented a mix of political systems." Each body paragraph focused on the student's interpretation of a single law as indicative of dictatorship, democracy, or theocracy. The student provided claims and supporting reasoning for his interpretation and concluded that this evidence demonstrated that the Code represented a mix of political systems.

On the other hand, the 15 students who wrote Reports took up these prompts by focusing on descriptions, but without an overarching claim. For example, one student responded with a multi-part macro-Theme suggesting that the political system "applied dictatorship, a rigid system, and communism on [its] people." In other words, the political system was described as having three sub-classes, and each body paragraph corresponded, in order, to one of these (e.g., "First of all, Hammurabi was a dictator…"; "Secondly, Hammurabi has a rigid punishment system…"; and "Finally, Hammurabi applied communism in his community.…"), with no effort to tie the paragraphs together as support for an overall characterization of the system to create a unifying argument.

Although these students did not write Arguments, they nonetheless made interpretations and inferences in order to create the labels for the sub-classes (e.g., "a rigid system," "communism") because these labels did not exist in the source text. Furthermore, while the use of interpersonal resources was, on the whole, less frequent and less effective in the Reports, some students incorporated ENGAGEMENT moves to integrate and explicate evidence in support of claims about the individual sub-classes ("if we returned to code 23, *we can see*how he is practicing communism when he forced all the people in his community to pay back the stolen money"). Thus, even in the Reports that lacked the key stages of Argument, the Argument Facilitative Source Text appears to have conditioned uptakes that had some features of argumentative writing and analysis.

4.3. Argument Conditioning Prompt + Non-Argument Facilitative Source Text

While nearly all of the students responded with Argument to the Argument Conditioning Prompt about Hammurabi's Code, the McNeill text resulted in proportionally fewer Argument uptakes when combined with Argument Conditioning Prompts, M-Q1 and M-Q3. Both prompts are framed in terms of degree, a framing Coffin (2006) suggests is favorable for triggering Argument, and M-Q3 has the additional element of direct address ("do *you* find"), which makes this prompt especially well suited to the uptake of Argument (Llinares & Pascual Peña, 2015). For M-Q1, four students wrote Arguments, and three wrote Consequential Explanations. For M-Q3, only one student wrote Argument, while the other five wrote Factorial Explanations (Table 5).

Table 5. Genres produced in response to McNeill, Questions 1 and 3 (M-Q1, M-Q3).

Prompt	Argument	Explanation	Historical Account	Total
M-Q1: According to McNeill, to what degree does disease influence culture (i.e., religion)?	4	3	0	7
M-Q3: How compelling do you find McNeill's evidence that the settlement of Southern China was slowed by the "disease gradient"?	1	4	0	5
Total	5	7	0	12

In the five Arguments in response to M-Q1 and M-Q3, students took up the prompt by making an overarching claim that fully answered the prompt and following the stages of Argument. For example, for M-Q1, students who responded with Argument made an overarching claim about the idea of degree (e.g., "…we can see that diseases have had some effect on influencing some regions"), and either forecasted or followed up evidence in body paragraphs with summarizing statements that tied back to the thesis (e.g., disease affected culture "somewhat" or "greatly"). However, three of the five Arguments were underdeveloped versions of this genre, lacking important features of fully developed Arguments. These essays made statements about degree either at the beginning or end of most paragraphs, but with other sentences in the paragraphs written as if they were telling facts or explaining causes and effects factually, and thus more closely resembled the language of an Explanation in significant portions of the essay.

For both prompts, students who wrote Explanations elided some of the prompt wording and turned the prompts into a question for explanation (Dalton-Puffer, 2007). In M-Q1, students who wrote Explanations apparently took up the prompt by answering the question, "*how* does disease influence culture?", ignoring the idea of degree. In M-Q3, students who wrote Explanations focused on a re-presentation of McNeill's discussion of the consequences of the disease gradient; they did not take up the invitation to evaluate his evidence, but rather wrote about it as if it were factual. Students did not organize Explanations around a central claim, but rather focused on explaining multiple causes and effects. They made little use of interpersonal resources to anticipate and navigate possible resistance from the reader.

For example, in response to M-Q1, one student wrote in her introduction: "The establishment of empires and close knit societies led to the spread of new diseases.... This in turn led to the diseases' influence on culture such as the spread of Buddhism in India after 500 B.C., the transcendentalism in Indian religions, as well as belief in larger families in Chinese culture." Each body paragraph elaborated one of these effects of disease on culture, foregrounding causal relations, without an argument about degree. Similarly, for M-Q3, although several students included an evaluating claim in the introduction, such as "I feel McNeill is right," or "McNeill gives conclusive evidence," none supported this claim or even referred to it throughout the essay. In these cases, the response to the framing of degree was only nominal.

Thus, in contrast to the Hammurabi text, the McNeill text resulted in a wider uptake profile when combined with Argument Conditioning Prompts; it appears that the conditions created by the source text made it more challenging for students to write Arguments, even with these prompts. The McNeill text is a macro-genre that includes claims supported by evidence from multiple sources. In making his argument, McNeill describes events in chronological time, establishing his interpretation of events and evaluating them. Different from the Hammurabi text, which lacked an explicit argument, the features of the McNeill text facilitate the re-presentation of its content as if it were factual, sometimes in the same order as the source text.

4.4. Non-Argument Conditioning Prompt + Non-Argument Facilitative Source Text

M-Q2 is a question for facts, a type Llinares and Pascual Peña (2015) found most commonly elicited Accounts and Explanations. Our analysis is consistent with these findings, as only one of 12 students wrote an Argument, while six wrote Consequential Explanations, and five wrote Historical Accounts. Thus, we categorized M-Q2 as a Non-Argument Conditioning Prompt (Table 6).

Table 6. Genres produced in response to McNeill, Question 2 (M-Q2).

Prompt	Argument	Explanation	Historical Account	Total
M-Q2: What happened when the "four divergent disease pools" (p. 124) began to mix at the beginning of the Christian era?	1	6	5	12

In the single Argument, the student went beyond what the prompt asked by evaluating the consequence of the mixing of disease pools in the Thesis stage: "McNeill argues that with areas or regions that have not previously experienced such diseases, the outcome was lethal." This student made use of many interpersonal resources to position the reader as someone needing to be aligned to the thesis, rather than presenting it as factual information (e.g., "It is *extremely crucial for one to understand* that endemics have evolved..."; "*Acknowledging this difference is fundamental* to understanding the effects certain diseases had..."). Furthermore, she returned to her thesis as she presented evidence from the text ("McNeill refers to this process as 'homogenization.' This would definitely become more devastating").

The students who wrote Consequential Explanations took up the prompt as an invitation to explain consequences of the mixing of disease pools. One student started off with a seemingly viable claim in the introduction: "He argues that in the beginning of the Christian era the four civilized diseases occur or come into existence and these diseases affect people and cultures and had an influence on certain aspects." However, the rest of the essay foregrounded causal relations, emphasizing one major consequence and using facts from the source text without much use of interpersonal resources (e.g., "These diseases become 'epidemic disasters' because the population number or density become less and less so, there is a rapid decay in the population density"), and with no reaffirmation of the thesis or recurring reminders to the reader about the point of evidence presented.

The students who wrote Historical Accounts took up the prompt as an invitation to tell a story. These essays were organized by a focus on time, which was revealed in the marked Themes of many clauses (e.g., "Before the Christian era"; "Not long before the Christian era"; "At the beginning of the Christian era"; "During the first millennium"). In the elaboration of what happened during these time periods, the students used language that explained causal relationships, with the causes realized within clauses (e.g., "trade *created* new chains of infection"; "infections could easily *affect*"; "this helped *open up* development").

Thus, it appears that the conditions created by the Non-Argument Conditioning Prompt in combination with the Non-Argument Facilitative Source Text made it challenging for students to write Arguments. In contrast with a source text like Hammurabi's Code (which does not describe events happening over time), students who wrote Explanations and Accounts based on the McNeill text were able to find McNeill's discussion of the mixing of the disease pools and re-present it in their essays as if it were fact.

5. Discussion

Drawing on the concept of uptake (Freadman, 1994, Freadman, 2002) and previous linguistic descriptions of history genres (e.g., Coffin, 2006), this study examined the intertextual relationship of prompts and source texts with student writing. In writing their history essays, students responded to what we found to be Argument Conditioning Prompts and Non-Argument Conditioning Prompts, in combination with what we found to be an Argument Facilitative Source Text and a Non-Argument Facilitative Source Text. Although the professor expected students to write Arguments in response to all prompts and source texts, many students instead wrote less-valued genres—Accounts, Reports, or Explanations—engaging in "knowledge telling" rather than "knowledge transformation" (McCarthy Young & Leinhardt, 1998). Our analysis indicates that this variation in uptake was conditioned by features of the prompt and source text, independently and in combination, which were invisible to the professor.

Although the professor wanted students to write arguments based on all the prompts, we found that some prompts were not well suited for argument. These prompts had wider uptake profiles (Bawarshi, 2008) than only Argument, resulting in several non-argument uptakes. For example, the Non-Argument Conditioning Prompt "What happened when the four disease pools…"? (M-Q2), is a question for facts (Dalton-Puffer, 2007) that, for the most part, was not taken up with Argument. The use of prompts that are not well aligned with the intended uptake is not unique to the classroom in our study, as Llinares and Pascual Peña (2015) found an over-reliance on factual questions in their study of history oral discussions when the instructor›s overall goal was for students to produce Arguments. Similarly, Horowitz (1986) found that even when instructors aim to have students write argumentative essays, many prompts ask students to describe, explain, or discuss.

To write an Argument from a Non-Argument Conditioning Prompt, students had to go beyond what was being asked in the prompt. For example, M-Q2 ("What happened when the 'four divergent disease pools'…began to mix…"), resulted mostly in Accounts (telling what happened chronologically), or Explanations (explaining multiple consequences of the mixing). The student who wrote Argument went beyond what the prompt was asking by evaluating the mixing as being "lethal" and supporting this evaluation with evidence. Although there were Non-Argument Conditioning Prompts for both texts, nearly half of students responding to those about Hammurabi produced Arguments, while only one responding to McNeill produced an Argument. These differences in uptakes point to the importance of the intertextual relationships between source texts and student writing.

We suggest that the Hammurabi text is an Argument Facilitative Source Text because, as a list of laws without an overarching claim or explicit argument, the students were unable to simply re-tell the source text author's point of view. There is no place in the source text where the author makes an explicit assertion about, for example, Babylon's social structure, so even students who wrote Reports had to make inferences and draw logical connections between the content of a law and the corresponding interpretation of the society. In effect, this absence of argument in the source text seemed to push students toward the kind of interpretation and analysis that is necessary for writing Arguments. Another noteworthy aspect of the uptake of this source text was the complete lack of Historical Accounts, which could be attributed to the fact that Hammurabi's Code does not describe historical events in chronological time. Overall, the features of this source text created conditions that were well aligned with the instructor's goal of the students' uptake of Argument.

Among the prompts about the Hammurabi text, the prompt that was most successful in eliciting Argument (and selected by the most students) was H-Q4. Part of this prompt's success may have been its inclusion of a direct address ("What sort of picture do you get?"), making it a question for opinion, the type of question that Llinares and Pascual Peña (2015)found most successful in eliciting Argument. In addition, the topic of the prompt—asking students to praise or blame what the laws reveal about the treatment of women—may have been more accessible than having to characterize abstract entities like a political system or social structure. Accessibility and familiarity with the topic may shape how effectively students write from source texts (Yu, 2009) and may also be a reason for the high percentage of students who elected to respond to this prompt.

In contrast, we suggest that the McNeill text is a Non-Argument Facilitative Source Text. It included claims supported by evidence and described events in chronological time, so students could re-present its content as if it were factual, in the form of Accounts and Explanations, sometimes in the same order as the source text. This is consistent with Keck's (2014) conclusion that expository texts result more often than narrative texts in students mirroring "the sequence of source text paragraphs" (p. 17). We also note that the McNeill text was longer and more complex than the Hammurabi text. While Li and Casanave (2012)argue that difficult source texts may lead to inappropriate textual borrowing, we did not find inappropriate borrowing in our data. Rather, our finding may be evidence of Tardy's (2009)claim about intertextuality in which she points out that genres "are born out of prior texts and retain traces of those texts" (p. 14): the factual re-presentation of information from the McNeill text may be explained as the traces of the source text that remained in students' uptakes.

The unfavorable conditions that the McNeill text created are particularly evident in the uptakes to Argument Conditioning Prompts (M-Q1 and M-Q3), in which some students elided key aspects of the prompt and produced non-argumentative genres. For example, M-Q1 asked, "According to McNeill, to what degree does disease influence culture (i.e., religion)?"; this exact phrase—*to what degree*—is one that Coffin (2006) suggests can be used to elicit Argument. However, almost half of the students seemed to elide this portion of the prompt, taking up a prompt asking *How does disease influence culture (i.e., religion)?*, and producing Consequential Explanations. Ackerman (1990, quoted in Kroll & Reid, 1994) notes that "in many cases the assignment [or topic] given by an instructor and the assignment [or topic] taken by a student are not a reciprocal fit" (p. 236), creating unexpected intertextual relationships between prompt and student uptake. The wording in the history professor's prompts that was meant to cue Argument as the appropriate uptake seems not to have been reciprocal with what some students took up. This resonates with Reid and Kroll's (1995) suggestion that prompts be designed to explicitly indicate the genre expected in students' responses.

Even the few students who attempted to write Arguments in response to McNeill did so with mixed results. Three of the six Arguments were underdeveloped versions of this genre. While they had the stages of Argument and some features of this genre, they also exhibited features that looked more like Explanations. Whereas some of the Reports in response to Hammurabi's Code exhibited features of Argument, students responding to McNeill seemed to be pushed in the opposite direction.

Clearly, the Hammurabi and the McNeill texts created different conditions for Argument uptake. Out of 59 essays in response to Hammurabi, 43 (72.9%) were Arguments; of 24 in response to McNeill, only six (25.0%) were Arguments. Of the 13 students who responded to both texts, six wrote an Argument for Hammurabi but not McNeill, and only one wrote an Argument for McNeill but not for Hammurabi. These results are especially notable because the Hammurabi text was the first reading of the course, when students had less experience with university-level academic writing, whereas the McNeill reading was the fourth of the semester, when one might expect students to have a better understanding of assignment expectations and argumentation.

6. Implications

Our study contributes to the growing interest in intertextuality, with a focus on understudied aspects of the relationships between course materials and student writing. By applying Freadman, 1994, Freadman, 2002 and Bawarshi, 2003, Bawarshi, 2008 work on uptake to a history course in an English-medium university in the Middle East, we have shown the usefulness of this concept in an L2 setting. Furthermore, by combining Freadman's and Bawarshi's theoretical orientation toward intertextuality and genre with an SFL-based framework for detailed linguistic analysis of genre, we have shown how these two schools of thought may be profitably integrated. Finally, our focus on undergraduate L2 writers is particularly important given their challenges when producing argument, as discussed in the literature (e.g., Hirvela, 2013). The conditions created by writing prompts and source texts can contribute to the challenges students encounter when writing arguments, which merits further study.

The intertextual relationships among source text, prompt, and student writing should be taken into account to improve alignment between an instructor's goals and expectations, assignment design, and the writing students produce. Three important pedagogical implications for L2 writing instruction emerge from this study. First, faculty should carefully select source texts that create conditions favorable for the expected uptake. In this study, we found a source text that lacks an explicit overarching claim allowed many students to do the knowledge transformation that is necessary for argumentative writing. In contrast, a source text that includes its own claims and support may be more challenging for L2 writers, both in terms of reading comprehension and facility with producing an Argument.

Second, faculty must carefully construct prompts that make the expected genre clear to students (see also Reid & Kroll, 1995). This may be particularly important for L2 writers, for whom genre expectations may be less clear. We found some prompts were not well aligned with the professor's desired uptake of Argument. For example, if Argument is expected, the instructor may ask, *How compelling do you find McNeill's evidence...? Evaluate McNeill's evidence and provide support for your argument.* Or, if Factorial Explanation is expected, the instructor may choose a frame such as: *Explain the causes of...*. Prompts should then be unpacked with students during class, explicitly teaching students how prompts are meant to cue specific genres. For instance, teachers should be explicit about how a frame like *How compelling...* is inviting students to make an evaluation and consistently support that evaluation. In our study, we found that students produced non-Argument genres when they ignored key parts of the Argument Conditioning Prompts. When genre expectations are not made explicit, students must "draw upon the same... knowledge of genre that the test constructor did" in order to successfully "decode" prompts (Horowitz, 1989, p. 23), and L2 writers in particular may not have such knowledge. For example, L2 writers might be more likely to read prompts more literally than L1 writers, failing to see prompts such as *explain* or *discuss* as an invitation to argue (Kroll & Reid, 1994). Similarly, cultural differences may cause some L2 writers to feel that they do not have authority to write critically of others (Ramanathan & Atkinson, 1999) as would be required to critique the claims or evidence in a source text. L2 writers responding to prompts such as *How compelling do you find McNeill's evidence...?* may need explicit instruction and encouragement to understand that this is an invitation to challenge authorial authority. Thus, strong prompt design requires faculty to be keenly aware of how prompt wording may condition student uptake.

A third implication of this study is that faculty can guide students toward producing Arguments through a carefully planned sequence. For example, an instructor might begin the semester by assigning a reading like the McNeill text and using prompts that are intended to produce Explanations or Reports to check students' reading comprehension. Then, the instructor could progress to asking for Arguments by providing only suitable prompts, aided by an Argument Facilitative Source Text, and supplemented with explicit instruction about how the targeted genres differ. Finally, the instructor could target Arguments in response to more complex source texts (using only prompts designed to elicit Argument), with explicit discussion of how such source texts can be challenging for students and how to avoid producing Explanations and Reports. At each stage of this sequence, the instructor should deconstruct sample essays that did and did not respond with the desired uptake.

To implement these suggestions, faculty need to be aware of the genres in their field, the stages of these genres, and their linguistic features. An instructor who is aware of genre features is better equipped to provide students with additional linguistic resources for meeting the goals of the expected genre(s), and this is particularly important for L2 writers (Johns, 1997). With such awareness, faculty can also better recognize the genres that students produce and how these do and do not fit the expected genre(s). Because not all faculty across the curriculum are well equipped to teach writing with a focus on genre features, we recommend collaboration between faculty in the disciplines and faculty with more language expertise. While the specific suggestions outlined above may be particular to history, we are working with faculty in other disciplines using a similar approach, focusing on analyzing, categorizing, and deconstructing key features of the genres students are expected to produce.

The findings presented here are revealing about the intertextual relationship between prompts, source texts, and L2 student writing, yet further research is needed, both within history and in other disciplines. For example, we need more knowledge about how other features of source texts condition students' uptakes. We also need to know more about how differences among students, such as prior genre experience and language background, may affect how students interact with source texts and prompts. The application of introspective methods such as think-aloud protocols could provide insight into how students interpret a prompt and what steps they take to respond. Such research would provide further knowledge about how writing prompts and source texts influence student writing.

REFERENCES

Abasi, A. R., Akbari, N., & Graves, B. (2006). Discourse appropriation, construction of identities, and the complex issue of plagiarism: ESL students writing in graduate school. *Journal of Second Language Writing, 15*, 102–117.

Allison, H. (2009). High school academic literacy instruction and the transition to college writing. In M. Roberge, M. Siegal, & L. Harklau (Eds.), *Generation 1.5 in college composition: Teaching academic writing to U.S.-educated learners of ESL* (pp. 75–90). New York: Routledge.

Aull, L. (2015, Spring). Linguistic attention in rhetorical genre studies and first-year writing. *Composition Forum, 31*.

Bawarshi, A. S. (2003). *Genre and the invention of the writer: Reconsidering the place of invention in composition.* Logan, UT: Utah State University Press.

Bawarshi, A. S. (2008). Genres as forms of in (ter) vention. In C. Eisner & M. Vicinus (Eds.), *Originality, imitation, and plagiarism* (pp. 79–89). Ann Arbor, MI: University of Michigan Press.

Bawarshi, A. S., & Reiff, M. J. (2010). *Genre: An introduction to history, theory, research, and pedagogy.* West Lafayette, IN: Parlor Press. Brisk, M. E. (2014). *Engaging students in academic literacies: Genre-based pedagogy for K-5 classrooms.* New York: Routledge.

Christie, F., & Derewianka, B. M. (2008). *School discourse: Learning to write across the years of schooling.* New York: Continuum.

Coffin, C. (2000). *History as discourse: Construals of time, cause and appraisal* (Unpublished doctoral thesis) Australia: University of New South Wales.
Coffin, C. (2006). *Historical discourse: The language of time, cause and evaluation*. New York: Continuum.
Coffin, C., & Hewings, A. (2004). IELTS as preparation for tertiary writing: Distinctive interpersonal and textual strategies. In L. J. Ravelli & R. A. Ellis (Eds.), *Analysing academic writing: Contextualized frameworks* (pp. 153–172). London: Continuum.
Dalton-Puffer, C. (2007). *Discourse in content and language integrated learning (CLIL) classrooms*. Amsterdam: John Benjamins.
Davis, M. (2013). The development of source use by international postgraduate students. *Journal of English for Academic Purposes, 12*, 125–135. Dreyfus, S. J., Humphrey, S., Mahboob, A., & Martin, J. M. (2015). *Genre pedagogy in higher education: The SLATE project*. London: Palgrave Macmillan. Educational Testing Service (2015). *TOEFL for institutions: Compare TOEFL scores*. Retrieved from https://www.ets.org/toefl/institutions/scores/compare/
Eggins, S., Wignell, P., & Martin, J. R. (1993). The discourse of history: Distancing the recoverable past. In M. Ghadessy (Ed.), *Register analysis: Theory and practice* (pp. 75–109). London: Pinter.
Feez, S. (2002). Heritage and innovation in second language education. In A. M. Johns (Ed.), *Genre in the classroom: Multiple perspectives* (pp. 43–72). Mahwah, NJ: Lawrence Erlbaum.
Freadman, A. (1994). Anyone for tennis? In A. Freedman & P. Medway (Eds.), *Genre and the new rhetoric* (pp. 43–66). London: Taylor & Francis.
Freadman, A. (2002). Uptake. In R. M. Coe, L. Lingard, & T. Teslenko (Eds.), *The rhetoric and ideology of genre: Strategies for stability and change* (pp. 39–53). Cresskill, New Jersey: Hampton Press.
Freedman, A., & Medway, P. (Eds.). (1994). *Genre and the new rhetoric*. London: Taylor & Francis.
Halliday, M. A. K., & Mathiessen, C. M. I. M. (2004). *An introduction to functional grammar*. London: Routledge.
Hammurabi. (1754 B.C.). *Hammurabi's Code of Laws* (L.W. King, Trans.). Retrieved from http://www.ohio.edu/people/uhalde/1210/hammur-txt.htm Hamp-Lyons, L., & Mathias, S. P. (1994). Examining expert judgments of task difficulty on essay tests. *Journal of Second Language Writing, 3*, 49–68. Harklau, L. (1994). ESL versus mainstream classes: Contrasting L2 learning environments. *TESOL Quarterly, 28*, 241–272.
Harklau, L. (2001). From high school to college: Student perspectives on literacy practices. *Journal of Literacy Research, 33*, 33–70. Hinkel, E. (2002). *Second language writers' text: Linguistic and rhetorical features*. New York: Routledge.

Hirvela, A. (2013). Preparing English language learners for argumentative writing. In L. C. de Oliveira & T. J. Silva (Eds.), *L2 writing in secondary classrooms: Student experiences, academic issues, and teacher education* (pp. 67–86). New York: Routledge.

Hirvela, A., & Du, Q. (2013). "Why am I paraphrasing?.": Undergraduate ESL writers' engagement with source-based academic writing and reading. *Journal of English for Academic Purposes, 12,* 87–98.

Horowitz, D. (1986). Essay examination prompts and the teaching of academic writing. *English for Specific Purposes, 5,* 107–120. Horowitz, D. (1989). Function and form in essay examination prompts. *RELC Journal, 20,* 23–35.

Johns, A. M. (1997). *Text, role, and context: Developing academic literacies.* New York: Cambridge University Press.

Johns, A. M. (2011). The future of genre in L2 writing: Fundamental, but contested, instructional decisions. *Journal of Second Language Writing, 20,* 56–68. Keck, C. (2006). The use of paraphrase in summary writing: A comparison of L1 and L2 writers. *Journal of Second Language Writing, 15,* 261–278.

Keck, C. (2010). How do university students attempt to avoid plagiarism?. A grammatical analysis of undergraduate paraphrasing strategies. *Writing & Pedagogy, 2,* 193–222.

Keck, C. (2014). Copying, paraphrasing, and academic writing development: A re-examination of L1 and L2 summarization practices. *Journal of Second Language Writing, 25,* 4–22.

Kobrin, J. L., Deng, H., & Shaw, E. J. (2011). The association between SAT prompt characteristics, response features, and essay scores. *Assessing Writing, 16,* 154–169.

Kroll, B., & Reid, J. (1994). Guidelines for designing writing prompts: Clarifications, caveats, and cautions. *Journal of Second Language Writing, 3,* 231–255. Kuiken, F., & Vedder, I. (2008). Cognitive task complexity and written output in Italian and French as a foreign language. *Journal of Second Language Writing, 17,* 48–60.

Li, Y., & Casanave, C. P. (2012). Two first-year students' strategies for writing from sources: Patchwriting or plagiarism. *Journal of Second Language Writing, 21,* 165–180.

Llinares, A., & Pascual Peña, I. (2015). A genre approach to the effects of academic questions on CLIL students' language production. *Language and Education, 29,* 15–30.

Martin, J. R. (1992). *English text: System and structure.* Amsterdam: John Benjamins.

Martin, J. R., Maton, K., & Matruglio, E. (2010). Historical cosmologies: Epistemology and axiology in Australian secondary school history discourse. *Revista Signos, 43,* 433–463.

Martin, J. R., & Rose, D. (2008). *Genre relations: Mapping culture*. London: Equinox.

Martin, J. R., & White, P. R. R. (2005). *The language of evaluation: Appraisal in English*. New York: Palgrave Macmillan.

McCarthy Young, K., & Leinhardt, G. (1998). Writing from primary documents: A way of knowing in history. *Written Communication, 15*, 25–68.

McNeill, W. H. (1976). *Plagues and peoples*. New York: Anchor Books.

Miller, C. R. (1994). Genre as social action. In A. Freedman & P. Medway (Eds.), *Genre and the new rhetoric* (pp. 20–36). London: Taylor & Francis.

Miller, R. T., Mitchell, T. D., & Pessoa, S. (2014). Valued voices: Students' use of Engagement in argumentative history writing. *Linguistics and Education, 28*, 107–120.

Oliver, E. I. (1995). The writing quality of seventh, ninth, and eleventh graders, and college freshmen: Does rhetorical specification in writing prompts make a difference? *Research in the Teaching of English, 29*, 422–450.

Ong, J., & Zhang, L. J. (2010). Effects of task complexity on the fluency and lexical complexity in EFL students' argumentative writing. *Journal of Second Language Writing, 19*, 218–233.

Pecorari, D. (2003). Good and original: Plagiarism and patchwriting in academic second-language writing. *Journal of Second Language Writing, 12*, 317–345.

Plakans, L., & Gebril, A. (2013). Using multiple texts in an integrated writing assessment: Source text use as a predictor of score. *Journal of Second Language Writing, 22*, 217–230.

Ramanathan, V., & Atkinson, D. (1999). Individualism, academic writing, and ESL writers. *Journal of Second Language Writing, 8*, 45–75.

Reid, J., & Kroll, B. (1995). Designing and assessing effective classroom writing assignments for NES and ESL students. *Journal of Second Language Writing, 4*, 17–41.

Schleppegrell, M. J. (2004). *The language of schooling: A functional linguistics perspective*. Mahwah, NJ: Lawrence Erlbaum.

Schleppegrell, M. J., Achugar, M., & Oteı́za, T. (2004). The grammar of history: Enhancing content-based instruction through a functional focus on language. *TESOL Quarterly, 38*, 67–93.

Shaw, P., & Pecorari, D. (2013). Source use in academic writing: An introduction to the special issue. *Journal of English for Academic Purposes, 12*, A1–A3. Shi, L. (2012). Rewriting and paraphrasing texts in second language writing. *Journal of Second Language Writing, 21*, 134–148.

Silva, T. (1993). Toward an understanding of the distinct nature of L2 writing: The ESL research and its implications. *TESOL Quarterly, 27*, 657–677.

Tardy, C. M. (2009). *Building genre knowledge*. West Lafayette, IN: Parlor Press.

Veel, R. (1997). Learning how to mean—scientifically speaking: Apprenticeship into scientific discourse in the secondary school. In F. Christie & J. R. Martin (Eds.), *Genres and institutions: Social processes in the workplace and school* (pp. 161–195). London: Continuum.

Weigle, S. C., & Parker, K. (2012). Source text borrowing in an integrated reading/writing assessment. *Journal of Second Language Writing, 21*, 118–133.

Wette, R. (2010). Evaluating student learning in a university-level EAP unit on writing using sources. *Journal of Second Language Writing, 19*, 158–177.

Wu, S. M., & Allison, D. (2005). Evaluative expressions in analytical arguments: Aspects of appraisal in assigned English language essays. *Journal of Applied Linguistics, 2*, 105–127.

Yu, G. (2009). The shifting sands in the effects of source text summarizability on summary writing. *Assessing Writing, 14*, 116–137.

Acknowledgments

We would like to thank the anonymous *JSLW* reviewers and Christine Tardy for their helpful and insightful comments on previous versions of this manuscript. We would also like to thank Caroline Coffin, Shoshana Dreyfus, Susan Hagan, Sue Hood, David Kaufer, and Benjamin Reilly for their valuable input. This publication was made possible by NPRP grant # 5-1320-6-040 from the Qatar National Research Fund (a member of Qatar Foundation). The statements made herein are solely the responsibility of the authors.

Ryan T. Miller is an Assistant Professor in the English Department at Kent State University. His research areas are second-language reading and writing. His research investigates development of academic and discipline-specific writing skills and genre knowledge, and dual-language involvement and support of reading and its sub-skills.

Thomas D. Mitchell is an Assistant Teaching Professor of English at Carnegie Mellon University in Qatar. His research interests include academic writing development, and the relationship between discourse, identity, and place.

Silvia Pessoa is an Associate Teaching Professor of English and Sociolinguistics at Carnegie Mellon University in Qatar. Her research areas include literacy, academic writing development, and immigration studies. She has investigated the socio-cultural factors influencing literacy development in various settings and with various populations including immigrant adolescents in the U.S., college students in the U.S. and in Qatar, and migrant workers in Qatar.

Notes

1. All study procedures were approved by the university's institutional review board. All participants gave informed consent.

2. Although two history professors teach at this campus, this course is consistently taught by the same professor, who is originally from the United States., has English as his first language, and received his Ph.D. in history in the United States. He has extensive undergraduate teaching experience and had taught at this university for five years.

3. As a part of the larger study from which we draw these data, we interviewed the professor and 30 students multiple times. Due to space constraints, we do not report on specific interview findings, since our main focus is on the analysis of student writing. Nonetheless, our analysis is informed by our interview data.

4. Coffin found the Report genre in student history writing but did not include it in her genre typology for school history writing because it was "not pivotal in fulfilling the aims of the secondary history curriculum" (Coffin, 2000, p. 86).

5. Martin (1992) distinguishes between *elemental* genres and *macro-genres*. Elemental genres are ones like those found in Table 1, and macro-genres are typically longer texts comprising multiple elemental genres. Despite this complexity, macro-genres may be characterized by an overarching purpose.

KB JOURNAL

KB Journal takes as its mission the exploration of what it means to be "Burkeian." To this end, *KB Journal* publishes original scholarship that addresses, applies, extends, repurposes, or challenges the writings of Kenneth Burke, which include but are not limited to the major books and hundreds of articles by Burke, as well as the growing corpus of research material about Burke. It provides an outlet for integrating and critiquing the gamut of Burkeian studies in communication, composition, English, gender, literature, philosophy, psychology, sociology, and technical writing.

KB Journal is on the Web at http://kbjournal.org/

The Syrian Civil War, International Outreach, and a Clash of Worldviews

Peter C. Bakke and Jim A. Kuypers skillfully apply dramatism to help readers understand the seemingly unending Syrian Civil War, where the two (or more) sides are absolutely divided even as they share a common history, space, and religion. How does each side explain its actions? Bakke and Kuypers apply Burke's pentad to the terministic screens of the Syrians on all sides to show how motive is attributed, and thus they avoid the trap of analyzing the conflict strictly from a Western (or US) perspective.

The Syrian Civil War, International Outreach, and a Clash of Worldviews

Peter C. Bakke and Jim A. Kuypers

Abstract: We present a dramatistic analysis of the discourse of Syrian President Assad and his opposition in the ongoing Syrian civil war. Comparing terministic screens and world views expressed in the discourses, we find that the Assad regime believes it is not responsible for the current conflict, and is justified in the use of violence against rebel groups. Rebel groups overtly reject Western values and seek to depict their current and planned violence as morally justified.

Disclaimer

The views represented in this article are those of the authors and are not intended to officially or unofficially represent the position of the U.S. Army or U.S. Government.

Introductory Note

We originally undertook this project in the fall of 2013 – a time when the Assad Regime seemed to be gaining ground in the Syrian Civil War and rebel groups appeared to be fractured. Tension between the Syrian regime and the West was particularly high due to rebel allegations that the Syrian military was employing chemical weapons. ISIL (then known as the Islamic State of Iraq and al-Sham) was still jockeying for dominance with the Nusrah Front (al-Qaeda in Syria) within the trans-national Al-Qaeda power structure, and the refugee crisis was not nearly as intense as in late 2015. Throughout 2013, the Assad regime appeared to make a coordinated effort to portray itself as an ally in "Global War on Terror." When Assad appeared on Fox News to make such a case, we wondered whether he was trying to sell the U.S. public a "bill of goods." As Kenneth Burke might say, we wondered what kind of "medicine" the "medicine man" was prescribing. To gain a better perspective of the regime's position, we began examining the discourse of the disparate rebel groups fighting against Assad's forces to see if it lent any validity to his message. Coincidentally, many of the rebel groups we examined began collapsing under the umbrella of the "Islamic Front." In November of 2013, the "Islamic Front" issued a statement calling for the continuation of Jihad against the regime and the establishment of a Salafist Sunni Islamic state in Syria. Given this development, we felt that a two-sided analysis of the conflict's discourse would help uncover the motives of each side. We later added some examples of ISIL activities to demonstrate how ignoring rhetorical justifications for inhumane behavior (on both sides) can have serious implications.

* * *

The Islamic State, coined "ISIS" or "ISIL" by the U.S. news media, has recently garnered the attention of the U.S. and Western publics. Islamic State brutality against Yazidi Christians in the north of Iraq, seizure of crucial Iraqi infrastructure, and barbaric beheadings of American journalists James Foley and Steven Sotloff have resulted in the Obama administration's call for an international coalition to defeat the organization in Iraq and Syria. Coalition efforts have already required U.S. military commitment to meet the President's stated goal of "degrading and destroying" the Islamic State, and thwarting their objective of establishing an international caliphate. However, in order to make a new war palatable, as well as defend previous policy decisions, the Islamic State seems to be portrayed as a new and emerging threat, one differentiated from former adversaries who "pulled" us into previous conflicts. Thus, dominant administration and media narratives seem to push the idea that "ISIS" materialized from the ether to become a threat "even more extreme than Al-Qaeda" ("David Gregory"). U.S. Secretary of Defense Chuck Hagel, for instance, described the organization as "beyond anything we've seen," and Attorney General Eric Holder stated that ISIS's plans were " 'more frightening than anything I think I've seen as attorney general. . . . It's something that gives us really extreme, extreme concern....'" (Ritger, "Chuck Hagel"; Holder qtd. in Francis, "Why the Long Arm"). Suddenly, it seems the U.S. is faced with an enemy whose brutality tames our perception of those who attacked the U.S. in 2001 and may force our collaboration with the "blood soaked" regime of Bashar al-Assad. In the words of an Al-Qaeda aligned Syrian opposition fighter, "Your news makes it seem like [ISIL] appeared out of nowhere... [slamming his hand on the dashboard]. You want to talk about [ISIL]? Ask a Syrian!" (Day, "Syrian Fighter").

Presidential candidates and pundits now debate whether we should have armed earlier "a more moderate Syrian opposition" and whether collaboration with Assad is acceptable (Goldberg, "Hillary Clinton"). Such characterizations and suggestions, however, require a closer look at the recent history and discourse of the conflicts in Iraq and Syria. Such analysis would suggest that we have seen "ISIS" on the battlefield before (in Iraq 2003-2010), that "ISIS" and Al-Qaeda are the same movement, and that "ISIS"-like jihadist discourse permeates the influential branches of the very Syrian opposition the U.S. sought to aid in its rebellion against the Assad Regime (MacFarQuhar and Sadd, "As Syrian War Drags On").

Examining the discourse of the Syrian conflict is vitally important because the parties in conflict represent larger warring factions throughout the Middle East. Such sectarian conflict defies U.S. conceptions of allies and adversaries, because some of each may fall on either side of the sectarian divide, and much of the animus traces its roots back to the beginnings of Islam. Thus, it becomes important to understand how the conflict discourse of individual groups is indicative of motivation and actions that can potentially impact the security of American citizens and regional stability. An understanding of how extremism and violence manifest on both sides of the regional conflict can only encourage a more effective foreign policy.

Flowing out of dramatism is the idea that people universally use symbols to explain their actions in similar ways. In "The Rhetoric of Hitler's Battle," for instance, Kenneth Burke demonstrated how application of a dramatistic perspective allowed him to discover "what kind of 'medicine' this medicine-man [Hitler] has concocted, that we may know... exactly what to guard against, if we are to forestall the concocting of similar medicine in America" (Burke, "The Rhetoric of Hitler's Battle" 191). Burke's implication is clear: we should examine the speech-acts of those outside of the "American" world view, as well as critically compare such content with that of our own domestic political discourse. Other scholars since Burke have used dramatism and the pentad as starting points for the examination of non-U.S. and non-

Western discourse. For example, Adriana Angel and Benjamin Bates examined Columbian radio conversations, Xing Lu examined the rhetoric of Chinese nationalism, Pedro Patron-Galindo examined the political marketing strategies of Peruvian President Alejandro Toledo, and Colleen E. Kelley wrote on the rhetoric of Soviet leader Mikhail Gorbachev (Angel and Bates; Lu; Patron-Galindo; Kelley). In general, the operating assumption of such studies is that Burkean dramatism is cross-culturally applicable, but the essays stop short of explaining why this is so or how one might efficaciously apply dramatistic principles most fruitfully in a cross-cultural context. In this paper, we demonstrate how this process, combined with an in-depth knowledge of recurrent cultural narratives flowing within a foreign discourse, can establish a framework that allows the dramatistic pentad to function as an effective cross-cultural analytical tool. Further, this dramatistic analysis of foreign discourse allows for an effective critical comparison between both the motives of a speaker with a foreign world-view and his or her representation in U.S. political discourse.

The nascent means for such a comparison (situational contextualization, explanation of cultural metaphor, application of the pentad, comparison with domestic discourse) are found in Burke's analysis of *Mein Kampf*, which includes all of these elements without specifically including them in the framework of dramatism. Burke contextualizes Hitler's anti-Semitic writing, for instance, by providing rich descriptions of the political conditions of Pre-World War I Vienna and Post-World War I Munich. Further, he describes the Christian and German mythology that functioned as a common language between Hitler and his potential base of supporters. This added knowledge allows his explanation of Hitler's foreign world-view to function cross-culturally. How else might one of Burke's readers of the 1930s (English speakers) be able to understand the particularly German flavor of Hitler's strongly anti-Semitic persuasive campaign? We believe that the application of dramatistic principles to the discourse of those with non-U.S. world-views is as relevant today as it was when Burke wrote of Hitler. As a contemporary extension to Burke's ideas, we examine the rhetoric of the still evolving sectarian conflict in Syria and Iraq, and then discuss how the reflection of such discourse in domestic politics holds serious implications for U.S. foreign policy. We accomplish this in five stages: first, we contextualize the nature of the conflict in Syria; second, we explore the different cultural narratives of President Assad and the Islamic Front; third, using a dramatistic analysis we analyze the internationally aimed discourse of Assad and the Islamic Front; fourth, we specifically look at the metaphor underpinning Assad's outreach to the United States; finally, we conclude with an exploration of Syrian clashing world views and implication for dramatism and U.S. policy in the region.

Contextualization: The Nature of the Syrian Conflict

The Syrian conflict, much as the Syrian population at large, comprises numerous groups and alliances. A 74% majority of Syrians are Sunni Muslims of Arab descent. A large portion of the Sunni-Arab population lives in rural areas throughout the country. The minority Syrian population consists of 12% Alawite-sect Shia Muslims (to which the Assad family and ruling class belong), with the remaining 14% of the population consisting of Christians, Jews, Kurds, and Druze ("Syria—People and Society"). For the purpose of discussion, we characterize the conflict within Syrian borders as one between the Sunni majority and ruling Alawite-Shia minority. However, sectarian and ethnic alliances within Syria spill well outside its borders. For example, Alawites maintain strong ties with their Shia neighbors in Iran and Lebanon, as well as certain militant/terrorist groups such as Hezbollah; the Sunni majority finds kinship among other Sunni-Arab dominated nations such as Saudi Arabia and Jordan, as well as support from transnational jihadist groups (Al Qaeda, for example) throughout the Middle East (Fassihi, Solomon, and Dagher, "Iranians Dial up Presence in Syria"). Therefore, the Alawite-Shia versus Sunni conflict within Syria can be viewed as part of a larger pan-Islamic sectarian struggle with implications for all nations involved. Further, undertones of secularism versus Islamism color the brutality inflicted by both parties.

Aron Lund provides insight into the ethno-religious sectarian nature of the conflict, writing, "revolutionary demands originally focused on democracy and economic reform but the new opposition movement did not arise in a social vacuum." In socio-economic terms, he describes the uprising as an "ideologically motivated uprising of the Sunni working class against the Alawite military ruling elite" (Lund, 8). As the conflict entered its second year in 2012, increasing numbers of foreign fighters (Salafi-Sunnis) joined the fray ("Syria Profile"). Although Sunni Syrians comprised the bulk of the opposition, further backing arrived from in the form of foreign ideologues and Islamic extremists—namely al-Qaeda (AQ). In May of 2013, analysts from the Rand Office for External Affairs provided testimony for the House Homeland Security Committee designating Jabhat-al-Nusrah as the Syrian arm of AQ. Analyst Seth Jones testified that "Jabhat al-Nusrah (JN) grew out of AQ in Iraq (AQI)." After a 2013 split with AQI, JN pledged allegiance directly to AQ senior leadership in Pakistan. The remainder of AQI maintained allegiance to Abu-Bakr al-Baghdadi and became known as the Islamic State of Iraq and the Levant (Syria) or "ISIL / ISIS." The point here is not to trace the linage and development of groups making headlines in the U.S.; rather, we wish to demonstrate a common sectarian interest between groups labeled "moderate" and those implementing the most perverse interpretation of Sunni Islam imaginable. When interacting with each other, JN and ISIS might be enemies. However, in the context of the sectarian war, they should be considered estranged brothers.

Burke demonstrated how one ideologue (Hitler) used language to set the German people on a path to destruction. Because conflict had yet to unfold, he needed to analyze only one voice, Hitler›s. The Syrian situation differs in that it has evolved into a conflict with many parties. As such, we proceed by choosing an Alawite-Shia voice and a Sunni voice we feel most representative, the "embodiment," of each side. The ruling Alawites have been led and represented by the Assad family since the 1970›s. Hafez al-Assad (now deceased), and his son Bashar have represented the Alawite-Shia grip on Syrian power for nearly 40 years. Likewise, they serve as a lightning rod for the animosity of a frustrated Arab-Sunni population. Thus, Bashar al-Assad is our chosen voice for the Alawite-Shia faction.

In November 2013, The Syrian Islamic Front, elements of the Free Syrian Army, and Islamist elements formerly operating under Supreme Military Command united under the banner of one group – the Islamic Front. ISIS and JN have formerly allied with the Islamic Front. Despite current estrangement between the groups, the Islamic Front provides the voice for the Sunni-Arab faction of the conflict. We selected the Islamic Front for two reasons: (1) it is directly opposed to Assad and (2) U.S. politicians indirectly cite them as "moderate" due to their estrangement from "ISIS."

Read Monitor 360's "Country Report: Syria" at http://kbjournal.org/sites/default/files/OSC-SyriaMasterNarratives.pdf

Clashing Cultural Narratives

Having established some situational context, we now turn to the undercurrents of Syrian dialogue. In 2012, the Director of National Intelligence's Open Source Center (OSC) published Master Narratives Country Report: Syria. The report is intended to facilitate an understanding of the language used by various groups within Syria. The report details eight master narratives and subordinate themes, which interact or stand-alone, to shape each groups understanding of events. We use this document as our initial touchstone for understanding Syrian cultural narratives. Similar to how Burke expounded on Hitler's perversion of religion, we seek to use Syrian cultural narratives as an example of the "baseline" from which each side deviates. These "master narratives" are the threads with which Syrians tell stories and sometimes act as a lens through which they interpret events. Much as the German of the 1930's found familiarity in the liturgical rhythm of Nazi repetition, the Sunni-Arab Syrian might find familiarity in reference to the "Greater Levant." Much as the German blamed his economic problems on the tangible Jew, the Sunni-Arab narrative might provide a pre-ordained scapegoat in the Alawite.

Assad Narrative

Syrian President Bashar al-Assad attempts to convey his popularity. Courtesy of NPR.org.

Assad's explanation of current events, contained in his September 2013 news media interview with Dennis Kucinich and Greg Palkot, displays three prominent narratives common among the groups that he represents (Al-Assad). The included narratives are (1) Alawite Survival, (2) Conspiracies All Around, and (3) Greater Syria (United States, "Open Source Center" Executive Summary). According to the OSC, the "Alawite Survival" narrative centers around the Alawite rise from Sunni oppression by virtue of their "superior achievements." This narrative maintains that the Alawites hold a rightful place in the halls of leadership but always remain threatened by "fanatical Sunni's who wish to destroy them" (United States, "Open Source Center" 33). The core themes of "Alawite Survival" are the concepts of encirclement, existential fear, and survival. Assad addresses the themes of existential fear and encirclement through his characterization of the conflict.

His description of foreign backed terrorists working in conjunction with fanatical jihadists toward an ideologically closed society invokes the possibility of Alawite destruction. A "new kind of war" also elicits the fear of the unknown, in which alliances among individuals and nations threaten a small core of Syrians dedicated to preservation of the state.

The "Conspiracy" narrative, as expressed by Assad, is particularly salient when used in conjunction with "Alawite Survival." The narrative is based upon Syria's turbulent history and espouses a worldview where "secretive cabals inside the country, scheming Westerners and envious Arab neighbors conspire against the people" (United States, "Open Source Center" 13). For his part, Assad alleges not only a terrorist threat but also raises the specter of faceless enemies who agitate the rebellion from afar. He names al-Qaeda among the conspirators but also accuses other Western and Arab nations of fomenting unrest.

Here we can establish a relationship between Assad's heavy use of scenic descriptions or grounded terminology (explained in the next section) and the wide array of Alawite cultural narratives that support them. Hostile Sunni's, terrorists, and foreign-led cabals create an environment where the secularist Alawites' struggle to survive. Such survival depends on Alawite ability to combat forces beyond their control. Thus, the Alawites are not responsible for the conflict. This demonstrates consistency between contemporary scene driven explanations and environmentally dominated Alawite cultural narratives. It also suggests that Assad's characterization of conflict is an attempt to sway listeners toward his real worldview.

Assad's self-described end-state for the conflict embraces the "Greater Syria" narrative. This narrative stems from the belief that Syria is the cradle of civilization. After having been fractured by the West, Syrians must seek to "restore their pride by reinstating Syria as a homeland for all creeds and the vanguard of the Arab World" (United States, "Open Source Center" 20). The core themes of this narrative are exceptionalism, restoration, and tolerance. Therefore, when Assad speaks of Syria in the interview as a "melting pot" and accuses his opposition of trying to create a closed and radicalized society, he is calling upon Syrian exceptionalism and accusing his enemies of violating the very essence of being Syrian.

The "Greater Syria" narrative is tied to Assad's explanation of specific brutal acts in which he highlights purpose. That is, when he is willing to assume responsibility for an act within the conflict, he invokes the only narrative able to vindicate such behavior. It is impossible to know for sure if a purpose-driven explanation for brutality is linked with a genuine worldview regarding Syrian greatness, or whether the weaving of this narrative into an explanation is a rationalization. However, it does provide perspective regarding the logic he uses to excuse his actions.

Islamic Front

As with the Assad Regime, the rhetoric of the Sunni opposition has deep roots within sectarian narrative ("The Islamic Front's Founding Declaration"). The central narratives of the Sunni majority within Syria are that of the "Alawite infidel" and "Greater Syria". The "Alawite infidel" is unique to the rural Sunni population and reflects the group's resentment toward minority rule. The narrative explains that Alawites, often referred to using derogatory slurs, connived their way to power during the period of French occupation of Syria. Following the French exit in the 1920's, the Alawites maintained their power through brutal oppression of the innocent. The narrative calls for vengeance against the ruling regime and by "pushing the Alawites and their supporters into their graves." Core themes include (1) intolerance, (2) revenge, and (3) righteous cause (United States, "Open Source Center" 5).

Note the group's objectives and goals as stated in their foundational charter: "To topple the existing regime in its entirety, with all its obscure remnants, to wipe them out of Syrian existence completely, and to defend the underdogs, their honor and wealth. Toppling the regime means detaching and terminating all its judicial, legislative, and executive authorities along with its army and its security institutions, in addition to prosecuting those who are involved in bloodshed along with their supporters…." ("Islamic Front- Founding Declaration," 7th Clause, 1). This goal contains many of the"Alawite infidel" components, and one can see the narrative origin of such language seeking the destruction of the regime. As included in the narrative, the Islamic Front's goal promises that vengeance will be extended toward Alawite supporters. Additional language within the document includes historically based slurs against ethnic Alawites, as well as the promise of protecting the rights of groups unjustly persecuted by the regime.

The language of the document support use of a purpose-driven explanation of future acts – in this case, the creation of an Islamic state and massacre of enemies. Embracing "Greater Syria" in terms of an Islamic State encompassing the whole Levant (including Iraq and Jordan) justifies brutality en route. The Islamic Front wishes to characterize the conflict as the ultimate struggle to achieve their conception of a utopian state. This ideology as identical to that of the Islamic State (ISIS). Because the Levant exists within cultural narratives, certain aspects do not require further explanation for regional audiences. Further, achievement of an Islamic State controlling the Levant excuses the killing of enemies. There is no need to deflect responsibility. In fact, regional Sunni narratives already support a negative view of the Alawite. Thus, killing them requires less justification that that already provided in the "Greater Syria" purpose-driven explanation of intent. Again, we can see worldviews in cultural narratives and consistency in how worldviews manifest in persuasive attempts through a dramatistic lens.

Important to our purpose here, both Assad and the opposition seem to understand the importance of influencing multiple audiences. Both sides struggle for popular support among the Syrian people, their sectarian allies, and the international community. Leadership of both sides routinely engage in dialogue and interviews, and also maintains websites stating their objectives. To better understand the rich rhetorical nuances of the various discourses operating in this civil war, we further examine the content of the September 2013 news media interview between Syrian President Bashar al-Assad, Dennis Kucinich and Greg Palkot, as well as the foundational video-statement produced and published by the Islamic Front, the most powerful opposition group as of this writing. Thus, we hope to gain an appreciation of the worldview and motivations of each by analyzing specifically the dramatistic elements presented in their dialogue as well as draw comparisons between their content and ethnic narratives.

Assad and the Opposition: A Contrast in Drama

Burke provides insight into analyzing texts to find the implied worldview of their authors. One way involves looking for what he called terministic screens: "even if any given terminology is a *reflection* of reality, by its very nature as a terminology, it must be a *selection* of reality; and to this extent it must function also as a *deflection* of reality" (Burke, *Language as Symbolic Action* 45). Taking this into consideration, we can look for how the Islamic Front and Assad's choice of words and phrases act to orient listeners' attention toward a particular view of reality. For Burke, "there are two kinds of terms: terms that put things together, and terms that take things apart" (Language as Symbolic Action 49). This process acts to create either or both continuity and discontinuity; we can see how discourse creates moments for composition as well as division. Viewed dramatistically, we can see that "whatever terms we use ... constitute a ... kind of screen...." This screen "directs" our "attention to one field rather than another. Within that field there can be different screens, each" acting to focus our attention on various elements within a given situation: "All terminologies must implicitly or explicitly embody choices between the principle of continuity and the principle of discontinuity" (Burke, *Language as Symbolic Action* 50).

In our present case, we can look specifically at the discourses of the opposition and of Assad to see how their choice of terms opens up possibilities for unity or division with each other and with the international community. Are there true moments for consubstantial co-existence? Or instead, do the discourses operate to shut out such consubstantial moments by stressing division? On this point Lawrence Prelli and Terri S. Winters write, the "notion of terministic screens enables us to scrutinize how efforts to come to terms with problematic situations often involve similarities and differences about what meanings to reveal and conceal, disclose and foreclose. At stake in efforts to 'screen' meanings terminologically is the adequacy of underlying perspectives in depicting a situation's reality" (Lawrence and Winters, 226).

Screens point us toward certain elements of what Burke described as a dramatistic pentad—agent, act, scene, agency, purpose—and these different elements have differing degrees of influence upon ourselves and others. How we describe these elements provides insight into how we view the workings of the world. Andrew King describes the utility of Burke's work in this area as a "method of discovering why people do what they do." He writes further, "the dramatic frame features a battle over meanings, perspectives and values" (King, 168-9). In order to uncover the speaker's motivation and perspective, Burke suggested that each of the pentadic elements represents a way of explaining or rationalizing a specific event. Thus, when examining a speaker's explanation of an action, one examines the degree to which he or she juxtaposes other pentadic element against the action – the elemental ratio.

The ratio itself represents the interpretation a speaker offers to his or her audience. For example, if a speaker explains an act in terms of the environment in which it occurs (scene-act ratio), he or she might seek to frame the event as inevitable – or to deflect responsibility (Burke, *A Grammar of Motives;* King). Thus, the elemental ratios used by Assad and his opposition should provide some clue as to how they view their role in the conflict, or at least how they wish us to perceive it.

By discovering the elements of the terministic screens operating, we shed insight into the motives, or underlying worldviews, operating in the discourses of both the Assad regime and the opposition. Specifically, we look for how the various terminologies used acts to reflect the inner worldviews of the parties. Armed with this knowledge, we are then in a position to offer insights into how these worldviews operate to increase or decrease opportunities for consubstantial moments with each other as well as the international community.

Bashar Al-Assad's Interview with Kucinich and Palkot

Bashar Al-Assad's Interview with Kucinich and Palkot is on YouTube at https://youtu.be/wiFToslKyyM

By August of 2013, the conflict in Syria had raged for over two years. Islamic Front momentum seemed to have shifted to a stagnant but deadly equilibrium, if not somewhat to the Assad Regime. On August 21st, hundreds of Syrian civilians perished in an opposition-held suburb of Damascus. A United Nations investigation attributed the deaths to the employment of a chemical nerve-agent (a violation of international law), known as Sarin (United Nations Mission). Furthermore, the concentration and delivery system for the nerve-agent seemed to implicate Alawite regime forces. The United States immediately threatened retaliatory military action against the Assad Regime while Syrian allies such as Russia and China scurried to broker a diplomatic agreement to prevent such action. On September 12th, the same day U.N. made the investigation public, the Syrian regime agreed to disarm its chemical arsenal. It was in light of these events that Bashar al-Assad addressed the international community via his September 13, 2013 interview with Fox News contributor and former Democratic Congressman Dennis Kucinich. Assad ostensibly conducted the interview to deny his part in the chemical attack and to state his commitment to the U.N. chemical disarmament mandate. However, his status as the Syrian President and member of the Alawite minority placed him in a position to serve as a spokesman for the regime and his sect. His verbal engagement with Kucinich provides an ample number of examples from which we can better understand Alawite characterization of the entire conflict, their perceived role in it, and motivation behind their actions.

Early questions focus on the chemical attacks, and Assad wryly admits that the presence of his chemical weapons stockpile "is not a secret anymore" (Al-Assad). He denies that his forces were responsible for the attacks and suggests that his enemies engineered the attack. As the interview progresses, Assad engages in a broader discussion of the conflict and the character of the opposition. For example, when Kucinich asks about the future of a secular Syria and whether the country is engaged in a civil war, Assad describes his country as a tolerant "melting pot" of many ethnicities and religions. He describes the threat to the status quo as "extremism, terrorism and violence," the result of which would be an "ideologically closed... more fanatic" society (Al-Assad). Assad emphatically denies the conflict is a civil war. The ideological shift threatening Syrian society, he says, can be directly attributed to foreign-backed "terrorists." He states, "A civil war should start from within. A civil war doesn't need to have 80 or 83 nationalities coming to fight within your country supported by foreign countries. What we have is not a civil war. What we have is a new kind of war" (Al-Assad). When elaborating on the composition of the opposition fighters, he estimates that they are 80% "terrorists or Al Qaeda," who cross the border into Syria with funding and weapons provided by ideologically motivated individuals (Al-Assad). Thus, Assad provides us with the Alawite and regime characterization of the conflict. That is, they are engaged in a fight for the survival of a secular, multi-cultural Syria, against foreign backed terrorists who have ignited jihadist motivations among certain elements of the Syrian population.

Dramatistic Elements of Assad's Interview

If one looks at the entirety of Assad's interview through the lens of Burke's dramatic pentad, we can see deeper into the Alawite characterization of the conflict and their justification for violence. Assad certainly places the element of "scene" at the forefront; he would have his audience believe that he has no choice but to involve himself in a struggle with foreign backed terrorists who seek to undermine the secular nature of his country. In doing so, he not only denies responsibility for the conflict but also extends this denial to Syrian opposition groups who have been "duped" into rebellion by foreign conspirators. Such denial of responsibility can serve a threefold purpose; first, it saves face for the regime in the sense that it allows foreign influence – rather than the regime's own policies - to have caused the rebellion; second, it allows both parties to negotiate a settlement without either "being at fault"; third, it recognizes that the majority Sunni population cannot be vilified if the Alawites wish to remain in power.

However, when discussing particular actions, rather than characterizing the conflict, Assad places "purpose" at the forefront. Thus, when questioned about the thousands of casualties incurred since the beginning of the conflict, Assad cannot deny involvement; rather, he asserts that his actions are justified given the nature of his opponents and the extremist agenda they will visit upon the Syrian people. As a former medical doctor, Assad relates that his actions are humanitarian in nature in the sense that he is "extracting a limb to save the patient." By privileging purpose, his discourse assumes a logic where the ends justify the means. This represents a break with his overall denial of responsibility for the conflict. He is assuming responsibility for brutal actions, which he wants us to view as necessary, for the restoration of Syrian governance. Taken as a whole, we can infer that Assad wished audiences to view his role as reactionary yet strong and appropriate. He did not start the fight but will take the necessary means to resolve it properly.

For Burke, a dominance of scene suggests a sense of materialism operating in the discourse. He believes materialism to be "that metaphysical theory which regards all the facts of the universe as sufficiently explained by the assumption of body or matter, conceived as extended, impenetrable, eternally existent, and susceptible of movement or change of relative position" (Burke, *A Grammar of Motives* 131). It is "the theory which regards all the facts of the universe as explainable in terms of matter and motion. . . ." (Burke, *A Grammar of Motives* 131). Important here is that Assad›s discourse scenic reliance threatens to «downplay free choice and emphasize situational determinism,» and that it is *from* scenic domination that Assad›s purpose flows: «The dramatistic concept of purpose answers the question *why* an action should or should not take place and is, as such, moralistic in tone. Since purposive thinkers concentrate on the goal of an act, they understand small acts and decisions in light of a larger program» (King, 174; Fay and Kuypers, 207). In this sense, Assad is justifying deadly force as necessitated—compelled even—due to the scenic pressures. However, the focus on purpose also allows for the move toward a transcendent aspect of Assad's active use of deadly force: a greater, multicultural, and secular Syria (King, 170-171). Thus, Assad is willing to sacrifice lives and fortunes to save not himself, but a greater Syria. From Burke's point of view, the "sacrificial principle is intrinsic to the nature of order" because sacrifice leads to ultimate fulfillment and rewards ("Dramatism" 450).

The Islamic Front's Foundational Statement

> **Syria Document: Founding Declaration of the Islamic Front**
>
> On November 22, seven leading factions united as the "Islamic Front", one of the most significant realignments of the insurgency in Syria's conflict.
>
> See **Syria Analysis: Why and How Insurgent Formation of an Islamic Front Changes the Conflict**
>
> Read the "Founding Declaration of the Islamic Front" in PDF format.

Read this document at http://kbjournal.org/sites/default/files/Syria-Document-Founding-Declaration-of-the-Islamic-Front.pdf

The Islamic Front ratified their founding principles and goals on November 22, 2013. These principles were announced in an online video, in which the leadership of all subordinate factions surround the speaker, Ahmed Issa al-Sheikh ("Islamic Front- Founding Declaration"). Issa al-Sheikh is the former military commander of a powerful Jihadist fighting force and served as the Islamic Front's leader. Particularly relevant due to its timing, the statement is rife with sectarian undertones, ethno-religious narratives, and is clearly meant to address a diverse audience. The statement comes in the wake of recent pro-regime victories against several key Jihadist fighting groups and the killing of a key Islamist opposition leader. Subordinate groups of like ideology recognized the need to unify their forces and clearly articulate a vision for a future Syria. Their exigency became even more salient in the wake of the internationally brokered deal preventing U.S. intervention against the Assad regime.

Issa begins the statement by defining the Islamic Front as "a comprehensive Islamic, social, political, and military formation. Aiming to a complete toppling of Assad regime in Syria, and building an Islamic state in which the lordship will be for the almighty God Sharia (law)...." ("Islamic Front- Founding Declaration," Introduction). With this statement, Issa breaks the silence, intentionally maintained by many Jihadist groups, regarding their end-game for a post-Assad Syria. The remainder of the statement takes on the nature of a governing document. Fifteen clauses distinctly outline the group's ideology, goals, rules for membership, characterization of other groups, and codes of behavior. In broad terms, the statement attempts to strike a balance between vehement advocacy for the implementation of Sharia law and understanding the concerns of Syrian citizens who would exist under it. Further, the speaker defines the Islamic Front's central role within the conflict, while directly and indirectly naming its enemies.

Issa is very clear regarding the group's intentions for governance. His desire is "to establish an independent state in which God's faithful Sharia will reign sovereign...." ("Islamic Front- Founding Declaration," 1st Clause). He further rejects any form of secularization, stating "Religion without policy is a kind of monasticism that is forbidden in our religion and policy without religion is rejected secularization." His moderating tone shows up in his address of how such a system might be implemented. To the Syrian people (and perhaps the international community) he relays the group's commitment to work "for political progress, to create unified visions and positions compatible with societal issues; along with the civilian side, it revives and activates society's various capacities in preparation for rebuilding the desired new Syria, the state of Islam, justice, and advancement." The speaker further highlights elements of class and sect by stating that in the "new Syria" the group will "defend the underdogs" and their honor ("Islamic Front- Founding Declaration," 7th Clause, 1).

When discussing its enemies, the group directly addresses the Alawite-Shia Assad Regime as well as indirectly addressing supporters of an Arab style secular state. With respect to the regime, the groups stated goal is "to topple the existing regime in its entirety, with all its obscure remnants, to wipe them out of Syrian existence completely" ("Islamic Front- Founding Declaration," 7th Clause, 1). The statement addresses regime supporters by stating that following the dismantling of all governmental institutions, they should receive an "equitable trial" ("Islamic Front- Founding Declaration," 7th Clause, 1), although one might assume that such trials would occur based upon the Islamic Front's interpretation of Sharia Law. The other take-away from the statement, is the frequency with which the speaker denounces secularism. Without naming anyone, the group is sending a clear message to elements of the opposition who have not yet aligned with them, as well as rejecting the influence of foreign powers. Finally, the group stakes its claim to legitimacy by citing its member-groups successful participation since the beginning of the "revolution" and paying homage to its own military prowess.

Dramatistic Elements of Opposition Discourse

The speaker's words within the video indicate that the group advocates the destruction of the Assad Regime and the establishment of an Islamic State governed by Sharia Law. However, the meaning of the speaker's words extend beneath the surface regarding the Islamic Front's role in the formation of the Islamic State, and the likelihood it will carry out its agenda against Assad regime supporters. Here the *act* of the Islamic Front is the establishment of an Islamic State and the conduct of retribution. Throughout the text there is a mingling of *purpose* and *agent* with this *act*. This varies by clause within the document, with some assuming an *act-purpose* ratio and others assuming an *act-agent*ratio. These ratios interanimate to form a general sense of *act* to *purpose/agent* emphasis. The speaker›s interchanging emphasis on *purpose*and *agent* with respect to the *act* of establishing an Islamic state demonstrate their ambition to rule such a state as well as a willingness to justify violence in order to establish it.

The strong domination of act in the discourse of the Islamic Front implies an undercurrent of philosophical realism operating in the discourse. Burke describes realism as a belief "in the real existence of matter as the object of perception (natural realism); also, the view that the physical world has independent reality, and is not ultimately reducible to universal mind or spirit." Importantly for understanding the discourse of the Islamic Front, this realist underpinning also suggests "the existence of objects in the external world independently of the way they are subjectively experienced" ("Realism"). The act of the Islamic Front fuels their very conception of self: "things are more or less real according as they are more or less *energeia* [activity] (*actu*, from which our 'actuality' is derived). [F]orm is the *actus*, the attainment, which realizes the matter" (Burke, *A Grammar of Motives* 227).

Agent and purpose work together to legitimize the Islamic Front's central role in the conflict, qualify them for leadership, and promoting ideology. As agents, the leaders of the Islamic Front view themselves as fighting for a larger cause, and their discourse suggests that they take on a larger than life persona. Certainly the dramatistic agent can be viewed as a heroic person, one willing and able to take on the most difficult of circumstances. This aspect of the Islamic Front's discourse could be particularly appealing to Western cultures where, as Andrew King points out, "the charismatic leader who triumphs in spite of obstacles, setbacks, and enemies" has long been celebrated (170). The reliance on purpose in the discourse serves to highlight the larger context in which the Islamic Front views their *actions*. Since purpose answers the question *why* an action should or should not take place, we have a greater sense of how the Islamic Front sees its individual acts of violence are seen in relation to a much larger program of the imposition of Sharia Law within a Middle East Caliphate. This emphasis on *purpose* within the text reflects concerns of mysticism. On this point King writes that «in the extreme example of this kind of rhetoric means are subordinated to ends... for the sake of higher or divine law» (172). The speaker›s consistent emphasis upon the use of violence for the sake of Islam and Sharia Law certainly fits here. For example, with regard to necessarily justified action the speaker states that, «the Islamic Front believes that the way to achieve its targets cannot be realized unless the armed military movement actively undertakes the Assad regime›s toppling.» The document additionally explains that this entails wiping the Assad regime from existence. The justification for intended brutality remains the establishment of the Islamic state. The speaker views such actions as acceptable in light of «an independent state in which God›s faithful Sharia will reign sovereign.»

As noted by King, persons who expect charismatic leaders to solve their problems tend to emphasize the agent in their discourse (171). The speaker in the Islamic Front video places the Islamic Frontas the agent for taking action and solving the problems of its advocates. The statement's sixth paragraph provides the following example; "Islamic Front sons were the first to revolt against the Assad regime's tyranny and protected the people from its injustice. The most prominent military victories over the Assad regime are theirs, so they are part of the Syrian people and interpret Syrians' aims and hopes." In this telling example, the speaker clearly designates the central nature of Islamic Front within the conflict and offers their suitability to "protect the underdog [and] his honor," and to represent the Syrian people.

Metaphor and "Selling" of the Alawite Case to the U.S.

An examination of Bashar al-Assad's interview can inform us about the perception and motivations of the group he represents. A juxtaposition of history, events, narrative, and dramatistic pentad show an Alawite ruling class which believes it is locked in conflict with a sectarian enemies bent on its destruction; events of the conflict are beyond their control as evidenced by a conspiratorial relationship between their neighbors, ideologically motivated individuals, and Western nations. Because they argue that the conflict is not of their making, Alawite rulers feel justified in using violence on those they perceive as not being *truly Syrian*. They also believe that in destroying their opposition and reincorporating certain factions of the rebellion, they will be resurrecting "Greater Syria." Given the difference between Syrian and Western narratives, understanding regarding the nature of the conflict, and preconceived Western notions of a "tyrannical regime," how does Assad try to influence U.S. opinion?

Throughout the interview, Assad chooses to explain his case using carefully selected language understood by Westerners, particularly Americans. The language used—metaphors—translates central ideas using words that produce wide meaning and invoke sympathy among his audience. Thomas R. Burkholder and David Henry describe a metaphor as a speaker's means to "ask listeners to comprehend one thing, represented by the *tenor*, in terms of another, represented by the *vehicle*" (98). Metaphor, however, is more than just a description or comparison of one thing in terms of another. Michael Osborn describes how "the 'thought' of the subject (tenor) and the 'thought' of the item for association (vehicle)… in their meaningful action together, determine psychologically the appearance and sense of the metaphor" ("The Metaphor" 228). Thus, the metaphor is a process of thought and understanding on the part of the sender and receiver. In some cases, we might consider it a contextualization in the pursuit of persuasion. Osborn's later work describes such a process whereby "cues in the context include consciousness of recent events… susceptibility of listeners, and deeper cultural configurations that come into play" ("The Trajector," 80). In our present case, Assad is asking us to understand the *opposition and their actions* in terms of *terrorists and terrorism*.

A September 11, 2001, *terrorists* no longer only attacked small groups who chose to venture into dangerous lands, nor was their destruction limited to those unfortunates within the blast radius of a bomb. *Terrorists* could now pilot airplanes, destroy cultural landmarks, kill thousands in well-coordinated attacks, and do it where ordinary people live and work. *Terrorism* invokes visceral images of buildings collapsing with thousands trapped inside. It also elicits fear of a faceless enemy who violates the American sense of security, challenges ideals of tolerance, and seethes with incomprehensible hate. Further, with the exception of certain high-profile domestic cases, *terrorists are foreign*. The collective nature of emotion, fear, and suspicion described above comprise the Alawite understanding of the Syrian rebellion and the conceptualization he asks U.S. audiences to assume. Although he doesn't directly state the following, Assad seems to extend the metaphor toward *The Syrian Governments actions are a war on terror*. Such a metaphor permeates a barrier between the Syrian-Alawite and U.S. world-views that might have been impenetrable on September 10, 2001.

We believe that Assad understands the power characterizing *opposition as terrorists* based upon his frequency of use. It is important, however, to understand why he uses it. When engaging with U.S. audiences, the Alawite use of metaphor assumes certain ideographic characteristics as both a call for inaction and a justification for action. If the abstract of *terrorism* represents a collective commitment to a normative goal, that goal is combating terrorism. Following 9/11, the U.S. engaged in the War on Terror. Although the concept of War on Terror eventually led to military action, it was initially an ill-defined call to action against an unknown enemy (Kuypers). By characterizing 80% of the Syrian opposition as *terrorists*, Assad and his Regime seek to align themselves with this call to action – and justify their use of force. Similarly, if Regime forces are combating terrorism, the U.S. shouldn't intervene in their execution of a war on terrorism. The specter of terrorism warrants and excuses Regime actions while attempting to avoid U.S. involvement by invoking collective commitment to a common goal. It is powerful because it calls upon U.S. commitments and imparts an immediate and visceral understanding of the Alawite worldview - existential fear, encirclement, vigilance, and survival.

Additionally, Assad's metaphor of rebels as terrorists aligns his objectives with those of the U.S. By defining a common enemy he not only seeks to stem U.S. opposition, but to invite active support. At the time of his interview, the specter of terrorism in Syria proved insufficient for U.S. policy-makers to overcome the short-term political benefit of taking a hard line on the regime's brutality. However, the recent horrific actions of the Islamic State as well of the AQ affiliations of the Islamic Front have made it clear that Assad does indeed fight self-proclaimed enemies of the United States. Perhaps we can judge his previous appeals in a new light as we consider the way ahead in the larger regional conflict. In recent months, Secretary of State Kerry alluded to a possible tacit cooperation with Syrian forces fighting the Islamic State (Islamic Front is not specifically addressed) despite the U.S.'s official policy of arming and equipping the opposition. He noted, "we are working very hard with other interested parties to see if we can reignite a diplomatic outcome… we have to negotiate in the end" (Kerry qtd. in Gordon, "Kerry Suggests"). This shift does not necessarily represent support for the Syrian dictator or his Iranian allies. However, it seems to indicate a willingness to revaluate the application of economic and military pressure as policy makers refine their understanding of the conflict.

Clashing World Views: Dramatism and International Audience

Our analysis suggests that U.S. audiences use care when evaluating the discourse of potential allies in the Syrian conflict, as well as when applying the pentad to non-Western discourse. Three pitfalls can lead to oversimplification and misplaced sympathy toward either of the two sides. These pitfalls include: one, listening to what is being said about the groups involved rather than what *they themselves are saying;* two, listening to speakers who do not represent the warring parties; and three, imposing a U.S. understanding of the "underdog versus the tyrannical regime" upon the conflict itself. These pitfalls can, however, be avoided through the proper contextualization and use of primary sources, the analysis of cultural narratives, and the application of the pentad used to better understand worldviews. In particular, one must evaluate the discourse *of* the persuasive agent rather than discourse *about* a persuasive agent. For example, if one intends to evaluate Bashar al-Assad›s motives, a Western media outlet›s interpretation of his words would be an ill-advised source. Although such documents might contain quotes, those chosen might actually support a pre-existing U.S. culturally based interpretation (such as the «the underdog vs. the tyrannical regime»).

U.S. failure to hold a conversation regarding the actual discourse *of* Syrian (by extension Iraqi) partisans in context of the conflict is already leading it toward poorly advised «side-taking.» Never has U.S. publicdiscourse regarding Syria included a scenario where the U.S. intervenes on behalf of the Regime to prevent an internationally recognized terror syndicate from gaining control of the infrastructure of a developed country. This is not to imply that such strategies would be correct, but rather to highlight that a robust understanding of the parties involved ought to lead to questions regarding potential U.S. support for the opposition. Such questions, when they have been addressed in the public discourse, are answered by rhetoric that supports the "moderate" opposition. Such lines of logic conclude with the idea that the "extremists" are a minority, and support for the "moderates" will prevent others from filling a power void. However, a closer look shows that much of the "moderate" voice is either disregarded as irrelevant by representative opposition groups, if not used as a tool for bargaining by influential individuals with ties to those groups. Furthermore, the group now overseeing the "moderate" opposition (The Islamic Front) originates from the same cloth, holds the same ideology, desires the same goal, and uses similar narratives as the Islamic State (ISIS). The ethno-religious/sectarian nature of the conflict, as well as the role of terrorist groups within it, are not only ignored in public discourse, but also at times denied completely. For instance, U.S. Secretary of State John Kerry stated in September 2013, "I just don't agree that the majority of them are al-Qaeda and the bad guys" (Michaels, "Kerry"). However, the value of public knowledge informed by those who choose to agree/disagree with certain characterizations pales in comparison with realistic assessments based upon *what the groups themselves tell us*. On the contrary, when commentators and officials choose to ignore primary sources and make statements of opinion, they perpetuate mischaracterization by a public who relies on their judgment to inform foreign policy. We feel that in conflicts involving ideologies and worldviews completely foreign to most Americans, the public would do well to listen to words spoken by the combatants themselves.

Analysis of foreign discourse with respect to commonly used cultural narratives is a necessary first step for cross-cultural applications of the dramatistic pentad. For example, rural Sunni narratives tell us that those who are fighting against the Assad regime historically sought regional dominance and routinely discuss the destruction of the "illegitimate" Alawite regime. These are not motives in the Burkean sense. However, they do contextualize the "who" and "why" when applying the pentad. For example, if a fanatical Sunni seeks to cast "enemies of Islam" into their graves, we have some idea of who is first in line

(Alawites) and what sets of ambitions exist outside of the immediate discourse. Thus, if "freedom and democracy" are not part of the cultural repertoire of a rural Sunni rebel, we might not consider such an end-state among the menu of his or her possible motives.

Following our methodology, once we understand the speaker›s cultural repertoire, we can apply the pentad. As we have shown, the Islamic Front assumes a realist worldview by placing the *act* of creating a Syrian Islamic state governed by Sharia Law as the central component of their discourse. The act is achieved by the killing and expulsion of the Alawite Regime as well as imposing judgment on its supporters. The Islamic Front intertwines the use of *purpose* and *agent* with *act*, creating an act-agent/purpose ratio. This ratio provides us further insight regarding their worldview and motivation. Thus, we know that the Islamic Front's leadership feels justified in killing for the purpose of establishing a religious state. Further, they are the self-styled rulers of the future regime by virtue of their military prowess and righteousness. This is not the language of tolerance expected of governments in the West; future studies may show that it is quite similar to the language of the Islamic State (ISIS/ISIL).

The danger of imposing our perceptions upon the warring groups (rather than listening to the discourse) is that they might well pursue their ideological path to its logical conclusion, despite our fervent wishes to the contrary. As we have seen here, for some this includes the bloody disposal of all perceived enemies and the establishment of an ideologically narrow autocracy. To sympathize with the Islamic Front or Al-Nusrah because we do not perceive them to be as extreme as "ISIS," or with jihadists because they are fighting a bloody war against the Syrian state apparatus, is a failure to recognize the credibility of their motivations as portrayed in their own words (Sly, "Al-Qaeda"). Such groups tell us that they will kill their enemies according to (their interpretation of) Sharia Law and establish a caliphate. Perhaps the important question is not whether we can cooperate with (or even identify) a moderate opposition, but why the jihadist discourse of the Islamic Front and ISIS resonates so heavily with the regional Sunni population and potential allies. Understanding this might allow real dialogue with those who must eventually be part of the solution.

Application of the pentad provides the starting point for a truly contextualized policy discussion. As the final portion of our method discusses, we can now move beyond the immediate discourse of the partisans themselves. A starting point lies in the Islamic Front's *purpose*. What does a strict interpretation of Sharia Law look like to a Sunni extremist, and what does it tell us about the potential for partnership against "undesirable" elements in Syria? *Reliance of the Traveler and Tools for the Worshiper* (A Classic Manual of Islamic Sacred Law by Ahmad Ibn Naqib al-Misri) written in the 14th Century provides some insight. It is an authoritative manual on Sunni Islamic jurisprudence that dictates rules for interactions with non-Muslims, lists requirements of Jihad, details when killing is permissible, itemizes corporal punishment for various offenses, and so forth. Interpretations of this kind have serious implications for a potential alliance with any opposition aligned with the Islamic Front. The document makes clear that Jihad is obligatory, as is the killing of apostates in Muslim lands, or of Christians who criticize Islam. Additionally, any alliance with non-Muslims is prohibited, unless Muslims are outnumbered (Al-Misri, 246). The document does not leave any room for interpretation for strict followers. Thus alliances with the Islamic Front or subordinate groups might prove ultimately unreliable, as their law mandates a return to a strict Sharia interpretation once they have numerical superiority. Reference to such interpretations of Sharia (also used by ISIS/ISIL) might also be an underlying reason Arab nations are hesitant to cooperate in a ground coalition. Even if Jordanian and Saudi politicians do not use such documents to govern their actions, blatant violations might jeopardize their legitimacy with Sunni constituents. Unfortunately for the West and the U.S., there doesn't seem to be much choice between "ISIS" and other fighters who share their ideology in the larger sectarian conflict. Further, the "rules of the game" used by ISIS and the "moderate" rebels in Syria are the same as those used by the Charlie Hebdo attackers. A nuanced conversation might highlight the inanity of creating artificial pecking orders of evil (e.g. the Paris attackers and ISIS are really evil, Al-Qaeda is in the middle, and the Syrian rebels are "good").

The regime of Bashar al-Assad has been successfully fighting against such militants. His discourse has traditionally been that of defining a common enemy through the metaphor of terrorism. He justifies his brutal actions using a scene-act/purpose ratio to describe the inevitability of conflict, and to justify his methods. Uncovering the motivation behind his discourse, it *seems* that we have a willing and capable ally in the struggle against extremism. Be that as it may, his discourse indicates that the reverse may also be true. That is, he might attack and destroy U.S. trained «moderates» because he perceives them to be terrorists. What is to stop him from doing so when his demise is their primary stated objective? Unfortunately, this possibility has not frequently surfaced in U.S. domestic discourse – which seems to assume a one-on-one fight between «moderates» and «ISIS.» The ultimate question is whether we are willing to recast groups in a new light after listening to their discourse, or whether we will cling to old labels, impose U.S. narratives on the conflict, and develop untenable courses of action.

Moving beyond the finding of worldviews and sharing policy implications, this essay also demonstrates how the dramatistic pentad provides a fruitful analytic path into cross-cultural rhetorical criticism, and an effective rhetorical lens for understanding diverse worldviews. In order to navigate this path one must examine the speaker's actual discourse and draw context from the speaker's own culture. This requires the identification of primary sources to serve as artifacts for analysis and the examination of native historical-cultural discourse surrounding the artifacts. Close readings of such culturally related discourse can discover thematic cultural narratives that enhance understanding of the intended audience of a speaker, as well as more accurately account for the worldview of that speaker.

This is an important step since the supplantation of native (non-U.S.) narratives with U.S. narratives leads to miscues regarding a speaker's motive. For example, in our present case, both Assad and the Islamic Front tell us which of their cultural narratives are relevant by explaining them in terms of our own, U.S. narratives. When Assad describes the current conflict as a "fight against terror," we understand that he is describing a perceived existential threat. Thus, we can glimpse the worldview from which he is operating, and would have his audience enter into, by examining the narratives of existential threat. Native narratives provide such nuanced context for applying the pentad. As an additional example, rural Sunni narratives (those of the opposition) do not simply discuss humiliation and justice. Such narratives describe humiliation *at the hands of Alawites,* and justice *against Alawites.* It is with this insight that we can actually apply the pentad. Native narrative and use of metaphor allow us to properly identify the pentad's elements. Thus, the *act,* or "medicine" the Islamic Front (for example) asks us to take is the extermination of Alawites and the establishment of a caliphate in Syria. We would not, however, arrive at this conclusion by applying the pentad through the lens of our own sacred narratives (e.g. equality, tolerance, and justice for the oppressed). As Burke demonstrated in his early unveiling of Hitler's sinister intent, uncovering motive through application of the pentad requires understanding of the other's history, culture, and the surrounding discourse. Only when this is accomplished can we begin the intuitive work of understanding how each element fits together to provide meaning.

Works Cited

Al-Assad, Bashar. Interview with Dennis Kucinich and Greg Palkot. *You Tube*. Fox News Incorporated 13 Sept. 2013. Web. 9 Jan. 2016. http://www.youtube.com/watch?v=qmMmGZQaVsc

Al-Misri, Ahmad Ibn Naqib. *Reliance of the Traveler*. Trans. and Ed. Nuh Ha Mim Keller. Beltsville, MD: Amana Publications, 1994.

Angel, Adriana, and Benjamin Bates. "Terministic Screens of Corruption: A Cluster Analysis of Colombian Radio Conversations." *KB Journal* 10.1 2014. Web. 9 Jan. 2016. http://kbjournal.org/angel_bates_terministic_screens_of_corruption

Burke, Kenneth. *A Grammar of Motives*. 1945. Berkeley, CA: U of California P, 1969. Print.

—. "Dramatism," *International Encyclopedia of the Social Sciences*. Ed. David L. Sills and Robert K. Merton. New York: Macmillan and Free Press, 1968: 445-52.

—. *Language as Symbolic Action: Essays on Life, Literature, and Method*. Berkeley, CA: U of California P, 1966. Print.

—. "The Rhetoric of Hitler's 'Battle.'" *Readings in Propaganda and Persuasion: New and Classic Essays*. Ed. Garth S. Jowett and Victoria O'Donnell. Thousand Oaks, CA: SAGE , 2006. 149-68.

Burkholder, Thomas R., and David Henry. "Criticism in Metaphor." *Rhetorical Criticism, Perspectives in Action*. Ed. Jim A. Kuypers. New York: Lexington, 2009. Print.

"David Gregory: Al-Qaeda Cast off ISIS as Too Extreme." *The Tampa Bay Times* 13 August 2014. Web. 9 Jan. 2016. http://www.politifact.com/punditfact/statements/2014/aug/13/david-gregory/david-gregory-al-qaida-cast-isis-too-extreme/

Day, Anna Therese. "Syrian Fighter: We are the Western Front against ISIL." *Mashable.com* 24 June 2014. Web. 9 Jan. 2016. http://mashable.com/2014/06/24/syrian-fighter-we-are-the-western-front-against-isil/

Fassihi, Farnaz, Jay Solomon, and Sam Dagher. "Iranians Dial up Presence in Syria." *Wall Street Journal* 13 Sept. 2013. Web. 9 Jan. 2016.http://on-

line.wsj.com/news/articles/SB10001424127887323864604579067382861808984
Fay, Isabel, and Jim A. Kuypers. "Transcending Mysticism and Building Identification Through Empowerment of the Rhetorical Agent: John F. Kennedy's Berlin Speeches on June 26th, 1963." *Southern Communication Journal* 77.3 (2012): 198-215.
Francis, David. "Why the Long Arm of ISIS Has Eric Holder Spooked." *The Fiscal Times*. 15 July 2014. Web. 9 Jan. 2016. http://www.thefiscaltimes.com/Articles/2014/07/15/Why-Long-Arm-ISIS-Has-Eric-Holder-Spooked
Goldberg, Jeffrey. "Hillary Clinton: 'Failure' to Help Syrian Rebels Led to the Rise of ISIS." *The Atlantic* 10 Aug. 2014. Web. 9 Jan. 2016. http://www.theatlantic.com/international/archive/2014/08/hillary-clinton-failure-to-help-syrian-rebels-led-to-the-rise-of-isis/375832/
"The Islamic Front's Founding Declaration; Full English Text" *Democratic Revolution, Syrian Style*. 28 Nov. 2013. Web. 9 Jan. 2016. http://notgeorgesabra.wordpress.com/2013/11/29/full-english-text-of-the-islamic-fronts-founding-declaration/
Kelley, Colleen E. "The Public Rhetoric of Mikhail Gorbachev and the Promise of Peace." *Western Journal of Speech Communication* 52 (1988): 321-34.
Kerry, John. qtd. in Michael R. Gordon. "Kerry Suggests There Is a Place for Assad in Syria Talks." *The New York Times* 15 March 2015. Web. 9 Jan. 2016. http://www.nytimes.com/2015/03/16/world/middleeast/kerry-suggests-there-is-a-place-for-assad-in-syria-talks.html?_r=0
King, Andrew. "Pentadic Criticism: The Wheels of Creation." *Rhetorical Criticism, Perspectives in Action* Ed. Jim A. Kuypers. New York, NY: Lexington Books, 2009. Print.
Kuypers, Jim A. *Bush's War: Media Bias and Justifications for War in a Terrorist Age*. Lanham, MD: Rowman and Littlefield, 2006. Print.
Lu, Xing. "A Burkean Analysis of China Is Not Happy: A Rhetoric of Nationalism." *Chinese Journal of Communication* 5.2 (2012): 194-209.
Lund, Aron. *Syria's Salafi Insurgents: The Rise of the Syrian Islamic Front*. Swedish Institute of International Affairs: UI Occasional Papers No. 17. March 2013. Web. http://www.ui.se/eng/upl/files/86861.pdf
MacFarQuhar, Neil, and Hwaida Saad. "As Syrian War Drags On, Jihadists Take Bigger Role." *The New York Times* 29 July 2012. Web. 9 Jan. 2016. http://www.nytimes.com/2012/07/30/world/middleeast/as-syrian-war-drags-on-jihad-gains-foothold.html?pagewanted=all&_r=0
Michaels, Jim. "Kerry: Syrian Rebels have not been Hijacked by Extremists." *USA Today* 5 Sept. 2013.
Osborn, Michael M., and Douglas Ehninger. "The Metaphor in Public Address." *Communications Monographs* 29.3 (1962): 223-34.
Osborn, Michael M. "The Trajectory of My Work with Metaphor." *Southern Communication Journal* 74.1 (2009): 79-87.

Patron-Galindo, Pedro. "Symbolism and the Construction of Political Products: Analysis of the Political Marketing Strategies of Peruvian President Alejandro Toledo." *Journal of Public Affairs* 4.2 (2004): 115-24.
Prelli, Lawrence, and Terri S. Winters. "Rhetorical Features of Green Evangelicalism." *Environmental Communication* 3.2 (2009): 224-43.
"Realism," *Oxford English Dictionary*, 2nd Edition (OED2). Web.
Ritger, Clara. "Chuck Hagel: ISIS is 'Beyond Anything' the US has Seen." *The National Journal* 21 Aug. 2014. Web. 9 Jan. 2016. http://www.nationaljournal.com/defense/chuck-hagel-isis-is-beyond-anything-the-u-s-has-seen-20140821
Sly, Liz. "Al-Qaeda Disavows any ties with Radical Islamist ISIS Group in Syria, Iraq." *The Washington Post* 3 Feb. 2014.
"Syria—People and Society." *The World Factbook*. Central Intelligence Agency, n.d. Web. 9 Jan. 2016. https://www.cia.gov/library/publications/the-world-factbook/geos/sy.html
"Syria Profile," *BBC News*. BBC, 9 Dec. 2015. Web. 9 Jan. 2016. http://www.bbc.com/news/world-middle-east-14703995
"United Nations Mission to Investigate Allegations of the Use of Chemical Weapons in the Syrian Arab Republic: Report on the Alleged Use of Chemical Weapons in the Ghouta Area of Damascus on 21 August 2013. United Nations. 12 Sept. 2013."http://www.un.org/disarmament/content/slideshow/Secretary_General_Report_of_CW_Investigation.pdf
United States. Central Intelligence Agency. Director of National Intelligence Open Source Center (OSC). *Open Source Center Master Narratives Country Report: Syria*. Reston: Open Source Center, 2008.

This work is licensed under a Creative Commons Attribution-NonCommercial-NoDerivatives 4.0 International License.

LITERACY IN COMPOSITION STUDIES

Literacy in Composition Studies is a refereed open access online journal sponsoring scholarly activity at the nexus of Literacy and Composition Studies.

Literacy in Composition Studies is on the Web at http://licsjournal.org

With literacy and composition as our keywords we denote practices that are deeply context-bound and always ideological and recognize the institutional, disciplinary, and historical contexts surrounding the range of writing courses offered at the college level. Literacy is often a metaphor for the ability to navigate systems, cultures, and situations. At its heart, literacy is linked to interpretation—to reading the social environment and engaging and remaking that environment through communication. Orienting a Composition Studies journal around literacy prompts us to analyze the connections and disconnections among writing, reading and interpretation, inviting us to examine the ways in which literacy constitutes writer, context, and act.

'The Advantages of Knowing How to Read and Write': Literacy, Filmic Pedagogies, and the Hemisphere Projection of US Influence

Olson and Reddy's fascinating history of the partnership between the Office of the Coordinator of Inter-American Affairs (OIAA) and the Walt Disney Company in the mid-twentieth century was published in a special issue titled "The Transnational Movement of People and Information" which was guest edited by Rebecca Lorimer Leonard, Kate Vieira, and Morris Young. This article demonstrates that literacy was linked to claims of US superiority in the Disney films produced for and distributed to the Americas. As the special issue editors note, "through a careful analysis of archival materials, Olson and Reddy track the movement of literacy materials across space, time, and political regimes, as cartoons sponsored by the US government about the importance of literacy are broadcast into the neo-colonial context of Latin America, reinscribing ideologies of literacy that reinforce hemispheric hierarchies." Olson and Reddy bring together conversations in literacy studies and transnational rhetorics to characterize how the "developmentalist" framing in the Disney films promote ideological values such as modernity and efficiency specifically linked to the US and construct Latin Americans as literacy's Others.

"The Advantages of Knowing How to Read and Write:" Literacy, Filmic pedagogies, and the Hemispheric Projection of US Influence

Christa J. Olson and Madison Nancy Reddy

In his December 1940 "Arsenal of Democracy" fireside chat, Franklin Delano Roosevelt warned listeners that Axis aggression posed a grave threat to the American hemisphere. One year later, the United States experienced that hemispheric risk first hand at Pearl Harbor. Halfway between those two attention-calling moments, the demands of hemispheric security precipitated a less military sort of action: an educational partnership aimed at enacting Roosevelt's call for a democratic arsenal that would defend not just the United States but the whole of the Americas. Starting in June 1941, the Office of the Coordinator of Inter-American Affairs (OIAA) and the Walt Disney Company made a series of films projecting good neighborliness and benign development southward across the hemisphere. The partnership resulted in animated features, good-will tours, and training filmstrips, all aiming to "strengthen the bonds between the United States and the other American Republics" at a time when such bonds were critical and in doubt ("Memorandum" 1).

While the feature films *Saludos Amigos* and *The Three Caballeros* are the best-known outcomes of the partnership between Disney and the OIAA, the educational films they produced circulated nearly as widely. Those films, which Disney later described as "edutainment," combined audience appeal and instructional purpose to address matters of health, development, literacy, and history (Van Riper 2). However, they were above all concerned with promoting hemispheric union. Some even carried tellingly "American" titles (e.g., "Health for the Americas" and "Reading for the Americas"), and their narration was often well salted with the language of American values.

Matters of transhemispheric movement infused almost every aspect of the Disney-OIAA films. In service of the OIAA's goals (and Disney's commercial interests), the films and their creators traveled widely, strengthening bonds with allied American republics and seeking to entice more recalcitrant ones. The films themselves were shown in classrooms from the United States to Argentina, from Guayaquil, Ecuador, to Rio di Janeiro, Brazil. Walt Disney animators, US-based educators, and OIAA employees traversed the Americas gathering sources and promoting US interests. Latin American artists and musicians and their creative work traveled northward to enrich the American visions that Disney and the OIAA circulated.[1] Latin American political elites and civic leaders welcomed OIAA delegations and sent reactions north to the Office of the Coordinator. Articles published in Latin American newspapers made their way back to Washington, DC, where they were translated and placed in the files of the OIAA. In the midst of all that circulation, caught in the glare of inter- American cooperation and US technical expertise, the average Latin American appeared resolutely immobile, a subject always in need of education and development.

That contrast between a mobile, modern United States and a stagnant Latin America is poignantly visible in the materials at the heart of this article: the archives of a Disney-OIAA literacy and hygiene project that flourished briefly toward the end of World War II. While the OIAA and Walt Disney touted their goal of reaching every Latin American citizen with film-based literacy training, their depiction of those recipients as passive and a-modern marked them always as literacy's others and, consequently, as America's others.

Engaging that Disney-OIAA literacy project, this essay illuminates how literacy and film served the US government as "navigational technolog[ies]" that directed and constrained access to modern mobility (Vieira, "Consequences" 27). Produced in a moment when literacy, democracy, and development were tightly linked in popular discourse and literacy scholarship, the Disney-OIAA literacy films carried the assumption of US expertise in modern life outward to the "other American republics" (e.g., Bromage, Gross, Lynde). Literacy became [US] American property in much the way that Prendergast sees literacy emerge as white property within the United States (7-8). Ultimately, though US officials imagined filmic literacy linking the Americas through common values, their always pre-existing claim to literacy simultaneously reinscribed familiar hierarchies that placed the United States at the head of the hemisphere.

In addressing how themes of movement and stagnation pervade the Disney-OIAA literacy project, we call attention to the intertwined possibilities and consequences of literate mobility. We build on scholarship in literacy studies and transnational rhetorics, approaching the Disney-OIAA literacy campaign as a matter of both educational practice and political purpose, as a means of projecting both local skills and wide-ranging ideological import (e.g., Vieira, "American by Paper"; Brandt and Clinton; Lorimer Leonard; Dingo, *Networking*; C. Olson, "Contradictions of Progress"; L. Olson,). Recent discussions of literacy's consequences have moved us productively beyond the terms of the literacy myth and into the question of literacy's social and material effects on those relegated to the category of "illiterate" (e.g., Brandt; Mortensen, "Figuring Illiteracy," "Reading Material"; Prendergast; Prendergast, and Ličko; Stuckey; Vieira, "American"). Extending that conversation into Latin America, we suggest that under a developmentalist frame, literacy education creates literacy's others even as it seeks to extend literacy. In that paradigm, literacy moves and prevents movement; it circulates and constrains access to circulation.

The coming pages offer first a general overview of the OIAA and its partnership with Disney, highlighting the hemispheric spirit mobilized by both organizations to serve US interests. Then, turning to the 1943-45 Disney-OIAA literacy project, we examine the specific literate mechanisms of that transnational nationalism. As OIAA staff, Disney animators, literacy experts, and local respondents discussed the goals and implementation of their work, the particulars of literacy and pedagogy were subsumed to ideologically inflected matters of modernity, development, and efficiency. Ultimately, the "advantages of knowing how to read and write" so touted by the films became advantages that accrued primarily to those in the North and in each American republic who were already established as *letrados, modernos,* and *Americanos* (Alstock).

HEMISPHERIC UNITY AND MOVING PICTURES

The Office of the Coordinator of Inter-American Affairs was created by executive order on July 30, 1941.[2] The agency, housed within the Office for Emergency Management, was headed by Nelson

A. Rockefeller through the bulk of World War II.[3] In response to the threat of Axis economic, cultural, and political influence in Latin America, the OIAA was charged to "formulate, recommend, and execute programs in the commercial and economic fields which, by the effective use of governmental and private facilities, will further the commercial well-being of the Western Hemisphere" and promote the "effective realization of the basic cultural and commercial objectives of the Government's program of hemisphere solidarity" (Roosevelt, "Executive"). Concerned, as Roosevelt had suggested in the "Arsenal of Democracy," that Axis intervention anywhere in the American hemisphere would pose a significant threat to US security, the OIAA was to promote political stability, commercial cooperation, and democratic solidarity throughout the Americas. Through propaganda campaigns, "Coordination Committees" staffed by US citizens living abroad, and educational projects, the OIAA amplified Roosevelt's Good Neighbor message across the continent. After the war, responsibility for Inter-American Affairs was absorbed into the State Department, and the OIAA ceased to exist. In the intervening years, the OIAA was a small but far-reaching agent of hemispheric influence. It facilitated both "softer methods of persuasion and attraction and harder strategies of coercion to achieve given foreign policy goals" (Cramer and Prutsch 806).

While the activities that fell under the OIAA's responsibility shifted over time, the agency's most consistent role was rhetorical coordination. Throughout the war it maintained "a watchful eye on Axis nationals and sympathizers, particularly in the media and communication sector" (Cramer and Prutsch 791). While the agency had some covert responsibilities, "information and propaganda was
 ... one of its most important assignments throughout the war" (794). The OIAA "employed some two hundred journalists, editors, translators, visual artists, photographers, and clerks, and it turned out a large variety of publications, including posters, pamphlets, comics, journals, and magazines" (794). It also "employed some of [Communication Studies'] foremost researchers to gauge public opinion in Latin America and to devise propaganda strategies to achieve specific objectives" (802).

In 1942, Rockefeller extended the OIAA's responsibilities outward in a public call to educators for a "union of our intellectual forces" to produce "an American renaissance of unlimited possibilities" that would engulf the entire American hemisphere (Rockefeller 143). That project demanded a broad-based effort to educate people in the United States about their Southern neighbors. Rockefeller asserted, "We need the aid of parents ... the assistance of Boards of Education and of our schools and colleges" to increase the US public's awareness of Latin America (Rockefeller 143). Reaching audiences in the other American republics required an equally wide-ranging effort. So, the OIAA was given a mandate that included responsibility for facilitating activities among "such fields as the arts and sciences, education and travel, the radio, the press, and the cinema" in order to disseminate a [US] American message across the continents (Roosevelt, "Executive"). The collaboration with Disney at the heart of this essay was just one part of that dissemination, but it was a particularly natural partnership given the Walt Disney Company's own interest in education, its global reach, and its fascination with American values.

Walt Disney believed that film could provide social benefit and argued regularly that its capacity for entertainment was a natural aid to education. After the war, he reflected that "[t]he generation that used the motion picture to help train its fighters and its workers into the mightiest nation in history, is not apt to ignore the motion picture as an essential tool in the labor of enlightenment, civilization, and peace" (Disney 125). Though that "essential tool" could not operate on its own—"educational pictures merely offer a new tool for the educator's kit"—it was inextricably and evocatively tied to modernity (Disney 122). Because of the exigency of war, Disney asserted, "we have been compelled to reject any move that had no purpose, any method that was cumbersome or slow, any means that could not guarantee results. The watchword was to retain whatever was efficient and swift, and to cast off whatever was not effective" (Disney 119). The motion picture, under this rubric, was a model for modern education. It "took a leading part in all phases of wartime education—propaganda and information as well as training. It explained and supported ideas, it showed with impartial fidelity the course of events, it made hidden phenomena visible, and it demonstrated the way to control them" (Disney 119). For Disney, films' capacity for unveiling truths, circulating knowledge, and connecting people was unmatched and synecdochally connected to modern power. Added to the toolkit of the United States, films gave greater heft to the prowess of the emerging superpower.

The OIAA was not the first or the only US government agency to contract with the Walt Disney Company during the war years. Disney produced training films for the armed services, propaganda films for circulation within the United States and abroad, and edutainment shorts for the civilian population. By 1943, government and military contracts accounted for ninety-four percent of Disney's output (Roe 15). Walt Disney was a fierce advocate for [US] American values and a savvy businessman. His relationship with the US government served both purposes. Disney films projected "the unmixed blessings of technology, the exceptional status of the United States, the benevolence of authority figures and the virtues of submitting to them" (Van Riper 2). These ideas were "preached, openly and explicitly, in Disney edutainment films" (Van Riper 2). The films fit neatly into a worldview where US values and US good will were paramount.

American ideals of capitalist success and business efficiency also permeated Disney's relationship with the OIAA. In a prefatory interview appended to the 1942 documentary *South of the Border with Disney* that showcased that partnership, Disney notes that the films they produced needed no government subsidy: "that little thing went out and it did a heck of a business and the United States government didn't have to put up one nickel … it was actually a good will tour for the government" (*South of the Border*). Disney's claim to have needed no subsidy is questionable, given that the OIAA paid for Disney's expenses and equipment for the good-will tours. At the same time, OIAA officials recognized the larger benefits accruing from collaboration with the Walt Disney Company, thanks to the font of good feeling that Disney and his work could provide and that the United States desperately needed in Latin America. Both Disney's tour and the films he produced would tether "Disney's good will and prestige which are unique the world over" to the interests of the United States of America (*Project Authorization,* 4). That effort to provide a pleasing Disney facade to US government activities wasn't always successful, but it was a key strategy in disseminating [US] American visions and [US] American interests widely across the hemisphere.

"READING FOR THE AMERICAS"

Disney and the OIAA formalized their shared motion picture work starting in the summer of 1941. Their effort to combat illiteracy in the other American republics began somewhat later, on the suggestion of Dr. Enrique Sánchez de Lozada, a Latin American exile who had organized previous social campaigns in his native Bolivia and was hired by Rockefeller as a speechwriter and regional expert. Interested in promoting education and development in Latin America, de Lozada recommended in October 1942 that the OIAA embark on a literacy campaign in cooperation with the other American republics. De Lozada was specifically interested in film's ability to disseminate literacy more widely than traditional methods made possible, and the OIAA turned to Disney "in view of the high calibre of the training films and materials produced by the Walt Disney Studios for the Army and Navy" (de Lozada 1).

The next step in the process—a seminar on literacy education held in May and June 1943 with educators from both Latin America and the United States—examined an array of possible teaching methods, including the use of audio-visual material. De Lozada's original proposal had been to include "about ten Latin American illiteracy experts" and "an equal number of outstanding teachers and technicians in the United States" (de Lozada 1).[4] It is unclear from available records exactly who ultimately participated in the seminar, but it is possible they included some of the experts who later advised the project: Mexican teachers Eulalia Guzman (who directed a Mexican literacy campaign in 1923), Estele Soni(Directorofthe Escuela Cristobal Colon), Guadalupe Cejudo(Supervisorof Schools in Mexico City), and "Professor Piña" (an "adult education specialist ... of Indian extraction"); US educators Dr. Mildred Wiese, ("authority on the teaching of adult illiterates in the US"), Dr. George Sánchez ("professor of education, University of Texas"), Eleanor Clark ("representative of the Motion Picture Division"), Dr. Antonio Rebollado ("Professor of Education of Highlands University, New Mexico"); and Puerto Rican professor Dr. Ismael Rodríguez Bou (Superior Council of Education, University of Puerto Rico) (de Lozada 5; Cutting Personnel-9).[5]

Based on the outcomes of the Summer 1943 seminar, de Lozada urged a joint Latin American- US literacy project in which films were "the central device ... strengthened with related printed material, recordings and slides" ("Adult Literacy in the American Republics," qtd. in de Lozada 1) Even in that early articulation, the use of film was believed to promise greater efficiency (it would reduce the need for specially trained teachers) and access to modernity (in addition to teaching reading and writing, the films would "impart some practical simple improvement in the students' knowledge of living") (de Lozada 1-2).

Over the next year and a half, Disney and the OIAA put together a panel of advisors; produced a series of four films designed to teach reading, writing, and hygiene; and prepared a testing program intended to assess the effectiveness of the films. The six films to be shown as part of the testing program included two shorts drawn from the "Health for the Americas" series—"The Human Body" and "The Unseen Enemy"—and four made specifically for the "Reading for the Americas" project— "La Historia de José" and "La Historia de Ramón," each in two parts. In the reading films, new Disney characters José and Ramón taught reading and writing through their health and hygiene choices. José, a light-skinned, clean-shaven, well-muscled young man who OIAA employee Ryland Madison describes as "the strong, aggressive, alert type of person," "eats well" and so learns well. On the other hand, flabby, dark-skinned, mustachioed Ramón, as the title of his second film declares, "is sick." His "inferiority complex" and insipid personality combine with bad hygiene habits to leave him well behind the accomplishments of his adept, healthy, educated counterpart (Madison, "Can Films" 3). As the films introduced their main characters, descriptions of their actions "flashed on the screen a whole sentence at a time" and then were "repeated slowly by the sound device" while the audience joined in (Albornoz 28). The goal was for audience members to recognize the written words as they spoke them aloud and then associate those words with the Disney characters and their actions while also picking up basic health habits.

It is worth noting that this manner of teaching Spanish-language literacy was itself both a source of controversy and a point of pride for the Disney-OIAA organizers. Their commitment to film as a vehicle for technical modernity influenced their pedagogical choices, particularly the decision to teach reading using the "modernized global method," rather than the phonetic method used by Latin American educators.[6] In that method, Madison explains enthusiastically, "whole sentences are first learned, then broken down into individual words, rather than the phonetic system of teaching whole vowels and letters to develop word pictures" ("Can Films" 1). This emphasis on modern pedagogy— in both method and medium—did not go unquestioned, however. In a memo written after an April 1943 trip to Mexico, John

Cutting—who appears to have been an OIAA staff member—criticized the choice of the global method as blatantly disregarding Latin American expertise in the teaching of their own language. Cutting explained, acerbically, that "the Ministry of Education in Mexico is using the method they are ... not because they are living in the Dark Ages and are ill-informed about modern teaching methods; but because they have found that definite results are achieved by the work they are doing" (7). Despite such objections, however, the film program proceeded with the global method. As accounts of the program make clear, Disney and OIAA staff saw that pedagogical approach as part of a new and more efficient style that was linked inextricably to the equally modern efficiency of the motion picture.

To corroborate that belief in pedagogical and technological innovation, OIAA staff turned to a wide array of mostly US-based experts in education and literacy to evaluate the quality of the "Reading for the Americas" films. Those outside consultants—university professors, literacy educators with international experience, and executives from educational film programs—consistently supported OIAA claims that film was well-suited to literacy instruction and applauded the methods. In addition to providing the entertainment and motivation presumed to be necessary for the program's prospective students, they argued, film's sequential nature fit well with the requirements of reading pedagogy. Dr. William S. Gray, described in OIAA material as an "authority on the teaching of reading," for example, emphasized that each film should be devoted to "a specific step in the teaching of reading" (E. Clark, "Literacy Film Showings" 2). He offered to send a list of these steps and their proper order, presenting learning to read as a universal process that would proceed in an orderly and linear fashion. Film equally linear and orderly form provided an ideal medium through which to disseminate that step-by-step literacy.

Film also appealed to experts like Gray and Dr. Mildred Wiese because it allowed the teaching of reading to be systematized and standardized in classrooms across Latin America. While official, public-oriented documents produced by the OIAA emphasized the role of Latin American educators in developing and implementing literacy instruction, internal discussions among OIAA staff and the US-based consultants they engaged showed substantial skepticism about relying on instructor expertise. They tended to position the films themselves as the central vehicles for literacy learning, with instructors playing only a limited role, typically restricted to guiding discussion of material presented by film. Moreover, these US-based experts tended to have a dim view of the training and ability of Latin American teachers. They noted, for example, that one of the benefits of films in which the steps for learning reading were presented sequentially was that "the teacher learns the methodology as she teaches" (E. Clark, "Literacy Film Showings" 1). These pedagogical experts preferred, in other words, to trust the authority of US-made films rather than fallible teachers to correctly transfer literacy knowledge to students. Inherently modern and literate, film, it seems, could be relied on to carry accurate, systematic instruction throughout the Americas.[7]

Equipped with what they believed to be cutting edge technology and pedagogy, the staff of the Disney-OIAA literacy pilot project headed south in the summer of 1944. They showed the six pilot films to large audiences in Mexico, Honduras, and Ecuador. Eleanor Clark and Dr. Rodríguez Bou were the primary OIAA point people for the testing phase, traveling to Latin America in July 1944 to make preliminary arrangements. They were joined in Mexico later that year by Dr. Ryland Madison— representing the health and sanitation division of the OIAA—, Dr. Antonio Rebolledo—professor of education—, and Daniel MacManus—a Disney animator ("Regarding" 1). Over the course of a three week testing period in Mexico, the films were shown to "nearly 5,000 people," including army conscripts, school children, and adults and children in a manufacturing town and a rural area (Madison, "Results" 1). These communities were chosen because they made up "a representative cross-section of Mexico" (Madison, "Can Films" 3). Before the film screenings, audiences were tested on both general health knowledge and literacy skills, with the same tests repeated after the films were shown. For the group of conscripts, both sets of films were shown repeatedly, with the health films screened three times and the literacy films four times (2-3).

Subsequently, the testing program moved to Honduras and then to Ecuador. There is little information available about the Honduras pilot, but the tests in Ecuador were well documented by the OIAA, largely thanks to their positive reception in the Ecuadorian press. There, the Disney-OIAA group collaborated with a literacy-training program operated by the Ecuadorian Journalists Union (UNP, Unión Nacional de Periodistas). That partnership aligned the developmentalist interests of the United States with those of Ecuador's elites, and may be responsible for the glowing terms in which Ecuadorian journalists portrayed the pilot's success. In Ecuador, the films were shown to some 6,500 people in fifteen provinces ("6.500"). For showings in Quito, the audience included military conscripts, indigenous laborers, and convicts—not a representative sample of the population, but certainly indicative of how the OIAA and their Ecuadorian partners pictured the population of illiterate American others ("New Method").

Early reports on the success of the pilot project were overwhelmingly positive. The Mexican portion of the testing concluded on September 15, 1944, and a memo from Madison dated September 16 eagerly asserts that "both the Health films and the Literacy films have been successful far beyond our expectations" ("Results" 1). Madison describes the audiences as "tremendously enthusiastic" and goes on to explain that Mexican government officials present at the screenings were similarly impressed ("Results" 1,3). A month later, a newspaper article published in Ecuador touted the efficient pedagogy that film provided, noting "This new method makes the teaching of reading easy because it does not require the illiterate person to submit to the slow process of learning to read letter by letter." The article praised the project as, "one more method available to incorporate large groups of literates into the great group of civilized people in the world, thus fulfilling a dictate of humanity and social service" ("Important Motion Pictures"; "Demonstration"). After the testing finished in Ecuador, an article that circulated first to US diplomats and then to potential English- speaking tourists described the success of even just one film session as a "personal miracle" for the attendees (Albornoz 28). Those enthusiastic celebrations of the literacy project spoke readily to the existing assumptions of US audiences. They relied on a synecdochic movement in which acquisition of literacy and hygiene stood in for a larger encounter with the progressive energy of [US] American life. That such skills were attained through the bright light of film only amplified the power of that synecdochic modernity.

MOVING LITERACY, IMMOBILIZING LATIN AMERICA

Perhaps not surprisingly, the "Reading for the Americas" project inspired copious amounts of writing in its short life. OIAA and Disney staff, US and Latin American educators, and Latin American journalists and diplomats all helped the Disney-OIAA films move across the hemisphere through the words they composed about it. These interlocutors, though speaking to varied goals and audiences, consistently imagined the literacy project in service to modern development, national pride, and hemispheric union. Because the film-literacy project provided an opportunity to spread US American assumptions about hemispheric unity and democratic progress across the hemisphere, it also did important work in furthering the larger aims of the OIAA. In internal reports, public presentations, and local responses literacy education was imagined as a means of performing American unity. It tied governments together and fostered human development. It gave elites across the continents a common role and a common challenge framed in terms amenable to the interests of the United States. Access to literacy and the panoply of opportunities that literacy supposedly opened became synonymous with access to American promise and American progress.

This celebration of filmic literacy followed a consistent pattern, often recycling language across formats and purposes. Three elements of that pattern are particularly evocative for our purposes and will be easily recognized as familiar tropes by literacy scholars: 1) Discussions of the literacy project repeatedly presented illiterate adults as permanently childlike yet lacking the vigor of childhood, tapping into available assumptions about literacy and development. 2) The project made an essential link between matters of hygiene and the acquisition of literacy, binding them together as concomitant matters of modernity and American-ness. 3) Assessments of the program attributed near-miraculous effects to its use of motion pictures, imagining them as not only effective but life- changing—mimicking in a safer, more democratic and capitalistic way the effects of revolutionary fervor. Taken together, those three elements tightly linked acquisition of literacy to capacity for movement—in both a rhetorical and a circulatory sense. Through them, illiteracy stood stagnant and immobile, and the benefits of literacy accrued inevitably to those already understood as mobile. Whether withheld or extended, literacy served notions of economic development, consumption, and docility that privileged the interests of the US government, US companies (like Disney), and Latin American elites eager to align with them.

Childlike Learners

In texts outlining the film program, adult Latin American literacy learners are frequently imagined as childlike, and film as uniquely capable of grasping and maintaining their attention. As one memo explained: "Adult illiterates, after a hard day's work, cannot be attracted, and their interest cannot be sustained, unless we offer entertainment as an inducement. This is proven beyond any doubt ... by the numerous attempts made in different countries to carry on literacy campaigns, which campaigns have failed invariably, because the ways and means through which they were carried on were tiresome and uninteresting to the adult illiterate" (Clark and de Lozada 2). Latin American literacy learners would not, in other words, pursue education for its own sake. Rather, they must be enticed and rewarded with pleasure, receiving literacy with sugar coating.

While that same memo's authors emphasize that their students will be adults, and so explicitly object to the use of teaching methods designed for children, the "Reading for the Americas" films were not precisely "adult" in style. Disney's animation gave even adult characters a childlike look, and the films' sing-song narration assumed an audience of ingénues. Even more tellingly, OIAA memos and public relations materials repeatedly depict adult literacy learners as lacking maturity: unable to help themselves, awed by the light and sound of film, easily swayed for good or ill, and limited to a basic level of learning. Following a pattern well established for treatment of Latin America's racial others, the Disney-OIAA literacy films approached their audience as adult children or, at least, as childlike adults (O'Connor). Acquisition of literacy wouldn't change that status.

The panel of literacy experts attending the May 1945 screening of the health and literacy films at the University of Chicago, for example, imagined literacy learners as recalcitrant children whose attention must be carefully attracted and monitored. These experts—education professors, a professor of Spanish, and a member of the board of directors for an educational film company—were enthusiastic about film as a vital tool for motivating adult illiterates. A memo from Eleanor Clark summarizing the discussion lists the use of music and color to "increase the student's enjoyment'" as a particularly salient point of agreement among the experts. Remarking on the special problem of motivating Latin American literacy learners, Dr. Paul Witty, Professor of Education at Northwestern University and former director of the US Army Literacy Program, noted that "he was not faced with the same incentive problem with students in the Army as we are with our prospective students." Military discipline, a classic marker of manhood, distinguished his students from the resistant, petulant Latin American. Film, however, would bring those childish students to attention, the Chicago experts agreed (E. Clark, "Literacy Film Showings" 3).

Latin American newspaper accounts of the pilot project likewise emphasized this image of the childlike illiterate entranced by the modern technology of film. Referring to the "pedagogical problem of holding the student's interest," one Ecuadorian newspaper article reported that "the attention of the adult student is completely monopolized by the pictures" while others used the language of hypnosis to describe how susceptible adult literacy learners were to the power of film (G. Vacas 3; "Important Motion Pictures").

Beyond problems of motivation, discussions among OIAA staff and their US-based consultants also consistently highlighted the childlike limitations of their chosen students. The health films, for example, were designed "to arouse interest and awareness rather than teach detailed facts" on the assumption that their audience had neither the patience nor the intellectual capacity to retain complex or abstract information. Clem Thompson, an authority on adult illiterate education who attended the Chicago showing, emphasized the need to provide students with a limited kind of material. He recommended that motivation for learning be "very concrete and immediate to the life and livelihood of the student" (E. Clark, "Literacy Film Showings" 3). Thompson was not alone in that emphasis on the thoroughly concrete orientation of literacy learners. Other respondents similarly characterized illiterates as lacking the ability to think in abstractions. They recommended that "the vocabulary presented in the first films should consist principally of nouns, as they are easily picturable" (E. Clark, "Literacy Film Showings" 1). Two Chicago participants commented on the difficulty that abstract topics, such as "health," would pose for adult literacy learners, recommending instead that films approach more practical topics, such as the cure of a specific disease (E. Clark, "Literacy Film Showings" 1, 3). Making a parallel assumption, articles describing the pilot project illustrate the response of literacy learners using examples that are striking in their childish simplicity—from an actual child who announces that spitting on the ground spreads tuberculosis to grown men who laugh with delight at recognizing a word or suddenly know to wash their hands (Madison, "Can Films" 4; Albornoz 28, 27).

Though the pedagogical point of these admonitions was to eschew the abstract in favor of the applicable, the frequency with which such commentary circulated makes clear that focus on the simplistic was not simply a matter of educational best practices. It also indexed the enclosed and stagnant world in which literate Americans believed their illiterate compatriots lived. Comments from one participant in an internal OIAA viewing of the films are indicative of a general presumption of Latin American limitation in comparison with US development. He noted that the one commonality among their prospective students was the fact that they had "no foundation of scientific facts on which our modern medicine is based" and so could not progress far in their learning (Harrison 2).

Even when the illiterate subjects of the literacy pilot tests developed new skills through the program, their learning was still presented by experts and journalists in terms that reinforced a sense of dependence and limitation. The causes of such progress were rarely located in learner's own intellectual movement. An article published in *El Comercio*, one of Quito's leading newspapers, portrayed health and literacy instruction delivered through film as having a transformative effect because it essentially took over its subjects. The unhygienic bodies of illiterate Quiteños filling the room for the showings "emitt[ed] an acrid odor" that reeked of stagnation and lack of modern understanding. As those bodies were inhabited by the modern technology of film and the power of literacy, however, they were transformed: "they spoke the words in a firm and cheerful voice as if the first gleam of intelligent comprehension was shining from their dull eyes" (G. Vacas). It is hard to escape the impression that the light coming from the eyes of those odiferous literacy learners was emitted not by their own minds but by the film projector located in the back of the room.

And yet, in hortatory celebrations of the value of literacy, its *imagined* impact on students remained powerful. Madison, in his September 1944 report, claimed that "the audiences have not only thoroughly understood the material presented" but have also "been quick to adopt the new thoughts presented to them" ("Results" 1). Literacy, represented in the familiar terms of the literacy-orality divide, might just eventually move those childlike audiences from concrete to abstract thinking. That movement, in turn, offered the possibility of moving adult illiterates from childish dependency to adult citizenship. Another article in *El Comercio*, for example, explained that the Ministry of Education supported the program so that "it may continue to make progress in its work of teaching those Ecuadoreans who have not yet been able to take their places as well-prepared citizens" ("New Method"). Similarly, a letter celebrating the program that was sent to Nelson Rockefeller in 1944, describes the films as "a valuable addition to the protection of the health of the people who live in a primitive state as far as hygiene is concerned, in these countries of South America" (Vallejo Larrea and Arellano Montalvo).

Such dramatic movement was always placed just beyond the grasp of the actual students profiled in these reports, a common move in developmentalist literature of the time (A. Kim Clark, "Racial Ideologies"; Prieto). That did not deter the effusive celebration of literacy's potential within the Disney-OIAA project, however. Its task, after all, was less tied up in the specifics of reading and writing and far more concerned with the unification of a modern hemisphere. The shape of that larger orientation is particularly visible in the next element persistently present in discussions of the literacy project: the intimate connection between literacy and hygiene as synecdoches for modernity.

Hygiene & literacy

OIAA materials initiating the literacy project do not to offer an explicit justification for linking health and literacy. Instead, from the beginning of the project the two were assumed to be naturally intertwined. In fact, though disseminating literacy across the hemisphere was ostensibly the central objective of the project, OIAA officials imagined the health material as more essential than the films explicitly teaching reading and writing. A letter sent to Dr. Rodriguez Bou in 1945, for example, reminds him that "the health films can be shown without the literacy films, but not the literacy films without the health films" (Black).

This emphasis on health information as a necessary vehicle for transmitting literacy education invokes, of course, the well-worn notion that reading and writing are not themselves content areas. It also, however, reveals the underlying assumptions about civilization and development that drove the OIAA's efforts in Latin America: both literacy and health serve primarily as indexes for modernity. "This modern means of teaching by movies" would directly transmit both health and literacy knowledge to illiterates, shaping them into modern subjects (Madison, "Can Films"). Lacking that, the a-modernity that suffused the illiterate, unhygenic majority of Latin Americans separated them from the assumed spheres of American-ness—democracy, consumption, and modern life itself— and made them a troublingly internal American other.[8]

From official reports to newspaper accounts of the Disney-OIAA project, the belief that literacy and hygiene were deeply imbricated in the broader experience of modernity was inescapable. Indeed a drive toward American advancement consistently took precedence over the specifics of literacy learning itself. A July 1945 report to the OIAA and the Inter-American Educational Foundation (IAEE) by the Conference on Community Education in Latin America with Special Reference to Literacy, for example, framed its work in terms of three overall objectives. The first two placed literacy within a frame unapologetically focused on American progress, as literacy training aimed "to raise the standard of living and to promote enlightened public opinion" and "to develop inter- American understanding" ("Report of the Committee").[9] Similarly, an article published in Guayaquil, Ecuador asserted that access to literacy would "kindle a light" in the mind of the illiterate person and so "[open] up a new horizon in his life, and as a final result, [add] a really useful member to the community as a whole" ("Campaign"). Individual literacy mattered, in this sense, to the extent that it moved a larger public body toward active citizenship and consumption.

A memo from OIAA staff coordinating the pilot project explains, for example, that the project they propose "is not to be a literacy program in a narrow sense, but in a broad sense. Learning to read and to write will be the basis of instruction, but the subject matter ... will enrich the adults' lives." "Literacy in a broad sense" was, in other words, an ideological project. And so, literacy expanded to contain "instruction on health habits, agricultural techniques, crafts, and other subjects relating to the world in general, and the students' environments in particular" (Clark and de Lozada 1). Accessing literacy opened learners to an enriched life and incorporated them into a larger public body.

Ultimately, efforts to increase access to health and hygiene were not simply humanitarian activities. Rather, improved health and hygiene were fundamentally linked to democracy and prosperity. As one

OIAA staff member explained in a memo about a parallel hygiene campaign in Ecuador: "A nation sick physically is sick economically, politically and socially" and so "is neither a good source of materials efficiently produced nor a good market for goods from other countries" and furthermore, "cannot be a democratic nation cannot hope for the political stability [sic] needed for optimum international relations" (F. Adams 1). In a similar, though more progressive tone, Dr. Rodriguez Bou suggested to the UNP in Ecuador that while "all can learn," "we cannot expect all to learn with equal quickness and speed. People who are sick, ill-nourished individuals, alcoholics, those accustomed to receiving orders and to having others think for them, cannot react as promptly as those who eat properly, live well, and fully enjoy what the undernourished produce" ("Excerpts"). Illiteracy was an infection that putrefied modern life, a contagious form of public ill health. It infested the public body and prevented it from accessing social, political, and economic benefits. Persistent illiteracy and lack of hygiene enervated key American values such as democratic participation and capitalist consumption.

Latin American elites, aligning themselves with American modernity and education if not with the United States, used similar language to discuss the value of literacy and hygiene instruction. A letter to the OIAA from Ecuador's UNP asserted the efficacy of the Disney films for changing audience members' behavior, noting that "the day following the showing the students arrived clean and with quite a different appearance from that of the previous day" (Vallejo Larrea and Arellano Montalvo). Likewise, an article about the project by Miguel Albornoz, an Ecuadorian diplomat, suggested that literacy changed a smelly, dirty man into a model subject: "he very obviously had a bath. Moreover, his fingernails and hair had been trimed [sic]. Rafael also wrote to the local paper, saying that at last he felt like a man, and he would urge all his friends to become literate" (27). These students, becoming clean and learning to read, remained subject to surveillance by outside elites who placed their own literacy and modernity always one step ahead of that attained by literacy learners. Illiterate Latin Americans were, in other words, caught in the same double bind that A. Kim Clark identifies trapping indigenous Ecuadorians in their political organizing and Catherine Prendergast illustrates with regard to African Americans and education in the United States: already identified with a category presumed deficient, they are unable to escape the mark of deficiency. The status travels with them no matter how much literacy they acquire (A. Kim Clark, "Race" 201; Prendergast 33).

Across internal memos and published reports, literacy and hygiene were fundamentally connected to modern life for the OIAA. And yet, literacy learning and hygiene education simultaneously calcified a category of Latin American others fundamentally separated from modernity. Always positioned as literacy learners, the majority of Latin Americans remained just outside the realm of equal participation. Institutional factors, political investments, and racist structures that blocked access to effective education and undermined anti-poverty efforts ensured that those other Americans stayed profoundly other. Their lack of movement toward healthful literacy reinvigorated US American and elite Latin American assumptions of distinction and reinforced the sense that those always literate elites held a higher claim to modernity, progress, national responsibility, and— in a word—Americanness.

The Miraculous Effects of Film (and Literacy)

While depictions of adult literacy learners emphasized their permanent childishness, their persistent failures of hygiene, and their inevitable lack of modernity, discussions of the Disney-OIAA literacy program celebrated its scientific maturity, its technological brightness, and its powerful ability to transform its subjects. Literacy learners presented in reports and news articles were passive, immobile subjects energized by the activating force of motion picture literacy. If they were moved by their encounter with the films, it was motion picture technology that inspired them, not their own learning. The effects of motion picture literacy were sure, grounded in modern teaching methods and crafted by the leading experts in educational film. That scientific confidence that pervades accounts of the program was based, however, on an untested faith in the miracle of film and of American ingenuity. One Ecuadorian author, in his laudatory account of the pilot program, recognized as much, not only describing the literacy project as "a profoundly revolutionary experiment in pedagogical technique" but also emphasizing its use of "that magic realistic art ... that is, motion pictures" (G. Vacas).

OIAA records for the literacy program exude confidence about the ability of film to convey literacy and health information, but they are generally vague on specifics. Vacas may have been the only one to literally invoke the "magic" of film, but other accounts share his sense that there was something special but unknowable about the power of motion pictures. Anecdotal accounts of similar projects and their success sit alongside supportive commentary from US based experts in literacy, education, and film. The scholars and business consultants participating in the University of Chicago screening, for example, were in unanimous agreement about the films' capacity to "play a valuable part in the stimulation of literacy among adults" (E. Clark, "Literacy Film Showings" 1). Likewise, the OIAA official who introduced the "Reading for the Americas" films at a screening for OIAA department and division heads expressed a vague hope for the potential of film to directly transmit literacy and health knowledge, noting that "direct learning through pictures might be possible" because "extensive tests in South America have shown that this is possible" (Harrison 2).

Accounts of the testing program emphasized two aspects of films' power. First, and most consistently, they noted the motivational effects of motion pictures. Moving pictures moved illiterate adults to interest in learning and thus in modernity. As a report from the Conference on Community Education in Latin America with Special Reference to Literacy put it in July 1945, "the Literacy Program ought to seek to bring to bear upon the available resources of the community the content of modern science with a view towards integrating the rural folk of Latin America with the larger world" ("Report of the Committee" 2). Film, like literacy, motivated development.

Early discussions of motion picture literacy also, however, celebrated the potential for film to directly transmit literacy and health knowledge, suggesting that the films would have an almost instantaneous impact on the lives of their audiences. As an article published in Guayaquil, Ecuador explained it, teaching by film "instills the knowledge not only into the mind of the learner but into his consciousness as well" ("Important Motion Pictures"). The immediate efficacy of the films was similarly described in a report by Gustavo Vallejo Larrea, President of the UNP, who noted that "we can vouch for the results obtained with the teaching of hygiene," because of the participants changed appearance the following day (Vallejo Larrea and Arellano Montalvo).

Perhaps because of that pervasive, near-magical faith in film, early reports from the pilot program emphasize affective response and anecdotal evidence. Although the project authorization characterized the testing program as "an opportunity to measure scientifically the teaching effectiveness ... of the Disney health films," initial reports sent back to the OIAA emphasized audience reaction as a telling measure of efficacy. Madison reported that "everywhere they were shown, the films elicited the greatest interest and enthusiasms" ("Can Films" 3). Recounting the screening for Mexican army conscripts, Madison claimed that they were "elated over the showings" ("Can Films" 2). Clark, similarly, describes a Puerto Rican woman in New York who "chuckl[ed] with pleasure at her success" in reading aloud with the films (E. Clark, "Summary" 4). Madison presents as typical the example of an old man in El Salto, who requested the films be shown again because they have "shown me how easy it is to read" ("Can Films" 3). Albornoz similarly reports the gratitude of "one old peon" who "said sturdily that his employers could not fool him on the payroll any more" after he had seen the films a few times (28). Such reports assume that film and literacy, offered together, could effect change so wide-reaching that it needed no proof other than audience reaction. In fact, there were no plans to formally assess literacy learning for the proposed Brazilian portion of the testing program, as the experts asserted that "it will be possible to observe the reaction of illiterates to those teaching films on a purely subjective basis" ("Regarding" 1).

These overwhelmingly positive early reports reflect great confidence in the power of film and US ingenuity to fluidly and efficiently move Latin American audiences toward literacy, cleanliness, and modernity. They authorize and evince the pervading OIAA assumption that the United States was essential to the forward progress of Latin America. In this view, the United States alone had the technological capacities and economic wherewithal to project literacy into the lives of its southern neighbors. This inevitable success would come relatively easily, spurred forward by whole sentences, efficient methods, and the transformative light of the motion picture.

ENDINGS AND CONTINUITIES

Those visions of motion picture miracles came to a rather abrupt end. When the results of the test project were finally calculated several months after Madison's confident reports, they were not encouraging. Although scores in both test groups increased "significantly" on health and reading, direct instruction by teachers was markedly more effective than the films were. Students taught by a teacher scored higher in all areas, and the testers concluded that "a teacher is probably better than films alone" (Holland 1). However, despite these rather discouraging results, and against all evidence to the contrary, the report insisted that "we are very sure that films are a useful teaching instrument" (Holland 1). Faith in the power of film was resilient.

Still, a December 19, 1945 meeting of the Board of Directors for the OIAA-affiliated Inter- American Educational Foundation (IAEF) effectively spelled the end of the film program. The Board expressed concerns about the expense of the project and concluded that "there are not, therefore, sufficient funds available to carry out the project, even had the results of the testing been favorable to film" (Holland 1). The revised approach to literacy they advocated emphasized cooperation with the successful literacy campaigns already underway in Latin America. Although these new efforts would be made in cooperation with local authorities, the United States would retain a central role in creating and distributing instructional materials, including printed materials, film strips, and (once again) motion pictures, reinforcing its identity as the central location from which literacy should be disseminated.

Even in light of the disappointing test results, IAEF discussions still characterized film instruction as valuable for its ability to engage students, and the December 19 report described the motion picture as "a useful and attractive medium for creating popular interest in, and information about, an educational problem like that of literacy" (Holland 4). What persisted beyond the film literacy program, in other words, was a vision of American elites—US experts and Latin American program coordinators—united by their informed action against the pervasive stagnation of illiteracy and poor hygiene. Film, it seemed, just ought to be powerful enough to move those stubbornly un-modern masses forward.

Latin American coverage of the Disney-OIAA program likewise emphasized inter-hemispheric cooperation for progress as the ultimate effect of literacy training. One article remarks on Dr. Rodriguez Bou's ambition to "see a united America in which democracy will no longer be the privilege of only a few individuals." It notes as well Rodríguez Bou's desire "to leave bonds of real solidarity among our educated classes who likewise think and dream as he does of a better, more united and prosperous America" ("Effective"). Similarly, a report from

Honduras specifically invokes American foreign policy to characterize the benefits of the film literacy program, noting that "we have been receiving in full measure benefits of the Good Neighbor Policy, translated into important material and cultural accomplishments." These articles, alongside letters written by government officials and Army leadership, were collected and archived at the OIAA. As Latin American elites allied themselves with the rhetorical aims of the program, their voices became part of the official record celebrating the modern impulse of motion pictures.

However, this cooperation came at a cost. The conversations generated by the Disney-OIAA literacy program reinscribed the otherness of those Latin Americans not already possessing literacy. Without literacy, they lacked access to literate movement and literate affiliation; the hemisphere connected by filmic literacy simultaneously wrote literacy learners out. As one newspaper article from Ecuador tellingly suggested, those without literacy lived within America yet separate from it: literacy training "[helped] the people of Ecuador escape from the disgrace ... of having two million illiterate inhabitants" ("New Method"). The language of the article begs two questions: who are those two million inhabitants if not Ecuadorian people? and What does it mean for a people to be inhabited by illiterates? Seemingly, the more attention paid to illiteracy, the more experts who circulated intent on studying it, the more technology developed for eradicating it, the more fully were Latin American "adult illiterates" separated from the image of America. While the literate, modern hemisphere moved forward, those without literacy remained stuck behind. Like the audience in rural Ecuador described by Albornoz, they were transfixed by moving pictures, tantalizingly close to the health and modernity promised to those who gained "the advantages of knowing how to read and write," but never quite able to claim those advantages for their own.

NOTES

1. The feature films Disney produced in its collaboration with the OIAA—most notably *Saludos Amigos* and *The Three Cabelleros*—highlight easy movement from the United States to Latin America and celebrate warm American connections. See, for example, the hop-skip-jump depictions of plane travel from the United States to Brazil and the immediate connection between José Carioca and Donald Duck in *Saludos Amigos*. It's worth

noting as well that travel among the other American republics is shown as more risky— the sketch about Pedro the airplane's trip across the Andes in *Saludos Amigos* is laden with myth (the personified threat of the mountain Aconcagua) and difficulty (the height and frigidity of the Andes). See Dale Adams, "*Saludos Amigos*," for more on Hollywood and FDR's Good Neighbor policy.

2. The Office of the Coordinator of Inter-American Affairs took over the work of its predecessor agency, the Office for Coordination of Commercial and Cultural Relations Between the American Republics, which was established in August 1940 by the Council of National Defense. In 1945, the agency's name was changed once more, to the Office of Inter-American Affairs. The records of the agency held at the National Archives are under that final title, and for consistency's sake, we also use that acronym to refer to the agency throughout its existence.

3. The Coordinator position was almost certainly designed for Rockefeller. The name of the agency was changed to omit the "Coordinator" just before Rockefeller left the office, and the executive order creating the OIAA specifically states that "[t]he Coordinator shall serve as such without compensation but shall be entitled to ... expenses incidental to the performance of his duties" (Roosevelt "Executive"). Surely only someone with the independent wealth of a Rockefeller could have undertaken such arduous public service without remuneration.

4. From the perspective of our interest in assumptions of US modernity, there is something telling about de Lozada's choice to describe Latin Americans as "illiteracy experts" and US Americans as "outstanding teachers and technicians."

5. Cutting's memo to Walt Disney, though stapled into a single document, contains three separately paginated sections—an overview of concerns related to the literacy program, a "Memo on Personnel," and a "Diary." When referring to the document, we will give pages as "Memo-#," "Personnel-#," or "Diary-#" for maximum clarity.

6. At least one Latin American educator left the project in light of this choice, feeling that her expertise had been ignored. She later publicly criticized the pilot project during its time in Mexico (de Lozada).

7. As forthcoming work by Kelly Ritter suggests, this sense of film's ability to control the spaceof the classroom and promote not only literacy but also uniform American values was not limited to films with an international mission. Educational films made for US classrooms evince similar assumptions and serve similar ends (Ritter).

8. For more on this question of the nation and its internal others, see chapter four in C. Olson, *Constitutive Visions*.

9 The Inter-American Educational Foundation was one of five subsidiary corporations spun off from the OIAA to [facilitate] the undertaking

of larger-scale operations that required close cooperation with Latin American authorities and were financed through bilateral funds or dependent on longer-term budgetary commitments" (Cramer and Prutsch 788).

WORKS CITED

"6500 Illiterate Adults in the Republic of Ecuador Learn to Read and Write." OIAA Translation of "6.500 Analfabetos Adultos en Toda la República Aprenden a Leer y Escribir." *El Comercio* [Quito] 9 Aug. 1944. Record Group 229, Entry 77, Box 959, Folder "Literacy Program * Miscellaneous OEMcr-107-305." Washington, DC, 4 June 1945. US National Archives, College Park.

Adams, Dale. "Saludos Amigos: Hollywood and FDR's Good Neighbor Policy." *Quarterly Review of Film & Video* 243 (2007): 289-95. Print.

Adams, Frances McStay. "Campaña para la Salud del Ecuador." Report Prepared for Wyman R. Stone. June 1944. Record Group 229, Entry 111, Box 1388. US National Archives, College Park.

Albornoz, Miguel. "Alphabet in the Andes." *Ecuador* Sept-Oct 1949: 27-28. Print.

Alfaro Arriaga, Alejandro. "Excerpts of Letters Received by Miss Clark from Individuals Who Had Been Connected with the Testing of the Health and Literacy Films." In Clark and Ryland.

Alstock, Francis. Letter to Roy Disney. Record Group 229, Entry 77, Box 958, Folder "Disney Trip to Mexico." Washington, DC, 7 Dec. 1942. US National Archives, College Park.

Black, Ruby. Letter to Ismael Rodríguez Bou. Record Group 229, Entry 77, Box 959, Folder "Literacy Program * Miscellaneous OEMcr-107-305." Washington, DC, 4 June 1945. US National Archives, College Park.

Brandt, Deborah. "Literacy Learning and Economic Change." *Harvard Educational Review* 69.4 (1999): 373-94. PDF.

Brandt, Deborah, and Katie Clinton. "Limits of the Local: Expanding Perspectives on Literacy as a Social Practice." *Journal of Literacy Research* 34.3 (2002): 337-56. Print.

Bromage, Arthur W. "Literacy and the Electorate." *The American Political Science Review* 24.4 (1930): 946-62. Print.

"Campaign Against Illiteracy." OIAA Translation Number 34729, originally published in *El Telegrafo* [Guayaquil] 20 Aug. 1944. In Clark and Ryland.

Carias G., Filomena. "Excerpts of Letters Received by Miss Clark from Individuals Who Had Been Connected with the Testing of the Health and Literacy Films" in Clark and Ryland.

Clark, A. Kim. "Race, 'Culture,' and Mestizaje: The Statistical Construction of the Ecuadorian Nation, 1930-1950." *Journal of Historical Sociology* 11.2 (1998): 185-211. Print.

---. "Racial Ideologies and the Quest for National Development: Debating the Agrarian Problem in Ecuador (1930-1950)." *Journal of Latin American Studies* 30.2 (1998): 373-93. Print.

Clark, Eleanor. "Literacy Film Showings, University of Chicago, May 17, 1945." Letter to Wallace K. Harrison, 30 May 1945. Record Group 229, Entry 77, Box 959, Folder "Literacy Program * Miscellaneous OEMcr-107-305." US National Archives, College Park.

---. "Summary of my Activities Relating to the Literacy Program During your Absence." Letter to Kenneth Holland, 19 Apr. 1945. Record Group 229, Entry 77, Box 959, Folder "Literacy Program * Miscellaneous OEMcr-107-305." US National Archives, College Park.

Clark, Eleanor, and Enrique de Lozada. "Adult Literacy Program (Basic Adult Education)." Memo to Wallace K. Harrison, 12 Mar. 1945. Record Group 229, Entry 77, Box 960, Folder "Health and Literacy Program." US National Archives, College Park.

Clark, Eleanor F., and Ryland R. Madison. "Addition to Appendix of Subjective Report on Health and Literacy Film Testing Trip." Tegucigalpa, Honduras, 19 Dec. 1945. Record Group 229, Entry 77, Box 959, Folder "Literacy Program * Miscellaneous OEMcr-107-305." US National Archives, College Park.

Cramer, Gisela, and Ursula Prutsch. "Nelson A. Rockefeller's Office of Inter-American Affairs (1940- 1946) and Record Group 229." *Hispanic American Historical Review* 86.4 (2006): 785-806. Print.

Cutting, John. Memo to Walt Disney. Record Group 229, Entry 77, Box 959, Folder "Literacy Program * Miscellaneous OEMcr-107-305." c.1943. US National Archives, College Park.

de Lozada, Enrique. "Adult Literacy Program." Memo to Harold B. Gotaas, et al. 2 Jan. 1946. Record Group 229, Entry 77, Box 959, Folder "Literacy Program * Miscellaneous OEMcr-107-305." US National Archives, College Park.

"Demonstration of a New Method for Teaching Reading Which Will Be Begun Next Monday under the Auspices of the U.N.P. with the Help of Delegates from the United States." OIAA Translation Number 34740, originally published in El *Comercio* [Quito] 21 Oct. 1944. In Clark and Ryland.

Dingo, Rebecca. "Linking Transnational Logics: A Feminist Rhetorical Analysis of Public Policy Networks." *College English* 70.5 (2008): 490-505. Print.

---. *Networking Arguments: Rhetoric, Transnational Feminism, and Public Policy Writing*. Pittsburgh: U of Pittsburgh P, 2012. Print.

Disney, Walt. "Mickey as Professor." *The Public Opinion Quarterly* 9.2 (1945): 119-25. Print. "Effective Missionaries of Pan-Americanism."

OIAA Translation Number 34735, originally published in *El Comercio* [Quito] 9 Nov. 1944. In Clark and Ryland.

"Excerpts from the Address Delivered Yesterday by Dr. Rodríguez Bou to the Newspapermen of Quito. 'Everyone in America Can Learn,' Said the Head of the Coordinator's Mission Against Illiteracy." OIAA Translation Number 34736, originally published in *El Comercio* [Quito] 9 Nov. 1944. In Clark and Ryland.

Graff, Harvey J. *The Literacy Myth: Cultural Integration and Social Structure in the Nineteenth Century.* New Brunswick: Transaction, 1991. Print.

Gross, John O. "Adult Education in Democracy." *Peabody Journal of Education* 20.6 (1943): 351-58. Print.

Harrison, Wallace K. Memorandum to All Department and Division Heads, Office of Inter- American Affairs. 20 June 1945. Record Group 229, Entry 77, Box 959, Folder "Literacy Program * Miscellaneous OEMcr-107-305." US National Archives, College Park.

Hesford, Wendy S., and Eileen E. Schell. "Introduction: Configurations of Transnationality: Locating Feminist Rhetorics." *College English* 70.5 (2008): 461-70. Print.

Holland, Kenneth. "Motion Picture and Visual Education Materials, B-EF-62 Change Order No. 2." Memo to the Board of Directors, Inter-American Educational Foundation, 18 Dec. 1945. Record Group 229, Entry 77, Box 959, Folder "Literacy Program * Miscellaneous OEMcr-107-305." US National Archives, College Park.

"Important Motion Pictures Illustrating Modern Teaching Methods Were Shown Yesterday in the Assembly Hall of the Office of the Coordination Committee." OIAA Translation Number 34732, originally published in *El Telegrafo* [Guayaquil] 17 Oct. 1944. In Clark and Ryland.

Lorimer Leonard, Rebecca. "Multilingual Writing as Rhetorical Attunement." *College English* 76.3 (2014): 227-47. Print.

Lynde, Samuel Adams. "Light for Men in Darkness." *Phylon* 6.2 (1945): 129-35. Print. Madison, Ryland. "Can Films Conquer Illiteracy? Here's how Jose and Ramon Tackled the Problem in Mexico." 16 Jan 1945. Record Group 229, Entry 77, Box 959, Folder "Literacy Program * Miscellaneous OEMcr-107-305." US National Archives, College Park.

---. "Results of the Health-Literacy Testing Program in Mexico." Memo to George C. Dunham,16 Sept. 1944. Record Group 229, Entry 77, Box 960, Folder "Health and Literacy Program." US National Archives, College Park.

"Memorandum of Agreement," Contract No. NDCar-110. 5 Aug. 1941. Record Group 229, Entry 77, Box 959, Folder "Gracias Amigos 4041 OEMcr218." US National Archives, College Park.

Mortensen, Peter. "Figuring Illiteracy: Rustic Bodies and Unlettered Minds in Rural America." *Rhetorical Bodies*. Eds. Jack Selzer and Sharon Crowley. Madison: U of Wisconsin P, 1999. 143-70. Print.

---. "Reading Material." *Written Communication* 18.4 (2001): 395-439. Print.

"The New Method of Teaching Illiterates Will Be Begun on Friday." OIAA Translation Number 34731, originally published in *El Comercio* [Quito] 19 Oct. 1944. In Clark and Ryland.

O'Connor, Erin. "Helpless Children or Undeserving Patriarchs? Gender Ideologies, the State, and

Indian Men in Late Nineteenth-Century Ecuador." *Highland Indians and the State in Modern Ecuador*. Eds. A. Kim Clark and Marc Becker. Pittsburgh: U of Pittsburgh P, 2007. 56-71. Print.

Olson, Christa J. *Constitutive Visions: Indigeneity and Commonplaces of National Identity in Republican Ecuador*. University Park: Pennsylvania State UP, 2014. Print.

---. "Contradictions of Progress: Visions of Modernity, Infrastructure, and Labor in Late Nineteenth- Century Ecuador." *JAC: A Journal of Rhetoric, Culture, Politics* 33.3-4 (2013): 615-44. Print.

Olson, Lester C. "Resisting Rape: Rhetorical Re-Circulation of a Print Series Portraying the Boston

Port Bill of 1774." *Rhetoric & Public Affairs* 12 1 (2009): 1-36. Print.

Prendergast, Catherine. *Literacy and Racial Justice: The Politics of Learning after Brown v. Board of Education*. Carbondale: Southern Illinois UP, 2003. Print.

Prendergast, Catherine, and Roman Ličko. "The Ethos of Paper: Here and There." *JAC: A Journal of Rhetoric, Culture, Politics* 29.1-2 (2009): 199-228. Print.

Prieto, Mercedes. *Liberalismo y Temor: Imaginando los Sujetos Indígenas en el Ecuador Postcolonial, 1895-1950*. Quito: Abya Yala, 2004. Print.

"Project Authorization: Walt Disney Field Survey and Short Subjects on the Other American Republics." 16 June 1941. Record Group 229, Entry 77, Box 959, Folder "Gracias Amigos 4041 OEMcr218." US National Archives, College Park.

"Regarding Testing of Literacy and Health films." Memo to Nelson A. Rockefeller, et al. 30 June 1944. Record Group 229, Entry 77, Box 960, Folder "Health and Literacy Program." US National Archives, College Park.

"Report of the Committee." Report from the Office of Inter-American Affairs and the Inter- American Educational Foundation, Inc. Conference on Community Education in Latin America with Special Reference to Literacy. 11 Aug. 1945. Record Group 229, Entry 77, Box 959, Folder "Literacy Program Miscellaneous OEMcr-107-305." US National Archives, College Park.

Ritter, Kelly. *Reframing the Subject: Postwar Instructional Film and Class-Conscious Literacies*. Pittsburgh, PA: U of Pittsburgh P, forthcoming 2015.

Rockefeller, Nelson A. "For New Americas." *The Modern Language Journal* 26.2 (1942): 143. Print. Roe, Bella Honess. "The Canadian Shorts: Establishing Disney's Wartime Style." *Learning from Mickey, Donald and Walt: Essays on Disney's Edutainment Films*. Ed. A. Bowdoin Van Riper. Jefferson, NC: McFarland, 2011. 15-26. Print.

Roosevelt, Franklin D. "Executive Order 8840 Establishing the Office of Coordinator of Inter- American Affairs." Eds. Gerhard Peters and John T. Woolley, *The American Presidency Project*. 30 July 1941. Web. 3 May 2014.

---. "Fireside Chat". 29 Dec. 1940. *The American Presidency Project*. Eds. Gerhard Peters and John T. Woolley. 21 July 2014. Web. 3 May 2014

South of the Border with Disney. Dir. Walt Disney. Walt Disney Productions. 1942. Film. Stuckey, J. Elspeth. *The Violence of Literacy*. Portsmouth, NH: Heinemann, 1991. Print.

Vacas G., Humberto. "Magic and Varied Teaching Methods in the Post-War Period. Experiment in Teaching Ecuadorean Illiterates by Means of Motion Pictures. This Method Has Also Been Tried in Mexico and Honduras." OIAA Translation Number 34739, originally published in *El Comercio* [Quito], 5 Nov. 1944. In Clark and Ryland.

Vallejo Larrea, Gustavo, and P. Arellano Montalvo. Letter to Nelson A. Rockefeller, 21 Nov. 1944. "Excerpts from a Letter to the Coordinator of Inter-American Affairs from Gustavo Vallejo Larrea, President of the Union Nacional de Periodistas, and P. Arellano Montalvo, Director of Literacy Campaign, Quito, Ecuador." In Clark and Ryland.

Van Riper, A. Bowdoin. "Introduction." *Learning from Mickey, Donald and Walt: Essays on Disney's Edutainment Films*. Ed. A. Bowdoin Van Riper. Jefferson, NC: McFarland, 2011. 1-13. Print.

Vieira, Kate Elizabeth. "'American by Paper': Assimilation and Documentation in a Biliterate, Bi- Ethnic Immigrant Community." *College English* 73.1 (2010): 50-72. Print.

---. "On the Social Consequences of Literacy." *Literacy in Composition Studies* 1.1 (2013): 26-32. Print.

Wan, Amy J. *Producing Good Citizens: Literacy Training in Anxious Times*. Pittsburgh: U of Pittsburgh P, 2014. Print.

PHILOSOPHY AND RHETORIC

Philosophy and Rhetoric is on the Web at https://muse.jhu.edu/journal/151

Philosophy and Rhetoric is dedicated to publication of high-quality articles involving the relationship between philosophy and rhetoric. *Philosophy and Rhetoric* has a *longstanding* commitment to interdisciplinary scholarship. It publishes articles on such topics as the relationship between logic and rhetoric, the philosophical aspects of argumentation (including argumentation in philosophy itself), philosophical views on the nature of rhetoric held by historical figures and during historical periods, psychological and sociological studies of rhetoric with a strong philosophical emphasis, and philosophical analyses of the relationship to rhetoric of other areas of human culture and thought, political theory and law.

Seeming and Being in the "Cosmetics" of Sophistry: The Infamous Analogy of Plato's Gorgias

Reames's article considers the infamous passage in Plato's *Gorgias*, in which Socrates compares rhetoric to cosmetics. This passage is a decisive moment in which the apparent dichotomy between seeming and being makes rhetoric forever suspect. Reames argues that the key term, "kommōtikē," is derived from an Egyptian term that pulls its meaning away from appearance and toward profligate consumption of foreign goods. The ripple effect of this modification moves Plato's critique from a polemic against rhetoric, predicated on a fundamental distinction between seeming and being, to a particular polemic against a cultural shift in Athens that was in the process of occurring during the dramatic dating of the dialogue and that threatened the very existence of the Athenian polis as such. It is a shift that undermines an accepted and canonical doctrine, which makes it worthy of inclusion in this volume.

Reames, Robin. "Seeming and Being in the 'Cosmetics' of Sophistry: The Infamous Analogy of Plato's Gorgias." *Philosophy and Rhetoric*, 49.1 (2016): 74-97. Copyright © 2016 by Penn State University Press. This article is used by permission of The Pennsylvania State University Press.

Seeming and Being in the "Cosmetics" of Sophistry: The Infamous Analogy of Plato's *Gorgias*

Robin Reames

Abstract: The earliest record of the term "kommōtikē," commonly translated as "cosmetics" or "self-adornment," occurs in the "most famous passage" of Plato's dialogue Gorgias (Kennedy 1994, 37). There, Socrates compares rhetoric to cookery and sophistry to "kommōtikē" (464b–66a). This marks a decisive moment in the Platonic corpus, a moment when rhetoric and sophistry are associated with seeming and appear- ance and therefore distanced from being and reality. I outline the reasons why this translation is incomplete if not misleading. I propose an adjustment that pulls both the analogy and the dialogue away from a Platonist distinction between seeming and being and toward a distinction between foreign profligacy and domestic austerity. This transformation discharges the vulgarization of appearance as mere appearance and mere seeming that has long infected and hampered both our understanding of Plato's thought and of early rhetoric.

Only all the effete latecomers, with their overly clever wit, believe that they can be done with the historical power of seeming by explaining it as "subjective," where the essence of this "subjectivity" is something extremely dubious.

—Martin Heidegger *Introduction to Metaphysics*

Introduction

The *Gorgias* dialogue is widely recognized as the source of Plato's harshest condemnation of rhetoric. In it, he ultimately concludes (465a) that rhetoric is not "a *technē* but a knack, because it can give no rational explanation of the thing it is catering for, nor of the nature of the things it is providing, and so it can't tell you the cause of each. And I don't give the name '*technē*' to something which is unreasoning" (Plato 2010, 30; translation modified).[1] Perhaps less widely recognized than the harshness of the criticism, however, is the fact that the dialogue also marks the place in the Platonic corpus where rhetoric and sophistry most explicitly come to be associated with seeming and appearance and therefore distanced from being and real- ity. This association with seeming (and alienation from being) arises from "the most famous passage in the dialogue" (Kennedy 1994, 37): the analogy (464b–66a) in which Socrates distinguishes between two kinds of *technai* (a term that means "arts," "sciences," or perhaps more accurately, "ways of doing and making things"): *technai* that concern political life (*psychē politikē*/ ψυχῇ πολιτικὴν) and *technai* that concern bodily life (*sōmati*/σώματι).[2] He further divides these into two branches: one dealing with the health- ful maintenance of the polis and the body— legislation and gymnastic— and the other dealing with curing ills in the polis and the body—justice and medicine.[3] He then matches each of these four *technai* with a false counterpart, which does not offer true maintenance or healing but "attaches itself" to maintenance and healing by means of "flattery."These false coun- terparts may lead us to believe they are the thing they simulate but in fact they are not. We might imagine this analogy as a grid:

	maintenance (being | seeming)	cure (being | seeming)
polis	legislation | sophistry	justice | rhetoric
body	gymnastic | *kommōtikē*	medicine | cookery

Sophistry is the false counterpart of legislation, rhetoric of justice, cookery of medicine, and "cosmetics, "self-adornment," or *kommōtikē*/ κομμωτική, of gymnastic.

Upon initial investigation, the "falseness" of sophistry, rhetoric, cookery, and cosmetics seems to be a species of the familiar Platonic distinction between appearance and reality. As E. R. Dodds explains, "The most important element in the present passage is the distinction- of principle which Plato draws between 'scientific' and 'unscientific' procedures (see 465a2–5). *It is one form of that distinction between being and seeming, inner reality and outward appearance, which runs through the whole of the dialogue from this point*" (Plato 1959, 227, emphasis mine). Dodds's description accurately summarizes over a century of scholarship on the analogy: rhetoric is relegated to an inferior status, and that status is deter- mined by rhetoric's relationship to seeming or appearance and its con- sequential divorce from being and reality. Brian Vickers makes the same point: "Binary oppositions were extremely common in Greek thought, of course, but their function in Plato's hands is to relegate rhetoric to the inferior, the lowest possible category" (1988, 113). In other words, gym- nastic *is* healthful maintenance of the body, or so the story goes, while cosmetics *seem like* healthful maintenance. Legislation *is* healthful main- tenance of the polis, while sophistry only *seems like* healthful maintenance, and so on. The false practices deal in "images or reflections" (Kennedy 1999, 62), appearances, opinion, or what seems to be, and not in reality, knowledge, or truth. As Ilman Dilman writes, "The counterfeit varieties of these arts aim only at the *appearance* of what their genuine counterparts aim at—apparent beauty, apparent well-being, apparent knowledge" (1979, 24). The false arts are designated as such, in other words, on the basis of their association with seeming or appearance and their alienation from being or reality.[4]

I would like to suggest that this foundational distinction between seem- ing and being and the persistent view that the critique of rhetoric is predi- cated on this distinction naturally dictate (albeit tacitly) that the critique is universal in its application. The universality of Plato's critique follows from the fact that the distinction between seeming and being, as it emerged in Greek thought, was crucial in the development of a metaphysics of tran- scendence and the notion of universal truth. As being was split from seem- ing (and in the same stroke truth from appearance) in Greek philosophy, being (and therefore truth) was accorded a supersensory, transcendent sta- tus that would create the template for metaphysics in the West.[5] Insofar as Plato's critique of rhetoric is taken to be a species of the traditional Platonic distinction between seeming and being, truth and appearance, it is likewise taken to be, in the words of Vickers, "a universally valid critique of rhetoric" (1988, 88).

The focus of this article is a single term within the analogy that I believe has determined the fate of the analogy as such and, by extension, the dialogue as a whole. I begin by explaining the difficulty as well as the importance of the term "kommōtikē," commonly translated as "cosmetics" or "self-adornment."I outline the reasons why this translation is incomplete if not misleading, a point of particular concern, since the interpretation both of this analogy and of the dialogue as a whole is informed by an implicit opposition between seeming and being on the basis of this single term. None of the other seven terms carries a connotation of appearance or seeming. Through "cosmetics" alone, rhetoric and sophistry anachronisti- cally are linked to seeming and appearance and dissociated from being and truth.

However, I suggest that Plato constructed this term not, as is commonly believed, from Greek terms referring to hair care and self-adornment (*komaō*/κομάω) but from an Egyptian term referring to gums and unguents (*kommi*/κόμμι).[6] This seemingly minor translation adjustment creates ripple effects throughout the dialogue, since it pulls us away from a presumed Platonic distinction between seeming and being and toward a historical, economic problem of profligate consumption of foreign goods that imper- iled Athens, making Socrates' analogy concerning rhetoric and sophistry accord better with the larger themes of political justice, domestic austerity, and temperance that are the focus of the rest of the dialogue. This transformation discharges the vulgarization of appearance as *mere* appearance and *mere* seeming that has long infected and hampered both our understanding of Plato's thought and of early rhetoric.

In what follows, I summarize the place of the analogy within the dramatic structure of the dialogue as a whole. I then discuss two interpretive problems that arise from the traditional interpretation of *kommōtikē* as cosmetics, hair care, and outward adornment: the first is that these common interpretations do not sufficiently alter the meaning of "komaō" (the presumed root for the neologism), rendering the neolo- gism superfluous, and the second is that standard interpretations fail to account for Plato's insertion of a double *mu* (or μμ). I then propose an alternate interpretation, which links "kommōtikē" not to "komaō," but to the Egyptian term for gum, "kommi," used in the production of perfume, a costly and exotic but also much-demanded good in fifth-century Athens, emblematic of Athens's thirst for foreign and expensive luxury items. Finally, I explain how this adjusted interpretation is supported by the dramatic context of the Peloponnesian War, explicitly referenced throughout the dialogue. I develop the latter two points through reading *Gorgias* along- side two contemporaneous texts: Xenophon's *Symposium* and Thucydides' *History of the Peloponnesian War*. By deuniversalizing Plato's critique in this way,

I suggest that the true target of the attack in the *Gorgias* was a set of specific, historically situated linguistic and cultural practices. Accordingly, Socrates' critiques of rhetoric and Athenian greed in the *Gorgias* dialogue are knitted into a single critique of the acquisitiveness that led Athens into a war of imperial domination. The effect is that we can no longer so easily assume that *Gorgias* is a timeless, universal condemnation of rhetoric and sophistry as such.

The Gorgias Dialogue and the Role of the Analogy

At the opening of his 1959 commentary, E. R. Dodds poses the question that confronts every investigation of this dialogue: how is rhetoric rendered in the *Gorgias*? The centrality of this question is inescapable, given the fact that, since antiquity, the *Gorgias* has carried the second title "ἢ περὶ ῥητορικῆς," or "concerning rhetoric." Indeed, if R. G. Hoerber's hypoth- esis is correct, that the second title originated with Plato himself, then we are correct to seek to understand how it is that rhetoric unites the diverse and sometimes meandering themes of the dialogue, many of which are seemingly irrelevant to rhetoric, including war, justice and injustice, freedom and slavery, wealth, power, desires (both satiable and insatiable), moderation, and the ultimate "ends" of life.[7]

The thematic development of the dialogue is mirrored by conversational shifts, so that the dramatic structure supports the content structure. These shifts are marked by three turns in the conversation, from Gorgias to Polus to Callicles. Beginning with Gorgias, the interlocutors set out to define "rhetoric"—this ineffable thing at which Gorgias excels to wide acclaim, prompting even Socrates to remark that it "comes across as something supernatural, a divine power" (Plato 2008, 19; translation modified [456a]). Gorgias's student Polus then steps in and changes the direction of the discussion (461a–b) by accusing Socrates of using sophisms with Gorgias. He shifts the focus from Gorgias's definition of rhetoric to Socrates'. It is at this point that Socrates offers the crucial analogy, defining rhetoric and sophistry analogically by comparing them to cookery and *kommōtikē* (464e–65b). He then discusses the uses and misuses of this power, conclud- ing with his famous claim that suffering wrong is superior to doing wrong (469c). In the final turn of the conversation, Callicles steps in (481b) to chal- lenge as stridently as he can Socrates' moral vision, bringing

Socrates ulti- mately to link the exercise of power with the aims of self-satisfaction and acquisitive pleasure, and the moral life with self-discipline and restraint. This calls into question the ultimate aims of life, which cannot be defined as the mere prolongation of life (511b–c), since the end of life is death. The close of *Gorgias* reverberates with the timbre of the *Phaedo*, where Socrates claims that philosophy is ultimately a preparation for death.

Given both the second title and the prominence of the analogy's place- ment, it is no surprise that the analogy concerning rhetoric and sophistry has had such a profound impact on the disparagement of rhetoric in the history of ideas. As Robert Wardy suggests, "The *Gorgias* falls little short of the *Republic* in the continuous influence it has exerted on Western intellectual and political history" (1996, 56). Within that history, the place of rhetoric is notorious: as George Kennedy writes, *Gorgias* is "the earliest example of the identification of rhetoric with flattery and deceit, a view that has recurred throughout western history" (1999, 66). As a result, we are driven alongside Gorgias himself "to the humiliating admission that the master of oratory lords it only over those who do not know: ever since, philosophers have approached the wiles of rhetoric with circumspection, while its self-professed champions have indignantly denounced Plato's defamation as apiece of shoddy rhetoric" (Wardy 1996, 57). In other words, the future fate of rhetoric is determined first and foremost in this analogy from the *Gorgias* dialogue.

Given both the pride of place and the hefty impact of this analogy, it is worth careful attention, as well as extensive quotation. As I have noted, Plato makes an initial distinction between those *technai* that concern political life (*psychē politikē*) and those that concern bodily life (*sōmati*) ([464b–c]). The former are legislation and justice, while the latter are gymnastic and medicine. As laws and gymnastic maintain respectively the health of the group and the individual, so the courts and medicine cure their ills. "These four sciences, two taking care of the body of the two of the *psychē*, and always with a view to what is best" (Plato 2010, 30 [464b–c]), are not left inviolate.[8] Rather, each is corrupted by "sycophancy," which

> divides itself into four, attaching itself to each of the subdivisions, and *makes itself out/over to be the very thing it attaches itself to* [ὑποδῦσα ὑπὸ ἕκαστον τῶν μορίων, προσποιεῖται εἶναι τοῦτο ὅπερ ὑπέδυ]. It has no concern with what is best, but

uses the plea- sure of the moment to ensnare and deceive folly, masquerading as something of the greatest value. . . . Under medicine, as I say, lies the sycophancy that is cookery; under fitness training, in just the same way is *kommōtikē*, since it is pernicious, illusory, demeaning, and slavish, deceiving with shapes and colours smooth skin and clothes. *It makes people import an alien beauty and neglect that beauty of their own which comes from gymnastic,* . . . [for] as *kommōtikē* is to gymnastic, so cookery is to medicine. And moreover, as *kommōtikē* is to training, so the skill of the sophist is to the science of the legislator; and as cookery is to medicine, so rhetoric is to justice. (Plato 2010, 30; translation modified, emphases mine [464c–65c])[9]

"Kommōtikē" is the only truly confounding term in this section. Plato's use of "rhētorikē" in the analogy has received serious scholarly attention owing to the fact that, as Edward Schiappa (1990) has argued, it is here that he may have coined the term. But the meaning of "rhētorikē" is not so very perplexing given the widespread use of the root "rhētor" prior to the *Gorgias* dialogue. Rather, the more unusual terminology is the rhyming tail to the newly minted *rhētorikē*'s head: *kommōtikē*.

This term has long puzzled translators, who, for a time, opted to remove it from the dialogue entirely. This omission may be seen, for example, in Aristotle's implicit reference to the analogy, found in his *Rhetoric* (1.2.1):

Let rhetoric be [defined as] an ability, in each [particular] case, to see the available means of persuasion. This is the function of no other art; for each of the others is instructive and persuasive about its own subject: for example, medicine about health and disease . . . and similarly in the case of the other arts and sciences. But rhetoric seems to be able to observe the persuasive about "the given" so to speak. That, too, is why we say it does not include technical knowledge of any particular, defined genus [of subjects]. (Aristotle 2006, 37 [1355a])

On the basis of Aristotle's elision, Thompson suggested in his 1871 commen- tary that the term "kommōtikē" should routinely be struck from the *Gorgias* dialogue, a view that was influential for a time but ultimately short-lived.[10] There is a reasonable explanation for why both Aristotle and modern commentators might be inclined to strike "kommōtikē" from the text. In brief, it's possible that no one, not even Aristotle, had seen the word before, since there is no record of the term's use prior to its appearance in the *Gorgias* dialogue. Although a few terms with the root "komm–" did exist (which I discuss below), Plato's term is unique. The newness of the term is not itself strange—it was not unusual for Plato to innovate with language.

What makes the term puzzling, rather, is the fact that, unlike other terms Plato coined (such as "rhētorikē"), "kommōtikē" did not begin circulating as linguistic currency. It never appears again in the Platonic corpus, and the next instances of its use do not occur until the first and second centuries CE with the emergence of Neoplatonists such as Plutarch (see fr. 147).[11] Although the term does see widespread use in the Platonist tradition from late antiquity through the Middle Ages by authors who were self- consciously taking up Plato's vocabulary, there is no record of the term's use before the *Gorgias* dialogue nor for nearly five hundred years following it. This absence indicates that term's meaning was likely to have been puzzling to Plato's own readers and followers.

Since the term's definition is uncertain, we must consider what neigh- boring Greek terms Plato would have been drawing on to construct it. In other words, which familiar source terms would have helped his audience glean the meaning of the neologism? Most modern scholarship concurs that, despite the term's "uncertain lineage" (Plato 1973 [1871], 147), Plato probably constructed this term out of the homophonously rooted words referring to care and tendance (the verb *komeō*/κομέω and the noun *komidē*/κομιδή), hair (*komē*/κόμη) and ostentatious grooming or letting the hair grow long (*komaō*/ κομάω, *komeō*/κομέω [Ionic]). The similarity between Plato's neologism and the terms for self-care, hair, and hairstyling moved Olympiodorus in the sixth century CE to suggest that the term refers to when one "adorn[s] the hair with an artificial elegance and colour" (14.2.131). Most modern transla- tors and commentators follow Olympiodorus's lead. Gonzalez Lodge, for example, in his 1890 commentary, suggests that the term refers "not only to finery in dress, but also hair—curling, ointments, cosmetics, etc." (Plato 1890, 81). While typical English translations for this term are "self-adornment" or "cosmetics," these translations grew out of an early preference to interpret the term as a linguistic descendent of "komaō" and therefore as an implicit reference to a form of self-adornment that involved hairstyling.¹² This theory about the origins of the neologism faces two problems, however, which I discuss in the following section.

THE TWO PROBLEMS: SUPERFLUOUS MEANING AND THE DOUBLE μ

The first problem arises from the fact that if Plato's neologism is to do any work in Socrates' critique, then its meaning ought to exceed (even if only slightly) what's already denoted by the original term. Otherwise, there would be no need for Plato to improvise on it. If the dominant etymological accounts of "kommōtikē" are correct, and the term is, in fact, derived from the homophonously rooted "komaō" or "komeō," and intended to refer to a controversial manner of self-adornment or cos- metic enhancement, then we encounter a curiosity. The commentators and translators attribute to the new term a definition that was already present in the old term. Namely, the root term is sufficient in itself for evoking the concept of excessive self-adornment—even to a shameful and socially controversial degree—without etymological adjustment of any kind.

Komaō referred not only to letting one's hair grow long but also to being arrogant and haughty and to putting on airs, a meaning derived from the fact that wearing one's hair long was an aristocratic habit. Indeed the term was associated with a set of aristocratic practices that were controver- sial in the fifth century and even more so from the view of fourth-century posterity.¹³ If it is the case that this terminological root referred to the very practices that the translators and commentators assign also to Plato's neol- ogism and if, moreover, these practices were not only common during the dramatic date of the dialogue but also retrospectively controversial at the date of composition, then what need would Plato have had for a neologism? In other words, if this is in fact the source of Plato's neologism, then he doesn't need a neologism. Or, if Plato was drawing on "komaō" primarily to nominalize these cultural practices, he might have made the term far less ambiguous by simply writing "komatikē" rather than "kommōtikē," which brings us to the second problem: the former would have been far more recognizable and more in keeping with the construction of the companion term "rhētorikē."

I believe it is important to attend precisely to what is new about Plato's neologism in order to define its possible meaning. While the commentators may be correct that Plato expected his readers to borrow from the meaning of "komaō" in order to make sense of his neologism, his basic innovation includes the bizarre appearance of a double μ, an unusual and relatively young development in Greek at the time of Plato's writing. Gemination in itself is not strange—adding or removing letters was particularly common in poetic compositions. Letters could be added or removed at the discretion of the writer to lengthen or shorten the sound of words in the service of greater parity and harmony. This convention makes it particularly strange, then, that Plato uses a double μ in his term "kommōtikē," since the addi- tional μ makes the term less not more similar to the terms he uses in

conjunction with it, and the overall effect is greater dissonance and less harmony not only visually but also aurally.

The possible significance of this dissimilarity is even more striking when we consider what pains Plato took to create terminological similarity in his analogy. All eight terms are given the rhyming stem "-ikē," six terms have four syllables, and two have five syllables. He introduces first the four legitimate *technē* (*gymnastikē*, *iatrikē*, *nomothetikē*, *dikastikē*) in sequence and follows them with their counterparts (*kommōtikē*, *opsopoïkē*, *sophistikē*, and *rhētorikē*). The close proximity of these terms emphasizes their assonance, homophoneity, and rhythmic regularity. It is all the more strange, then, that Plato uses a double μ here, given that it sets the term apart as the only term of the eight to contain a geminated consonant. Although a minority of scholars link "kommōtikē" to other fifth-century terms that also contain the root "komm–" (which, if these scholars are correct, would imply that the gemination does not originate with Plato), these accounts still do not explain the source of the geminated μ in the first place.

There is a term that, with only one exception, has been overlooked by both ancient and modern commentators alike, which I believe is the hid- den root of the neologism. I suggest that a fuller appreciation of the verbal source of Plato's neologism severs the word from seeming and appearance by binding it to foreignness and profligacy.

The *kommi* in *kommōtikē*: Athenians and Luxury

I wish to explore an etymological source for *kommōtikē* that to my knowledge has been proposed only once before, in Platonic scholia. Thompson notes this attribution but then immediately dismisses it:

"The word κομμοῦν is of somewhat uncertain lineage," Thompson writes. "A scholiast derives it from κόμμι, gummy [sic] which can hardly be true" (Plato 1973 [1871], 147).[14] I believe there is good reason for this proposal, given the probable way in which this term and its material referent entered Athenian culture and the Greek tongue.

The term "kommi"/κομμί means "gum," "paste," or "unguent" (and is the precursor to the English word "gummy"). It was first transliterated into the Greek tongue as a result of commerce with Egypt, and, I believe, would have been relatively young in Greek at the time Plato wrote *Gorgias* in the early fourth century. I speculate that, because of its recent introduc- tion from Egypt, it would have carried natural associations not only of foreignness but also of luxuriousness—particularly the luxury of perfumed unguents that came to Greece through trade with Egypt and Phoenicia (Forbes 1955, 35; Pliny, *Natural History* 11.59; Herodotus, *Histories* 3.107–12) and that were closely associated with cosmetic and medicinal self-care and luxurious, costly pampering. In this way, both the word and its matter are of a foreign extraction for the Greeks.

The earliest appearance of the term "kommi" in Greek literature is in the *Histories* of Herodotus, who in using the term also offers a defin 2. It was more likely to have gained wide circulation through association with the perfume trade, given the fact that *kommi* bore an essential connection to the manufacture of perfume, an Egyptian good that was an object of trade and highly valuable in Athenian society. This relation would have been established through the material process by which perfumes were made and through the fact that the perfumes themselves, in their finished form, were solid gums or emulsions, suggesting that the term itself could have functioned metonymically for perfume.[15]

Ultimately, it is through the perfume trade with Egypt and the consequent widespread use of perfume in Athens that, I believe, this term acquired its significance as a component of Plato's neologism "kommōtikē." Once trade both linguistic and material of Egyptian *kommi* began with Greece, perfume use in Greece became more widespread. Jean-Pierre Brun recounts how, in the earliest days of the trade, only the wealthiest Greeks could afford it. But in the seventh and sixth centuries BCE, when the trade center began moving from Alexandria to Corinth, it became more widely available. Brun also notes how the nature of the trade changed during this time—instead of importing perfumes that had been manufactured abroad and packaged in small alabaster vials the Greeks began importing the raw materials (such as *kommi*) from abroad and manufacturing and packaging the perfumes domestically. It is likely that this material shift is what led to the assimilation of the Egyptian term into the Greek language.

There is a remarkable amount of ancient testimony that provides insight into the symbolic social status and significance of perfumes and perfum- eries in Athens from the classical to the Hellenic period. While this may seem to be a detour of sorts, I believe the material and economic association of the Egyptian term "kommi" with perfume is essential for understanding the social controversies that inflect Plato's neologism, controversies that are not captured by the concept of self-adornment alone. Athenaeus cites texts from the fourth through the second century BCE that all attest to the exor- bitant cost of such perfumes, sums that were relatively equal to more than five hundred days of citizen dues, and at the same time to the widespread popularity of perfume in Athens (15.691): "When the price of perfumes was exorbitant . . . they did not abstain from their use any more than we do nowadays" (Athenaeus 1941, 205). He cites evidence from Demosthenes and Lysias to show not only the social popularity of the perfume market (the perfumers' shops near the agora were popular meeting places) but also the remarkable function of perfume as a status symbol. Athenaeus describes a speech by Lysias (13.612e) in which Lysias derides Aeschines for going into debt so that he could acquire a perfume shop—Lysias accuses him of being morally corrupt in his endeavor to promote "himself from the condition of peddler to that of perfume-seller" (Athenaeus 1941, 301).[16] Elsewhere, Athenaeus quotes Antiphanes, the late fifth-/early fourth- century BCE playwright, who points to Egyptian perfume as a particularly expensive type (15.690a). This testimony demonstrates the class- and status- consciousness that would have been associated with the use of perfumes. In addition, these perfumes, which, again, had the material consistency of *kommi*, were also used in aristocratic hairstyling trends of the fifth century (Griffith 2006), linking the Egyptian term not only homophonically but also materially and practically to its assonant sister "komaō."

Finally, the potential relevance of Egyptian *kommi*, essential in the production of Egyptian perfumes traded with Athens, for Plato's neolo- gism is made all the more likely given a passing remark about perfumes made by Socrates in Xenophon's *Symposium*. The text, which dates to the same time as Plato's *Gorgias*—380 BCE—recounts a feast hosted by the wealthy Callias, a great patron of the sophists, that was attended by (among others) Antisthenes, who was a follower not only of Socrates but also of Gorgias. In this text, both perfume and sophistry are topics of conversation, and they are treated, albeit obliquely, as similar practices by Socrates.

At the outset of the dialogue (1.5), Socrates responds to Callias's invitation by drawing attention to Callias's patronage of the sophists: he has "paid a good deal of money for wisdom to Protagoras, Gorgias, Prodicus, and many oth- ers" (Xenophon 2006, 537), Socrates says in a show of false admiration. This prompts Callias to respond that if Socrates comes to the feast, he will indeed demonstrate that he is "a person of some consequence" (Xenophon 2006, 537).

It is in an effort to prove his consequence and wealth that Callias offers to share perfumes with his guests. After a performance by a male and a female dancer, Socrates praises his host, both for the excellent food and the excellent entertainment. Callias responds by suggesting that they feast not only on food and dance but on aromas as well. He will bring in his perfumes, he says (2.3–4). Socrates stops him:

> No indeed! . . . For just as one kind of dress looks well on a woman and another kind on a man, so the odours appropriate to men and to women are diverse. . . . The odour of the olive oil, on the other hand, that is used in the gymnasium is more delightful when you have it on your flesh than perfume is to women, and when you lack it, the want of it is more keenly felt. (Xenophon 2006, 542–45)

Twice Socrates condemns the perfumers in this dialogue, blaming them even (through a quote from Theogenes) for the corruption of society (2.4): "Good men teach good; society with bad will but corrupt the good mind that you had" (Xenophon 2006, 543–45). He recommends against the use of foreign, feminine perfume in favor the more appropriate and truly Athenian, male, gymnastic practice of using olive oil. Here we see an explicit indication that Socrates saw the use of perfume as, on the one hand, an opponent to gymnastic (the same opposition we find in *Gorgias* between *kommōtikē* and *gymnastikē*) and, on the other hand, a source of alien cor- ruption in the polis. Following this refusal of his host's hospitality, he pays him an additional insult by accusing the sophists Callias follows of a similar kind of corruption

(4.57–62): they "teach only the *words* that tend to make one attractive" (Xenophon 2006, 593–97).

Several things overlap in this bricolage. Not only is it clear from the ancient testimony and from Socrates' statements that perfume, made from *kommi*, occupied a controversial place in Athenian society as a sort of cultural corruption in itself, but the archaeological record also confirms that it was widely desired and used in practices of self-adornment that had become popular among both men and women. Socrates laments these practices because they corrupt cultural purity and austerity with profligate self-indulgence. Aligned with this critique is his further critique of foreign sophistry, which is hidden in his analogical and ironic praise of pimps, who dress and coif their clients to greatest advantage. It is not self-adornment alone that is problematic; rather, it's the use of expensive, foreign goods in the act of self-adornment that is problematic.

Taking this economic and societal context into consideration, we can see that "kommi" inflects "kommōtikē" with a meaning that is much more complex than what is captured in the words "cosmetics" and "self-adornment" alone. The *kommōtikē* that comes from *kommi* is suspect not because it alters the appearance or causes people to seem different from how they are, but because it makes them different from how they are through the use of for- eign goods that can only be obtained at great cost—foreignness makes it expensive, which it turn makes it undemocratic and necessitates imperial reach. In fact, Plato provides something like a clue that his neologism is drawing on a foreign term. The hint is supplied in the passing definition he offers soon after using the term "kommōtikē": it "*makes people import an alien beauty* [ὥστε ποιεῖν ἀλλότριον κάλλος ἐφελκομένους τοῦ οἰκείου] *and neglect that beauty of their own which comes from gymnastic*" (465b). In my view this explicit reference to importing or dragging in alien goods that are not properly one's own binds the term "kommōtikē" to the foreign- sounding word "kommi," adding to the concept of *komaō* the consumption of expensive, luxurious, foreign goods in the practices of self-adornment— the imported, perfumed gums of the wealthy as opposed to the native olive oil of the gymnast.

It is altogether possible that Egyptian "kommi" is also the source of other inflections of the root "komm–." Other terms similarly demonstrate that this root term is consistently associated with profligate pampering, suggesting therefore that the derivation from the foreign and expen- sive κόμμι is not entirely unlikely. For example, the term "κομμώτρια," meaning "ladies' maid," "dresser," or "tire woman," appears in *Republic* during a discussion of the bloated, enlarged city, filled with a multitude of unnecessary comforts (373b). To supply the city with these items neces- sarily requires manufacturers of excess, especially those having to do with feminine adornment (373c): cooks, nurses, maids, κομμώτρια, and many other pampering servants.The term also appears Aristophanes'*Ecclesiazusae* in a similar context. Here a character is arranging an imaginary stock of luxurious belongings and indulgent attendants: a sunshade carrier, a water carrier, a flute girl, a perfume carrier, and a κομμώτρια (734–44). In both of these examples, which satirize and ironize fifth-century profligacy and self-indulgence, the term relates to a constellation of activities defined pri- marily by their wasteful extravagance and not by a relation to appearance and seeming (the example from Aristophanes' *Ecclesiazusae* even makes explicit reference to a phial of oil or perfume).[17] All of these inflections con- firm that the root term "komm–" was young in the fifth century and that despite the uncertainty regarding its origins (which has baffled numerous philologists), it was routinely used to refer to the self-indulgent excesses of fifth-century Athenian society. These excesses may well be linguistically and materially explained by the surge of imported goods during the fifth century, including Egyptian perfume and Egyptian *kommi*.

War: The Historical Context and the Critique of Rhetoric

To conclude this article, I propose that the altered definition of "kommōtikē" indicates that the critique offered in *Gorgias* is not nec- essarily a univer- sally applicable polemic against rhetoric, predicated on a fundamental distinction between seeming and being, but a particular polemic against a cultural shift in Athens that was in the process of occurring during the dramatic dating of the dialogue and that threatened the very existence of the Athenian polis as such.

In the very first lines of the dialogue (447a), Callicles says "You're in nice time, Socrates. For a war or a battle, as the saying goes." Socrates responds, "Does that mean we're too late? Have we missed the feast, as they say?" (Plato 2010, 7). I propose that these two themes—warring and feasting—cut through every discussion, from Gorgias's claim that, through the *polemos* of rhetoric, he can make a feast of his opponent, to Socrates' inquiry toward the end of the dialogue (491d) whether it is better to "rule the pleasures and desires within [oneself]" (Plato 2010, 67) than to relent- lessly pursue material pleasure and bodily desires. This essential contrast reflects some basic conditions of existence for a fifth-century Athenian and fourth-century survivor of the Peloponnesian war. Is it better to feast without limitation, which requires going to war to fill Athens's walls with consumable goods? Or is it better to limit one's appetite, which would nullify both the appetite and the need for war?[18] This tension between greed and collective responsibility may be seen clearly in Thucydides' account of the Peloponnesian war, a dramatic setting that should not be overlooked given the copious references to the war in the *Gorgias* dialogue.[19] Indeed, all the historical references contained in the dialogue refer to events that occurred during the war—Plato poetically suspends this conversation with Gorgias, which only could have occurred during his one and only visit to Athens (427 BCE), across the historic span of the war: Pericles's death in the plague at the beginning of the war (429 BCE) is described as "recent" (503c) and the trial of the generals that took place at the end of the war in 405 is referred to as having occurred only "last year"(473e). In a way, Gorgias's visit to Athens reinforces this temporal suspension, since Athens received two Sicilian ambassadorial delegations— one four years after the start of the war in 427 BCE, and another eleven years before the end of the war in or around 415 BCE. These deliberately impossible temporal references emphasize the importance of the war as a backdrop for the dialogue.

It is in the war that the tension between greed and justice is thrown into relief. Plato's contemporary Thucydides, writing what he hoped would be the true and accurate history of the same events that serve as dramatic setting for the *Gorgias* dialogue, shows how the general response in Athens to the second Sicilian campaign demonstrated precisely this problematic clash of values. This is most evident in the conflict between the Athenian general Nicias and his opponent Alcibiades. In his speech to the Athenian assembly (6.12), Nicias warns against listening to Alcibiades, who "advises you to set sail, when he is only looking out for his own interests . . . and really hopes to benefit from the prerequisites of his office while being admired for his fine stable of horses" (Thucydides 1998, 238). In response, Alcibiades offers a defense for the greed of the "1 percent", claiming that his extravagances are ultimately good for the polis (6.16): "All things that make me notorious are really an honor to my ancestors and to me, as well as an advantage to the state" (Thucydides 1998, 239).

The sophist is fitted into the barrier between the two sides of this dichotomy that unite the beginning and end of the dialogue. The sophist in this case, historically and situationally, is Gorgias, and not sophistry and rhetoric writ large. In other words, this is not "a universally valid critique of rhetoric"(Vickers 1988, 88) but a situationally contingent critique of Gorgias, a wealthy and profligate foreigner who enchanted Athens with his verbal sorcery, luring the city to seek a greater imperial reach and giving its citizens a thirst for war, whetted by the promise of filling their purses and bellies. Gorgias, by this interpretation, is not symbolic of a timeless, universal insti- tution of "rhetoric" or "sophistry," predicated on a metaphysics of being as opposed to seeming. Rather, as a historical figure, he evokes the immanent lure of foreign riches, the answer to Athenian acquisitiveness and greed, and serves as the counterweight to a more appropriate Athenian austerity, par- simony, and domesticity. He stands between Nicias and Alcibiades just as he stands between Callicles' two citizens (484a): the democrat who believes that "equality is admirable and right" (Plato 2008, 66) and the Nietzschean antecedent who will "shake off these limitations, shatter them to pieces, and win his freedom; he'll trample all our regulations, charms, spells, and unnatural regulations into the dust. This slave will rise up and reveal himself as our master, and then natural right will blaze forth" (Plato 2008, 66). It is not a universal critique of rhetoric and sophistry as such, in other words, but a particular critique of the wealthy Gorgias's sophistry that aimed to exploit Athens's desire for a power capable of "producing pleasure and enjoyment" (462c). Gorgias promises to deliver this pleasure by teaching Athens his arts of rhetoric; employing these arts, they will be able to squeeze whatever they want from whomever they want: "As for the businessman, it will become clear that he is not in business for his own benefit, but for someone else's— yours, since you are the one who has the ability to speak and persuade large groups of people" (Plato 2010, 14–15 [452d–e]).

Gorgias is an ideal symbol for the dangers that would come from ful- filling such a promise, since the Sicilian delegations succeeded in making Athens do Syracuse's bidding by provoking its greed. Of the first delegation, we know from Thucydides'account (2.65) that it succeeded in persuading the Athenians to send ships by tapping into their desire for "prestige and profit" (Thucydides 1998, 83): "The Athenians did send ships, allegedly because of their long-standing relationship, but really. . . to feel out whether it would be possible to take control of things in Sicily" (Thucydides 1998, 132 [3.86]). The first Sicilian campaign, of which Gorgias was a part, became typologi- cal in the war itself, prefiguring the very thing Thucydides calls Athens's "biggest mistake": the second campaign in 415 during which Athens would lose its navy and ultimately destroy itself (2.65). In the second campaign, the admonitions of the likes of Nicias (which mirror those of Socrates) failed. Instead, Athens was persuaded by the lure of riches promised by the likes of Gorgias and Alcibiades (and their mirror Callicles).

As we know, the Sicilian campaign fails miserably, crushing Athens. It would be impossible for any fourth-century reader of the dialogue, which refers to the first of the two Sicilian diplomatic envoys that bookend the war, not to think—cringing—of the war as a backdrop of the dialogue. The devastating defeat at Sicily, Alcibiades' treachery, the fall of Athenian democracy, and the installation of the tyrants in Athens would necessarily be evoked from the very outset of the dialogue.

Socrates' critique of sophistry and rhetoric cannot be detached from the disasters that are necessarily summoned by this explicit reference to the first Sicilian ambassadorial visit. To define precisely Socrates' criticism, we must acknowledge the role the sophists played in exploiting the greed that would ultimately lead to Athens's downfall. The term "kommōtikē" serves as a subtle reference to that greed, indicating that the "universal critique," if it can still be called that, has more to do with greed and acquisitiveness than with sophistry and rhetoric as such.

Conclusion

For Plato's Socrates and Thucydides' Nicias, the greed that promotes imperial domination is the same greed lurking beneath the demand for foreign luxury goods, including foreign perfumes. Thucydides explic- itly blames Athenian acquisitiveness for the destruction brought about through the war; Plato explicitly makes the war the dramatic backdrop and then explicitly critiques Athenian acquisitiveness for making Athens pursue pleasure rather than justice. In the end, the definition of rheto- ric and sophistry offered in the analogy coheres with this larger critique of Athenian appetites and imperial policies precisely because the term "kommōtikē" is capable of reflecting these wedded critiques: that of the consumption of goods and that of foreign entanglements. A *kommōtikē* derived from Egyptian *kommi* is capable of connoting both imperial domi- nation and profligate consumption; *kommōtikē* derived solely from Greek *komaō* is not.

Although translations of the *Gorgias* regularly impose a distinction between seeming and being in a way that is consistent with Dodds's read- ing, which suggests that the analogy introduces a metaphysical opposition that is recurrent and upheld throughout the rest of the dia- logue, the analy- sis here suggests the distinction is less firm than it is often presumed to be. Insofar as it may be found in the dialogue, it is probably more accurate to say that Plato, through the depiction of the conflict between Gorgias and Socrates, was in the process of develop- ing what would later come to be a firm distinction between seeming and being and the basic architecture of Western metaphysics. But here, it is at best nascent.

When Plato finally introduces the myth of the afterlife at the end of *Gorgias*, it is to add valuative force to the contrast he's developed between a life that pursues pleasure and a life that aims instead at self- discipline and the avoidance of wrongdoing. Up to that point, both seem as though they may be viable accounts of what is good. But the myth reminds us that both end in death; in death, both are stripped of their clothing and every other luxury (523c)—"attractive bodies, noble birth, and wealth" (Plato 2008, 130) are shed.[20] What remains are the products of the *psychē* (525a): "the scars which every dishonest and unjust action imprinted on it, utterly crippled by lies and arro- gance and warped by a truth-free diet" (Plato 2008, 131). The dia- logue has set up a contrast not between truth and its appearance but between two equally alluring models of goodness: the Calliclean (later Nietzschean) lion who takes what he wants and the Socratic citizen who disciplines what he wants. It's the myth of the afterlife that allows the reader to subordinate the former to the latter. This is one indica- tion among others that the ostensive critique of rhetoric in *Gorgias* is not predicated on a distinction between seeming and being and that therefore it is not a universally applicable critique of rhetoric. Rather it is a critique that passes *through* the medium of the sophist's rhetoric and arrives ultimately at its true target: the use of power for acquisitive gain and the greed that necessitates imperial expansion—a critique, I might add, that remains powerfully relevant today.

Department of English
University of Illinois at Chicago

Notes

I am very grateful to four anonymous readers who offered helpful feedback on an early version of this essay and to Professor Manfred Kraus who provided invaluable etymo- logical advice at an early stage of this research. I am likewise grateful to Professor Nanno Marinatos for sharing her love of Thucydides with me.

1. The harshness of the criticism is identified by numerous scholars. James Doyle notes that the tone of the dialogue is more acrimonious than any other and that it even degenerates to "naked hostility" (2006, 89). Alessandra Fussi suggests that Plato must have been "enraged" when he wrote the dialogue (2000, 39).

2. My translation of this passage differs from most, which render the analogy as a Platonic distinction between the soul and the body, a difference that turns on Plato's use of the term "psychē." Plato writes "τὴν μὲν ἐπὶ τῇ ψυχῇ πολιτικὴνκαλῶ, τὴν δὲ ἐπὶ σώματι." Here I believe Plato drops "psychē" in the second phrase, which amounts to a distinction between what we would call the life of the polis and that of the body rather than a distinction between soul and body. This translation is far more plausible, given that "πολιτικὴν" is an adjective modifying "ψυχῇ" in this phrase and is implied with the dative "σώματι" in the second phrase. Amending the translation in this way solves the seeming imbalance in the analogy, pointed out by Dodds, of one set of practices pertaining to the individual and the other to the group (Plato 1959, 227).

3. This analogy is an elaboration of the one offered originally by Gorgias in his *Encomium of Helen* (DK82b11.14): "The effect of speech upon the condition of the *psychē* is comparable to the power of drugs over the nature of bodies. For just as different drugs dispel different secretions from the body, and some bring an end to disease and others to life, so also in the case of speeches, some distress, others delight, some cause fear, others make the hearers bold, and some drug and bewitch the soul with a kind of evil persuasion" (Gorgias 1972, 53). Dodds suggests that this analogy predates even the historical Gorgias, since its antecedent occurs in Aeschylus, who has Oceanus say, "Do you not know then, Prometheus, that words are the

physicians of a disordered temper?" (Plato 1959, 379–80). Plato repeats the analogy between medicine and rhetoric in *Phaedrus* (270b).

4. See Plochmann and Robinson 1988, 65–67, Bernardete 1991, 33, and Stauffer 2006, 49. The influence of the distinction between seeming and being is also on display in the translations of the dialogue. For example, in his analysis of the analogy (464c–d), Socrates says "the art of flattery[,] which . . . divides itself into four, plunges itself into each of the subdivisions, and makes itself out to be the very thing it has crept into" (my transla- tion). Griffith and Waterfield translate "attaches" or "plunges" ("ὑποδῦσα") as "impersonates." Griffith and Lamb translate "makes out to be" ("προσποιεῖται εἶναι") as "pretends." Similarly, at the end of the dialogue (527b), Socrates presents the famous maxim that "we have to take greater care to avoid doing wrong than we do to avoid suffering wrong, and that above all else we must concentrate not on making people expect [δοκεῖν] that we're good, but on being good" (Plato 2008, 134). Lamb translates this as a distinction between "seeming good" and "being good." While these translations may seem very close to the essential meaning, they nevertheless reflect a firm distinction between seeming and being that is arguably not present in the text.

5. This interpretation belongs to Martin Heidegger (2000, §75–88), who claims that in early Greek thought, and even in Plato, seeming and appearance had not been fully dissociated from being and truth. Rather, Heidegger insists, the Greek understanding of being was fully predicated on concepts related to appearance and presence. Although Heidegger identifies Plato's attack on the sophists as an important moment in the eventual rupture between seeming and being and the development of a metaphysics of transcen- dence, he denies that the rupture was complete with Plato. The rupture is only completed once the Latin tongue and later Christian metaphysics take hold of Platonic thought. The aftereffect of this is that being and truth are thought of as enduring, permanent, unchanging, constant, and so forth. Thus, by contrast, seeming and appearance supply the inverse: change, impermanence, temporariness, nonbeing. In other words, that which only appears or seems to be *is not*. Seeming can only be false, in a universal, absolute sense. In this way, a rhetoric that is predicated on seeming and appearance can only be universally and absolutely false.

6. There are a handful of commentators and translators who link "kommōtikē" to other terms with the root "komm–," but the majority relate it to "komaō"/κομάω.

7. Diogenes Laertius records the second titles of most works in the Platonic corpus and indicates that Thrasylus also used the second titles. R. G. Hoerber notes, however, that the use of second titles for the works dates to as early as the fourth century, perhaps even originating with Plato himself (1957, esp. 19–20).

8. In this instance, Plato drops the terminology explicitly referring to the polis, although the immediately preceding text at 464b indicates that "psychē" here refers to the polis.

9. Griffith points out that sycophancy refers to members of the Athenian polis who had no legitimate trade of their own but made their living by bringing law suits against other citizens. In this way, the term refers to a dubious practice of exploiting the Athenian legal and political structures for self-gain (Plato 2010, 28n26).

10. For Thompson's recommendation that it be struck, see Plato 1973 [1871], 147. Dodds mentions that it was a common practice among many scholars toward the beginning of the twentieth century to strike the phrase that included "kommōtike" from 465c (Plato 1959, 231). As far as I can tell, Dodds's commentary marks the end of the practice; he reintroduces the term and defends its strangeness, arguing that it "is intelligible in light of what has preceded it" (Plato 1959, 231). Nevertheless, "what has preceded it" is simply the same strange, possibly indecipherable word, and not an explanation of the word's meaning.

11. See also Galen, *De compositione medicamentorum secundum locos libri* 5.12.439–512.

12. In the many editions of Lamb's translation published between 1925 and 1983, the term is rendered either as "self-adornment" or "personal adornment." Griffith uses the term "fashion" (Plato 2010, 30). Waterfield uses "ornamentation" (Plato 2008, 32). Kennedy uses "cosmetics" in his summaries of the analogy (1994, 37; 1999, 62).

13. The broader cultural significance of the practices associated with *komaō* is discussed in a recent article by Mark Griffith (2006), who shows that the hairstyling denoted by these terms was a common practice among upper-class Athenians. Griffith notes that it was regarded with particular suspicion in the fifth century. See especially 308–10. There is also evidence of the identification of hairstyling with both Asianism and excess in Plato's contemporary Thucydides, who offers direct evidence to support the probability that in period in which the *Gorgias* is set, the upper classes styled their hair elaborately and wore adornments, both of which were associated with *komaō* (1.6). Furthermore, Thucydides' example indicates that in the period following the one the dialogue is set in—in other words, at the time the dialogue was written—this *komaō* was subject to the critique of posterity, both for its excess and its foreignness. Although Thucydides does not use the exact term, what he describes would have been synonymous with it.

14. The scholiast who derived the term from "kommi" was referring not to the *Gorgias* but to *Republic* 373c, recorded in both the Greene (1938) and the more recent Cufalo (2007) editions. The scholiast defines "kommōtikē" by claiming it is related to the contempora- neous term "kommōtriōn," a ladies' maid or dressing woman. Both of these terms, the scholiast suggests,

come from the term "kommi." This derivation arises originally as a result of the fact that "kommi," a gum that oozes out of a tree, was used as a hairstyling product in order to make one's hair seem more effeminate, and, it seems, it was most valuable when used unmixed and pure, straight from its source. The etymology is as fol- lows: κομμωτριῶν. κόμμι λέγεται τὸ ἐκ τῶν δένδρων ἅτε δὴ δάκρυον ἀπορρέον ὑγρόν, ᾧ χρῶνται πρὸς τὰς τρίχας τῶν γυναικῶν ὥστε μὴ διαχεῖσθαι ἀλλὰ μένειν ὡς ἄγαν συνημμένας ἐφ' οὗ βεβούληνται σχήματος αἱ κομμώτριαι, παρ' ὃ καὶ ἀπὸ τοῦδε τοῦ κόμμεος λέγονται, καὶ ἡ τέχνη κομμωτική

15. Archaeologist Jean-Pierre Brun has recounted how gums and unguents were inte- gral to the ancient Egyptian perfume-making process, dating to the second millennium BCE. In this process, fats were heated in order to be made astringent, and then they were mixed with aromatic plants and "fragrant woods, gums [*kommi*], and musk" (2000, 277). This suggests that the *kommi* may even have been the source of the perfume's scent!

16. For a full account of the speech against Aeschines, see Lysias 2000, 342–46.

17. I am grateful to Professor Manfred Kraus for drawing my attention to the poten- tial relevance of these terms. It may be the case that both "κομμοῦν" and "κομμώτρια" both are derived from "κομμώ," as speculated by both Immanuel Bekker (1814, 273) and Felix Solmsen (1901, 501). Bekker defines "κομμώ" as "ἡ κοσμοῦσα τὸ ἕδος τῆς Ἀθηνᾶς," or the name for a priestess who adorned the statue of Athena in the Acropolis. Nevertheless, this attribution still does not explain the geminated μμ. Solmson speculates that the μμ in these terms may result from an "affectionate" lengthening of the sound (504), but this explanation is uncertain, particularly since it would be unusual for one to speak with affection of such self-indulgent activities. In any case, Solmson's attempt to account for the gemination only reinforces its strangeness. Similarly, the verb "κομμόομαι" ("to be clean, decorate or embellish") also begins appearing in the fifth century. Frisk's etymology suggests that its origin is unknown and notes that it may have been a "fashionable new creation or a borrowed term" ("eine modische Neuschopfung oder Englehnung zu sein") (1954–72, 1:109). Frisk's attribution of this verb to improvisation and borrowing further supports the possibility that the root comes from another language, perhaps Egyptian (κόμμι). All of these examples indicate neologisms that date to the fifth century, whose μμ gemination has been unaccounted for.

18. This same tension between "acquisitiveness and injustice" (Balot 2001, 179) makes an appearance in Aristotle's *Politics* (1256b–66b), but as Ryan Balot discusses, it has its roots in the sixth century in Solon's laws and poems (fr. 13.71, 4c, 34.7–9). On Solon's view, acquisitiveness is suspect precisely because it compromises justice. It is perhaps not incidental that one of Solon's laws banned the selling of perfume in Athens. Aristotle in the fourth

century, with Solon in the sixth century, "is urging the rich to observe self-restraint for the sake of Athens as a whole" (Balot 2001, 58). Balot shows how these Athenian values reached a peak of con- cern between Solon's and Aristotle's time, as it were, in the late fifth century, when "a unified discourse on greed arose in response to the changing social, economic, and military conditions in Athens. . . . In the intellectual controversies of the time, as well as in the two oligarchic revolutions at the end of the century, Athenians played out conflicts between rich and poor and between individual self-interest and collective responsibility" (179).

19. Arlene Saxonhouse (1983, 1992) rightly insists that Thucydides is essential background reading for *Gorgias*.

20. While this myth is often read as though it were another manifestation of the distinction between seeming and being (since the clothes project an appearance and what underlies is the reality), there is no terminology to suggest that this distinction is at work in the story. Rather, it may be read instead as yet another critique of foreign luxuries and fashions that corrupt the unadorned Athenian aesthetic. One cannot help but notice the parallel between the adorned aristocrat and the ideal nude Athenian gymnast.

Works Cited

Aeschylus. 1926. *Prometheus Bound*. Trans. Herbert Weir Smith. Cambridge, MA: Harvard University Press

Aristophanes. 2002. *Ecclesiazusae*. Trans. Jeffrey Henderson. Cambridge, MA: Harvard University Press.

Aristotle. 2006. *On Rhetoric*. Trans. George A. Kennedy. New York: Oxford University Press.

Athenaeus. 1941. *The Deipnosophists*. Vol. 7. Trans Charles Burton Gulick. Cambridge, MA: Harvard University Press.

Balot, Ryan. 2001. *Greed and Injustice in Classical Athens*. Princeton, NJ: Princeton University Press.

Bekker, Immanuel, ed. 1814. *Anecdota graeca*. Vol. 1. Berlin: Nauck.

Bernardete, Seth. 1991. *The Rhetoric of Morality and Philosophy: Plato's "Gorgias" and "Phaedrus."* Chicago: University of Chicago Press.

Brun, Jean-Pierre. 2000. "The Production of Perfumes in Antiquity: The Cases of Delos and Paestum." *American Journal of Archaeology* 104 (2): 277–308.

Carey, Christopher. 2007. *Lysiae orationes cum fragmentis*. Oxford: Oxford University Press. Cufalo, Domenico, ed. 2007. *Scholia graeca in platonem*. Scholia ad dialogos tetralogiarum, Vol. 1. Rome: Edizioni di storia e letteratura.

Dilman, Ilman. 1979. *Morality and the Inner Life: A Study in Plato's "Gorgias."* New York: Macmillan.

Doyle, James. 2006. "The Fundamental Conflict in Plato's *Gorgias.*" *Oxford Studies in Ancient Philosophy* 30 (Summer): 87–100.
Forbes, R. J. 1955. *Studies in Ancient Technology.* Vol. 5. Leiden: Brill.
Frisk, Hjalmar. 1954–1972. *Griechisches etymologisches Wörterbuch.* 3 vols. Heidelberg.
Fussi, Alessandra. 2000. "Why is the *Gorgias* So Bitter?" *Philosophy and Rhetoric* 33 (1): 39–58.
Gorgias. 1972. "Encomium of Helen." In *The Older Sophists*, ed. Rosamond Kent Sprague, trans. George Kennedy, 50–54. Columbia: University of South Carolina Press.
Greene, William Chase, ed. 1938. *Scholia platonica.* Philological Monographs, Vol. 8. Haverford, PA: American Philological Association.
Griffith, Mark. 2006. "Horsepower and Donkeywork." *Classical Philology* 101 (4): 307–58. Heidegger, Martin. 2000. *Introduction to Metaphysics.* Trans. Gregory Fried and Richard Polt. New Haven, CT: Yale University Press.
Herodotus. 1928. *The History.* Trans. George Rawlinson. New York: Tudor.
Hoerber, R. G. 1957. "Thrasylus' Platonic Canon and the Double Titles." *Phronesis* 2 (1): 1–20.
Kennedy, George. 1994. *A New History of Classical Rhetoric.* Princeton, NJ: Princeton University Press.
—. 1999. *Classical Rhetoric and Its Christian and Secular Tradition: From Ancient to Modern Times.* 2nd ed. Chapel Hill: University of North Carolina Press.
Lysias. 2000. *Lysias: Translations into English.* Trans. Steven Charles Todd. Austin: University of Texas Press.
Olympiodorus. 1998. *Commentary on Plato's "Gorgias."* Trans. Robin Jackson, Kimon Lycos, and Harold Tarrant. Leiden: Brill.
Plato. 1890. *Gorgias.* Ed. Gonzalez Lodge. Boston: Ginn and Company.
—. 1959. *Gorgias.* Ed. E. R. Dodd. Oxford, UK: Clarendon Press.
—. 1973 [1871]. *Gorgias.* Ed. William H. Thompson. New York: Arno Press.
—. 1983. *Gorgias.* Trans. W. R. M. Lamb. Cambridge, MA: Harvard University Press.
—. 2008. *Gorgias.* Trans. Robin Waterfield. Oxford, UK: Oxford University Press.
—. 2010. *Gorgias.* Trans. Tom Griffith. Cambridge: Cambridge University Press. Plochmann, George Kimball, and Franklin E. Robinson. 1988. *A Friendly Companion to Plato's "Gorgias."* Carbondale: Southern Illinois University Press.
Saxonhouse, Arlene. 1983. "An Unspoken Theme in in Plato's *Gorgias*: War." *Interpretation* 11 (1983): 139–69.
—. 1992. *Fear of Diversity: The Birth of Political Science in Ancient Greek Thought.* Chicago: Chicago University Press.

Schiappa, Edward. 1990. "Did Plato Coin *Rhētorikē*?" *American Journal of Philology* 111 (4): 457–70.
Solmsen, Felix. 1901. "Zwei Nominalbildungen Auf –μα." *Rheinisches Museum für Philologie* 56: 497–507.
Stauffer, Devin. 2006. *The Unity of Plato's "Gorgias": Rhetoric, Justice, and the Philosophic Life*. Cambridge: Cambridge University Press.
Thucydides. 1998. *The Peloponnesian War*. Trans. Walter Blanco. New York: Norton. Vickers, Brian. 1988. *In Defence of Rhetoric*. Oxford, UK: Clarendon Press.
Wardy, Robert. 1996. *The Birth of Rhetoric: Gorgias, Plato, and Their Successors*. London: Routledge.
Xenophon. 2006. *Symposium*. Trans. O. J. Todd. Cambridge, MA: Harvard University Press.

PRESENT TENSE

Present Tense is on the Web at http://www.presenttensejournal.org/

Present Tense: A Journal of Rhetoric in Society is a peer-reviewed, blind-refereed, online journal dedicated to exploring contemporary social, cultural, political and economic issues through a rhetorical lens. In addition to examining these subjects as found in written, oral and visual texts, we wish to provide a forum for calls to action in academia, education and national policy. Seeking to address current or presently unfolding issues, we publish short articles ranging from 2,000 to 2,500 words, the length of a conference paper. For sample topics please see our submission guidelines. Conference presentations on topics related to the journal's focus lend themselves particularly well to this publishing format. Authors who address the most current issues may find a lengthy submission and application process disadvantageous. We seek to overcome this issue through our shortened response time and by publishing individual articles as they are accepted. We also encourage conference-length multimedia submissions such as short documentaries, flash videos, slidecasts and podcasts.

Implicating the State: Black Lives, A Matter of Speculative Rhetoric

andré carrington's "Implicating the State: Black Lives, A Matter of Speculative Rhetoric" was published in late fall 2015 as part of *Present Tense's* powerful and timely special issue on Race, Rhetoric, and the State. Using speech act theory, carrington analyzes the utterance of "Black Lives Matter" in order "to assess the efficacy of rhetoric that purports to confront the problem of state-sanctioned lethal violence against Black people." carrington argues that the effectiveness of such an utterance is speculative; therefore, the choice of how we use and understand the phrase is pivotal to politics and discourse about race. We believe this essay is a great example of our journal's dedication to excellence in rhetorical scholarship on the most salient current social issues.

(c) 2015 by Fibonacci Blue. Creative Commons Attribution License. https://www.flickr.com/photos/44550450@N04/20000371679/

Implicating the State: Black Lives, A Matter of Speculative Rhetoric

andré carrington

In the wake of spectacular acts of violence in which state actors have killed or legitimated the killing of Black Americans, including Trayvon Martin, Rekia Boyd, Aiyana Stanley Jones, Miriam Carey, Tamir Rice, Michael Brown, and Freddie Gray, activists have invoked the phrase "Black Lives Matter" to uphold the value of Black life in the face of its apparent devaluation. Following the dissemination of the maxim as a hashtag and in grassroots mobilizations, supporters and detractors have reiterated this mantra, occasionally altering it in order to articulate distinct, sometimes competing, understandings of violence and state power. The President said Your Life Matters in his 2015 State of the Union Address. A *Twitter*user posited Blue Lives Matter to defend police officers' actions. After coining the phrase along with her colleagues Alicia Garza and Opal Tometi, Patrisse Cullors has insisted on All Black Lives Matter to resist marginalizing tendencies among activists that propagate the notion that cisgender, heterosexual Black men are the sole targets of racial profiling. Sometimes, as a rebuttal to the discomfiting reminder that Black vulnerability to state violence maintains White supremacy, White interlocutors will proclaim that #AllLivesMatter on social media. These confounding circumstances have made it vital to continue saying "Black Lives Matter" in conjunction with actions that seek to turn the tide of a violent history in which Black life does not seem to matter to representatives of American social institutions and political leadership. This essay analyzes the prototypical utterance of "Black Lives Matter," based on firsthand accounts of its origins, in order to argue for applications of speech act theory that allow us to assess the efficacy of rhetoric that purports to confront the problem of state-sanctioned lethal violence against Black people.

I interpret the implications of saying "Black Lives Matter" in terms of performativity, rhetoric, and pragmatics, which come together to shed light on politics and communication in new ways in recent years. Scholars and teachers can learn how to make more effective discursive interventions against racism, in educational contexts and in everyday life, from the organic intellectual practice of the Black women who coined "Black Lives Matter." By contextualizing the phrase's meaning in the work of activists engaged in ongoing social movements, we can provide more salient examples of the work rhetoric performs in contemporary politics, and we can maintain attention to the role of institutions—as well as to our own roles as speakers and listeners—in determining the meaning of what we say and, by extension, what we do to each other. By recognizing how this speech act is distinctive in its aims and effects, we can participate in a rigorous critique of the state and the acts carried out with its legitimation. By understanding that the efficacy of this statement is speculative in nature—its implications are uncertain—we might conceptualize the choice to use the phrase in the way its originators intended as a matter in which we have some agency as custodians of its meaning.

Spectacle, Violence, and Performativity

One factor that accounts for disparate reactions to the assertion "Black Lives Matter" and for the structural critique it entails is the commonplace tendency to identify racism as a character flaw, a matter of individual dispositions. This manner of thinking often leads White interpretants who do not want to see themselves as racist to take a defensive posture when their interlocutors subject whiteness to scrutiny. Highlighting the shortcomings of individualistic accounts of racism, scholars and teachers who practice a "pedagogy of whiteness" scrutinize individualistic accounts to emphasize how focusing on personal culpability for racist acts "removes non-overtly racist individuals from feeling any responsibility for addressing diversity issues since they do not see their role in larger discriminatory practices" (Hytten and Adkins 444). Whereas individuals may hold themselves blameless for racist acts perpetrated in the past or by other persons, a thorough appreciation of rhetoric reminds us that the positions of bystanders, spectators, and listeners are integral to the process of making meaning and inspiring action. When motivated to move from the sidelines into active positions in determining what the ongoing legacy of racism means, present-day White interlocutors sometimes enter into critical discourse on racism through the process of identification that Melanie Kill describes as "uptake" (218). Eventually, by internalizing a desire to resist racism, those erstwhile bystanders can learn to take up "positive white identities."

"Black Lives Matter" is a critical formulation of the call to resist racist violence because it places Black subjects at the center of its analysis and it implicates the state. Unlike the imperative of cultivating positive White identities, which emphasizes individual transformation, it employs a collective mode of address. While sustaining diverse coalitions is a part of working toward social transformation, satisfying individual coalition members in emotional and cognitive terms (e.g., cultivating empathy and pursuing common interests) is an insufficient strategy on its own, because it relies on the notion that allies' desire to avoid feeling bad will motivate them toward constructive action (Jurecic 11). With personal rather than structural goals in mind, the actions to which allies commit will be those that assuage their own concerns even if they leave the status quo intact.

Institutions may embrace a more systematic understanding of racism in official pronouncements, but the rhetoric with which they do so matters as well. Sara Ahmed cites a recent pattern in the United Kingdom, where "(in particular, the police) have either recognized themselves as being institutionally racist or have adopted a definition of institutional racism within their race-equality policies" (106). She refers to these statements as "nonperformative," because although they acknowledge responsibility for past errors, they disavow the need for further redress (107). Further, Ahmed cites the inaction countenanced by such statements as a feature, rather than a flaw: "In my model of the 'nonperformative,' the failure of the speech act to do what it says is not a failure of intent or even circumstance, but it is actually what the speech act is doing" (105). In politics, we judge speakers' pronouncements as ineffectual when they dispense with action in favor of "mere rhetoric." This critique underlies political scientist Cathy Cohen's call to distinguish between actions that offer substantively affirmative responses to the question "Do Black lives matter?" and gestures of "performative solidarity" that consist only of saying "Black Lives Matter."

Since taking up J. L. Austin's defining work of speech act theory, *How to Do Things With Words*, critics have devoted heightened attention to the political possibilities of language that not only means something but also *does* what it says. Although performative utterances sometimes fail to bring about their desired effects, it is instructive, in political matters, to attend to the implications of pronouncements that are both rhetorical and speculative in nature. Examples of these utterances include provocations, incitements, and assertions; these aspirational, defiant, and even utopian statements can motivate social action and thereby cross the threshold between meaning and doing. By asking what is at stake when speakers use the phrase "Black Lives Matter," in its original context as well as in its subsequent iterations, we might work toward understanding—but not prescribing—what this rhetorical act makes possible.

Making Speech Acts Meaningful

When Alicia Garza read reports of George Zimmerman's acquittal for killing Trayvon Martin in July 2013, she drafted a *Facebook* status decrying the injustice. Her initial message, which she describes as a "love letter to Black folks," culminated thusly: "Black people. I love you. I love us. Our lives matter" (King). Garza's friend, prison abolition activist Patrisse Cullors, reiterated the message of grief and hope, adding the hashtag #blacklivesmatter, on *Facebook*. From an expression of shared condolences that Cullors shared on the *Facebook* walls of her friends, which they in turn shared with their contacts, #blacklivesmatter became the first term of, in Garza's words, "a proposition: 'twin, #blacklivesmatter campaign? can we discuss this? I have ideas. I am thinking we can do a whole social media/ all out in the streets organizing effort'" (King). After the pair contacted a third interlocutor, Opal Tometi of the Black Alliance for Just Immigration, the three women coined the hashtag #BlackLivesMatter, and it spread virally on Twitter before appearing on banners at demonstrations across the country. Mobilizations of diverse participants under the herald of #BlackLivesMatter have underscored the inherent value of coalitions among constituencies otherwise divided by class, color, citizenship, age, gender, and ability. In a PBS interview, Tory Russell of Hands Up United highlighted this difference between the current activism and the conventions of familiar American social movements:

> "This is not the Civil Rights Movement . . . [T]his is the oppressed people's movement. So when you see us, you're gonna see some gay folk, you're gonna see some queer folk, you're gonna see some poor black folk, you're gonna see some brown folk, you're gonna see some white people, and we're all out here for the same reasons."

Through this expansive formulation, like Cullors's reminder that "All Black Lives Matter," these organizers intend to ward off tendencies toward hierarchy along gendered and sexual lines and instead return attention to the mantra's origins in the variegated, heterogeneous context of Black women's discourse (Henderson 5). In Tometi's words, "The movement is about creating a multiracial democracy that works for all black folks. We have to stand up for all marginalized people—black transgendered [sic] people, black immigrants, black people struggling in poverty" (Milloy B1).

The ongoing deaths that result in reminders that "Black Lives Matter" substantiate the speakers' belief in the statement's necessity and attest to the urgency of the demands it conveys. Through its utterance and repetition, users of the phrase form a circle of protection to encompass those interlocutors for whom the utterance is imperative. In addition, the *assertion*, as the particular form this utterance takes, anticipates a response to its conditions of possibility—even if it cannot name that response in advance. As a statement made to and for someone, the assertion is a particular kind of speech act: "grounded in an occasion, an assertion is a purposive act entraining very real effects" (Munro 27). In the case of "Black Lives Matter," the assertion calls for a change in the conditions that make its utterance necessary. It is at once axiomatic and speculative; grounded in the occasion of state-sanctioned violence, the statement is not just the invocation of a self-evident truth in which the speaker avers belief but also, in a special sense, a promise to uphold this truth, to make the implications of knowing it manifest in the future in ways that are not apparent in the present. Understanding the hope with which Garza, Cullors, and Tometi coined "Black Lives Matter" requires that we link a race-conscious analysis of past state violence to ongoing, collective responses in the present and future.

As an assertion, "Black Lives Matter" entails both an "illocutionary force"—the deed of professing solidarity that is more or less accomplished in the act of saying these words—as well as some "propositional content" or "perlocutionary effects" (Lycan 179). There is a speculative quality to this aspect of the statement's meaning. As a perlocutionary act, its implications are inchoate in the moment of its utterance and can only be fulfilled through further actions. Andrew Munro calls the investigation of this speculative dimension of meaning "perlocutionary inquiry" (31). I would argue that it is their simultaneously rhetorical and speculative nature that makes perlocutionary acts so confounding for speech act theory. Making perlocutionary utterances requires a speaker to speculate about the listener's response: "a listener's passive comprehension of a speaker's meaning is a 'scientific fiction,' as all real and integral understanding constitutes nothing other than the initial preparatory stage of a response (in whatever form it may be actualized)" (Bakhtin qtd. in Kill 220). Thus, perlocutions do not necessarily assume that listeners will demonstrate a successful "uptake" of their meaning; rather, they give listeners the responsibility to *make* them meaningful.

The Meanings Speech Acts Make

Perlocutionary utterances like "Black Lives Matter" not only do what they say (assert a belief), but they also aim to persuade, and all persuasion runs the risk of failure. Whether I mean it or not, I might say "Black Lives Matter" enjoining you to accept or reject my statement's implications. Such is the power of the assertion "I love you"—which we now know to be implicit in the prototypical utterance of "Black Lives Matter"—that it forms the basis for Jacques Derrida's signature contribution to the theory of performativity (Miller 232). In similar fashion, fiction writer and critic Samuel Delany notes the discourse of desire is so powerful and the "terror of rejection" so great that actually saying to the object of one's desire "I like you. Do you like me?" seems unthinkable (16). These meaningful assertions are fraught with the risk of conveying truths about the speaker—truths that might place one at odds with the state or with one's beloved—and implicating the addressee in their consequences.

To profess one's love for Black life in the face of armed indifference engages a speaker and addressee in a profound undertaking. It is daring to make the statement's truth known, its presence felt, by the state and the public and thereby challenging their power to devalue Black lives through violence and its legitimation; however, depending on the speaker's identity and the listener's judgment, any given speech act can take on radically different meanings. "It is normal," empirically speaking, "for different hearers to assign to the same speaker a high, moderate, or low credibility" (Marcu 1727). Furthermore, "the relevant features of the speaker," which qualities of the speaker will facilitate a given listener's assent and which qualities will mitigate persuasion, "are influenced by the groups to which the hearer belongs or wants to belong." We are all addressed in various ways by the phrase "Black Lives Matter," whether we are likely listeners, skeptics, or joining in as "unintended hearers" (Kang 61). Part of what is at stake in the utterance is the listener's willingness to join a struggle initiated by Black women and to maintain the rigorous commitment to inclusion it entails. Our varied investments in state power, the groups to which we belong or want to belong, play a critical role in what we are willing to demand of the state as well.

To believe that "Black Lives Matter" means something unique to each of us and to reiterate it accordingly is to join in the risky undertaking that Charles Peirce called "speculative rhetoric," to act on the knowledge that the implications of our words are subject to "different uptakes effected by rhetorical agents with diverse pasts and disjunctive present purposes" (Munro 31-2). We may choose to reject the proposition that saying "Black Lives Matter" necessarily implicates the state, or even try to deny the urgency of saying it, but that will not make the utterance meaningless. Not all speakers and listeners acknowledge that "#BlackLivesMatter as a rallying call was meant to undermine all forms of state violence" against all Black people (Cullors). But we can choose to make that what it means.

Works Cited

Ahmed, Sara. "The Nonperformativity of Antiracism." *Meridians: Feminism, Race, Transnationalism*7.1 (2006): 104-26. Print.
Allen, James, and John Littlefield. *Musarium: Without Sanctuary: Lynching Photography in America*. Twin Palms Publishers, 2000-2005. Web.
Berman, Mark, and Wesley Lowery. "The 12 Key Highlights from the DOJ's Scathing Ferguson Report." *Post Nation*. The Washington Post, 4 Mar. 2015. Web.
Cohen, Cathy. "#DoBlackLivesMatter? On Black Death and LGBTQ Politics." CLAGS: The Center for LGBTQ Studies. The Graduate Center of the City University of New York. 12 Dec. 2014. Kessler Award Lecture.
Cullors, Patrisse. "All Black Lives Matter: #BlackLivesMatter Co-founder Patrisse Cullors on De-Centering Cis-Sisters and Brothers and Making the Movement Trans-inclusive." *Ebony*. Ebony Magazine, 18 Dec. 2014. Web.
Delany, Samuel. "The Rhetoric of Sex/The Discourse of Desire." *Shorter Views: Queer Thoughts and the Politics of the Paraliterary*. Middletown, CT: Wesleyan UP, 2000. 3-40. Web. 31 Mar. 2015.
Gadbois, Barry (BarryGadbois). "Cops have a right to defend themselves and an obligation to protect you. #BlueLivesMatter #Ferguson." 25 Nov. 2014, 12:19 a.m. Tweet.
Henderson, Mae. "Speaking in Tongues: Dialogics, Dialectics, and the Black Woman Writer's Literary Tradition." *The Scholar and Feminist XXX: Past Controversies, Present Challenges, Future Feminisms*. Spec. issue of *Scholar & Feminist Online* 3.3/4.1 (2005). Web. 6 Aug. 2015.
Hytten, Kathy, and Amee Adkins. "Thinking Through a Pedagogy of Whiteness." *Educational Theory* 51.4 (2001): 433-50. Print.
Ifill, Gwen. Interview with Molly Greiber, Tory Russell, and Jessica Pierce. "Why Do You March? Young Protesters Explain What Drives Them." *Washington Week*. 9 Dec. 2014. Web.
Jurecic, Ann. " Empathy and the Critic." *College English* 74.1 (2011): 10-27. Print.
Kang, Qiang. "On Perlocutionary Act." *Studies in Literature and Language* 6.1 (2013): 60-4. Print.
Kill, Melanie. "Acknowledging the Rough Edges of Resistance: Negotiation of Identities for First-Year Composition." *College Composition and Communication* 58.2 (2006). Print.

King, Jamilah. "#blacklivesmatter: How Three Friends Turned a Spontaneous Facebook Post into a Global Phenomenon." *The California Sunday Magazine*. California Sunday, 1 Mar. 2015. Web.

Kurzon, Dennis. "The Speech Act Status of Incitement: Perlocutionary Acts Revisited." *Journal of Pragmatics* 29 (1996): 571-96. Print.

Lycan, William. "Speech Acts and Illocutionary Force." *Philosophy of Language: A Contemporary Introduction*. London, Eng.: Routledge, 1999. 173-86. Web. 23 Mar. 2015.

Marcu, Daniel. "Perlocutions: The Achilles' Heel of Speech Act Theory." *Journal of Pragmatics* 32 (2000): 1719-41. Print.

Miller, J. Hillis. "Performativity as Performance/Performativity as Speech Act: Derrida's Special Theory of Performativity." *South Atlantic Quarterly* 106.2 (2007): 219-35. Print.

Milloy, Courtland. "Marginalized Black Women Are at Heart of the Matter." *Washington Post* 20 May 2015: B1. Print.

Munro, Andrew. "Reading Austin Rhetorically." *Philosophy and Rhetoric* 46.1 (2013): 22-43. Print.

Obama, Barack. "Clip from 2015 State of the Union Address." *C-SPAN*. 20 Jan. 2015. Web. 4 June 2015.

Trawalter, Sophie, Kelly Hoffman, and Adam Waytz. "Racial Bias in Perception of Others' Pain." *PLoS One* 7.11 (2012): n. pag. Web. 6 Aug. 2015.

Worthen, W.B. "Drama, Performativity, and Performance." *PMLA* 113.5 (1998): 1093-107. Print.

REFLECTIONS

Reflections is on the Web at https://reflectionsjournal.net/

Reflections, a peer reviewed journal, provides a forum for scholarship on public rhetoric, civic writing, service-learning, and community literacy. Originally founded as a venue for teachers, researchers, students and community partners to share research and discuss the theoretical, political and ethical implications of community-based writing and writing instruction, Reflections publishes a lively collection of scholarship on public rhetoric and civic writing, occasional essays and stories both from and about community writing and literacy projects, interviews with leading workers in the field, and reviews of current scholarship touching on these issues and topics.

The Challenges Faced by African Americans in the 19th Century

Michelle Hall Kells's article is one of the most powerful rhetorical personal narratives we've received from an author. As she said to the *Reflections* editor, this was one of the best and most difficult articles she's ever written given she was working with "transgenre resources of the personal academic essay to examine the politics of gender and questions of privilege across academic and public spheres." Focusing on how Writing Across Communities developed from her personal experiences with her son's disabilities and hardships and her experiences working with communities within and outside of academia, she takes readers on a poignant journey.

A Prison Story: Public Rhetoric, Community Writing, and the Politics of Gender

Michelle Hall Kells

Abstract: This article enacts the transgenre resources of the personal academic essay to examine the politics of gender and questions of privilege across academic and public spheres. The author interweaves prose, poetry, criticism, and argument to interrogate the practice of transcultural citizenship and the transdisciplinary project of Writing Across Communities.[1]

Despair

Crumpled newspaper, the bags he carries, the clothes he wears.
Stiff as an old woman's knees, shambling through security,
scanning the boarding gate. A trembling animal in a crate,
caged, frightened, he searches for the exit.

There are no quaint messages to send, no Christmas newsletters,
no charming receptions, no cut-glass bowls, no yellow paper napkins,
no proper etiquette, only this brittle young man on my arm,
silent, the thread of spittle is a pearl on his lip.

No longer an infant in a clear, plastic incubator, jaundiced and bawling, no
longer the toe-headed child, deep and soulful, no longer the college boy I
waved off to Chile, with ski poles,
two volumes of Neruda, my dictionary, a year's supply of lithium.
Shell-shocked, panicked, he reaches across the aisle, "I'm sorry, Mom. Please take me home."

This essay grows out of a story. It is offered in response to the urging of the participants in my Community Writing Conference workshop, "Citizens Scholars and the Cultural Rhetorical Ecology of Writing Across Communities," in Boulder, Colorado on October 15, 2015.[2] During this workshop, we engaged six dimensions of institutional culture as generative themes or *topoi* for cultivating cultural ecologies of writing (Appendix A). Invoking an alliterative laundry list of talking points I coined in terms of *Principles; Privilege; Partnerships; Populations (People & Places); Pedagogies & Practices; Programs and Projects*, I presented a series of inductive moments to map the development of the University of New Mexico Writing Across Communities initiative (Gallegos). Through cross-talk with the twenty-five workshop participants around these six *topoi*, the initial purpose of the workshop was framed as helping emergent leaders build engaged infrastructure for community writing in their home institutions. Toward these purposes, I argued that implementing Writing Across Communities as a hermeneutic project that cuts across disciplinary, institutional, and intellectual boundaries, can help to efficaciously enact both deliberative democratic practice and the transformational possibilities of agonistic pluralism toward the inclusion of historically underrepresented populations in the work of community writing across academic, public, and professional spheres.

But in the process of telling the origin story of Writing Across Communities, I confessed to my workshop participants that the reasons that I maintain my commitment to the work of Writing Across Communities remain embedded in a personal narrative. I have looked to poetry more often than to prose to describe the ineffable experience of losing my child to mental illness and the prison system.

NCWAC 2012 Summit Group

I first publically recounted the catalyzing moment of becoming an advocate of community writing in the climate of radical intimacy at the 2012 Summit of the National Consortium of Writing Across Communities (NCWAC) in Santa Fe, New Mexico on July 15, 2012 (Writing Across Communities Resource Site). In the rustic, wood-plank banquet room of the Cowgirl BarBQ on Guadalupe Street in historic Santa Fe, the city of "blessed faith," a group of thirty junior and senior scholars from across the nation deliberated together for three days about the role of community writing in the field of Composition Studies.

Homeless Woman at UC Boulder Community Writing Conference

Three years lapsed between the first telling and the re-telling of this story at the workshop for University of Colorado, Boulder Conference on Community Writing on that early October 15, 2015 morning. The black, mentally ill homeless woman pushing her shopping cart across the UC Boulder campus at 7:30 a.m. as I parked my car moved me to speak. The only other person of color I would meet over the next few days on campus or around Boulder was the young black man from Jamaica, a custodian and international work study student, who was taping electrical cords to the floor of my conference room. I invited him to join our workshop, which he enthusiastically did, still dressed in his janitorial uniform sitting among us predominantly white academics. His presence demanded an equally authentic and vulnerable act as the guest to his campus. So I took the risk of self- disclosure. Meanwhile, over the three years since I first told my story, the conversations changed, the actors transformed, and the narrative kept evolving while the issues, the *topoi*, the places where my arguments for the hermeneutic project called "Writing Across Communities." rested in silence—living and breathing at the heart of a prison story.

As scholar, teacher, and educational advocate, I am interested in the writing lives of students beyond the classroom. The transcultural, translingual, and transnational universe in which our students live and write in the 21st century, finds expression through polyvocalic, shape- shifting rhetorics and *trans-genred* discourses. There are no stable texts. The language and literacy practices of vulnerable communities and ethnolinguistically diverse populations represent the primary sphere of concern for which Writing Across Communities as an advocacy project has been directly engaged (politically, rhetorically, pedagogically, and theoretically) since 2004.

In February 2004 during my job talk at UNM, I offered this proposal: "Our classrooms have been think tanks for science and industry for decades. What might our classrooms look like if we cultivated think tanks for citizenship?" Writing Across Communities at UNM became part of that answer. Deploying the military term of the "think tank" was not a purely serendipitous metaphor. The long standing alignment of UNM with Los Alamos and Sandia Laboratories in New Mexico called for, in my mind, an educational counter-discourse in the cultivation of citizens and scholars. The UNM Department of English Professional Writing Program had strong historical ties to Sandia Laboratories. I simply wondered aloud if we might cultivate other community alignments not engaged in the business of making nuclear arsenal.

The conversation for Writing Across Communities (WACommunities) began in earnest at UNM during my first semester as an assistant professor in the Fall 2004, in my graduate- level practicum, ENGL 537 and my undergraduate advanced expository writing course ENGL 320, Writing Across Academic and Pubic Cultures. I adopted the organic term of "cultural ecologies of writing" as the conceptual metaphor for Writing Across Communities to begin to seed a local counter-discourse. The strategic use of this organic conceptualization system and organizing model, manifested itself over time in the multiple generative ways that WACommunities took root locally and nationally for the next decade. On a campus visit to UNM in 2009, Linda Adler Kassner described us as growing ivy. During a guest lecture at UNM, Juan Guerra, two years later, depicted the Writing Across Communities project as rhizomatic, a deep network below the surface of earth emanating from a single root system. Cultivating a project identity, a shapeshifting ethos resilient and responsive enough to endure the vicissitudes of a volatile decade of mobilization and institutionalization, represents one of the greatest strengths of WACommunities.

A growing constellation of stakeholders and scholars has since traced this local, national, and transnational conversation in a number of books and journal articles (Writing Across Communities Workshop Working Papers Resources). Several of these WACommunities scholarly articles have been anthologized. One received a national journal award. The forthcoming Oxford University Press TESOL Encyclopedia will include an entry for "Writing Across Communities." Trust me, there was no blueprint for any of this. The inauspicious beginning of the national WACommunities conversation happened at a 2005 CCCC panel presentation in San Francisco in the basement of an old convention hall contemplating the possibilities of what I audaciously proposed as "Writing Across Communities" with a handful of participants. It was a moment without apparent consequence.

The synchrony of the moment, however, was more efficacious for the field of Composition Studies than I realized. It was in this time and place that same year that Michael Moore and John Warnick launched the *Journal of Community Literacy*. WACommunities as a construct and a emergent advocacy movement indexed a change in progress, a paradigm shift, a political turn in the field first articulated by Steve Parks and Eli Goldblatt in their 2000 *College English* article, "Writing Beyond the Curriculum: Fostering New Collaborations in Literacy." Four years after that uneventful presentation positing the invention of the UNM Writing Across Communities project, I presented a paper once again extolling the need for a new model of community- based writing across the curriculum at the 2009 CCCC, also hosted in San Francisco. It was an occasion when the political became personal for me, the personal become political, and professional turn of our field brought me from the CCCC convention hall to the prison cell.

Why Study Disability? 313

POLITICAL CONSCIOUSNESS AND
TRANS-GENRED REALITIES

The phone call came as I sat in the 2009 CCCC convention ballroom in San Francisco listening to Mike Rose's featured speaker presentation on working class academics. I remember thinking to myself before my cell phone rang, "Why do so few women academics tell their stories?" While the list of masculine narratives of academic life abound, I still remain hard pressed to list an equal number of feminine narratives. Elaine Richardson's *PHD to Ph.D: How Education Saved My Life* and Nancy Welch's *Living Room: Teaching Public Writing in a Privatized World* are among the few to come to mind. Issues of authority and gender seem to constrain the act of *trans-genred* writing among women academics. And I am beginning to understand why. I silenced my cell phone as I left the ballroom to take the call from the chaplain of the Monterey County Jail. My son Jacob, incarcerated and suffering from bipolar disorder, was on suicide watch. The chaplain asked me to come. I stood stunned and alone. My son had disappeared more than three years before this moment, living among the homeless on unknown streets, resurfacing, and disappearing again. I had searched for him in every street, in every city I traveled—unconsciously and consciously calling his name wherever the professional conference circuit took me.

I found my way to the hotel concierge desk. There are things a mother imagines she will do for a child. I had done them all: the piano lessons, the band concerts, the soccer games, the commencement ceremonies, the celebrations, the comings-and-goings of youth. This was not one of those things. I simply could not bear the thought of seeing my son. With the help of a beautiful young woman named Beatriz at the concierge's desk at San Francisco Marriott, I made the journey to the Monterey County Jail to claim the shell of the young man that was my son. Uncertain if I should make the trip after the chaplain informed me that Jacob had refused all visitors for the past few months, Beatriz told me, "Go. The guards will call his name and tell him that his mother is there for him. I was an inmate at the Monterey County Jail myself. A stupid mistake. A DUI. I was too afraid and ashamed to tell my family where I was. And I waited until my mother came and called my name, 'Beatriz, *mi'ja*!' *Por eso* you must go." And so with the help and guidance of Beatriz, a bright angel, who reserved for me the last rental car available on St. Patrick's Day weekend in San Francisco and located the prison unit and the visiting hour schedule for the Monterey County Jail, I found Jacob.

Death of a Son

To the woman in the social office who dismissed the felony charges
for the bottle of water he stole from her purse.

To the officer who found him in a gutter
howling, a coyote to the L.A. moon.

To the truck driver
who saw him walking down the side of a
freeway, a somnambulist without shoes.

To the nurse
in the Colorado pysch
unit who tried to find
his mother.

To the medics who wrapped him
tightly, carried him from home,
thank you.
Final snapshot of a son.

In *Tragic Sense of Life*, philosopher Miguel de Unamuno contends: "Consciousness (*conscientia*) is participated knowledge, is co-feeling, and co-feeling is com-passion. Love personalizes all that it loves. Only by personalizing it can we fall in love with an idea" (120).

The idea of "Writing Across Communities" took form over the course of a ten-year trajectory around a set of principles, a hermeneutic project that has lived and grown on the margins of the academy—a counter-discourse to the neoliberal rhetoric of education as property. As the university emptied out our classrooms and the field of Composition Studies dis-embodied the teaching of writing into the digital sphere, WACommunities pressed us as students, community members, and faculty into closer contact with one another. Falling in love with the idea of Writing Across Communities for me coincided with the emergence of consciousness. As Miguel de Unamuno asserts consciousness "is only reached through an act of collision, through suffering more or less severe, through the sense of one's own limits" (120).

WACommunities is and remains an act of imaginative fiction—the kind of Midrash or emergence narrative pressing against the limits of the legal imagination of the academy. In the *Abraham Joshua Heschel: Essential Writings,* this evocative Jewish theologian writes of radical amazement. Heschel contends that the "greatest hindrance to knowledge is our adjustment to conventional notions, to mental clichés" (58). "Wonder," Heschel writes, "goes beyond knowledge" (59). Spiritually and intellectually "we cannot live by merely reiterating borrowed or inherited knowledge" (59). As an intellectual project, WACommunities resonates with the emergent consciousness that my dear friend and colleague Chuck Schuster so graciously indulged some twenty years ago with the publication of *Attending to the Margin: Writing, Researching, and Teaching on the Front Lines* (1999) and *Latino/a Discourses: On Language, Identity, and Literacy Education* (2004). For reasons both personal and professional, I have been writing and teaching from places that Victor Villanueva once termed "Edge City" for more than two decades, irrepressibly moved to engage the counter-narratives of the field (Villanueva). These marginal tendencies, however, are more than a romantic fascination or fetishizing of difference. These are *trans-genred* realities.

The term WACommunities denotes a principled and systemic institutional response to linguistic imperialism in K-16 literacy education across and beyond the disciplines informing curriculum development, administrative advocacy, assessment, research, and extra-institutional initiatives in support of ethnolinguistic minority populations (Kells "Linguistic Contacts" and Kells, Ballester, Villanueva "Latino/a Discourses").

WAC as a construct is simply too narrow for the work we need to be doing on behalf of historically underserved writers. However, Community Writing as a recently termed subfield is no more capacious in my mind. "Community Writing" as a cover term is an overly neutral construct, de-politicized container, an empty trope, and a vague conceptual metaphor. Searching for a robust conceptual umbrella to describe this work remains a thorny question for those of us in the field. My criticism of "Community Writing" as a subfield echoes my critique of traditional WAC: both subfields privilege white, English-speaking academics voyeuristically engaging curricular genre and discourses in and beyond elite universities.

First, all writing is community writing. All writing—academic, professional, civic writing—is cultural and community-based. Every discipline and every institution is saturated with culture and constituted as a polyglot discourse community. Secondly, "community writing" is a noun, passive, fixed, product-centered. Finally, "community writing" situates writers outside of spaces of institutional power. In my experience tackling the prison industrial complex and mental health system on behalf of my son, helping marginalized citizens to situate themselves *insides spaces of institutional power* in order to rewrite their lives, is the only way to help them access the resources for social well-being and civic participation.

So what are we really talking about when we talk about "Community Writing" and the public turn in Composition Studies toward writing beyond the curriculum? Are we talking about the (uneven) exercise, circulation, and concentration of privilege, power, and position across writing communities within and beyond academic institutional structures? Are we talking about a resistance movement away from our fetishized pre-occupation with first year college writers and curricular-based writing? Are we talking about the need for the field of Composition Studies to step away from our over-determined focus on entry-level college writers as the be-all-and-end-all of college literacy education? Are we trying to climb out of our own occupational neurosis as Compositionist, move beyond the classroom, and engage the writing lives of students and their communities of belonging in more meaningful ways?

WACommunities, in contrast, represents a free-floating gerund form of the verb "to write;" it is active, and process-centered. WACommunities promotes critical pedagogies and practices across a spectrum of discourse communities (academic, civic, and professional) using writing to learn as well as writing for engagement practices. WACommunities is political, seeking to align and coordinate institutional resources toward enhancing transcultural citizenship and cultivating rhetorical agency among historically excluded groups through writing practices across students' multiple spheres of belonging (Guerra, "Enacting Institutional Change" and "Language, Culture, Identity, and Citizenship"; Zawacki and Cox).

This initiative has functioned as an intellectual commonwealth, nationally and internationally, circulating WACommunities principles and practices to other sites and institutions for more than ten years.

There are no trademarks or copyrights. Of note, Baltimore Community College recently adopted the WACommunities construct as did Broward College System QEP. WACommunities programs (curricular, administrative, cross-institutional and extra- institutional) seek to extend writing support for ethnolinguistically diverse and other vulnerable populations vertically and horizontally throughout the entire process of literacy education in and beyond the curriculum. Site-specific applications of WACommunities approaches expand the limits of traditional WAC/WID models by integrating WACommunities principles and practices into traditional institutional structures.

Writing Across Communities evolved in the disturbance ecology of my own institution at the UNM, surviving the turbulence of four different presidential regimes, the unrelenting chaos in my own Department of English, alongside the devastating global economic shifts of the Great Recession. WACommunities is all about process— deliberative, generative, disruptive, and restorative processes. I have extolled the successes and celebrated the possibilities of Writing Across Communities in nearly a dozen conference presentations and an equal number of articles. But I won't be writing about these outcomes in this article. Instead, I want to talk about the dissonances, the shadow ecology of doing "WAC with a difference."

Writing in and through Disturbance Ecologies

The phone call came at 7:30 a.m. on the morning of March 10, 2010. Chuck Paine, my friend and colleague at UNM. Our colleague, Hector Torres, and his lover, Stefania Gray, a UNM graduate student in our program, had been stalked and murdered by her jealous ex-husband. The department grappled with the trauma and the aftermath of this violence over the next year. Faculty retired and moved away. Consequently, the UNM Rhetoric and Writing Program was reduced to two tenured faculty members: Chuck Paine and myself, the lone survivors.

Meanwhile, my own son remained incarcerated at Monterrey County Jail, psychotic and in a solitary confinement—deemed incompetent to stand trial for stealing a vegetable truck, casting heads of lettuce in his wake across a California highway from Salinas to Gilroy, the Garlic Capital of the world. Trauma and violence creates a rupture that community seeks to fill.

In the wake of these losses, several faculty members in the Department of English organized a UNM symposium on Domestic Violence to honor our fallen colleagues in September 2010. The following year, UNM graduate student, Brian Hendrickson, and the Writing Across Communities graduate-student governed WAC Alliance, coordinated the 2011 UNM Civil Rights Symposium on Mental Health and Social Justice. Transformation emerges out of death in uneven and unpredictable ways.

Ofrenda Table in Honor of Hector Torres and Stefania Gray

Grief

The anguish of loving falls
like grit into a perfect cup of tea,
children born and lost in the slow decay
of living, we write
new poems, make
desert from ash, stirring
dreams out of the piñon-scorched morning
on this blue-snow mesa.

In *The Power of Identity*, Manuel Castells elegantly theorizes the forms of institutional cycles of identity-building as conditioned by social power. Castells argues that the "construction of identities uses building material from history, from geography, from biology, from productive and reproductive institutions, from collective memory, and from personal fantasies, from power apparatuses, and religious revelations" (7). In brief, institutions and individuals draw upon these ideological building materials consciously and unconsciously. The theory works as an explanatory tool for understanding the process of identity formation of WACommunities as well. Castells offers three models to describe and identity these building formations: *legitimizing identity* (advanced by dominant institutional discourses); *resistance identity* (introduced by the counter-discourses of devalued and/or stigmatized groups); *project identity* (promoted toward new identity formations in order redefine the social position of historically excluded groups).

Over the course of the next decade, WACommunities migrated across all three of Castells' identity formations, reinventing itself through legitimizing institutional discourses, engaging resistance counter- discourses, and enacting project identities constellated through alternative discourse formations. The opportunity to interrogate these identity formation processes with other Community Writing, advocates inspired my decision to host the first summit of the loosely organized National Consortium of Writing Across Communities (NCWAC). Declaring the need for the formation of NCWAC in October 2010 during an invited speaker presentation at Auburn University, I proposed with WAC director Margaret Marshall, hosting the first NCWAC Summit in July 2012 in Santa Fe, New Mexico.

Drafting the work-in-progress vision statement of the National Consortium of Writing Across Communities signaled a move toward adopting a legitimizing identity by building alignments with other subfields across the national professional organization of CCC. The NCWAC vision statement emerged out of the conversation with a number of stakeholders and was drafted at Mary Mac's Tea Room in Atlanta during CCCC 2011. Seeking out this historically significant space, a safety zone for activists of the 1960s African American civil rights movement, my colleagues and I joined in conversation about the formation of NCWAC. This intimate and diverse cadre of community-engagement folks includeding Jackie Jones Royster, Juan Guerra, Steve Parks, Eli Goldblatt, Tiffany Rousculp, and Kevin Roozen. The following working statement ultimately set the terms and the agenda for the 2012 NCWAC Summit that convened more than a year later in July 2012, coinciding with the International Folk Art Festival in Santa Fe. The NCWAC vision statement reads:

> The National Consortium of Writing Across Communities represents a constellation of stakeholders locally and nationally centered around educational principles and cultural practices that promote the generative (creative and life-sustaining) ecological relationships of language and literacy to the maintenance and wellbeing of human communities. The NCWAC seeks to guide curriculum development, stimulate resource-sharing, support multi-modal approaches to community arts, cultivate networking, and promote research in language practices and literacy education throughout the nation to support local colleges and universities working to serve the vulnerable communities within their spheres of influence. (Kells, Writing Communities Newsletter 2011 and 2012; Writing Across Communities Workshop)

Invitations to scholars across subfields in WPA, WAC, Second Language Writing, Writing Centers, Community Writing, Basic Writing, and Service Learning/Civic Engagement followed. We reached out to graduate students and faculty at every corner of the nation, seeking a racially, ethnolinguistically, institutionally, and regionally diverse cohort of NCWAC Summit participants. We invited participants to deliver a five-minute position statement as a springboard for deliberation. The goals and objectives of the 2012 NCWAC Summit included the following action items:

> The five-minute position papers should respond in some way to the objectives for the Summit and/or the overarching goals of the Consortium. The objectives are as follows:
>
> Constitute the NCWAC vision/mission (goals/objectives) statement; Articulate and define the NCWAC organizational structure; Draft the NCWAC Intellectual statement with professional guidelines for scholars of community literacy and their institutions; Establish the terms/benefits of NCWAC membership as well as a plan for developing a membership

directory; Develop a plan for implementing the NCWAC resource website.

Guiding our achievement of the above objectives should be a consideration of the overarching goals of the Consortium to: Promote deliberative democratic practice in the public sphere and community literacy projects; Advocate for culturally- relevant, linguistically-informed approaches to literacy education for historically-underserved student populations; Promote curriculum development for Writing Across Communities approaches to First Year Writing, WAC programs, Writing Centers, etc.; Mentor graduate students and junior faculty (graduate school through tenure) so as to make it safe and feasible for them to do the scholarly work of community literacy; Promote resource-sharing and collaborative scholarly projects between faculty and graduate students across institutions. (Writing Communities and Writing Across Communities Workshop Working Papers)

The exigence and radical intimacy of the 2012 NCWAC Summit afforded me the rare occasion to discuss the reactive institutional cycles that subversive movements (in general) and WACommunities (more specifically) engender.

In addition to telling my own story, I invited colleagues and graduate students at the 2012 NCWAC Summit to grapple together over the vision statement that had framed our gathering. Among these aforementioned goals and objectives, I urged the group to achieve this single important outcome: the formation of a national network to make visible and public the work of community writing in and beyond the curriculum. I argued passionately that if we were going to mentor new leaders into the field—encourage graduate students and new professors to transgress boundaries of all kinds (institutional, disciplinary, intellectual, linguistic)—we need to be more transparent about the political implications and inevitable backlash this kind of work provokes.

WACommunities is a big idea with a sharp political edge. It is a capacious notion of WAC and Community Writing informed by Rhetoric, Sociolinguistics, Critical Theory, New Literacy Studies, and Composition Studies. This "big-ness" is both the source of its success as well as its marginalization as an educational movement locally here in New Mexico (and nationally). Aligning subfields such as

WAC and Community Writing alongside Second Language Writing, Service Learning, and Basic Writing in conversation to attend to the question of how to better serve marginalized writers, was the overarching impetus for the 2012 NCWAC Summit. The intersectionality of these subfields represented an occasion for both reflection and disputation. Moreover, the cross-pollination of these subfields was designed to complicate the conversation and diversify stakeholders racially, linguistically, politically, and regionally. Reflecting on his experience of the 2012 NCWAC Summit, Brian Hendrickson observes:

Writing Across Communities, then, makes an important contribution to the ongoing conversation calling for a radical reenvisioning of the academic mission in light of recent developments in fields invested in literacy advocacy and instruction. However, advocates for this re-envisioning, in performing public intellectual work in service to the most vulnerable communities within their spheres of influence, are likely to render themselves vulnerable to those forces in the academy invested in maintaining conventional modes of disciplinary knowledge-making and professionalization—modes that still hold sway over programmatic missions and tenure review boards inclined to apply to public intellectual work the pejorative *service*. ("The Hard Work of Imagining" 116)

I continue to puzzle over this conundrum as an educational activist and citizen scholar. Perhaps other scholars can help make better sense of this dilemma.

I look to Albert O. Hirschman's *The Rhetoric of Reaction: Perversity, Futility, Jeopardy* to help parse up the shadow ecology that has embattled the proponents of WACommunities locally and nationally. In *Language, Culture, Identity, and Citizenship in College Classrooms and Communities,* Juan Guerra poignantly represents the struggle of WACommunities advocates transgressing the limits of the rhetorical imagination of the academy. Reactive rhetoric, as feminist and civil rights activists have long asserted, is always an embodied discourse. The ad hominem attacks that characterize transgressive activists within and beyond the academy, women particularly, are embodied in some pretty revealing ways. Among the list of epithets lobbed across the political trenches of intellectual turf wars, the term "hard ass" is especially telling. I am reminded of the 1970s bumper sticker, "Well behaved women rarely make history."

The public representations of my work and professional *ethos* in the scholarship, however, might suggest a mostly happy journey without the grief, the loss, and the rupture (Guerra "Writing for Transcultural;" Enacting Institutional Change."). But leaving it at that would be an incomplete story—a story without exigence. If we are women, black, brown, indigenous, immigrant, non-native speakers of English, elderly, poor, uneducated, gay, mentally ill, incarcerated, we must learn to both endure and resist the micro-aggressions and violence to our dignity as part of the terrain of struggling to belong. Rhetorical listening as a "trope for interpretative invention and as a code for cross-cultural conduct" (1) that Krista Ratcliffe advances in *Rhetorical Listening: Identification, Gender, Whiteness* suggests one productive response to reactive rhetorics.

As I confessed to the participants of the 2015 UC Boulder Community Writing Conference workshop, the disturbance ecology of WACommunities represents a kind of parallel universe for me. The shadow ecology of my professional world mirrors the shadow ecology of my personal life. As a survivor, I exist in the tension between vulnerability and strength. Living in this New Mexico Zia cosmology, I have learned to accept the processes of disturbance ecologies as part of the natural cycle of life. The four sacred directions of the universe map onto the cycles of birth (east) and death (west), growth (south) and dormancy (north). Sometimes all we can do is just wait quietly. While rhetorical listening, like rhetorical silence, do have an important place in my experience, there is more to the story.

More than five years after my journey to the Monterey County Jail, my son's health, while stable and fully functioning as of October 2015, is ever-subject to change. Some might call it the "new normal." Ever living in the shadows of Edge City and residing precariously somewhere between the prison industrial complex, the mental health system, and the public education system, there are few constants for Jacob. He hasn't had a stable address for more than a year. A former research fellow at the United Nations, Jacob now lives and works among the indigent classes of this nation. The cycles of psychosis impact his entire universe of relationships—family, friends, neighbors, co-workers, and strangers. This is the body he inherited. This is the story he must live, this bitter, beautiful life. As he wrote in his 1998 Schreiner College honor's thesis titled, *Stepping In,* Jacob reflects on his journey in his poetic tribute to Santiago, Chile:

LUGARES

*Hay gente que trata de protegerse de
los cambios del corazón, Prefiero
experimentar los eventos internos mios y
visitar los lugares corrientes.*

Jacob in Chile

When healthy, Jacob is both a consumer and an employee serving as a service coordinator for the California State Department of Rehabilitation helping others with disabilities secure the public services toward health and wellbeing (MA thesis). He understands deeply the necessity of *la dignidad*, the social and spiritual values of supporting himself through his own labor and making his own contributions as a citizen to his community. As a gay man, surviving the revolving door of the prison system and the culture of incarceration, the trauma of sexual violence remains indelibly etched in his body and memory. Jacob's BA degree in English, his transcultural educational experiences in Latin America, bilingual literacy in Spanish, and MA degree in Economics, and professional background in non-profit organizational development—credentials cultivated throughout his college years before his ten-year struggle through the mental health and prison system from 2005 to 2015— have found a generative institutional space to grow.

Recently, Jacob helped his office in the Department of Rehabilitation coordinate a community civil rights celebration to mark the twenty- fifth anniversary of the Disability Act in Santa Rosa, California on August 2015. Jacob, and his biological father, who also suffers from bipolar disorder, have found common ground and degrees of wholeness living with their disabilities. However, I am sure that few of Jacob's cell mates, the countless young men of color lining the jails of this nation, have mothers with PhDs in public rhetoric to plead their cases. Even more importantly, white privilege continues to condition the outcome of criminal justice cases in our communities. Race, privilege, and civic literacy are inextricably linked. Neither WAC nor Community Writing as institutionalized models have effectively or historically aligned these political realities toward the promotion of writing across academic, civic, and professional spheres. WACommunities, nevertheless, continues to take up the conversation at the margins of the academy.

Within my own departmental sphere six years after the murder of Héctor Torres and Stefania Gray, the Héctor Torres Fellowship has generously funded a number of graduate student research projects, including the recent dissertation defended by WACommunities leader Christine Beagle García on the Chicana rhetoric of Dolores Huerta. The Department of English lounge, named in Héctor's honor, remains a poignant and painful reminder. However, Stefania Gray, a single mother of two young daughters, is all but forgotten, erased from institutional memory and the sordid story of murder and mayhem at UNM. Institutional memory, ever-shaped by institutional power, tends to cling the narratives that remake us all in its image. The civil rights symposia series sponsored by WACommunities at UNM has persistently advanced the argument that civic literacy is both a civil right and civic responsibility, tenaciously interrogating the teaching of writing in and beyond the institution (*Writing Communities* Newsletter 2011; 2012).

Trickster Tropes: Engaging the Rhetorics of Reaction

The public demand for openness, transparency, and inclusion that the WACommunities project demands is a threatening and radical rhetoric. Cultural critique without cultivation is an empty exercise. In the process, we must also turn the reflexive mirror back on ourselves. The 2015 University of Colorado, Boulder Conference on Community Writing, an occasion that stirred the re-telling of this story, both successfully and enthusiastically invigorated the national discussion on the work of public writing. However, the elite institutional location, the class privilege, and limited sub-disciplinary scope of the UC Boulder Conference on Community Writing regretfully privileged the participation of largely white intellectuals in a conversation from which historically-excluded communities remained conspicuously absent. Moreover, the two hundred dollar registration fee required for the 2015 UC Boulder Conference on Community Writing, prohibitively expensive to students of color, public school teachers, contingent faculty, the working poor, the homeless, and other vulnerable community members, consequently eliminated the dissonance and disputation that the 2012 NCWAC Summit sought to catalyze three years prior. Finally, the gift- giving economy advanced by the 2012 NCWAC Summit stands in stark contrast to the 2015 UC Boulder Conference on Community Writing's implementation of a capital accumulation economy and campaign of institution-building.

To be a generative, as well as aggravating force, is the solemn duty of the tenured professor. My colleague Kent Ryden, author of *Mapping the Invisible Landscape: Folklore, Writing and the Sense of Place*, calls himself a "paid contrarian." But it's even more than that. It is the charge for which the privileges of tenure afford us— the burden to push the boundaries of the social systems in which we live, the social biota of the academy and the intellectual life cycle of knowledge-making processes. Teaching is built upon this very paradox, this troubling contradictory dynamic, always conceived in the tension between transmitting received wisdom and engaging in the construction of new knowledge. Aggravation and agitation is our business.

What's at stake here? WACommunities as structure has no financial resources. It has operated entirely on a gift giving economy through donations of time and energy and grant support. WACommunities has no director. No reporting lines. No administrative staff. No tenure lines. No sanctioned institutional space. No commercial textbook contracts or royalties. Nevertheless, WACommunities organizers have sponsored over two dozen symposia, colloquia, conferences, Write On! Workshops, and Celebrations of Student Writing, serving thousands of students, faculty members, and local citizens in the past ten years—all completely free and open to the public with a banquet style-lunch included. Because of an organizational commitment to inclusion, all WACommunities events are completely open. There are no registration fees, no registration forms, no limits to participation. It's a come-as-you-are approach to democratic inclusion.

A sufficiency economic model or a kind parable of the loaves and fishes have shaped our ways of doing business. We build the moment and the community comes. We grapple with the ambiguities of providing for uncertain numbers as best we can, and then we make do with what we have. If we have more food than we need, we give it away to students. If we have less than we need, we share. Moreover, because of an organizational commitment to openness and transparency, all WACommunities events, expenses, grant-support sources, operating budgets, and outcomes reports remain public, posted annually to the UNM WAC website (WAC at UNM). What's at stake here is maintaining "an open space for democracy" in civic literacy education and public rhetoric in and beyond the university (Williams 41). What's at stake here is cultivating a cultural rhetorical ecology of writing that is generative and just.

Reflecting on her experiences working with students for the WACommunities sponsored Celebration of Student Writing at UNM, Genevieve García de Mueller notes:

> You don't want to devalue the kinds of things that students are already doing. They're civically engaged every day. They might not be doing the kinds of work that we think as civic engagement, but they are civically engaged at home talking about politics, talking about issues, trying to get their families to do certain things. . . .[As for] the Celebration of Student Writing—that's engaging with a certain community, that's engaging with freshmen and teaching them how to engage

the campus community and talk about their own writing and literacy practices. That's a form of civic engagement because we're asking them to do certain kinds of things which could be seen as political things because they're taking a stance on writing. (qtd in Guerra *Language, Culture, Identity, and Citizenship* 163)

So what's at stake here? What WACommunities generated through these organizing principles is rhetorical presence. As civil rights movements throughout history have revealed, transgressive power does not convert to acquired power without a price. The economies of dissent are costly. The places we need to be doing the work of community writing is in classrooms across the curriculum, in the prison system, in public health facilities, and at the edges of human suffering. This work is disruptive, disturbing, and distressing. Invoking Cornell West's notion of prophetic pragmatism, I see restorative justice as the most productive and most difficult response. As West reflects in *Democracy Matters*, "The tragicomic is the ability to laugh and retain a sense of life's joy—to preserve hope even while staring in the face of hate and hypocrisy—as against falling into the nihilism of paralyzing despair" (16). The emotional, intellectual, and spiritual labor demanded depletes and transforms us.

I wish to make a distinction here between advocacy rhetoric that WACommunities promotes vs. the kind of jeremiad rhetoric of the neo-liberal right that positions under-served student populations as a kind of "value added" property. As a rhetorical act, advocacy rhetoric stirs reactive rhetoric. As a spiritual act, advocacy rhetoric relies on a gift giving economy and a kind of coyote medicine— invoking trickster tropes that flip the script by changing the terms of the conversation. For example, trickster tropes in response to what Hirschman calls the *futility thesis* (the claim that change is useless/futile) promote a counter-discourse of open possibilities. Trickster tropes counter the *perversity thesis* (the claim that change is a distortion) with conceptually capacious alternatives. And trickster tropes battle the *jeopardy thesis* (the claim that change endangers the status quo) by foregrounding the positive potential of the unknown. Trickster tropes are shapeshifting discourses that help us navigate the shadow ecologies and allow us to lead through ambiguity rather than wait for ambiguity to be resolved in order to lead.

In closing, the provocative questions we need to be asking the leaders of our field and our institutions are: Who is benefitting from the way things are? How might the system be changed to better serve our most vulnerable communities? Who would be most impacted from these changes? Paul Farmer, international epidemiologist and social justice activist, argues in *Pathologies of Power* that our most vulnerable communities locally and globally are: the poor, prisoners, and students. As educators, our spheres of influence should attend to all of these. Because when we talk about the poor, we are talking about women, children, people of color, immigrants—the historically excluded. When we talk about prisoners we talk about the mentally ill, addicts, men and women of color, children, and the poor. When we talk about students we are talking about all of these—people in transition and poised with transformative potential.

WORKS CITED

Castells, Manuel. *The Power of Identity*. 2nd ed. Malden: Pearson/ Longman, 2010. Print.

Farmer, Paul. *Pathologies of Power: Health, Human Rights, and the New War on the Poor*. (Berkeley: U of California, 2003. Print.

Gallegos, Erin P. "Mapping Student Literacies: Reimagining College Writing Instruction within the Literacy Landscape." *Composition Forum* 27 (2013) Web 30 November 2015.

Guerra, Juan C. "Enacting Institutional Change: The Work of Literacy Insurgents in the Academy and Beyond." *JAC* 34. 1-2 (2014): 71-95. Print.

—. *Language, Culture, Identity, and Citizenship in College Classrooms and Communities*. Urbana: NCTE-Routledge, 2015. Print.

Hendrickson, Brian. "The Hard Work of Imagining: The Inaugural Summit of the National Consortium of Writing Across Communities by Albuquerque, NM." *Community Literacy Journal*. 7.2 (January 2013): 115-118. Print

Heschel, Abraham Joshua. *Abraham Joshua Heschel: Essential Writings*. 3rd ed. New York: Orbis, 2013. Print.

Hirschman, Albert O. *The Rhetoric of Reaction: Perversity, Futility, Jeopardy*. Cambridge: Harvard UP, 1981. Print.

Kells Jacob Hall Foss. *Stepping In*. English Honors Thesis. Schreiner College, Department of English. Kerrville, TX, August 1998. Print.

Kells, Michelle H. and Valerie Balester, eds. *Attending to the Margins: Writing, Researching, and Teaching on the Front Lines*. Heinemann-Boynton/Cook, 1999. Print.

Kells, Michelle H., Valerie Balester, and Victor Villanueva, eds. *Latino/a Discourses: On Language, Identity, and Literacy Education*. Heinemann-Boynton/Cook, 2004. Print.

Kells, Michelle H. "Linguistic Contact Zones in the College Writing Classroom: An Examination of Ethnolinguistic Identity and Language Attitudes." *Written Communication* 19.1 (2002): 5-43. Print.

—. "National Consortium of Writing Across Communities." *Writing Communities Newsletter* Spring 2011: 1-2. http://www.unm.edu/~wac/NewsLetter/WAC%20Newsletter_SP11.pdf.

—. "National Consortium of Writing Across Communities Meets July 2012 in Santa Fe." *Writing Communities Newsletter* Spring 2012: 1-2. http://www.unm.edu/~wac/files/WACommunities_%20Newsletter_SP12.pdf.

Parks, Steve, and Eli Goldblatt. "Writing Beyond the Curriculum: Fostering New Collaborations in Literacy." *College English* 62.5 (2000): 584-606. Print.

Ratcliffe, Krista. *Rhetorical Listening: Indentification, Gender, Whiteness*. Carbondale: Southern Illinois UP, 2005. Print.

Richardson, Elaine. *PHD to Ph.D.: How Education Saved My Life*. Anderson: Parlor P, 2013. Print.

Ryden, Kent C. *Mapping the Invisible Landscape*. Iowa City: U of Iowa P, 1993. Print

Unamuno, Miguel de. *Tragic Sense of Life*. New York: SophiaOmni P, 2014. Print.

University of New Mexico Civil Rights Symposium on Mental Health and Social Justice. Web 30 November 2015. <http://www.unm.edu/~wac/WAC 2011-2012 EventsMemo.pdf>

Villanueva, Victor "Edge City: Class and Culture in Contact." *Attending to the Margins: Writing, Researching, and Teaching on the Front Lines* Eds. Michelle H. Kells and Valerie Balester. Heinemann-Boynton/Cook, 1999: 1-5. Print.

WAC at University of New Mexico. University of New Mexico. Web 30 November 2015. http://www.unm.edu/~wac/

Welch Nancy. *Living Room: Teaching Public Writing in a Privatized World*. *Portsmith:* Heineman-Boynton/Cook, 2008. Print.

Williams, Terry Tempest. *The Open Space for Democracy*. Eugene: Wipf & Stock, 2004. Print.

Writing Across Communities Resource Site. University of New Mexico. 2005-2014. Web. 30 November 2015.

Writing in the Disciplines/Across the Curriculum and Communities. Community College of Baltimore County. Web. 30 November 2015. http://goo.gl/dqGSzV.

Writing Across Communities Workshop Working Papers Resources. Web 30 November 2015. https://sites.google.com/ site/resourcewac/

Zawacki, Terry M. & Michelle Cox, eds. *WAC and Second Language Writers: Research Towards Linguistically and Culturally Inclusive Programs and Practices*. Fort Collins, Colorado and Anderson, South Carolina: WAC Clearinghouse and Parlor Press. 2014. Print.

NOTES

1. Dedicated to the memory of Paolo Luka (December 12, 1982-February 12, 1983). *Gozarse uno la carne del alma.*

2. A special thanks to Cristina Kirklighter, Tobi Jacobi, Shannon Carter, and Michele Eodice for their encouragement and support in sharing this story.

APPENDIX

CITIZEN SCHOLARS AND THE CULTURAL RHETORICAL ECOLOGY OF WRITING ACROSS COMMUNITIES

MICHELLE HALL KELLS UNIVERSITY OF NEW MEXICO OCTOBER 15, 2015

COMMUNITY WRITING CONFERENCE UNIVERSITY OF COLORADO, BOULDER AGENDA

Thursday, October 15, 2015
8:45-10:45 a.m.

8:45-9:00   Preview of Workshop Agenda:

Writing Across Communities Resource Packet
- TESOL Forthcoming Encyclopedia Entry: "Writing Across Communities: Cultural Rhetorical Ecologies and Transcultural Citizenship;"
- WACommunities at UNM 2004 to 2014 (History);
- *Language, Culture, Identity, and Citizenship in College Classrooms and Communities* by Juan Guerra (NCTE-Routledge, 2015).

9:00-9:15   Introductions (Small Groups of 4):
- •Who are you?
- •Where are you from?
- •What questions do you bring with you?

9:15-9:30	Representative Anecdote: Kells
"Vicente Ximenes and the Civilian Conservation Corps: Literacy, Ecology, and Civic Engagement."

9:30-10:30	Growing Action Plans for Cultivating Cultural Rhetorical Ecologies of Writing In & Beyond the University
(Mapping the Six Dimensions of the Cultural Rhetorical Ecologies of Your Institutions)
- •Principles
- •Privilege
- •Partnerships
- •Populations (People & Places)
- •Pedagogies & Practices
- •Programs

10:30-10:45	Review of Workshop Agenda:
Small Group Reports What Next?
WACommunities Resource Workshop Working Papers
<https://sites.google.com/site/resourcewac/>

"Writing Across Communities" as a Hermeneutic Project: Cultivating Cultural Rhetorical Ecologies through Public Rhetoric & Community Literacy (Writing) In and Beyond Your Institutions

A Heuristic for Growing Action Plans: (Small Group Discussion)
(10 minutes/6 Dimension=60 Minutes)
Roles: Time Keeper; Facilitator; Recorder; Reporter.
1. Principles:

> What are the key principles and core values of your institution; writing program; department; how does your institutional mission and vision statement represent ethnolinguistic heterogeneity, cultural pluralism, and ideological pluralism? What are your first principles and core values? How does your vision and mission reflect, align, resist, and/or advance the values and principles of your institution?

2. Privilege:

> What populations does your institution privilege; what tropes (images, icons, and symbols) represent these privileged identities and social positions; who benefits from the way things are; who are the most vulnerable populations in your institution; writing program; department; how are these groups represented, reflected, or erased? who are the primary beneficiaries of your vision and action plan?

3. Partnerships:

> Who shares your key principles and core values in your institution? writing program; department? With whom do you stand in the field

(scholarship); who shares your sphere of concern (within the institution; outside the institution); who can help you expand your sphere of influence (within the institution; outside the institution)? What is your stake in this partnership/ project? How do you see your role?

4. Populations (People & Places):

   Which discourse communities shape the cultural rhetorical ecology of your institution; who are your students? What languages and literacy practices do they bring to the classroom? How does place (region; socioeconomic conditions; generational identification, etc.) influence your institution; writing program; department; how does your institution engage/ promote (or fail to engage and promote) ethnolinguistic heterogeneity, cultural diversity, and ideological/ intellectual pluralism;

5. Pedagogies & Practices:

   What are the current pedagogical practice for teaching writing and literacy at your institution; how do these pedagogies and practices reflect, align, conflict and/or resist your key principles and core values; whom does the curriculum privilege? Whom does it fail to serve? How do the ethnolinguistic identities and cultural diversity of your student populations inform current curriculum and pedagogical practice across the institution?

6. Projects & Programs:

   Which programs advance the key principles and core values about writing, language practice, and literacy education across your institution? What is your relationship to these programs? Who are the primary beneficiaries of these programs? How do

these programs engage and respond to the educational interests of your most vulnerable student populations? How does ethnolinguistic heterogeneity, cultural diversity, and ideological pluralism inform community engagement, curriculum development, and learning outcomes of your institution, writing program, or department?

Growing Action Plans: What Next?

Start a conversation (within your department; your classroom; your writing program; your institution);

- Build a narrative in the public sphere (create a public story);
- Construct an archive (document the journey; keep it open, transparent, and inclusive);

- Invite partnerships (across the institution; within the larger civic community; from the field of Rhetoric and Composition);
- Establish an intellectual commonwealth around your key principles and core values about language, writing, and civic engagement;
- Share your journey through multiple voices across different spheres (in scholarship; newsletters; digital media; colloquia series, etc.);
- Describe your collective experience (as change agents) to key stakeholders to enact institutional change (administrators; regents; legislators; journalists, etc.);
- Stir dissonance, recognize dissent, and engage difference (Note: Deliberative democracy grows out of engaged and agonistic pluralism; Social change, in turn, emerges out of shifting relationships within dynamic disturbance ecologies);
- Promote diversity as an index (assessment measurement) of a healthy cultural rhetorical ecology in your institution.

Hermeneutics represents the cross-disciplinary rhetorical practice of exegesis (the interpretation of texts); the act of producing and consuming written, verbal, digital, and nonverbal communication; the term hermeneutics is derived from the Greek deity Hermes—a messenger god; the god of networks, roads, commerce, and thieves; mythical figure who unabashedly transgresses boundaries.

Michelle Hall Kells is Associate Professor in the Department of English at the University of New Mexico where she teaches graduate and undergraduate classes in 20th Century Civil Rights Rhetoric, Contemporary and Classical Rhetoric, Writing and Cultural Studies, and Discourse Studies. She serves as Special Assistant to the Dean of the College of Arts and Science and Program Chair of the Writing Across Communities (WAC) initiative at UNM. Kells received the Lyndon B. Johnson Presidential Library Research Fellowship in 2008. She is a Senior Fellow at the Robert Wood Johnson Foundation Center for Health Policy at UNM. Kells' research interests include civil rights rhetorics, sociolinguistics, and composition/literacy studies. Kells is coeditor of *Attending to the Margins: Writing, Researching, and Teaching on the Front Lines* (Heinemann, 1999) and *Latino/a Discourses: On Language, Identity, and Literacy Education* (Heinemann, 2004). Her work is featured in the journals *JAC, Written Communication, Reflections,* and *Rhetoric & Public Affairs* as well as a number of edited books including *Cross-Language Relations in Composition, Dialects; Englishes, Creoles, and Education; Who Belongs in America?: Presidents, Rhetoric, and Immigration.* Kells is author of *Hector P. Garcia: Everyday Rhetoric and Mexican American Civil Rights* (Southern Illinois University Press, 2006). Her current book project is *Vicente Ximenes and LBJ's "Great Society": The Rhetoric of Mexican American Civil Rights Reform.*

TECHNICAL COMMUNICATION QUARTERLY

Technical Communication Quarterly is on the Web at https://www.tandfonline.com/toc/htcq20/current

Technical Communication Quarterly (*TCQ*) is the refereed journal of the Association of Teachers of Technical Writing (ATTW) published quarterly with support from Taylor and Francis, ATTW, and the East Carolina University English department. *TCQ* focuses on technical communication in academic, scientific, technical, business, governmental, organizational, and social contexts. *TCQ* articles combine theoretical and practical perspectives, have sound bases in theory, and include implications for teaching, research, and practice. Articles cover a range of topics including communication design, pedagogy, digital technologies, ethics, the rhetoric of professions, practices of publication management, research methods, and connections between social practices and professional discourse.

Food Fights: Cookbook Rhetorics, Monolithic Constructions of Womanhood, and Field Narratives in Technical Communication

In "Food Fights," the authors challenge traditional views of cooking as women's work and the production and use of cookbooks as not worth serious consideration as technical artifacts. They also critique more recent efforts to reclaim the whole of previously marginalized genres as technical documents without sufficiently acknowledging cultural and contextual complexities. According to reviewers, Moeller and Frost's article is "timely and effective" in demonstrating a necessary feminist critique in technical communication. The authors "analysis demonstrates clearly the cultural work that cookbooks can do in a particular cultural context— work that is heteronormative or that considers women as a homogenous group— rather than always inclusive and empowering." The consideration of cookbooks as a technical artifact in this way and the consideration of cookbooks in their use and not just their content is particularly needed in our field and reflects the kind of work that technical communication is well poised to contribute to feminist theory.

Food Fights: Cookbook Rhetorics, Monolithic Constructions of Womanhood, and Field Narratives in Technical Communication

Marie E. Moeller and Erin A. Frost

ABSTRACT: *Field narratives that (re)classify technical genres as liberating for women risk supporting the notion that feminism is a completed project in technical communication scholarship. This article suggests that technical communi- cators reexamine the impact of past approaches to critical engagement at the intersections of gender studies and technical communication; cook- books provide a material example. The authors illustrate how a feminist approach to cookbooks as technical/cultural artifacts can productively revise field narratives in technical communication.*

Tell me what you eat, and I shall tell you what you are.
—Jean Anthelme Brillat-Savarin (Fisher, p. 3)

This article about cookbooks and cookbook rhetorics could have gone in many critical directions. We might have, for example, analyzed how and why cookbooks are such a family affair and such a source of culture, especially for us as women, over multiple generations. However, we realized early on that this article isn't really about mothers, grandmothers, or even necessarily cookbooks, though such stories are part of the history of larger narratives about women and gender at play in the field of technical communication. Rather, it is those larger narratives—which we call "field narratives" because they portray the field's general or central feelings, discussions, or representations on a subject—to which this article responds and hails the field to reexamine initial discussions of the role and placement of cookbooks as a way of interrogating our critical engagement at the intersections of gender studies and technical communication. We relocate current discussions of cooking—and perhaps more importantly, its instruction set, the cookbook—outside of the liberatory narrative apparent in much current scholarship regarding cooking and cookbooks. This is not to lend an increased scientific legitimacy to cooking, nor is it to shift the discussion away from the cultural studies aspects of such technical texts. Quite the contrary, actually; by relocating cooking and cookbooks within the realm of the technical, we resituate these texts and narratives within a more critical technical communication framework.

This article is a response to recent narratives that herald cookbooks as liberatory documents (a carryover, perhaps, from early technical communication field discussions that we discuss shortly). In truth, we are not arguing the opposite; cookbooks may, indeed, be liberatory texts and cooking a liberatory activity. However, we recognize that context matters and so we are arguing that technical communicators must be careful to trouble narratives that (re)classify entire genres as liberating. We suggest that the cookbook genre is a physical manifestation of the intersections between representa- tions of womanhood and technology. Framings of cookbooks—and by extension other technologies including cooking-related composition, tools, and domestic spaces—as generally liberatory for women induce us to believe that domestic technologies are liberatory by nature. This belief authorizes us to ignore feminist critiques of domestic spaces; indeed, it authorizes us to ignore feminisms altogether. In this article, we show how much feminisms are needed in demonstrating what understandings about femininity, womanhood, and gender are at stake in cookbook writing.

As scholars and teachers committed to the practice of revision, we must continually make ourselves critical of past orientations to sites of inquiry. Of course, this is easier said than done; we tend to like to move forward, and on to the next field of inquiry. Especially when it comes to issues of gender and cultural locations of technical writing, we, as a field, and perhaps more generally as a public, are almost solely focused on forging new ground, analyzing new locations, and doing such analysis in new and innovative ways. An expedient approach to investigating the work, theory, and impact of technical writing, though quite effective—we traverse and theorize much work, and importantly so—also at times limits our commitment to reflective analysis and may potentially encourage us to believe that cultural sites of writing remain static. For example, readers may recognize a trend that we've identified at some technical communication conferences:

the sense, which we have heard explicitly articulated, that feminisms and gender studies in technical commu- nication have been "done," checked off our collective list, so to speak, and that it is time to move on to new frontiers. We resist this rhetoric of progress both because we are far from "done" and also because relevant technical texts that discipline us in how to think about gender and sex are constantly changing.

As feminist technical communication scholars, then, we feel particularly obligated to consistently lean reflexively into cultural sites that mask their continued commitment to gendered, raced, classed, and ability-based systems of oppression. Especially now—in a time when writers and pundits are throwing around terms such as post-feminism, in a time when we have seen our students over- whelmingly believe that equality in all forms has been achieved—teacher-scholars must pay attention to how cultural texts, in particular cultural texts that perform technical functions, support a hegemonic structure that feminizes positionalities considered "other." In this case, we argue, many cookbooks continually reinforce oppression, though–please excuse the metaphor–still feeding such sites to us as places of liberation, for our own good and happiness.

Seeking Inclusion through Cookbook Rhetorics

Our discussion of the field of technical communication's treatment of cookbook rhetorics begins with Durack's (1997) illustration in *Technical Communication Quarterly* of technical writing orga- nizations (specifically the Society for Technical Communication) categorically dismissing the tech- nical nature of cookbooks.[1] By extension, such a decision also provided commentary on the status of what was historically deemed "women's work," within the field, and more broadly, in terms of cultural capital. Such dismissal, Durack argued, metonymically represented technical communica- tion's narrow view of who does work in technical communication, how such work is done, and thus how power and legitimacy (in larger cultural representations of values and smaller representations of the field of technical communication) are assigned to labor and thus particular bodies.

Since Durack's (1997) call[2] to attend to the gendered nature of our inclusions and exclusions, a main narrative in feminist technical communication work has been historiographical (Bokser, 2012; Brasseur, 2005; Durack, 1998; E. A. Flynn, 1997; J. F. Flynn, 1997; Hallenbeck, 2012; Lippincott, 2003; Skinner, 2012; Sutcliffe, 1998; Tebeaux, 1998, 1999). Many scholars argued for this field to encompass texts previously considered outside the canon, including cookbooks, as a way to recog- nize women's contributions to technology (via household technologies) and the field at large. The reclamation of women's contributions to technical communication has been key to the inclusion of a discussion of gender issues in technical communication as well as in challenging the field to consider the potential for work in technical communication beyond what would be seen as common boundaries.

Indeed, many feminist technical communication scholars have done important work critiquing the ways in which we, as a field, determine what texts and artifacts matter. To return more fully to Durack's (1997) piece, she attaches the absence of women in technical communication to very specific notions of technology, work, and the workplace. She argues that technical communication historians employed "a peculiar set of cultural blinders" (p. 250) that resulted in imagining such terms in very specific, masculine historical ways. Women's technological advancements, she argues, have been routinely under-reported. Moreover, technological work that was once considered "women's work" was ignored and subjugated by the field itself.

> The periodic submittal (and rejection) of texts such as cookbooks to the Society for Technical Communication's annual publications competitions demonstrates the difficulty we have with considering as "work" a productive activity that is typically assigned to women and accomplished within individual households without benefit of financial compensation. (Durack, 1997, p. 255)

Thus, Durack pushed us to include such texts, texts from the public and the private spheres, within the corpus of technical writing.

This argument, published by *Technical Communication Quarterly* in 1997 as part of a special journal issue that made space for feminist scholars to talk about the histories of technical commu- nication, challenged us to think not only about our field's traditional documents, but also about what we were excluding and the implications of those decisions. Rightly so, Durack and others have encouraged the field to widen consideration of what is and could be technical writing, thus also widening the scope of practitioners, scholars, and teachers of technical communication. This was an important step, especially for women, as the professional field of technical communication had long been male dominated and a difficult field in which to find counter-narratives (Allen, 1994; Brasseur, 2005; Durack, 1997; Gurak & Bayer, 1994; Lay, 1991; Rauch, 2012; Ross, 1994; Royal, 2005; Thompson & Overman Smith, 2006).[3] Such steps were welcomed by feminist scholars as paving the way for further study of women and women's contributions to technical communication.

As an example of a relatively recent extension of this reclamation work, Fleitz argued in her 2010 article, "Cooking Codes: Cookbook Discourses as Women's Rhetorical Practices," that through cook- ing and cookbook work "women have participated in a practice that has allowed them throughout history to connect with other women and validate their own existence in the domestic sphere" (para. 1). Referencing scholars such as Marion Bishop (1997), Fleitz articulated that for women, using the process of writing and sharing recipes in the form of cookbooks and cooking Web sites allows women to construct a rhetorical situation in which they affirm "their worth not only as cooks but also as people" (para. 1). Additionally, she argued that because cookbooks have existed in the private space of the home, rarely have we considered such texts as culturally significant and worthy of consideration. Thus, she concluded that such forms of "women's writing" actually do work other than just convey a "list of rules and measurements" and that these forms of women's writing demonstrate the values and "desires of their authors and the communities they lived in" (para. 1). In other words, Fleitz argued that we should reclaim cookbooks as liberatory spaces for women writers and suggests that, as such, cookbooks and recipes and the rhetorical work they do should matter deeply to scholars.

Critical discussions of the cookbook as a woman's contribution to technical communication have yet to be taken up. However, the field continues to work with reclamation of a wide variety of women and women's work in technical communication. Brasseur (2005), for example, directs the field to continue feminist reclamation efforts and discussions with her germinal piece on Florence Nightingale's work with the rose diagrams, created by Nightingale to convey data and construct ethos in a situation hostile to her gender and social location. Additionally, Hallenbeck (2012), in her study of 19th-century women's bicycling manuals, articulates that to create social change, women bicyclists wrote extra-organizational manuals that provided instructions on riding bicycles (a mode of freedom) and wider commentary on women's roles and places in society (challenged societal notions of women's roles and activities). We build on such important work by shifting the direction of discussion a bit; we do not seek to shift away from reclamation, but—in the vein of Scott, Longo, and Wills' (2006) *Critical Power Tools: Technical Communication and Cultural Studies*— more toward the cultural work such documents do when we consider them as texts worthy of study within our field, and thus technical communication texts that do particular kinds of work in our world. In other words, we must take up, consider, and critique the cultural cache, location, and work of cookbooks as technical communication artifacts, rather than simply acknowledging, encompass- ing, and celebrating their existence. Uncritical celebrations of the reclamation of entire genres as technical documents highlight even further why we must consider how we include and discuss such texts, not just that they should simply be included or celebrated.

In the balance of this article, we provide a feminist approach for thinking about ways to consider cookbooks as technical artifacts and to be critical of the cultural work those artifacts do, and we provide specific examples of cookbook rhetorics that require such attention. We conduct this exercise in hopes of disrupting field narratives about cookbooks as always liberatory, recovered examples of women's technical writing and, further, in hopes of providing a model for disrupting similar field narratives in technical communication.

THEORIZING WOMANHOOD

To responsibly theorize how including cookbooks as articles of always-liberatory technical commu- nication can be potentially damaging to our understandings of who women are, how they think, what they do, and how they shape their lives, we situate ourselves at the nexus of several areas of study. We consider how a combination of work in cultural studies, anthropology, rhetoric, and queer theory provides a productive approach for a feminist resituation of cookbook rhetorics in technical communication and the meaning-making processes they represent.

We are engaging here in gynotechnic inquiry, a concept borrowed from anthropology that asks us to think of technologies as "system[s] of techniques for producing a specific material world" with attending ideas about women and gender systems (Bray, 1997, p. 277). This approach sets up a broad range of social rituals—including the production, distribution, usage, and celebration of cookbooks— to be understood as technologies and to come under the scholarly microscope for examination. Gynotechnic inquiry, then, demands that we consider how cookbooks, as a technology, produce particular and normative ideas about women.

We see gynotechnic inquiry—meaning, in this article, the call to consider how cookbooks as technology work to discipline and manage women—clearly intersecting with work from rhetorical scholar Scott (2003). Scott's (2003) work on HIV testing as disciplinary technology illustrates how HIV testing is "a tool for diagnosing and shaping subjectivity according to dominant culture" (p. 9); in other words, the HIV test is a technology for determining who is normal and who is not, for categorizing people, shaping public response, and thus managing bodily experiences/interactions/ actions. The HIV test, Scott articulated, is a "technology of surveillance and detection" (p. 4), of "reconnaissance" (p. 85). It induces us to simultaneously believe there is a single, cautionary way of responding to those it surveils and a single, cautionary way of being those it surveils. As Scott explained, "HIV testing practices also function in a more overtly ideological way to judge people as risky or clean, vulnerable or invulnerable, deviant or normal" (p. 7).

Cookbook rhetorics, we argue, function as a similar kind of technology to deem people deviant or normal. More specifically, cookbooks provide specific heuristics for the categorization of "women" and "men" and then encourage users to test themselves against those provided heuristics. These heuristics construct monolithic narratives of being as a way to easily manage cultural narratives of womanhood, and by extension material bodies and lives, in our current cultural milieu. Mohanty (1988) explained the problematic nature of creating and believing in such monolithic categories by arguing that the discursive formations favored by many White, Western feminists are damaging to women in the third world. She suggested that a monolithic interpretation of patriarchy "leads to the construction of a similarly reductive and homogeneous notion of what I shall call the 'third-world difference'" (p. 63). Mohanty said that the implications of her work are relevant for "any discourse that sets up its own authorial subjects as the implicit referent" (p. 64), which we argue holds true for cookbooks. Understandings of women as a homogenous group presuppose biological difference as a criterion for unity without making space for diversity among those who might identify as "women." Understandings of women's writing as always liberatory for all readers—without consideration of class, ethnicity, nationality, culture, social position, or politics—present the same problems. If we suggest that cookbooks are liberatory for women, we must also answer the question of which specific women we are talking about and, indeed, who gets counted as a woman. Acceptance and perpetua- tion of the idea that the celebratory inclusion of cookbooks as technical documents always works to the advantage of all women perpetuates understandings of monolithic womanhood.

To work against monolithic understandings of categories of people, we must pay attention to differences and to absences. We should more often recognize that technical documents restrict our understandings of how, where, and when we do things and how we understand ourselves. For example, Halberstam (2005) has addressed the issue of what a non-normatively gendered person is to do when confronted with spaces that are constructed according to gender, such as public bathrooms. The technical documentation that prescribes the location of bodies in such a circum- stance does not take into account transgender or alternately gendered individuals. Halberstam also argued that technical documents like marriage contracts reify normative perspectives about the timeline for a person's life. Thus, we must take into account how the places and times at which cookbooks are used affect the work they do. For example, just prior to her marriage to her male partner, Frost received piles of cookbooks as gifts, an experience that was familiar to many of her straight, female friends. This definitively marks a particular rite of passage and also induces women to believe that certain expectations exist for them in their new role as wife or partner. Cookbook rhetorics produce ideas about women based not just upon the content of their pages, but also their situation in space and time. The spatial, temporal, and social positioning of cookbooks, then, can be considered part of a technology that produces understandings of what women are or what they should be.

This transdisciplinary theoretical approach provides us with a way to think about how cookbook rhetorics and popular understandings of their empowering features might cause us to believe in a sort of homogenous womanhood. The approach we have utilized here makes way for us to critique technical artifacts that assume audience understanding in their representations and categorizations of subjects, and particularly of subjects identified as women.

COOKING DOWN COOKBOOK RHETORICS

By extending the above critiques and analyzing specific passages from modern cookbooks, we argue that a belief in cookbook rhetorics as necessarily liberatory for all women frames women in a number of problematic ways. First, this belief suggests that all women need to be liberated, and even that all women need to be liberated through literature associated with the domestic sphere. Second, this belief assumes equal access to cookbook rhetorics by all women, when in fact not all women have access to resources or situations that would allow them to own or even view cookbooks. Third, this belief presumes that all women (or, we might assume, all women who "matter") will recognize themselves in cookbooks, which largely represent women as middle class, White, and normatively gendered rather than recognizing the great diversity of people who self-identify as women or, indeed, the great diversity of nonwomen who might be cookbook users. This is not a comprehensive list, by any means, of the ways that cookbooks can and do construct womanhood. However, all of these claims are common and seem, to us, to be the most urgently in need of address. Thus, we attempt to make these problems apparent in the textual analysis below.

Rightly in many ways, Fleitz (2010) articulated that "cooking is and has historically been a gendered practice" (para. 5). This echoes Durack's (1997) concerns that texts such as cookbooks were omitted and subjugated because of their, and women's, historical place predominantly within the private, feminine sphere. In many ways, then, cookbooks are to be celebrated and held up as examples of the good to come from widening the scope of a field's canon. Yet, the blanket celebration of such texts also comes with a price. Fleitz argued that

> Since this community has traditionally existed in the private sphere, it has gone mostly unnoticed, allowing women to construct for themselves a vital, life-affirming community that respects their authority and experi- ence, something most women were unable to have in the public sphere of society. (para. 5)

If, as Fleitz argued, this community has gone unnoticed, then, as she claimed, we have technology such as the Food Network, cooking blogs, and celebrity media chefs to thank for making it more public. And, in making it more public, we are paying more attention to the work and place of the cookbook in modern society. However, with that attention comes some interesting effects. More than ever, the work of the text, the work of cooking, is defining us. And, if cookbooks reflect back to us a woman's life, a woman's place, a woman's community, as Fleitz claimed, the cookbooks we'll reference here reflect back to us an interesting and problematic idea of such "life-affirming" and authority-respecting communities.

Take, for instance, the by-women-for-women cookbook *The Little Black Apron: A Single Girl's Guide to Cooking with Style and Grace* (Citrin, Gibson, & Nuanes, 2007), which, in a section titled "Sodium: Salt in the Wound," used a hypothetical story about having a best guy friend to begin a discussion of the role of salt in the diet:

> Most of us have been there—explaining that we're still renting our studio apartments with pinkish brown carpet in the ghetto, still not married, still considering quitting our jobs, and still contemplating moving to India to become a yoga instructor. . ... Meanwhile, . . . [t]wo of your mutual friends just proposed to their girlfriends. After talking yourself out of pulling a Sylvia Plath and crawling into the oven, you regained your composure. You were doing fine with the other weddings. However, these two newly engaged individuals are boys. You refuse to refer to them as men, as it is inconceivable they know how to get married—or that they had the wherewithal to buy a ring, not to mention find a woman to marry. You started crunching the numbers and realized that most of your guy friends from high school and college are hitched. . ... You have eight weddings scheduled in the next twelve months and your year is beginning to resemble Cupid's calendar of love. Your bank statements reflect thousands of dollars of plane tickets and Williams-Sonoma gift registry items. Not fazed, you putter along in your existence. It's all just salt in the wound. (Citrin et al., 2007, pp. 105–106)

What does this cookbook, this technical communication artifact, tell us about life as a single woman in 2007 in the United States? That single women should be anxious about their lives if they are not partnered; that single women are likely on the edge—of life, of suicide, of the world? But mostly, that a single woman is not normal and won't be unless she becomes a member of partnered, compulsory heteronormative behavior patterns. Otherwise, she will (and should) feel isolated, ashamed, and able to do little else than putter along and wait for her "real life" to begin.

Contrary to Fleitz's (2010) argument, the representations of this community of women don't seem in the least bit supportive. In fact, this narrative is utterly disrespectful of difference and different women's experiences. Indeed, readers are to identify the single woman, and share or separate from the shame and isolation of singlehood, thus becoming a type of split community that works to reify heteronormative behavior. Interestingly enough, this work is done through a text whose primary goal is to nourish one's body. Indeed, though Durack and Fleitz articulated that little attention has been historically paid to the cookbook, we argue that we actually do, especially post- Food Network, pay very close attention to our cooking texts, and we tend to be less likely to critique them because of their seemingly altruistic endeavor of nourishment.

Consider Food Network star Nigella Lawson's (2001) introduction to her cookbook *How to Be a Domestic Goddess* (an interesting title in and of itself), where she said:

> This is a book about baking, but not a baking book—not in the sense of being a manual or a comprehensive guide or a map of a land you do not inhabit. I neither want to confine you to the kitchen nor even suggest that it might be desirable. But I do think that many of us have become alienated from the domestic sphere, and that it can actually make us feel better to claim back some of that space, make it comforting rather than frightening. In a way, baking stands both as a useful metaphor for the familial warmth of the kitchen we fondly imagine used to exist, and as a way of reclaiming our lost Eden. This is hardly a culinary matter, of course; but cooking, we know, has a way of cutting through things, and to things which have nothing to do with the kitchen. This is why it matters. (p. xii)

This is why it matters, indeed, though not in the way Lawson might have intended. This cooking book does cut through things, things that have nothing to do with the kitchen. For example, Lawson argued that cooking is a space of empowerment—a familiar narrative for feminist technical com- munication scholars—for women. She suggested that women's movements, that pushing back against oppression, has made such norms "frightening" to us, and that we should reembrace such normative spaces to find our "Eden" and indulge nostalgia for the way things once were. Of course, in this instance, Lawson seems to forget that the way things once were, prefeminist movement, when women were forcibly or ideologically confined to kitchens, wasn't exactly an ideal situation for any of us. It's unlikely we'll find Eden there.

To alter the approach from Eden to Elvira, we have cookbooks like *Skinny Bitch* that tell us that you can "Look hot. Feel great. Have fun while you cook. Do good to the earth" (Freedman & Barnouin, 2005, front inside cover). Fortunately, the implications of cultural demands for slender- ness have been well researched by feminist and gender studies scholars. Bordo (2003) suggested that the desire for slenderness reflects "powerlessness and contraction of female social space" (p. 26), a notion also represented in the 2007 cookbook *Crazy Sista Cooking* by LuLu Buffet, Jimmy Buffet's sister, who told us that to make burg- ers, you must:

1. Find a Helpful Man (if that's helpful).
2. Have him heat a charcoal or gas grill, whatever he prefers.
3. Mix him his favorite cocktail while he monitors the grill temp.
4. When he says the grill is ready, bring him the beautifully pat- tied burgers, arranged lovingly over waxed paper on a festive platter. Use waxed paper so that you can remove it after your Helpful Man has loaded the burgers onto the grill and, voila, you have a clean serving platter ready once they're cooked. (Buffet & Arnold, 2007, p. 154)

The recipe continues on in this fashion, reinforcing the notion that female autonomy is limited and that it is "his" comfort, preferences, and desires that will dictate how work is to be done.

Clearly, men are not exempt from the sorts of monolithic un- derstandings cookbooks encourage either. Much of our critique has focused on notions of womanhood because it is women who have his- torically been ignored, dismissed, and maligned. However, note that men are conspicuously absent as readers/users in these texts; often, cis-gendered men are eliminated from the user pool before they even finish reading the title because they won't identify as either a goddess or a bitch. In this way, cookbooks tell men they don't belong in this space. Further, men who do wish to engage in cooking are most often relegated to the outdoor world of the grill or to pre-prepared options, both of which tend to reinforce traditional and sexist notions of manhood and womanhood. Take *A Man, A Can, A Plan*: "Eggs are to be cooked until soft and jiggly, like Pamela Anderson. Then, they are flipped and cooked until crispy and golden brown, just like Pamela Anderson" (Joachim, 2002, p. 3). This text implies that men could not possibly engage in any cooking so sophisticated as to require more than a few ingredients from cans; simultaneously, men are taught to understand that they should have some sort of lecherous attachment to Pamela Anderson's body and, further, are encouraged to objectify women by comparing them to foods—objects that are, disturbingly, intended to be literally consumed.

Gender relations, as articulated and rearticulated by cookbooks, are deeply ingrained and deeply problematic. We need look no farther than the text *Will Cook For Sex: A Guy's Guide to Cooking* to learn that "a way to a man's heart is through his zipper. The way to a woman's heart is through her stomach" (Fino, 2010, p. 11). We also quickly learn that women who don't like chocolate aren't really worth the time it might take to seduce them with cooking prowess (p. 30), and all "guys" like red meat (p. 31). In contrast, Golden's (2011) attitude toward the "shewoman" (p. 70) is blatantly antagonistic, as evidenced by the following quotations: "Eat my balls" (p. 14), "Finally, you've found something easier than your little sister" (p. 48), and "quit being a pussy" (p. 78). Golden also acknowledged—and reinforced—the belief that women belong in the kitchen though men get extra points for being proficient cooks, "If you are a dude, wallow in accolades; if you are a shewoman, revel in the expectation that you won't fuck up" (p. 70). The author biography on the back cover continues in this vein, stating that the author "lives in Brooklyn, New York, with his girlfriend Sara and dog Oscar, both of whom he allows on the furniture."

Feminist and social-justice oriented critiques of cooking texts cannot and should not end with rhetorics that explicitly engage gender relations. Rhetorics such as "Procure some child labor to cheaply and efficiently cook" (Golden, 2011, p. 100) and "Pimpin' the Poultry"

(Coolio, 2009, p. 47) provide impetus for a variety of social critiques. Certainly, the world of cooking exists on the foundation of deeply culturally embedded understandings of race and class as well as sex and gender. Though we do not have space to do justice to these related critiques here, we encourage readers to take up this work.

All of these texts, clearly, do particular kinds of cultural work. When, as a field, our articles and research make statements such as "we must include women's texts in the canon" or "cookbooks are a space of empowerment and community for women," we must be critical of the implications of such generalizations. Rather than be satisfied with our sense that cookbooks are women's work and have now been accepted as liberatory, female-empowering technical artifacts, we must interrogate the cultural implications of those technical artifacts. Further, we must consider the effects of authorizing them within the technical communication corpus without taking them up more critically. We must look to their effects on the spaces in which we exist and we must continually push our field to return to itself critically and reflectively, to examine the spaces that in ways remain static in message but change rapidly in dissemination.

IMPLICATIONS

The work of cooking and the roles of cooks are ever present in the public imagination. Simultaneously, cooking remains a space with uniquely visible and impermeable gender stratifica- tions. Pollan (2013) undertook an organized exploration into the nature of cooking in his popular book *Cooked*, and he found that

> [B]arbecue pit masters are almost exclusively men, as are brewers and bakers (except for pastry chefs), and a remarkable number of cheese makers are women. In learning to cook traditional pot dishes, I chose to work with a female chef, and if by doing so I underscored the cliché that home cooking is woman's work, that was sort of the idea: I wanted to delve into that very question. We can hope that all the gender stereotypes surrounding food and cooking will soon be thrown up for grabs, but to assume that has already happened would be to kid ourselves. (p. 15)

Though Pollan himself has endured some feminist critique (Matchar, 2013), the observation he makes here is inarguable: Gender roles are deeply and publicly ingrained in cooking practices. Further, those roles have serious consequences for how we think of ourselves, which in turn affect how we cook and how we talk about cooking. This reality only increases the need for technical communication scholars to consider the ways in which technical artifacts like cookbooks contribute to this cycle.

Cookbooks are a genre that often includes examples of technical proficiency, misogynist rhetorics, humor, identification, and more. In short, they are complex documents that have potential to do many different kinds of work. Because cookbooks are often cast as a feel-good space, a space of recovery, they can be especially difficult to critique. However, we must also remember that cook- books are associated with histories of gender-based divisions of labor and sexual oppression. As scholars interested in technical communication, we are obligated to pay careful attention to the use of labels that create "a stable category of analysis" and that assume "ahistorical, universal unity among" group members "on a generalized notion of their subordination" (Mohanty, 1988, p. 72). We do not support the silencing of work on liberatory rhetorics, nor do we seek to quash historiographical recoveries of women's technical composition practices. However, we do support and seek to engage in critical analysis of the complexities involved with siting such analysis in spaces about domestic technologies. Once we start looking for the ways in which representation and categorization can be damaging, those transgressions are all too easy to find. We conclude by suggesting that critiques of categorization and representation are important and necessary, and therefore, feminists in technical communication need to develop methods for maintaining a difficult balance. We must foreground unity and pay attention to the positive aspects and inclusive spirit of feminist work in technical communication even as we carefully interrogate the parts of such work that may be problematic. We argue that current iterations of the cookbook genre and associated critiques have serious work to do if they are to accomplish more than perpetuating harmful cultural narratives.

Notes

1. Allen (1990) also notes this trend in a 1990 article in the *Journal of Business and Technical Communication*, "The Case Against Defining Technical Writing." Allen makes the point that we should not put hard limits on a definition of technical communication, as the effects of such limitations can close off our abilities to critically engage.

2. To be clear, a number of scholars had already done work at the intersections of feminisms and/or gender studies and technical communication prior to this publication (Allen, 1994; Bernhardt, 1992; Bosley, 1992, 1994; Brunner, 1991; Carrell, 1991; Dell, 1992; E. Flynn, Savage, Penti, Brown, & Watke, 1991; Gurak & Bayer, 1994; LaDuc & Goldrick-Jones, 1994; Lay, 1989, 1991, 1993; Neeley, 1992; Raign & Sims, 1993; Rifkind & Harper, 1992; Ross, 1994; Sauer, 1992, 1994; Tebeaux & Lay, 1992). Our point is that Durack's (1997) call widened the scope of such work and made possible some of the feminist work in technical communication that has emerged since (Haas, Tulley, & Blair, 2002; Herrick, 1999; Ingram & Parker, 2002; Koerber, 2000; Overman Smith & Thompson, 2002; Thompson, 1999; Wolfe & Alexander, 2005).

3. See research cited in the previous footnote for further discussions of feminist work in technical communication.

Notes on Contributors

Marie E. Moeller is an associate professor of technical and professional communication at the University of Wisconsin- La Crosse. Her research interests include disability and gender studies in technical communication, health commu- nication, and online writing pedagogy.

Erin A. Frost is an assistant professor of technical and professional communication at East Carolina University. Her research interests include feminisms and gender studies in technical communication, health care policy, risk commu- nication, and teaching with technology.

References

Allen, J. (1990). The case against defining technical writing. *Journal of Business and Technical Communication*, 4(2), 68–77. doi:10.1177/105065199000400204

Allen, J. (1994). Women and authority in business/technical communication scholarship: An analysis of writing features, methods, and strategies. *Technical Communication Quarterly*, *3*(3), 271–292. doi:10.1080/ 10572259409364572

Bernhardt, S. A. (1992). The design of sexism: The case of an army maintenance manual. *IEEE Transactions on Professional Communication*, *35*(4), 217–221. doi:10.1109/47.180282

Bishop, M. (1997). Speaking sisters: Relief society cookbooks and Mormon culture. In A. Bower (Ed.), *Recipes for reading: Community cookbooks, stories, histories* (pp. 89–104). Amherst, MA: University of Massachusetts Press.

Bokser, J. A. (2012). Reading and writing Sor Juana's arch: Rhetorics of belonging, Criollo identity, and feminist histories. *Rhetoric Society Quarterly*, *42*(2), 144–163. doi:10.1080/02773945.2012.659323

Bordo, S. R. (2003). *Unbearable weight: Feminism, Western culture, and the body* (10th ed.). Berkeley, CA: University of California Press.

Bosley, D. S. (1992). Gender and visual communication: Toward a feminist theory of design. *IEEE Transactions on Professional Communication*, *35*(4), 222–229. doi:10.1109/47.180283

Bosley, D. S. (1994). Feminist theory, audience analysis, and verbal and visual representation in a technical commu- nication writing task. *Technical Communication Quarterly*, *3*(3), 293–307. doi:10.1080/10572259409364573

Brasseur, L. (2005). Florence Nightingale's visual rhetoric in the rose diagrams. *Technical Communication Quarterly*, *14*(2), 161–182. doi:10.1207/s15427625tcq1402_3

Bray, F. (1997). *Technology and gender: Fabrics of power in late imperial China*. Berkeley, CA: University of California Press.

Brillat-Savarin, J. A. (1971). *The Physiology of Taste*. (M. F. K. Fisher, Trans.). New York, NY: Knopf. (Original work published 1825.)

Brunner, D. D. (1991). Who owns this work?: The question of authorship in professional/academic writing. *Journal of Business and Technical Communication*, *5*(4), 393–411. doi:10.1177/1050651991005004004

Buffett, L. A., & Arnold, A. (2007). *Crazy sista cooking: Cuisine & conversation with Lucy Anne Buffett*. Gulf Shores, AL: Already Done.

Carrell, D. (1991). Gender scripts in professional writing textbooks. *Journal of Business and Technical Communication*, *5*(4), 463–468. doi:10.1177/1050651991005004007

Citrin, J., Gibson, M., & Nuanes, K. (2007). *The little black apron: A single girl's guide to cooking with style and grace*. Avon, MA: Polka Dot Press.

Coolio. (2009). *Cookin' with Coolio: 5 star meals at a 1 star price*. New York, NY: Atria Books.

Dell, S. (1992). A communication-based theory of the glass ceiling: Rhetorical sensitivity and upward mobility within the technical organization. *IEEE Transactions on Professional Communication*, *35*(4), 230–235. doi:10.1109/ 47.180284

Durack, K. T. (1997). Gender, technology, and the history of technical communication. *Technical Communication Quarterly*, *6*(3), 249–260. doi:10.1207/s15427625tcq0603_2

Durack, K. T. (1998). Authority and audience-centered writing strategies: Sexism in 19th-century sewing machine manuals. *Technical Communication*, *45*(2), 180–196.

Fino, R. (2010). *Will cook for sex: A guy's guide to cooking*. Las Vegas, NV: Stephens Press LLC.

Fleitz, E. (2010). Cooking codes: Cookbook discourses as women's rhetorical practices. *Present Tense: A Journal of Rhetoric in Society*, *1*(1). Retrieved from http://www.presenttensejournal.org/vol1/cooking-codes-cookbook-dis courses-as-womens-rhetorical-practices/

Flynn, E. A. (1997). Emergent feminist technical communication. *Technical Communication Quarterly*, *6*(3), 313–320. doi:10.1207/s15427625tcq0603_6

Flynn, E. A., Savage, G., Penti, M., Brown, C., & Watke, S. (1991). Gender and modes of collaboration in a chemical engineering design course. *Journal of Business and Technical Communication*, *5*(4), 444–462. doi:10.1177/1050651991005004006

Flynn, J. F. (1997). Toward a feminist historiography of technical communication. *Technical Communication Quarterly*, *6*(3), 321–329. doi:10.1207/s15427625tcq0603_7

Freedman, R., & Barnouin, K. (2005). *Skinny bitch: A no-nonsense, tough-love guide for savvy girls who want to stop eating crap and start looking fabulous!* Philadelphia, PA: Running Press.

Golden, Z. (2011). *What the F*@# should I make for dinner? The answers to life's everyday question (in 50 F*@# recipes)*. Philadelphia, PA: Running Press.

Gurak, L. J., & Bayer, N. L. (1994). Making gender visible: Extending feminist critiques of technology to technical communication. *Technical Communication Quarterly*, *3*(3), 257–270. doi:10.1080/10572259409364571

Haas, A., Tulley, C., & Blair, K. (2002). Mentors versus masters: Women's and girls' narratives of (re)negotiation in web-based writing spaces. *Computers and Composition*, *19*(3), 231–249. doi:10.1016/S8755-4615(02)00128-7

Halberstam, J. (2005). *In a queer time and place: Transgender bodies, subcultural lives*. New York, NY: New York University Press.

Hallenbeck, S. (2012). User agency, technical communication, and the 19th-century woman bicyclist. *Technical Communication Quarterly*, *21*(4), 290–306. doi:10.1080/10572252.2012.686846

Herrick, J. W. (1999). "And then she said": Office stories and what they tell us about gender in the workplace. *Journal of Business and Technical Communication*, *13*(3), 274–296. doi:10.1177/105065199901300303

Ingram, S., & Parker, A. (2002). The influence of gender on collaborative projects in an engineering classroom. *IEEE Transactions on Professional Communication, 45*(1), 7–20. doi:10.1109/47.988359

Joachim, D. (2002). *Men's health presents a man, a can, a plan: 50 great guy meals even you can make!* New York, NY: Rodale Books.

Koerber, A. (2000). Toward a feminist rhetoric of technology. *Journal of Business and Technical Communication, 14*(1), 58–73. doi:10.1177/105065190001400103

LaDuc, L., & Goldrick-Jones, A. (1994). The critical eye, the gendered lens, and "situated"; insights—feminist contributions to professional communication. *Technical Communication Quarterly, 3*(3), 245–256. doi:10.1080/ 10572259409364570

Lawson, N. (2001). *How to be a domestic goddess: Baking and the art of comfort cooking.* New York, NY: Hyperion. Lay, M. M. (1989). Interpersonal conflict in collaborative writing: What we can learn from gender studies. *Journal of Business and Technical Communication, 3*(2), 5–28. doi:10.1177/105065198900300202

Lay, M. M. (1991). Feminist theory and the redefinition of technical communication. *Journal of Business and Technical Communication, 5*(4), 348–370. doi:10.1177/1050651991005004002

Lay, M. M. (1993). Gender studies: Implications for the professional communication classroom. In N. L. R. Blyler & C. Thralls (Eds.), *Professional communication: The social perspective* (pp. 215–229). Newbury Park, CA: Sage Publications.

Lippincott, G. (2003). Rhetorical chemistry: Negotiating gendered audiences in nineteenth-century nutrition studies. *Journal of Business and Technical Communication, 17*(1), 10–49. doi:10.1177/1050651902238544

Matchar, E. (2013, September 21). *Is Michael Pollan a sexist pig?* Retrieved from http://www.salon.com/2013/04/28/is_ michael_pollan_a_sexist_pig/

Mohanty, C. T. (1988). Under Western eyes: Feminist scholarship and colonial discourses. *Feminist Review, 30*, 61–88. doi:10.1057/fr.1988.42

Neeley, K. A. (1992). Woman as mediatrix: Women as writers on science and technology in the eighteenth and nineteenth centuries. *IEEE Transactions on Professional Communication, 35*(4), 208–216. doi:10.1109/47.180281 Overman Smith, E., & Thompson, I. (2002). Feminist theory in technical communication: Making knowledge claims visible. *Journal of Business and Technical Communication, 16*(4), 441–477. doi:10.1177/105065102236526 Pollan, M. (2013). *Cooked: A natural history of transformation.* New York, NY: Penguin Press HC.

Raign, K. R., & Sims, B. R. (1993). Gender, persuasion techniques, and collaboration. *Technical Communication Quarterly, 2*(1), 89–104. doi:10.1080/10572259309364526

Rauch, S. (2012). The accreditation of Hildegard von Bingen as medieval female technical writer. *Journal of Technical Writing and Communication, 42*(4), 393–411. doi:10.2190/TW.42.4.d

Rifkind, L. J., & Harper, L. F. (1992). Cross-gender immediacy behaviors and sexual harassment in the workplace: A communication paradox. *IEEE Transactions on Professional Communication, 35*(4), 236–241. doi:10.1109/47.180285

Ross, S. M. (1994). A feminist perspective on technical communicative action: Exploring how alternative worldviews affect environmental remediation efforts. *Technical Communication Quarterly, 3*(3), 325–342. doi:10.1080/10572259409364575

Royal, C. (2005). A meta-analysis of journal articles intersecting issues of Internet and gender. *Journal of Technical Writing and Communication, 35*(4), 403–429. doi:10.2190/3RBM-XKEQ-TRAF-E8GN

Sauer, B. A. (1992). The engineer as rational man: The problem of imminent danger in a non-rational environment. *IEEE Transactions on Professional Communication, 35*(4), 242–249. doi:10.1109/47.180286

Sauer, B. A. (1994). Sexual dynamics of the profession: Articulating the ecriture masculine of science and technology. *Technical Communication Quarterly, 3*(3), 309–323. doi:10.1080/10572259409364574

Scott, J. B. (2003). *Risky rhetoric: AIDS and the cultural practices of HIV testing.* Carbondale, IL: Southern Illinois University Press.

Scott, J. B., Longo, B., & Wills, K. V. (2006). *Critical power tools: Technical communication and cultural studies.* Albany, NY: State University of New York Press.

Skinner, C. (2012). Incompatible rhetorical expectations: Julia W. Carpenter's medical society papers, 1895–1899. *Technical Communication Quarterly, 21*(4), 307–324. doi:10.1080/10572252.2012.686847

Sutcliffe, R. J. (1998). Feminizing the professional: The government reports of Flora Annie Steel. *Technical Communication Quarterly, 7*(2), 153–173. doi:10.1080/10572259809364622

Tebeaux, E. (1998). The voices of English women technical writers, 1641–1700: Imprints in the evolution of modern English prose style. *Technical Communication Quarterly, 7*(2), 125–152. doi:10.1080/10572259809364621

Tebeaux, E. (1999). The emergence of women technical writers in the 17th century: Changing voices within a changing milieu. In T. Kynell-Hunt & M. G. Moran (Eds.), *Three keys to the past: The history of technical communication* (pp. 105–122). Stamford, CT: Ablex.

Tebeaux, E., & Lay, M. (1992). Images of women in technical books from the English Renaissance. *IEEE Transactions on Professional Communication, 35*(4), 196–207. doi:10.1109/47.180280

Thompson, I. (1999). Women and feminism in technical communication: A qualitative content analysis of journal articles published in 1989 through 1997. *Journal of Business and Technical Communication, 13*(2), 154–178. doi:10.1177/1050651999013002002

Thompson, I., & Overman Smith, E. (2006). Women and feminism in technical communication—An update. *Journal of Technical Writing and Communication, 36*(2), 183–199. doi:10.2190/4JUC-8RAC-73H6-N57U

Wolfe, J., & Alexander, K. P. (2005). The computer expert in a mixed-gendered collaborative writing group. *Journal of Business and Technical Communication, 19*(2), 135–170. doi:10.1177/1050651904272978

WLN: A JOURNAL OF WRITING CENTER SCHOLARSHIP

WLN: A Journal of Writing Center Scholarship is on the Web at https://wln-journal.org/

With Volume 40, the *Writing Lab Newsletter* was renamed as *WLN: A Journal of Writing Center Scholarship* to better reflect what it had long since become: a journal addressing questions of the theoretical, pedagogical, and administrative work of writing centers. Articles illustrate how writing centers work in an intersection of theory and practice, underpinned by theory, research, and scholarship. *WLN* aims to inform newcomers as well as extend the thinking of those who are more knowledgeable and experienced. Authors report on research and describe programmatic models that can be adapted to the varied contexts in which writing centers exist.

Service-Learning Tutor Education: A Model of Action

As opportunities for students to engage in service leaning and social justice are increasingly being folded into the mission of many universities, Zimmerelli and Brown's article extends this to show how writing centers can engage tutors in these roles. This article offers writing center directors both a tutor training model and a rationale for including tutors in social engagement. Moreover, the article demonstrates that writing centers are prime locations for educating student tutors about their responsibilities to society, thus enlarging the scope and mission of a writing center and adding yet another dimension to all that tutors gain in their educational experience.

Service-Learning Tutor Education: A Model of Action

Lisa Zimmerelli and Victoria Bridges

> *"It's the action, not the fruit of the action, that's important. You have to do the right thing.*
> *It may not be . . . in your time, that there'll be any fruit. But that doesn't mean you stop doing the right thing. You may never know what results come from your action.*
> *But if you do nothing, there will be no result."*
>
> — Mahatma Gandhi

Many writing centers, especially those in urban areas, have re- sponded to systemic and structural oppression in surrounding neighborhoods by extending their services beyond the campus community. For many of us, such engagement is consistent with the liberatory ideal of democratic education. However, adding service and a social justice component to writing center obli- gations can feel overwhelming. Indeed, early questions directors and staff face when considering community engagement can easily sideline a potential project into a mere "we should do this one day" wish. Basic questions (Where to start? How to get funding? Will tutors commit?) and complex questions (Will my department/institution support this? What is the need? How do we know it is the need? Are we making biased presumptions about the community and its literacy practices? Might we do harm?) point to ethical considerations of community engage- ment. And yet, as Mahatma Gandhi reminds us, "It's the action, not the fruit of the action, that's important;" we can also choose to respond to the equally ethical imperative to *act*, to do some- thing, even small, for the good of our community despite finan- cial, institutional, or psychic barriers.

> This essay is about our small action.1 We share the integration of service-learning in tutor education as one model for writing center community engagement. After providing our project context, we detail service-learning modifications made to our tutor education course, present benefits of service-learning, and identify what we see as four factors for success.

BACKGROUND

Dip a toe into service-learning scholarship, and you will find concerns over sustainability; this certainly is true for the two prominent community literacy models: the service-learning composition classroom and community-based writing centers.2 In service-learning composition classes, students engage in proj- ects thatrespond to a community need throughout the semester, and instructors link community engagement with coursework.3 Linda Adler-Kassner, Robert Crooks, and Ann Watters identify sustainability as a significant challenge to service-learning proj- ects; although the classroom environment provides a space for formalized, structured reflection (a key service-learning compo- nent), "class and term blocks can be a huge and even crippling obstacle" to the success of community-based service-learning writing projects (11). When semester and service end, the com- munity partner is left hoping another class will pick up where the previous class left off.

University-sponsored community-based writing/literacy cen- ters, usually off-campus and embedded in the community, pro- vide a range of support, from skills-based tutoring to publishing to literacy advocacy. Some, such as the Salt Lake Community College Community Writing Center—under Tiffany Rousculp's leadership4—and the Colorado State University Community Literacy Center—under Tobi Jacobi's leadership—enjoy tre- mendous institutional material sup- port, (i.e., devoted faculty and budget lines, permanent location and staff, etc.). Without such support, however, sustaining a community writing center is challenging. Tutors may struggle to commit consis- tently, es- pecially if the work is unpaid, and directors face the diffi- culty of lining up institutional support for what can be perceived as simply an add-on program, an important but disposable part of what the writing center and institution do.

COMBINED MODELS

To address the sustainability issue that plagues both ser- vice-learning models, we combined the class- and center-based models. Project sus- tainability was foremost in our minds be- cause we saw sustainabil- ity as an ethical imperative: if we were going to start the work, we wanted to ensure it continued. When we transformed our fall tutor education course, WritingCenter Practice and Theory, into a service-learning course, we knew that for at least one semester annually, the service would be mandatory and integrally tied to theory, praxis, and reflec- tion. Moreover, because our course is an extension of a larger, more comprehensive campus program—the writing center—we hoped our community engagement would be sustained by writ- ing center volunteers every spring. So while our service-learn- ing tutor education course provides a necessary theoretical and critical space to process the service, the writing center sustains the program all year by providing tutors (whether students in the tutor education course or tutors from our center).

PARTNERSHIP

We also sought a suitable community partner, which is key in creating an effective service-learning class. Our chosen part- ner, Bridges, spon- sored by St. Paul's School of Baltimore pro- vides a range of support services for Baltimore public school system students, including sum- mer bridge programs, tutoring, job training, and social services guid- ance.5 Formerly limited to elementary and middle school students, when Bridges grew to support high school students, it needed tutors to help those struggling academically.

The partnership arrangement, established during our first se- mester in 2011, is largely the arrangement we continue today. Every Wednesday evening our writing center closes early to accommodate Bridges students, who arrive on a bus driven by an Americorps intern. After grabbing pizza, tutors and students pair off for about two hours to work on homework, projects, SAT prep, and college essays. Lisa and Victoria are also present near- ly every week to work with students. And our plan for sustain- ability has worked: each spring, when our course is not offered, tutors volunteer to sustain the Loyola/Bridges program. Then, the class and program picks back up the next fall. In total, 46 tutors have tutored 40 high school students thus far.

TRANSFORMING TUTOR EDUCATION INTO SERVICE-LEARNING TUTOR EDUCATION

Modifications to our Writing Center Theory and Practice class to ac- commodate service learning include a weekly tutoring ob- ligation, readings, class discussion, and reflection assignments. Previously, tutors in the class committed four hours weekly to tutoring Loyola students. When we partnered with Bridges, we cut Loyola tutoring time to two hours weekly to allow two hours for Bridges' students. Tutors find that working with two different groups of students offers them an interrogated point of comparison; they wrestle with important issues of implicit bias, structural and systemic barriers to education, and the ef- fects of personal and family issues on writing process (to name a few examples).

Tutors in the class read writing center, service-learning, race and class privilege, literacy, and education texts. Each class we dis- cuss the readings in the context of our students' Bridges and Loyola tutoring experiences, and we weave Bridges into the class when we discuss composition and writing center theory and praxis. We also create opportunities for informal and formal reflection and critical engagement with the service experience. Within 24 hours of Bridges tutoring, our students post an on- line reflection visible only to each other and to Lisa and Victo- ria. These reflections are not graded and serve two purposes: a journal for the tutors and a mechanism for any needed interven- tion from Victoria. Because we work with high school students, we must communicate in a timely manner issues of concern with Victoria, who can relay information to the Bridges social worker (tutors, Lisa, and Victoria also meet briefly after each Bridges session expressly for this purpose). Additionally, tutors cull through their weekly reflections, looking for themes, de- velopments, and provocations for a final reflection paper. They select one or two essays from educational theory, local news, or service-learning or other relevant scholarship and put those essays in conversation with their reflections. Many tutors also extend their service-learning experience by tackling research topics that intersect with Bridges.

TUTORS AND BRIDGES STUDENTS' REWARDS

Collectively, the course mechanisms—weekly service, readings, class discussion, and reflection—help Loyola students connect their Bridges tutoring in various and often unexpected ways to the tutoring process. At the end of the semester, tutors often comment that their Bridges tutoring, not the writing center tu- toring, provided the most "hands-on" training and experience. As Lisa's teacher-research essay

"A Place to Begin: Service-Learn- ing Tutor Education and Writing Center Social Justice" attests, the rewards of community engagement are multifarious and powerful. Lisa's essay suggests that tutors increase their capac- ity for connection and empathy, learn to recognize and re- spect reciprocal learning, and expand their notions of literacy as social justice, all of which translate into the daily practice of their tu- toring.

Being mindful, however, of the danger of lopsided benefits for those engaged in service-learning, we instituted assessments with the Bridges students, asking them to complete surveys at each semester's start and close. But the Bridges students' survey responses tended to be overly positive and rather vague: they "LOVE" the program and tell us "not to change a thing" (well, ex- cept change the food from pizza!). We informally gauged Bridges students' GPA movement, but that measure hinges on so many factors that we hesitate to use it as a program efficacy marker. The next phase of the Loyola/Bridges part- nership (maybe an- other potential tutor research project) will be cre- ating a com- prehensive, meaningful assessment plan that factors in both Loyola tutors' and Bridges students' development and growth.

The feedback we have received, although suspect, has revealed some key findings. Almost all Bridges students cite study skills, time management, organization, and homework completion as areas where they develop most. Weekly, we witness the deep- ening of their under- standing of how to be successful students: they learn how to ask ques- tions about their work; they dialogue about how to approach teachers with questions they need an- swered; they examine their organization and develop a method for keeping track of assignments. Moreover, the opportunity to work with tutors on writing assignments is for many Bridges stu- dents their first encounter with writing as a process. From eval- uating the assignment prompt to exploring prewriting options to drafting alone to processing and analyzing teachers' grades and com- ments, students discover how much time and thought is necessary for a cogent and thorough piece of writing. Through ongoing dialogue with tutors, Bridges students develop self-re- flection and self-advo- cacy strategies as they evaluate their own writing and study practices.

Finally, we are struck by how much Bridges students love coming to and sharing our writing center space. By the end of each fall, they begin to consider themselves as belonging in our college campus cor- ner. They talk often to tutors about college life—both academic and social—and learn to interact with Lisa and Victo- ria, not as teachers, but as mentors. Writes one Bridges student, "Bridges/Loyola will help because of the simple fact that we are on a college campus with a college atmosphere and having a college tutor you could ask any questions [sic] may have or even get a feel of how difficult it is being a college student and what you could do to help you overcome it." For first-generation col- lege-bound students, this early college acculturation is invalu- able—and can be the first step in college retention and success.

FOUR SUCCESS FACTORS

Every service-learning project will be unique for that writing center and its community partner; nonetheless, we share the following four factors that ensured our program's success in the hopes that they will be helpful for others who begin a writing center community engagement project.

1) Presence

We recommend that directors consider carefully if they will participate in the service with their tutors. We believe our con- sistent engagement with the program has been critical for its success because our presence communicates to students that we value the program pedagogically and personally; it enables us to have our "eyes and ears on the ground," so we can respond to emerging issues; and it allows us to develop relationships, alongside our students, with all involved.

2) Flexibility

The first years of our service-learning partnership included ex- tensive trial and error. We tried different week days (holidays complicate Mondays in the spring), experimented with ways to begin the evenings (favorites include ice-breakers, tutor-led grammar lessons, and writing prompts), and troubleshot who should work where (we often had to ensure some particularly rambunctious Bridges participants were separated in the cen- ter). Moreover, we carefully considered who would work to- gether. Initially, we paired students at the start of the semester; this strategy only worked, however, if all Bridges students came weekly. We then moved to a more organic matching system; Bridges students write their names and homework on a white- board, and tutors sign up with a student). This semester we combined these approaches. The former approach fosters deep connections between students and a stronger commitment to the program over the semester; the latter helps generate a sense of group camaraderie.

3) Trust

We invite tutors and students to help inform and shape the program, and we trust that they can identify what the program needs and how it needs to grow. For example, one strong program addition is the tutor-recommended "College Night." Every semester a tutor panel answers Bridges students' college questions. Tutors then lead workshops on The Common Application, college discernment and selection, and financial aid. We began this program when a tutor learned that a Bridges student thought she did not qualify for college financial aid because she "wasn't on food stamps." We also invite Bridges students to tell us what they need, such as SAT prep books or readily available binders and folders, and we then provide these materials.

4) Fun

Although we have fun every week we work together, we also plan service and social events—e.g. tree plantings, basketball games, holiday parties, and end-of-year celebrations. For the holiday party, using funds donated by the Loyola Center for Community Service and Justice, the tutors and Lisa shop at the college bookstore, selecting t-shirts, hats, keychains, and other fun items for Bridges goodie bags. For the end-of-year celebrations, Loyola faculty donate books (novels, poetry, short stories), and Bridges students pick through the piles for their summer reading.

CONCLUSION

We posit that our small action, our service-learning tutor education program, is bearing fruit for one primary reason: we have made a permanent, ongoing institutional commitment to the program and to Bridges students. We are not simply dipping into Bridges students' lives to improve our students' tutoring skills; we will see many Bridges students throughout their high school careers, and those students will see many of our tutors throughout their college careers.

For us, this program cannot fail. It is not an option. Not sustaining the Loyola/Bridges partnership would be akin to not offering the tutor education course, or shutting down the writing center during midterms. This partnership is central, not peripheral to what we do, to our mission within the university and beyond. And we communicate it as such. Every annual report Lisa sub- mits includes a page reporting our Bridges work; every year at least one tutor presents on a service-learning project at a writ- ing center conference; every potential tutor that Lisa interviews commits at the outset to the weekly Bridges tutoring. Every week Loyola writing tutors and Baltimore City high school stu- dents gather to eat, write, and work together. This level of personal and professional commitment is sustained, in turn, by the small and big successes of the Loyola/Bridges program: Matthew settling into his work without prompting; Jason earning a "B" in Physics; Deeja hitting "send" on the com- mon app essay; Craig getting accepted with funding to Morgan State University; Angela landing her dream internship.6 And our tutors' successes are equally important: Gigi deciding to pursue urban healthcare; Alexa, a pre-law student, discovering what she calls her "civic identity and responsibility"; Kathleen carrying her Loyola/Bridges experiences into her own public school class- room. Every writing center tutor participates in Loyola/Bridges at least one semester, many more do so for two or three semes- ters. As the cornerstone of our tutor education, service-learning is foundational for our center and integral to the development of a thoughtful, intentional, and ethical tutoring identity.

Notes

1. For the sake of clarity and consistency of voice, we employed plural first person in this essay. Lisa Zimmerelli solely made some curricular and pedagogical decisions, and Victoria Brown solely made some logistical decisions, but our pro- gram is collaborative.

2. For recent scholarship on community literacy engagement, see Cella and Restaino; Deans; Deans et al.; Rose and Weiser; Rousculp; and Ryder. For scholar- ship that speaks about benefits of service-learning for tutor education, see Ashley; Condon; DeCiccio; Gorkemli & Conard-Salvo; Green; Moussu; and Spillane.

3. A description of service-learning at Loyola University Maryland is located at http://www.loyola.edu/department/ccsj/servicelearning. The Na-

tional Service- Learning Clearinghouse at <gsn.nylc.org/clearinghouse> offers the most compre- hensive list of service-learning resources.

    4. See Rousculp for a compelling reflection on her community writing center and the articulation of her discursive theory of literacy. See p. 28 for Hutchinson's review of her book.

    5. See <www.stpaulsschool.org/page.cfm?p=827> for more information.

    6. All Bridge's students' names have been changed. Loyola tutors have given permission to use their names.

Works Cited

Adler-Kassner, Linda, Robert Crooks, and Ann Watters, eds. *Writing the Community: Concepts and Models for Service-Learning in Composition.* Sterling, VA: Stylus, 1997. Print.

Ashley, Hannah. "The Idea of a Literacy Dula." ed. Laurie Cella and Jessica Restaino. *Unsustainable: Re-imagining Community Literacy, Public Writing, Service Learning and the University.* New York: Lexington, 2013: 179-194. Print.

Cella, Lauri, and Jessica Restaino, eds. *Unsustainable: Re-imagining Community Literacy, Public Writing, Service-learning, and the University.* Lexington, KY: Lexington, 2012. Print.

Condon, Frankie. "The Pen Pal Project." *Praxis: A Writing Center Journal* 2.1 (2004). Web. 15 May 2013.

Deans, Thomas. *Writing Partnerships: Service-learning in Composition.* Urbana: NCTE, 2010. Print.

Deans, Thomas, Barbara Roswell, and Adrian Wurr. *Writing and Community Engagement: A Critical Sourcebook.* Boston: Bedford/St. Martins, 2010. Print.

DeCiccio, Albert. "'I Feel a Power Coming All over Me with Words': Writing Centers and Service Learning." *Writing Lab Newsletter* 23.7 (1999): 1-6. Web. 15 May 2013.

Gorkemli, Serkan, and Tammy Conard-Salvo. "Professionalization, Tutor training, and Service Learning in the Writing Center." *Praxis: A Writing Center Journal* 4. 2 (2007). Web. 15 May 2013.

Green, Ann E. "The Writing Center and the Parallel Curriculum." *Praxis: A Writing Center Journal* 2.10 (2004). Web. 15 May 2013.

Moussu, Lucie. "Bridging Gaps—An Unusual Writing Center: Bringing Unusual High School Students to University." *Writing Lab Newsletter* 36.5-6 (2012): 7-10. Print.

Rose, Shirley and Irwin Weiser. *Going Public: What Writing Programs Learn from Engagement.* Utah State UP, Book 28, 2010. Web. <digitalcommons.usu.edu/ usupress_pubs/28>. 15 April 2015.

Rousculp, Tiffany. *Rhetoric of Respect: Recognizing Change at a Community Writing Center.* Urbana: NCTE, 2014. Print.
Ryder, Phyllis Mentzell. *Rhetorics for Community Action: Public Writings and Writing Publics.* Lexington, KY: Lexington, 2012. Print.
Spillane, Lee Ann. "The Reading Writing Center: What We Can Do." *Clearing House: A Journal of Educational Strategies, Issues and Ideas* 80. 2 (2006): 63-65. Print.
Zimmerelli, Lisa. "A Place to Begin: Service-Learning Tutor Education and Writing Center Social Justice." *Writing Center Journal* 35.1 (2015). Print.

www.ingramcontent.com/pod-product-compliance
Lightning Source LLC
Chambersburg PA
CBHW031419230426
43668CB00007B/359